Lenin Selected Writings:
On the National Question

On the National Question

VI Lenin

Selected Writings: 3

Wellred Books
London

On the National Question
Lenin Selected Writings: 3
VI Lenin

First edition
Wellred Books, December 2024

Publisher information:
Wellred Books Ltd, 4th Floor, 18 St. Cross Street,
London, EC1N 8UN, books@wellred-books.com

All material taken from the public domain
and Marxists Internet Archive

UK distribution: Wellred Books Britain, wellredbooks.co.uk
contact@wellredbooks.co.uk

EU distribution: 1917 Verlag e. U.
Lustkandlgasse 10/1, 1090 Vienna/Wien, Austria
william.haemmerle@gmail.com

USA distribution: Marxist Books, marxistbooks.com
sales@marxistbooks.com

DK distribution: Forlaget Marx, forlagetmarx.dk
Vermlandsgade 2, st., 2400 København NV
forlag@forlagetmarx.dk

Cover image: *Eyes East Towards Europe* by Richard Edes Harrison, for the
September 1940 edition of *Fortune*
Cover design by Jesse Murray-Dean

Layout by Wellred Books

ISBN: 978 1 916936 14 0

Contents

Part 2: Lenin, the Bund and 'Cultural-National' Autonomy

Part 3: During the Revolution and in Power

Appendices

Note on Dates

Until 14 February 1918, Russia used the Old Style (Julian) calendar, which was thirteen days behind the New Style (Gregorian) used in the West and which is standard today.

All dates referring to events and publications in Russia before 14 February 1918 are given in the Old Style, with all other dates using the Gregorian calendar.

Introduction

> Whatever may be the further destiny of the Soviet Union, the national policy of Lenin will find its place amongst the eternal treasures of mankind.
>
> – Leon Trotsky, *History of the Russian Revolution*[1]

The Russian Empire was described by Lenin as a prison house of nations. According to the last Russian census prior to the 1917 Revolution, just 43 per cent of the inhabitants of the Russian Empire were Great Russians, and they were concentrated in a few areas. In other words, the dominant national group in the bureaucracy of the tsarist empire was not a majority of the population.

Oppressed national groups were concentrated in the borderlands, at the farther reaches of the Russian empire. Some had clearly established national characteristics, while others, including nomadic tribes, still had their own identity, but could not be described as national groups.

All these different national and tribal groups were at different levels of economic development. Some of the oppressed nationalities were actually on a higher level of cultural and economic development than their oppressors. This was certainly the case with the Finns and the Poles. Others had not yet emerged from the nomadic state, or had only recently become sedentary. As a result, they had different levels of development of their national consciousness.

---

1 Trotsky, Leon, *History of the Russian Revolution*, Vol. 3, Wellred Books, 2022, p. 913.

The different aspects of the national question confronting the Russian Marxist movement were further complicated by the fact that some of these national groups which existed within the Russian Empire also had members of the same group living outside of the Empire. Not only this, but also, over a long period of time, some of these national groups had parts of their population emigrating to other parts of the Russian Empire, outside of their regions of origin. The Russian Empire had a deliberate policy of sending Great Russian colonists to go and settle in some of the Central Asian lands which were populated by other groups.

The development of industry in the Russian Empire also provoked the emigration of peasants into newly created industrial hotspots (in St. Petersburg, Baku, the Donbas coal mines, etc.) where they became proletarianised. In some cases this meant the migration of Russian workers into other nationalities, or the mixing up of workers from different national groups. Often, 'foreign' workers became dominant in the working class of oppressed nationalities.

So the national question in the Russian Empire was extremely complicated. It was a disintegrating factor. The revolutionary party had to get it right if it wanted to carry out a successful revolution in Russia. This problem affected mainly the peasant and petty-bourgeois masses, which were a majority of the population at that time. It was also closely linked to the agrarian question.

Leon Trotsky points out in his *History of the Russian Revolution* that it was the correct policy of the Bolshevik Party on this question "which in the long run guaranteed its victory".[2]

What was this policy and what did it mean in practice?

Most bourgeois historians of the Russian Revolution have shown their complete inability to understand this policy, and therefore they draw completely wrong conclusions from it. Historians such as Richard Pipes, for instance, claim that the Bolshevik policy towards the national question was cynical. He argues that during the struggle against the tsarist autocracy they promised the right of

---

2   Ibid, p. 904.

self-determination, as a ruse to get their support, but as soon as they came to power they implemented a policy of centralisation against the rights of different national groups. This is completely wrong, and it shows the inability of bourgeois historians to understand the dialectical approach Lenin had to this question.

Lenin's approach to the national question can be summed up in six different features:

— First of all, a defence of the democratic right of the nationalities to self-determination, meaning above all the right to set up an independent country.

— Second, that this was in order to guarantee the unity of the working class and remove any national animosity amongst workers of different nationalities.

— Third, the strictest unity within the party, which meant opposition to any attempt to organise it along federal, national lines.

— Fourth, the recognition that there is a difference between the nationalism of the oppressor nation and the nationalism of the oppressed nation (which contains a democratic and revolutionary kernel).

— Fifth, the need for the independence of the working class from the petty-bourgeois nationalists.

— Sixth, that the national question, being a democratic question, must always be subordinated to the class question.

Thus enunciated, these principles seem quite straightforward, but Lenin insisted that the national question was a *concrete* question and he always approached it in a dialectical manner, taking into account all the different aspects of a given national problem, its historical development, its relationship with the general interests of the working class movement, etc.

The Second Congress of the RSDLP, 1903

The general position of Marxism in regard to the rights of nations had been established in the decades previously. But it was at the Second Congress of the Russian Social-Democratic Labour Party in 1903 that many of the issues were first approached in a concrete form.

In particular, the discussions about Clause 7 (which became Clause 9 after the congress) of the programme and also regarding the position of the Jewish Bund within the party.

Clause 9 of the party programme clearly recognised the "right of self-determination for all nations included within the bounds of the state", and by this it meant the right of nations to form their own independent country if they so wished. The party programme also recognised:

> 3. Extensive local self-government; regional self-government for all localities which are distinguished by special conditions in respect of mode of life and make-up of the population.[3]

It also addressed the question of language rights:

> 8. Right of the population to receive education in their native language, to be ensured by provision of the schools needed for this purpose, at the expense of the state and the organs of self-government; the right of every citizen to express himself at meetings in his own language; use of the native language on an equal basis with the state language in all local, public and state institutions.[4]

In Lenin's view, the defence of the democratic rights of the oppressed nationalities was the only way to ensure the unity of the working class. The workers in the oppressed nations had to be reassured that the social-democrats (as the Marxists were known at the time) had nothing to do with the policy of national oppression carried out by the tsarist autocracy on behalf of the dominant Great-Russian nationality.

---

3 'Programme of the Social-Democratic Workers' Party', reproduced in *1903: Second Congress of the Russian Social-Democratic Labour Party*, New Park, 1978, p. 6.

4 Ibid.

Party unity versus federalism

In Lenin's view this meant that there should be one single Social-Democratic party, not separate parties for each national group united in a federation. In other words, that the Jewish social-democrats (known as the Bund), the Latvian social-democrats, the Ukrainian social-democrats, and so on, should all be part of one single united party, in common struggle against the tsarist autocracy.

This led to a polemic with the Jewish Bund, who demanded the sole right to speak to and on behalf of the Jewish workers. The position they had adopted was that of 'cultural-national autonomy' put forward by the Austro-Marxist[5] Otto Bauer. He regarded the national question from the point of view of culture and language, and devised a complex system in which every citizen of the country would be able to freely join a 'national association' as an individual, regardless of where he or she lived. In practice, this was both a capitulation to petty-bourgeois nationalism and also a way to avoid a genuine revolutionary solution to the national question in the Austro-Hungarian empire.

Such an approach suited the Bund, as Jewish workers, while more concentrated in certain geographic areas, were spread across the Empire, without a national territory they could call their own. In fact, one of the fathers of the idea of 'national cultural autonomy' was the Bundist ideologist Vladimir Medem, in his 1904 essay 'Social Democracy and the National Question'.

In arguing for the unity of the proletariat in one party Lenin explained that:

[In] the struggle against the autocracy, the struggle against the bourgeoisie of Russia as a whole, we must act as a single and centralised militant organisation, have behind us the whole of the proletariat, without distinction of language or nationality, a

---

5　Austro-Marxism was the leading tendency within the Social-Democratic Party of Austria, which attempted to reconcile reformism with revolutionary Marxism. It defended the position of 'cultural-national autonomy' in relation to the national question.

proletariat whose unity is cemented by the continual joint solution of problems of theory and practice, of tactics and organisation; and we must not set up organisations that would march separately, each along its own track; we must not weaken the force of our offensive by breaking up into numerous independent political parties; we must not introduce estrangement and isolation and then have to heal an artificially implanted disease with the aid of these notorious 'federation' plasters.[6]

The demand of the Bund for federal status within the RSDLP was rejected by all wings of the party. Lenin spoke against it, as did Martov and Trotsky. At Lenin's insistence, this question was taken at the beginning of the proceedings but a final vote was not taken until the 27th session. Only the five representatives from the Bund voted for their proposal and after losing the vote they walked out of the Congress.

In explaining the party programme on this question, Lenin insisted that the Bolsheviks were against nationalism. They were against *all* nationalism, both the nationalism of the oppressor nation and the nationalism of the oppressed nation. He explained that the Bolsheviks' position was mainly a *negative* one: they were against any privileges for any nations and against all oppression.

This meant that they were against the privilege of the oppressor nation, which at that point was the only one who had the right to form their own country, but they were also against any attempt of the bourgeois of the oppressed nation to acquire their own privileges.

The Bolsheviks did not adopt a preconceived position about the separation of any country. At one point, Lenin used the analogy with the right of divorce, which is a democratic right. If one of the two members of a couple wants to end the marriage, they have the right to do so, however this does not mean that in all instances we agitate for divorce.

---

6 Lenin, 'Does the Jewish Proletariat Need an 'Independent Political Party'?', 15 February 1903, in this volume, p. 189.

Lenin explained that the right of self-determination is a democratic right, not a socialist right, and therefore the right of self-determination should always be subordinate to the labour question, that is, to the class question. Throughout the history of the Bolshevik Party, Lenin always explained that the defence of the right of self-determination was the best way to guarantee the unity of the working class. The unity of different nations within one single state will only be a voluntary union.

This position was approved at the party congress in 1903, but this article in the party programme, Clause 9, was to provoke lots of polemics over many years, even after the October Revolution.

The debate between Luxemburg and Lenin

First of all was the debate with the Polish Social Democrats, led by Rosa Luxemburg. The Social Democracy of the Kingdom of Poland and Lithuania (SDKPiL) sent two visitors to the 1903 Congress, with the aim of conducting discussions leading to unity between the parties. However, the Fourth Congress of the SDKPiL, earlier in the same year, had passed a resolution which put forward certain conditions for this unity to go ahead. One of those was to replace the clause of the party programme on the right of nations to self-determination "by a precise formula incapable of interpretation in a nationalist spirit" and "autonomy to be demanded for the Polish and Lithuanian provinces".

The programme commission discussed the question and kept the original formulation which read: "Right of self-determination for all nations included within the bounds of the state." This was then adopted by the Congress. The two Polish delegates then left the congress making a statement to the effect that "unification will become possible *only if*" the congress adopted their wording of the clause, or if it left the question open for further discussion.

The position of the Polish social-democrats was then defended by Rosa Luxemburg in a series of articles in which she rejected the slogan of the right of nations to self-determination. She argued that in the epoch of imperialism this slogan could not be carried out, and that in any case it was the slogan of the bourgeois nationalists. Working-class socialists should instead stand for class unity, not separation. While rejecting independence for Poland and Lithuania, she nevertheless agreed with advocating their autonomy.

Lenin replied extensively to these arguments. To a certain extent it was understandable that Luxemburg, as a *Polish* social-democrat, would stress the need to not make any concession to the Polish bourgeois and petty-bourgeois nationalists, some of which attempted to give themselves a socialist colouring. Whether or not Polish social-democrats should argue for Polish independence or not was something which could be debated, according to concrete and specific circumstances.

However, Luxemburg and those who shared her views were demanding that the *Russian* Social-Democratic Party should not defend the *right* of nations to self-determination. That was wholly incorrect. Lenin said that the main task of the Great-Russian social-democrats was to fight against *their own* bourgeoisie and *their own* ruling class, which was guilty of oppressing the Poles and other nations, and therefore they had to guarantee and agitate for the *right* to self-determination. That was the only way to show the Polish workers and the Polish masses in general that the Russian social-democrats had nothing to do with the Great-Russian ruling class which was oppressing them.

The task of the *Polish* Social Democrats was slightly different. Their main task on the national question was to fight against the Polish bourgeois and petty bourgeois and against any attempt to put the national interests of Poland above the class interests of the Polish workers.

Imperialism and the ultra-left errors of Bukharin

Rosa Luxemburg's polemic on this question was later taken up, in 1915, by a group around Nikolai Bukharin in the Russian party, who advocated a similar position. The Baugy Group, as it was known after the Swiss town where they were based in exile during the First World War, was composed of Bukharin, Georgy Pyatakov, Yevgenia

Bosch and others. On this question they were also in agreement with Karl Radek, who had been involved in the Polish and German social-democratic movements.

In analysing imperialism and imperialist domination, Bukharin drew a series of ultra-left conclusions. From the general tendency towards state monopoly, militarism and the domination of the world by a few imperialist powers, he drew the conclusion that the party should abandon any agitation for the right of nations to self-determination and for democratic demands in general. He argued that these democratic demands could not be granted under capitalism and agitating for them would create false illusions amongst the workers. Under socialism, once the workers take power, these demands would be useless because they would have already been superseded. In 1915, in the 'Theses on the National Question' signed by Pyatakov, Bosch and Bukharin, they wrote:

> The slogan 'self-determination of nations' is first of all utopian, as it cannot be realised within the limits of capitalism. It is also harmful, as it is a slogan that sows illusions. In this respect it does not distinguish itself at all from the slogans of arbitration courts, disarmament, and so on which presuppose the possibility of so-called peaceful capitalism.

In opposing *in general* the slogan of the defence of the fatherland, which was correct, they abstracted themselves from the fact that there are oppressor nations and oppressed nations.

Lenin polemicised against them in a series of letters, describing them as "imperialist Economists", in reference to the polemic against the Economists in 1902-03, who argued that the proletariat should not concern itself with political demands, just economic demands.

The Baugy Group, similarly, argued that the workers should not concern themselves with political activity, but should 'simply' concentrate on the taking of power. In reality their argument was against democratic demands *in general*. The 'left-wing communists', including Bukharin himself, made the same points in debates in the Russian party and in the Communist International after 1917.

In answering them, Lenin explained how the struggle for democratic demands and the use of democratic institutions, however limited they may be, is an indispensable part of the necessary agitation of the revolutionary party in winning over the working class masses and broader layers of the population to the perspective of taking power.

The Russian Revolution

The question of the democratic demands of the oppressed nationalities played an important role in the Russian Revolution, both in February and in October 1917. This was the case particularly in Ukraine and Finland, but also in Poland, Georgia and Central Asia. In 1916, for instance, there had been a mass uprising in Central Asia, mainly of the Kyrgyz and Kazakh Muslim peoples, against conscription into the war.

In the period between February and October there was a lot of agitation again around this question, particularly in Ukraine, Poland and Finland. The Provisional Government was brought to power in February as a result of the abolition of tsarism and was meant to carry out the bourgeois-democratic revolution. But just as it was unable to carry out other democratic tasks, like land reform, a Constituent Assembly, etc., it did nothing to satisfy the national aspirations of the oppressed, even though the national democratic movement in most cases was also dominated by the bourgeois liberals.

Once the Bolsheviks took power, they immediately began rectifying this. Less than ten days after the October Revolution, the Council of People's Commissars, headed by Lenin, issued the 'Declaration of the Rights of the Peoples of Russia' on 15 November 1917, which stated very clearly its defence of:

> The right of the peoples of Russia to free self-determination, even to the point of separation and the formation of an independent state.[7]

This question, like all the others the Bolsheviks faced when coming to power, was not a simple, straightforward one. The national question

---

7   Lenin, 'Declaration of the Rights of the Peoples of Russia', 2 November 1917, in this volume, p. 332.

and the national aspirations of the oppressed peoples became completely enmeshed in the question of foreign intervention and the civil war, with foreign imperialist powers cynically attempting to use the national aspirations of oppressed nationalities against the October Revolution and Soviet power.

Nevertheless, in the first few years of the Russian Revolution, the Bolsheviks fulfilled their promise to the oppressed nationalities and put into practise the principle of the right of nations to self-determination. Five independent republics were recognised, including Finland, Latvia, Ukraine and Georgia. In addition, seventeen different autonomous republics were created within the Russian Soviet Federative Socialist Republic (RSFSR).

Finland

In Finland, the workers' movement was very strong, even before 1917. The Social Democratic Party had won a majority in the regional parliament even before the February Revolution. The Provisional Government of Kerensky, however, made an alliance with the Finnish bourgeois against the workers' parties and tried to suppress the movement. Within weeks of coming to power, on 18 December 1917, Lenin and the Bolsheviks recognised the independence of Finland, and by January 1918 there was a revolutionary uprising in Finland, in which the workers took power in the main cities.

Tragically, the leaders of the Social Democratic Party in Finland wanted to follow a parliamentary road to socialism, and instead of taking power, a lot of time was wasted in legalistic and democratic procedures. Meanwhile, the ruling class was organising to crush the workers' organisations and destroy any semblance of democracy. They created the murderous White Guards, brought in Swedish volunteers and smashed the working class in a brutal civil war, in which by some estimates as many as 100,000 workers were killed.

In this situation, there was a discussion about the convenience of Soviet intervention to help the Finnish. Luxemburg was very critical of the Bolsheviks. She had opposed the right of nations to self-determination and now said that all its implementation had led to was the creation of counter-revolutionary bourgeois governments, which attempted to smash the working-class revolution:

> While Lenin and his comrades clearly expected that, as champions of national freedom even to the extent of 'separation', they would turn Finland, the Ukraine, Poland, Lithuania, the Baltic countries, the Caucasus, etc., into so many faithful allies of the Russian Revolution, we have instead witnessed the opposite spectacle. One after another, these 'nations' used the freshly granted freedom to ally themselves with German imperialism against the Russian Revolution as its mortal enemy, and, under German protection, to carry the banner of counter-revolution into Russia itself.[8]

Lenin explained that this was not the case, that any attempt to deny national freedom to those oppressed nations *by force* would have been impossible. This would have been seen as a continuation of the oppression by Great Russian chauvinism under tsarism. By granting the oppressed nations their national democratic rights, the Bolsheviks were then in a better position to raise the common interests of workers and poor peasants against the petty bourgeois and bourgeois nationalists.

At the April conference in 1917, Lenin had said:

> Any Russian socialist who does not recognise Finland's and Ukraine's right to freedom will degenerate into a chauvinist.[9]

He was replying to Pyatakov and Dzerzhinsky, who argued against the right of self-determination and put the "hopelessly muddled" slogan of "no borders" as an alternative.

In Lenin's view, there was no contradiction between recognising the right of self-determination, which was necessary, and the workers' state coming to the aid of workers in other countries, even militarily. The only reason the Bolsheviks did not intervene militarily

---

8   Luxemburg, Rosa, 'The Russian Revolution', *Rosa Luxemburg Speaks*, Pathfinder Press, 1970.

9   Lenin, 'The Seventh (April) All-Russia Conference of the RSDLP(B)', 24-29 April 1917, in this volume, p. 290.

in Finland to help the Finnish workers was because *they did not have the means to do so*. The old tsarist army had collapsed at the end of the First World War, millions of peasants had gone back to the land, the masses were exhausted and did not want to fight any more wars. The Bolsheviks were still at war with Germany and trying to hold that front. Had they had the military forces to do so they would not have hesitated in coming to the aid of the Finnish workers.

Ukraine

In the case of Ukraine, the situation was further complicated. While Lenin always insisted that Ukraine was one of the countries which could exercise its right to self-determination, there was strong opposition to that idea from within the party, including prominent Bolshevik leaders in Ukraine such as Pyatakov, who were ultra-left on this question, as we have seen.

In the Donbas, an industrial mining area in the southeast of Ukraine, the base of the local Bolsheviks was mainly amongst mineworkers, who were from Russian and other nationalities which had emigrated to this industrially rich area to work. Many of these industrial and mineworkers were fiercely opposed to Ukrainian nationalism and opposed the right of self-determination.

Ukraine had never really existed as an independent country. It was composed of different national groups, and its territory had also been divided between different countries over a period of time. Among the most important social classes in the cities, i.e. the workers, the merchants, the petty bourgeois and so on, Ukrainian speakers were a small minority. Most of the city dwellers were either Great Russian, Jewish or Polish.

Ukrainian speakers were mostly concentrated in the countryside among the peasants. The national movement had an influence mostly or exclusively amongst a layer of petty-bourgeois intellectuals. After the February Revolution, the Ukrainian Central Rada was established, a bourgeois Ukrainian regional government. However, at the same time there was a powerful workers' movement in the industrial centres, in Kharkov, Odessa, Kiev and the Donbas.

On 20 November 1917, after the taking of power by the Soviets in Russia, a Ukrainian People's Republic was declared, led by petty-bourgeois and bourgeois nationalists, but at this stage it did not yet declare independence.

In December, Lenin and the Soviets issued the 'Manifesto to the Ukrainian People with an Ultimatum to the Ukrainian Rada' in which they reaffirmed the principle of self-determination and said they recognised the Ukrainian People's Republic and its right to secede or enter into a treaty with Russia, as they had done in the case of Finland. They also asked the Ukrainian People's Republic for clarification on a series of questions: about the disorganisation of the front with Germany, the Rada's collaboration with the reactionary rising of the Cadets and the recognition of the soviets in existence in Ukraine. They also asked the Ukrainian People's Republic to clarify their position on the activities of the counter-revolutionary armies of Kornilov and Kaledin in Ukraine. The Rada rejected the ultimatum on 20 December 1917. On 22 January 1918, Ukraine declared independence.

Simultaneously, the All-Ukrainian Congress of the Soviets in Kharkov declared the Ukrainian People's Republic of Soviets. Starting in Kharkov, which was an industrial centre, they marched all the way to Kiev and in the space of a few weeks established a Soviet government in Ukraine. The soviets gained a lot of support also from the peasantry, which was mainly Ukrainian-speaking, because of their agrarian policy.

However, this Soviet government only lasted a few weeks. The young Soviet Republic was still at war with Germany. During the peace negotiations in Brest-Litovsk, while the Bolsheviks were trying to buy time, the Germans advanced and took over Ukraine. They established a German puppet government called the Hetmanate. Later, when the Germans withdrew, the Rada was re-established, this time under the protection send as a puppet government of French imperialism.

This period showed in practice that Ukraine could exist as an independent country only in the form of a workers state along the lines of Soviet Russia. All other so-called independent Ukrainian governments were in reality puppets of different imperialist powers.

In Ukraine, Soviet power faced additional difficulties. The imperialist war had specific features in Ukraine, as did the civil war, which to a certain extent was a continuation of the former. Between 1919 and 1920, Ukraine was one of the main theatres of the civil war. This was not just a civil war between the Red and White armies. In Ukraine there were also the Greens, Makhnovite[10] troops which fought at different times on different sides of the civil war. There were also a number of Ukrainian-based communist groups. For a short period of time, there was also a Soviet Republic in the South East: the Donetsk-Krivoy Rog Soviet Republic. For two years the situation was extremely confused, with the class struggle and the national struggle completely overlapping each other.

This was not the end of the problems in Ukraine. When the civil war finished in 1921, the first head of the Ukrainian Soviet government was Pyatakov, who was ultra-left on the national question. He not only had a completely careless attitude in relation to the national question in Ukraine, he also had a very ultra-left policy on the agrarian question as well, which alienated many from the middle layers of the peasantry.

After a year, Pyatakov was replaced by Rakovsky, the Balkan internationalist. Initially, he also had a wrong position on the national question. He was very strongly influenced by his background in the Balkans where he had correctly defended the slogan of a Balkan Socialist Federation. As a result, he did not pay much attention to the concrete features of the national question in Ukraine. In effect, he had a very abstract internationalist position, which in practice led to a campaign of Russification in Ukraine.

Lenin was horrified by this. If one reads the writings of Lenin between 1918 and 1922 in relation to Ukraine, you will see that he had an extremely careful approach to the Ukrainian national

---

10 Nestor Makhno was a Ukrainian anarchist who led a peasant army during the civil war that followed the Russian Revolution. His forces took an alternating position between allying with the Red Army and opposing it.

question. In order to reverse the damage that had been done, he went as far as making some concessions to those who were leaning towards Ukrainian nationalism.

For instance, in Ukraine the left wing of the Ukrainian Party of Socialist-Revolutionaries, known as the Borotbists after the name of their central organ, *Borotba* (*Struggle*), wanted to join the Communist Party. In the discussions about the fusion, there were three different positions. One section wanted the Ukrainian Communist Party to be part of the Russian Communist Party. Others said the Ukrainian Communist Party should be separate from the Russian party and affiliate directly to the Communist International. There were others who argued that not only the Communist Party should be independent but that Ukraine should be independent and should not be a part of the Russian Soviet Federative Socialist Republic.

In this debate, Lenin showed his very careful approach to the national question. He insisted on the unity of the working class, but at the same time said that questions of demarcation of borders and the relative degree of autonomy of the party were not questions of principle but should be decided amicably within the Ukrainian party. He said:

> If a Great-Russian communist insists upon the amalgamation of the Ukraine with Russia, Ukrainians might easily suspect him of advocating this policy not from the motive of uniting the proletarians in the fight against capital but because of the prejudices of the old Great-Russian nationalism of imperialism.

> Such mistrust is natural and to a certain degree inevitable and legitimate, because the Great Russians under the yoke of landowners and capitalists had for centuries imbibed the shameful and disgusting prejudices of Great-Russian chauvinism.

> If a Ukrainian communist insists upon the unconditional state independence of the Ukraine he lays himself open to the suspicion that he is supporting this policy not because of the temporary interest of the Ukrainian workers and peasants in the struggle against the yoke of

capital, but on account of the petty-bourgeois national prejudices of the small owner.[11]

In making these observations, Lenin's main concern was the preservation of the unity of the working class:

> He who undermines the unity and closest alliance between the Great-Russian and Ukrainian workers and peasants is helping the Kolchaks, the Denikins,[12] the capitalist bandits of all countries. Consequently, we Great-Russian communists must repress with the utmost severity the slightest manifestation in our midst of Great-Russian nationalism, for such manifestations, which are a betrayal of communism in general, cause the gravest harm by dividing us from our Ukrainian comrades and thus playing into the hands of Denikin and his regime.[13]

His conclusion was that concessions were necessary *on the part of Great-Russian communists*:

> Consequently, we Great-Russian communists must make concessions when there are differences with the Ukrainian Bolshevik communists and Borotbists and these differences concern the state independence of the Ukraine, the forms of her alliance with Russia, and the national question in general.[14]

This sums up clearly the whole of Lenin's position in a practical, concrete example.

In November 1919, when the Red Army entered Ukraine, Trotsky issued an order to the troops which had exactly the same approach:

> The Ukraine is the land of the Ukrainian workers and working peasants. They alone have the right to rule in Ukraine, to govern it and to build a new life in it. Keep this firmly in mind: your task is not to conquer the Ukraine but to liberate it. When the reactionary bands of Denikin

---

11 Lenin, 'Letter to the Workers and Peasants of the Ukraine: Apropos of the Victories over Denikin', 28 December 1919, in this volume, p. 315.
12 Alexander Kolchak and Anton Denikin were generals in the White Army.
13 Ibid, p. 317.
14 Ibid.

have been smashed the working people of the liberated Ukraine will themselves decide on what terms they are to live with Soviet Russia. Long live the free and independent Soviet Ukraine.[15]

Here we see the dialectical character of the approach the Bolsheviks had to the national question when in power. At the same time that the Soviet troops were entering Ukraine to fight the counter-revolution, they were advocating a free Soviet Ukraine to decide for itself what relations it should have with Soviet Russia.

The debate at the Eighth Congress of the RCP(B), 1919

Contrary to what the ultra-lefts imagined, the national question, like any other democratic question, is not automatically resolved the day after the taking of power by the workers. On the contrary, it takes a very long time and requires the development of the material conditions for all the national prejudices and chauvinism to be eradicated, including the prejudices of an oppressor nation. This applies equally to the struggle for the liberation of women and to the struggle against the influence of religion.

This debate about the right of nations to self-determination did not finish with the October Revolution. The 'left-wing' communists continued to argue against self-determination at the Eighth Party Congress in 1919. Ironically, many of those arguing against the rights of oppressed nations came from oppressed nationalities themselves, including Georgians and Ukrainians.

Pyatakov, who at the time of the Congress was the secretary of the Communist Party of Ukraine, argued along the same lines that Luxemburg had a year earlier:

> The slogan 'the right of nations to self-determination' which our party has held to from time immemorial, has shown itself in practise, when it comes to the question of the socialist revolution, to be a slogan which is the rallying point for all counter-revolutionary forces.[16]

---

15 Trotsky, Leon, *How the Revolution Armed*, Vol. 2, New Park, 1979, p. 439.
16 Quoted in Smith, Jeremy, 'The Bolsheviks and the National Question, 1917-1923', PhD thesis, University of London, 1996.

Bukharin argued that the slogan was anachronistic in the period of the transition to socialism, and proposed an amendment to the party programme which said that the right of self-determination should be recognised as the self-determination "of the toiling masses", a formulation which he had borrowed from Joseph Stalin.

Lenin argued against this, and explained that the right of self-determination is a democratic right, not a socialist right and therefore affects *the whole nation*. You cannot simply decree the classes within a nation out of existence. He stressed that there should be absolutely no hint that the Bolsheviks intended to impose the soviet system by military force onto other peoples, or that they did not respect the right of each nation to decide their own future.

Military intervention?

In 1920, the issue of self-determination and military intervention was posed concretely in Poland. After the outbreak of the German Revolution in November 1918, the Bolsheviks repudiated the Brest-Litovsk agreement and were able to advance westward into the territories which had been abandoned by the German troops. Meanwhile, the Polish bourgeois nationalists, led by Józef Piłsudski, wanted to ensure the maximum territorial extension for Poland as well as domination over its neighbours in Ukraine, Belarus and Lithuania, amongst others.

In April 1920, the forces of the reactionary Polish nationalist Piłsudski allied with the Ukrainian People's Republic of Simon Petliura and launched an offensive on Kyiv. The Polish invasion of Ukraine and occupation of Kyiv had the effect of pushing the Ukrainian masses towards the Soviets. Piłsudski's forces were defeated and the Red Army started a rapid counter-offensive.

At this point there was a discussion among the Bolsheviks about whether to take advantage of this to continue chasing the reactionary Polish army all the way to Warsaw and help the Polish workers take power. The idea was that the Red Army advance would provoke or accelerate a rising of the Polish workers and peasants.

The advance of the Red Army was stopped, and the forces led by Tukhachevsky were defeated in the battle of Warsaw. For reasons of personal prestige, forces under the political command of Stalin refused direct orders to go to the aid of the Red Army advancing towards Warsaw and instead concentrated on a failed attempt at taking Lviv, which did not help matters.

More importantly, the rhythm and needs of the military offensive did not coincide with the rhythms of the class struggle and the advances in consciousness. The Polish masses were not ready. The question here was not that military intervention was ruled out as a matter of principle, but rather that one cannot impose Soviet power by the force of military intervention, when the conditions are not there. The impetus has to come from within, there has to be a genuine uprising of the workers and peasants. Only once that has happened, does the Soviet power in a neighbouring country have the right and the duty to help the workers in that country.

Central Asia

Central Asia was a completely different area. Most of the peoples and national groups in this region were extremely backward, some of them nomadic. Most of them did not have a written language, and the national movement in many of these places took place under the flag of Islam and even pan-Islamism or pan-Turkism.

Here, as well as in the Caucasus during the civil war, the Bolsheviks allied themselves as far as possible with the progressive modernising intelligentsia which existed in all these nationalities. In some cases these national movements were won over to the ideas of Bolshevism and became incorporated into the Communist Party. Enormous progress was made in these regions from the point of view of national development.

The Bolsheviks proceeded in a very cautious way. Part of the domination of the Russian Empire over these peoples was expressed in the question of religion, language and the script in which language was to be written. The tsarist empire imposed the Russian Orthodox Church, and oppressed other denominations and religions, like the

Armenian Church and Islam. In several cases, the Cyrillic script was imposed where bourgeois nationalists and progressive reformers in these nationalities were fighting for the restoration of the Arabic script in the writing of their languages.

The Bolsheviks reversed this policy completely. They allowed freedom of religion. They returned land and buildings that had been expropriated from the mosques. Uthman's Quran, a holy relic written possibly as far back as the seventh century, had been taken to the Imperial Library in St. Petersburg after the tsarist conquest of Samarkand. The Bolsheviks handed custodianship of it over to the All-Russian Muslim Council, located in Ufa (Bashkortostan, Russia), as an expression of this position.

On 24 November 1917 the Soviet government issued an 'Appeal to the Muslims of Russia and the East', which said:

> Moslems of Russia, Tatars of the Volga and the Crimea, Kyrghyz and Sarts of Siberia and Turkestan, Turks and Tatars of Transcaucasia, Chechens and mountain Cossacks! All you, whose mosques and shrines have been destroyed, whose faith and customs have been violated by the tsars and oppressors of Russia! Henceforward your beliefs and customs, your national and cultural institutions, are declared free and inviolable! Build your national life freely and without hindrance. It is your right. Know that your rights, like those of all the peoples of Russia, will be protected by the might of the revolution, by the Councils of Workers', Soldiers' and Peasants' Deputies![17]

The general progress of the development of the national culture and identity of these peoples was extraordinary.

The Bolsheviks proposed a school language policy, according to which in every school where there were twenty-five children in any age group who were speakers of one particular language, they should be taught in their own language, and this applied not only in the region of origin of this national group, but anywhere where they were settled. The actual implementation of this school

---

17 Lenin, 'Appeal of the Council of People's Commissars to the Moslems of Russia and the East', 3 December 1917, in this volume, p. 336.

language policy was curtailed by material and economic factors, but the intention was clear. By 1924, printing of books, textbooks and newspapers was being carried out in twenty-four different languages in the Soviet Union.

There was also a big debate about the question of the script in which the languages should be written. Lenin and Lunacharsky argued in favour of transforming all languages in Russia into a Latin script. Kemal Atatürk later on took the same position in Turkey, and for the same reasons: in order to modernise the country and bring it closer to the general current of world cultural development.

But in this question, like in many other questions pertaining to culture and education, Lenin did not impose his criteria on anyone. The decision should be taken by the people affected themselves. Many of the Central Asian peoples were Muslim and decided to adopt a simplified version of the Arabic script. This policy was later reversed under Stalin's bureaucratic counter-revolution when the Cyrillic script was imposed on all of these nations, whom had previously chosen either the Latin or Arabic script.

These cultural and education policies were accompanied by something that from the point of view of the Bolsheviks was even more important: economic development. There was a conscious policy of investing in these nations to develop infrastructure and industry, which was the only real way to bring these peoples out of backwardness and at the same time develop the proletariat.

There was also a conscious policy towards the 'nationalisation' of the local communist parties, which in many cases were made up only or mainly of Great-Russian workers. There was a campaign of recruiting communists from the national group concerned. A very careful and cautious approach was required, particularly on the question of religion, in order not to alienate them from Soviet power. Most of the work needed to be carried out on the basis of patient explanation, highlighting the class questions and through the practical demonstration of the material advantages of Soviet power.

At the time of the Revolution, the level of literacy in these regions was maybe 5 per cent, or even less. Even with very remote nomadic peoples in the north and in the Far East, the policy of the Bolsheviks was extremely careful. For instance the Yakuts, a very small tribal nomadic group in the north, were for the first time given a written language in the Latin script, which had no punctuation marks and no capital letters.

Lenin regarded the question of the establishment of soviet power in Central Asia and other Muslim lands of extreme importance, not only for the USSR, but more generally from the point of view of the world revolution. In a letter to the communists of Turkestan he explained:

> The attitude of the Soviet Workers' and Peasants' Republic to the weak and hitherto oppressed nations is *of very practical significance for the whole of Asia and for all the colonies of the world*, for thousands and millions of people. I earnestly urge you [...] to demonstrate to them by your actions *that we are sincere in our desire to wipe out all traces of Great-Russian imperialism.*[18]

The national question and the struggle against bureaucracy

In 1922, Stalin was far from being a conscious representative of the developing bureaucracy. But from his very first days as General Secretary he demonstrated a bureaucratic heavy-handedness in regard to the national question within the Soviet Union. In this context, one of Lenin's main struggles at the end of his life against the bureaucratisation of the Soviet Union and against Stalin was focussed on the issue of the national question.

There were two points in this struggle, the debate on the setting up of the USSR and the dispute over the 'Georgian affair'.

The first of these took place in 1922, during the discussion on the legal form that the Union of Soviet Socialist Republics was going to take. Stalin, who at the time was the People's Commissar for nationalities, proposed that the Constitution should be phrased in terms of the *entry* of Ukraine *into* the Russian Socialist Federative

---

18 Lenin, 'To the Communists of Turkestan', 7 November 1919, in this volume, p. 355.

Soviet Republic. Lenin opposed this formulation and insisted that the USSR should be the result of the *unification* of the Russian socialist republic with the others:

> Stalin has already consented to make one concession: in Clause 1, instead of 'entry' into the RSFSR, to put: "Formal unification with the RSFSR in a Union of Soviet Republics of Europe and Asia."

> I hope the purport of this concession is clear: *we consider ourselves, the Ukrainian SSR and others, equal,* and enter with them, *on an equal basis,* into a new *union,* a new federation, the Union of the Soviet Republics of Europe and Asia.[19]

In combating Stalin, Lenin described him as having a quasi-imperialist attitude towards oppressed nationalities. Despite his Georgian roots, Stalin was the very embodiment of the high-handed methods of the bureaucracy, which was saturated with Great-Russian chauvinism.

In this battle, Lenin counted on the support of people like Ukrainian Bolshevik leader Mykola Skrypnyk. He was a linguist and played a key role in developing the Ukrainian language, standardising its alphabet and orthography for the first time. Skrypnyk later became a Stalinist bureaucrat, but that did not save him from being purged by Stalin in 1933.

Lenin also had the support of Trotsky, Rakovsky and others in this debate. He was acutely aware of the oppressor-nation prejudices surviving amongst Bolshevik militants, including leading figures in the party. He said: "Scratch some communists and you will find Great-Russian chauvinists".[20]

The debate revealed two different approaches to the national question. On the one hand, that of Lenin, who was always extremely aware of the legacy of centuries of national oppression in the Tsarist Empire and went to great lengths to demonstrate to the oppressed

---

19 Lenin, 'On the Establishment of the USSR', 26 September 1922, in this volume, p. 368, emphasis added.

20 See Lenin, 'Eighth Congress of the RCP(B)', 19 March 1919, in this volume, p. 328.

nations that Soviet power had nothing to do with it. He did so with the aim of ensuring maximum unity of the working class. On the other hand, the high-handed approach of Stalin, Sergo Ordzhonikidze, Felix Dzerzhinsky and others, who were, in different degrees, opposed to the right of nations to self-determination, saw Lenin's approach as a nuisance and, behind Lenin's back, used their power to impose rather than convince. Despite the fact that many of them came from the oppressed nations themselves, they expressed the point of view of Great-Russian chauvinism.

The second issue in this struggle was the 'Georgian affair'. Georgia was a nation dominated by petty-bourgeois classes in the city and the countryside. For this reason, the Mensheviks were always the dominant party in the Georgian labour movement and the Menshevik Party had its main base in Georgia.

The issue of Georgia was very complex, as it was mixed up with the course of the civil war, foreign intervention and also the establishment of Soviet power in the neighbouring republics. But the truth is that Ordzhonikidze, who was the head of the Caucasian Bureau (Kavbiuro), was very impatient and displayed a bureaucratic attitude towards *imposing* revolution in Georgia. He staged a series of provocations, sent misleading information to the Politburo and, with the support of Stalin behind the scenes, created a *de facto* situation in which the Red Army invaded Georgia and installed Soviet power in February 1921. This led to all sorts of complications. Trotsky had advocated "a certain preparatory period of work inside Georgia, in order to develop the uprising and later come to its aid" and was not told of the decision to invade.

Even after the Red Army intervention in Georgia, Lenin insisted that a cautious policy of concessions to the petty bourgeois was necessary, and even raised the possibility of reaching an agreement with Noe Zhordania, the leader of the Mensheviks. Stalin on his part took a heavy handed approach against any "nationalist deviations", real or perceived, and opposed the formation of a Georgian Red Army (which Lenin specifically argued should be strengthened). At a meeting of Georgian communists in Tiflis in July 1921, he stated that the immediate task was "to eliminate nationalist survivals, to *cauterise them with red-hot iron*" and promised to "crush the hydra of nationalism". In a typical bureaucratic fashion, Stalin removed the head of the Revolutionary Committee Filipp Makharadze and replaced him with Polikarp Mdivani, whom he thought would be more pliable. Already here, we can see a very clear difference of approach between Lenin on one side and Stalin and Ordzhonikidze on the other.

During the debate on the formation of the USSR, some Georgian communists, led by Mdivani and others, first opposed the idea of a Transcaucasian Federation, raised by Stalin, and defended an independent Soviet Georgia to join the USSR. They were accused by Stalin of national deviations. Lenin sent a letter to Stalin arguing that while a Transcaucasian Federation was "correct in principle", its practical realisation should be delayed to allow for a proper discussion and a campaign of explanation in order to convince the workers and peasants of each of the republics.

In November 1922, it came to light that during a debate in Georgia, Ordzhonikidze had punched a Georgian communist, Akakii Kobakhidze, in the face. Lenin was furious. He demanded the expulsion of Ordzhonikidze from the party, but added that those really responsible for this incident were Stalin and Dzerzhinsky. He wrote a series of letters, his 'The Question of Nationalities or 'Autonomisation'', which he starts by saying:

I have been very remiss with respect to the workers of Russia for not having intervened energetically and decisively enough in the notorious question of autonomisation.

In my writings on the national question I have already said that an abstract presentation of the question of nationalism in general is of no use at all. A distinction must necessarily be made between the nationalism of an oppressor nation and that of an oppressed nation, the nationalism of a big nation and that of a small nation. In respect of the second kind of nationalism we, nationals of a big nation, have nearly always been guilty, in historic practice, of an infinite number of cases of violence;

furthermore, we commit violence and insult an infinite number of times without noticing it.

That is why internationalism on the part of oppressor or 'great' nations, as they are called (though they are great only in their violence, only great as bullies), must consist not only in the observance of the formal equality of nations but even in an inequality of the oppressor nation, the great nation, that must make up for the inequality which obtains in actual practice... In one way or another, by one's attitude or by concessions, it is necessary to compensate the non-Russian for the lack of trust, for the suspicion and the insults to which the government of the 'dominant' nation subjected them in the past.[21]

Lenin insisted that he was saying this not because he was in favour of the nationalism of the oppressed nation, but because this was the only way to achieve the maximum degree of unity and trust between the workers of both nations.

Throughout this period Lenin was ill, and this was used by the bureaucracy to attempt to hide information from him (for instance the full report on the Georgian incident), or to try to restrict his participation in party affairs. He considered this a crucial question. He asked Trotsky to defend his point of view at the forthcoming twelfth party conference and he wrote to the Georgian communists promising them support. He fought this vigorously and managed to leave his views in writing. It is not by chance that one of the crucial issues on which Lenin's struggle against bureaucratisation started was the national question.

Stalin's reversal of Lenin's policy

Lenin unfortunately died in 1924 before he could conclude this struggle. The reversal of Lenin's policy on the national question was not immediate. In 1923, the policy of *korenizatsiia* was formulated, meaning the indigenisation or nationalisation of the communist parties in the republics. Many of these were positive measures, which

---

21 Lenin, 'The Question of Nationalities or 'Autonomisation'', 30-31 December 1922, in this volume, p. 373.

were a continuation of Lenin's policy, but there was also a certain element which was never present in Lenin, an element of nation-building or developing nationalism. This was at the time of the right-wing turn of the nascent bureaucracy, when Stalin formulated the anti-Marxist, anti-Leninist policy of 'socialism on one country' and Bukharin talked of building socialism at a "tortoise pace", encouraging the kulaks to "enrich themselves".

However, not long after, the whole of Lenin's careful policy was reversed. The bureaucracy, having defeated the Left Opposition and afraid of the threat of capitalist elements which had grown out of the NEP, effected a sharp shift to the left. This was the period of forced collectivisation and the beginning of the process which led to the Great Purges.

The Stalinist purges throughout the late 1920s and 1930s had a particularly harsh impact on all the oppressed nationalities. For instance, all members of the Tajik Communist Party Central Committee were eliminated. In Ukraine, nine-tenths of all officials, heads of departments, ministers and all high officials were either arrested, deported or killed in the purges. It was also in these nationalities that the opposition against Stalinism was stronger, and this was the case particularly in Ukraine: in the industrial centre of Kharkov, amongst the Communist Youth, in the big factories, etc. as is described in detail in Pierre Broué's 2003 book *Communistes contre Staline (Communists Against Stalin)*.

There was a wholesale return to Great-Russian nationalism, which was in effect a continuation of the policy of the Tsarist Empire. Stalin's policy of national oppression created enormous accumulated grievances which remained for decades. Later on, during the Second World War, the Stalinist bureaucracy carried out mass deportation of whole peoples, who were branded as collaborators.

Nevertheless, for a whole period of time, on the basis of economic development, the national question subsided, and even what seemed to be deeply entrenched national conflicts (like that of Nagorno-Karabakh) were temporarily resolved or frozen.

Economic stagnation, particularly in the 1980s, which was the result of bureaucratic mismanagement, led to a new flare up of national sentiment, which had been suppressed for decades. The policy of the Soviet bureaucracy of Great-Russian national oppression was to play a big role in the breakup of the Soviet Union. This laid the basis for the dissolution of the Soviet Union, which from a formal point of view started with a referendum on independence in Ukraine.

As Marx and Engels explained, "no nation can be free if it oppresses other nations".[22] But equally important is the principle: "Workers of the world, unite!".[23] The two are inextricably linked, because the unity of workers from different nations, different religious and ethnic backgrounds, can only be achieved by guaranteeing democratic rights and eliminating any vestige of oppression. This was the basis of Lenin's approach to this question.

The policy of Lenin and of the October Revolution on the national question has left us an extremely rich and proud heritage, which we shall reclaim, explain and defend fully, because it is not commonly known, other than through distortions or generalities. It contains many lessons on how to deal with the question of national oppression, which remains strikingly relevant for communists today.

The national question was a fundamental part of the bourgeois revolutions. In those cases where the bourgeoisie was too weak and arrived late in the scene of history, some of the tasks of the bourgeois-democratic revolution were left unsolved. In some instances, the national question subsided for a whole period of time, but with the worsening of the organic crisis of capitalism it has come back to the fore with a vengeance.

The struggle against national oppression contains a democratic kernel which is progressive and can have revolutionary implications, but at the same time, there is the danger of reactionary chauvinism and division of the working class along national lines, with potentially bloody consequences. Studying Lenin's policy and practice on this question is therefore not merely a historical curiosity, but a current issue in revolutionary politics.

---

22 Karl Marx and Friedrich Engels, 'On Poland', *Marx and Engels Collected Works*, Lawrence and Wishart, 1977, Vol. 6, p. 389.

23 Marx and Engels, *The Communist Manifesto*, ibid, p. 519.

The study of Lenin's approach to the twin questions of the struggle against national oppression and the need for the unity of the working class also contains a valuable lesson on the method of Marxism, which is firm on its principles but flexible with its tactics. A careful study, both of Lenin's method and the Bolshevik attitude to the national question, will be a vital tool to arm revolutionary communists today.

Jorge Martín,
London,
December 2024

*Part 1:
Lenin, Luxemburg and
the Right of Nations to
Self-Determination*

On the Manifesto of the
Armenian Social-Democrats

Published 1 February 1903

A new social-democratic organisation has made its appearance in the Caucasus: *The League of Armenian Social-Democrats*. This League, as we know, began its practical activities over half a year ago and already has its own paper, published in Armenian. We have received the first issue of this paper, which is called *Proletariat* and next to its title carries the inscription 'Russian Social-Democratic Labour Party'. It contains a number of articles, commentaries, and reports dealing with the social and political conditions which have called into existence the League of Armenian Social-Democrats, and giving a general outline of the programme of its activities.

The leading article, 'Manifesto of the Armenian Social- Democrats', states:

In its activities, the League of Armenian Social-Democrats, as one of the branches of the Russian Social-Democratic Labour Party which extends the network of its organisations far and wide over the entire expanse of Russia, is in complete accord with the RSDLP, and will fight together with it for the interests of the Russian proletariat in general, and of the Armenian proletariat in particular.

Further, after referring to the rapid development of capitalism in the Caucasus and the monstrously powerful and manifold results of this process, the authors go on to speak of the present state of the working-class movement in the Caucasus. In the industrial centres of the Caucasus, such as Baku, Tiflis, and Batum, with their big capitalist establishments and numerous industrial proletariat, this movement has already struck deep roots. However, because of the extremely low cultural level of the Caucasian workers, their struggle against the employers has naturally been of a more or less instinctive, spontaneous nature till now. A force was necessary which could unite the workers' scattered forces, give their demands articulate form and develop class-consciousness among them. That force is socialism.

Then, after briefly setting forth the main theses of scientific socialism, the League explains its stand in relation to the present-day trends in international, and, in particular, Russian Social-Democracy.

> The attainment of the socialist ideal, [says the Manifesto] is, in our opinion, conceivable neither through the working class' efforts in the economic sphere, nor through partial political and social reforms; it is possible only by completely smashing the entire existing system, by means of a social revolution, to which the political dictatorship of the proletariat must be the necessary prologue.

Then, pointing out that the existing political system in Russia is hostile to every social movement, especially to that of the working class, the League declares that it sets itself the immediate task of politically educating the Armenian proletariat and drawing it into the struggle of the entire Russian proletariat for the overthrow of the tsarist autocracy. Without at all denying the need for the partial economic struggle of the workers against the employers, the League, however, does not consider it of importance in itself. The League recognises this struggle insofar as it improves the material condition of the workers and helps develop political consciousness and class solidarity among them.

Of particular interest to us is the League's attitude towards the national question.

Taking into consideration [says the Manifesto] that the Russian state is made up of many different nationalities at varying levels of cultural development, and believing that only the extensive development of local self-government can safeguard the interests of these heterogeneous elements, we deem essential the establishment of a *federative* [italics ours – *Lenin*] republic in the future free Russia. As to the Caucasus, in view of the extremely diverse national composition of its population, we shall strive to unite all the local socialist elements and all the workers of the various nationalities; we shall strive to create a united and strong social-democratic organisation, for a more successful struggle against the autocracy. In the future Russia we shall recognise the right of all nations to free self-determination, since we regard national freedom as being only one of the aspects of civil liberties in general. Proceeding from this proposition, and taking into account the above-mentioned diverse national composition of the Caucasus and the absence of geographical boundaries between the various nationalities, we do not find it possible to include in our programme the demand for political autonomy for the Caucasian peoples; we demand only autonomy in matters pertaining to cultural life, i.e. freedom of language, schools, education, etc.

We whole-heartedly welcome the 'Manifesto of the League of Armenian Social-Democrats' and especially its splendid attempt to give a correct presentation of the national question. It is highly desirable that this attempt be carried through to the end. Two fundamental principles by which all social-democrats in Russia should be guided in the national question *have been* quite correctly *outlined* by the League. These are, firstly, the demand for political and civil liberties and complete equality, rather than for national autonomy; and, secondly, the demand for the right to self-determination for every nationality forming part of the state. But neither of these principles is as yet quite consistently brought out by the League of Armenian Social-Democrats. As a matter of fact, is it possible *from the Armenian Social-Democrats' point of view* to speak of the demand for a *federative* republic? Federation *presupposes* autonomous national political units, whereas the League rejects the demand for national autonomy. To be fully consistent, the League should delete the demand for a federative republic from its programme, confining itself to the demand for a democratic republic in general. It is not the business of the proletariat to *preach* federalism and national autonomy; it is not the business of the proletariat to advance such demands, which inevitably amount to a demand for the establishment of an autonomous *class* state. It is the business of the proletariat to rally the greatest possible *masses* of workers of each and every nationality *more closely*, to rally them for struggle *in the broadest possible arena* for a democratic republic and for socialism. And since the state arena in which we are working today was created and is being maintained and extended by means of a series of outrageous acts of violence, then, to make the struggle against all forms of exploitation and oppression successful, we must not disperse but unite the forces of the *working class*, which is the most oppressed and the most capable of fighting. The demand for recognition of every nationality's right to self-determination simply implies that we, the party of the proletariat, must always and unconditionally *oppose any attempt* to influence national *self*-determination from without *by violence or injustice*. While at all times performing this negative duty of ours (to fight and protest against violence), we on our part concern ourselves with the self-determination of the *proletariat* in each nationality rather than with self-determination of peoples or nations. Thus, the general, basic and ever-binding programme of Russian Social-Democracy must consist only in the demand for equal rights for all citizens (irrespective of sex, language, creed, race, nationality, etc.) and for their right to free democratic *self*-determination. As to *support* of the demand for *national* autonomy, it is by no means a permanent and binding part of the programme of the proletariat. This support may become necessary for it only in isolated and exceptional cases. With regard to Armenian Social-Democracy, the League of Armenian Social-Democrats has itself recognised the absence of such exceptional circumstances.

We hope to return to the question of federalism and nationality.[1] For the time being we shall conclude by once again welcoming a new member of the Russian Social Democratic Labour Party – the League of Armenian Social Democrats.

1　See Lenin, 'The National Question in our Programme', in this volume, p. 9.

The National Question in Our Programme

Published 15 July 1903

Editor's note: In preparation for the Second Congress of the RSDLP in 1903, Lenin wrote a series of articles explaining different aspects of the questions which were to be debated, including the agrarian question, the organisational principles of the party, the attitude towards the Liberals, the differences between the social-democrats (as Marxists were known at the time) and the Socialist-Revolutionaries, etc.

Amongst these was the question of the party program in regards to the oppressed nationalities and why and how the social-democrats should defend the right of nations to self-determination. In this article, Lenin answers the arguments of the Polish Socialist Party, which was, despite its name, a petty-bourgeois nationalist party, founded in 1892.

* * *

In our draft party programme we have advanced the demand for a republic with a democratic constitution that would guarantee, among other things, "recognition of the right to self-determination for all nations forming part of the state". Many did not find this demand in our programme sufficiently clear, and in issue No. 33 [of *Iskra*],[1] in

---

1 *Iskra* (*The Spark*) was the first all-Russian illegal Marxist newspaper, founded by Lenin in 1900. It played a decisive part in the establishment of the RSDLP.

speaking about the 'Manifesto of the Armenian Social-Democrats', we explained the meaning of this point in the following way:

The social-democrats will always combat every attempt to influence national self-determination from without by violence or by any injustice. However, our unreserved recognition of the struggle for freedom of self-determination does not in any way commit us to supporting every demand for national self-determination. As the party of the proletariat, the Social-Democratic Party considers it to be its positive and principal task to further the self-determination of the proletariat in each nationality rather than that of peoples or nations. We must always and unreservedly work for the very closest unity of the proletariat of all nationalities, and it is only in isolated and exceptional cases that we can advance and actively support demands conducive to the establishment of a new class state or to the substitution of a looser federal unity, etc., for the complete political unity of a state.

This explanation of our programme on the national question has evoked a strong protest from the Polish Socialist Party (PSP). In an article entitled 'The Attitude of the Russian Social-Democrats Towards the National Question' (*Przedświt*, March 1903),[2] the PSP expresses indignation at this "amazing" explanation and at the "vagueness" of this "mysterious" self-determination of ours; it accuses us both of doctrinairism and of holding the "anarchist" view that "the worker is concerned with nothing but the complete abolition of capitalism, since, we learn, language, nationality, culture, and the like are mere bourgeois inventions", and so on. It is worth considering this argument in detail, for it reveals almost all the misconceptions in the national question so common and so widespread among socialists.

What makes our explanation so 'amazing'? Why is it considered a departure from the 'literal' meaning? Does recognition of the *right* of nations to self-determination really imply *support* of any demand of every nation for self-determination? After all, the fact that we recognise the *right* of all citizens to form free associations does not at all commit us, social-democrats, to *supporting* the formation of

---

2   *Przedświt* (*Daybreak*) was the magazine of the Polish Socialist Party.

any new association; nor does it prevent us from opposing and campaigning against the formation of a given association as an inexpedient and unwise step. We even recognise the *right* of the Jesuits to carry on agitation freely, but we fight (not by police methods, of course) against an alliance between the Jesuits and the proletarians. Consequently, when the *Przedświt* says: "If this demand for the right to free self-determination is to be taken literally [and that is how we have taken it hitherto], then it would satisfy us" – it is quite obvious that it is precisely the PSP that is departing from the literal meaning of the programme. Its conclusion is certainly illogical from the formal point of view.

We do not, however, wish to confine ourselves to a formal verification of our explanation. We shall go straight to the root of the matter: is Social-Democracy in duty bound to demand national independence always and unreservedly, or only under certain circumstances; if the latter is the case then under what circumstances? To this question the PSP has always replied in favour of unreserved recognition; we are not in the least surprised, therefore, at the fondness it displays towards the Russian Socialist-Revolutionaries, who demand a federal state system and speak in favour of "complete and unreserved recognition of the right to national self-determination" (*Revolutsionnaya Rossiya*,[3] No. 18, the article entitled 'National Enslavement and Revolutionary Socialism'). Unfortunately, this is nothing more than one of those bourgeois-democratic phrases which, for the hundredth and thousandth time, reveal the true nature of the so-called party of so-called Socialist-Revolutionaries. By falling for the bait presented by these phrases and yielding to the allurement of this clamour, the PSP in its turn proves how weak in theoretical background and political activities is its link with the class struggle of the proletariat. But it is to the interests of this struggle that we must *subordinate* the demand for national self-determination. It is this that makes all the difference between our approach to the national question and the bourgeois-

---

3　*Revolutsionnaya Rossiya* (*Revolutionary Russia*) was a paper of the Socialist-Revolutionaries (SRs), a petty-bourgeois party of agrarian socialists, who based themselves on the peasantry. They were the ideological heirs of the Narodniks.

democratic approach. The bourgeois democrat (and the present-day socialist opportunist who follows in his footsteps) imagines that democracy eliminates the class struggle, and that is why he presents all his political demands in an abstract way, lumped together, 'without reservations,' from the standpoint of the interests of the 'whole people,' or even from that of an eternal and absolute moral principle. Always and everywhere the social-democrat ruthlessly exposes this bourgeois illusion, whether it finds expression in an abstract idealist philosophy or in an absolute demand for national independence.

If there is still need to prove that a Marxist can recognise the demand for national independence only conditionally, namely, on the condition indicated above, let us quote a writer who *defended* from the Marxist viewpoint the Polish proletarians' demand for an independent Poland. In 1896 Karl Kautsky[4] wrote in an article entitled '*Finis Poloniae?*' ['The End of Poland?']:

> Once the proletariat tackles the Polish question it cannot but take a stand in favour of Poland's independence, and, consequently, it cannot but welcome each step that can be taken in this direction at the present time, insofar as this step is at all compatible with the class interests of the international militant proletariat.

> This reservation [Kautsky goes on to say] should be made in any case. *National independence is not so inseparably linked with the class interests of the militant proletariat as to make it necessary to strive for it unconditionally, under any circumstances.* [Italics ours. – *Lenin*] Marx and Engels took a most determined stand in favour of the unification and liberation of Italy, but this did not prevent them from coming out in 1859 against an Italy allied with Napoleon. (*Neue Zeit*,[5] XIV, 2, 5. 520.)

---

4   Karl Kautsky was one of the leading theoreticians of the Social Democratic Party of Germany (SPD) and the Second International. By the outbreak of the First World War, he had abandoned revolutionary Marxism and took up an indecisive position between revolutionary opposition to the war and patriotic support for the German bourgeoisie. As such, he became the theoretician of this 'centrism' in the socialist movement, and a bitter opponent of the Russian Revolution.

5   *Die Neue Zeit* (*New Times*) was the theoretical organ of the SPD, published in Stuttgart from 1883 to 1923.

As you see, Kautsky categorically rejects the *unconditional* demand for the independence of nations, and categorically demands that the question be placed not merely on a historical basis in general, but specifically on a class basis. And if we examine how Marx and Engels treated the Polish question, we shall see that this was precisely their approach to it from the very outset. *Die Neue Rheinische Zeitung*[6] devoted much space to the Polish question, and emphatically demanded, not only the independence of Poland, but also that Germany go to war with Russia for Poland's freedom. At the same time Marx, however, attacked Ruge,[7] who had spoken in favour of Poland's freedom in the Frankfurt Parliament and had tried to settle the Polish question solely by means of bourgeois-democratic phrases about 'shameful injustice', without making any attempt to analyse it historically. Marx was not like those pedants and philistines of the revolution who dread nothing more than 'polemics' at revolutionary moments in history. Marx poured pitiless scorn on the 'humane' citizen Ruge, and showed him, from the example of the oppression of the south of France by the north of France, that it is not every kind of national oppression that invariably inspires a desire for independence which is justified from the viewpoint of democracy and the proletariat.

---

6   *Die Neue Rheinische Zeitung* (*New Rhenish Gazette*) appeared in Cologne from 1 June 1848 until 19 May 1849. Marx and Engels were managers of this newspaper, Marx being editor-in-chief. As Lenin put it, the newspaper was "the best, the unsurpassed organ of the revolutionary proletariat". It educated the masses, roused them to fight the counter-revolution, and made its influence felt throughout Germany. Because of its resolute and irreconcilable position and its militant internationalism, *Die Neue Rheinische Zeitung* was from the first months of its existence persecuted by the feudal-monarchist and liberal-bourgeois press, and also by the government. Marx's deportation by the Prussian Government and the repressive measures against its other editors led to the paper ceasing publication on 19 May 1849.

7   Arnold Ruge was a German philosopher and associated with the Young Hegelians alongside Marx, Engels, Ludwig Feuerbach and others. He briefly edited the *Deutsch-Französische Jahrbücher* (*German-French Annals*), a paper published after the censorship of the original *Rheinische Zeitung*. The paper was discontinued due to the differences between Marx and Ruge, who was not sympathetic to socialism.

Marx referred to special social circumstances as a result of which:

> Poland [...] became the revolutionary part of Russia, Austria, and
> Prussia. [...] Even the Polish nobility, although their foundations were
> still partly feudal, adhered to the democratic agrarian revolution with
> unparalleled selflessness. Poland was already a seat of East-European
> democracy at a time when Germany was still groping her way through
> the most platitudinous constitutional and high-flown philosophical
> ideology. [...] So long as we [Germans] [...] help to oppress Poland,
> so long as we keep part of Poland fettered to Germany, we shall remain
> fettered to Russia and Russian policy, we shall be unable completely
> to smash patriarchal feudal absolutism at home. The creation of a
> democratic Poland is the primary prerequisite of the creation of a
> democratic Germany.[8]

We have quoted these statements in such detail because they
graphically show the historical background at a time when the
attitude of international Social-Democracy to the Polish problem
took shape in a way which held good almost throughout the second
half of the nineteenth century. To ignore the changes which have
taken place in that background and to continue advocating the old
solutions given by Marxism, would mean being true to the letter
but not to the spirit of the teaching, would mean repeating the old
conclusions by rote, without being able to use the Marxist method
of research to analyse the new political situation.

Those times and today – the age of the last bourgeois revolutionary
movements, and the age of desperate reaction, extreme tension of all
forces on the eve of the proletarian revolution – differ in the most
obvious way. *In those times* Poland as a whole, not only the peasantry,
but even the bulk of the nobility, was revolutionary. The traditions
of the struggle for national liberation were so strong and deep-rooted
that, after their defeat at home, Poland's best sons went wherever

---

8   Lenin is quoting from Engels, 'The Frankfurt Assembly Debates the Polish
    Question', first published in *Die Neue Rheinische Zeitung* in August-September
    1848. See *Marx and Engels Collected Works* (henceforth referred to as *MECW*),
    Vol. 7, Lawrence and Wishart, 1977, p. 337.

they could find a revolutionary class to support; the memory of Dąbrowski and of Wróblewski[9] is inseparably associated with the greatest movement of the proletariat in the nineteenth century, with the last – and let us hope the last unsuccessful – insurrection of the Paris workers. *In those times* complete victory for democracy in Europe was indeed impossible without the restoration of Poland. *In those times* Poland was indeed the bulwark of civilisation against tsarism, and the vanguard of democracy.

Today the Polish ruling classes, the gentry in Germany and in Austria, and the industrial and financial magnates in Russia are supporting the ruling classes of the countries that oppress Poland, while the German and the Russian proletariat are fighting for freedom side by side with the Polish proletariat, which has heroically taken over the great traditions of the old revolutionary Poland. *Today* the advanced representatives of Marxism in the neighbouring country, while attentively watching the political evolution of Europe and fully sympathising with the heroic struggle of the Poles, nevertheless frankly admit that:

> ... at present St. Petersburg has become a much more important revolutionary centre than Warsaw, and the Russian revolutionary movement is already of greater international significance than the Polish movement.

This is what Kautsky wrote as early as 1896, in defending the inclusion in the Polish social-democrats' programme of the demand for Poland's restoration. And in 1902 Mehring,[10] who has been studying the evolution of the Polish question since 1848, arrived at the following conclusion:

---

9   Jaroslaw Dąbrowski and Walery Wróblewski were prominent leaders of the Polish revolutionary movement in 1863-64, who emigrated to France after the suppression of the Polish uprising. In 1871 they were generals of the Paris Commune.

10 Franz Mehring was a German communist, historian and art critic who was a veteran of the SPD and later the Communist Party of Germany (KPD). He was in correspondence with Engels and edited various papers including *Die Neue Zeit*. He played a leading role alongside Rosa Luxemburg and Karl Liebknecht in founding the Spartacus League.

Had the Polish proletariat desired to inscribe on its banner the restoration of a Polish class state, which the ruling classes themselves do not want to hear of, it would be playing a historical farce; this may well happen to the propertied classes (as, for instance, the Polish nobility in 1791), but it should never happen to the working class. If, on the other hand, this reactionary utopia comes out to win over to proletarian agitation those sections of the intelligentsia and of the petty bourgeoisie which still respond in some measure to national agitation, then that utopia is doubly untenable as an outgrowth of that unworthy opportunism which sacrifices the long-term interests of the working class to the cheap and paltry successes of the moment.

Those interests dictate categorically that, in all three states that have partitioned Poland, the Polish workers should fight unreservedly side by side with their class comrades. The times are past when a bourgeois revolution could create a free Poland: today the renascence of Poland is possible only through a social revolution, in the course of which the modern proletariat will break its chains.[11]

We fully subscribe to Mehring's conclusion. We shall only remark that this conclusion remains unassailable even if we do not go as far as Mehring in our arguments. Without any doubt the present state of the Polish question differs radically from that which obtained fifty years ago. However, the present situation cannot be regarded as permanent. Class antagonism has now undoubtedly relegated national questions far into the background, but, without the risk of lapsing into doctrinairism, it cannot be categorically asserted that some particular national question cannot appear temporarily in the foreground of the political drama. No doubt, the restoration of Poland prior to the fall of capitalism is highly improbable, but it cannot be asserted that it is absolutely impossible, or that circumstances may not arise under which the Polish bourgeoisie will take the side of independence, etc. And Russian Social-Democracy does not in the least intend to tie its own hands. In including in its programme

---

11 Lenin is quoting Franz Mehring's introduction to the third volume of the *Collected Works of Karl Marx and Frederick Engels, 1841 to 1850*, published in 1902.

recognition of the right of nations to self-determination, it takes into account *all* possible, and even all *conceivable*, combinations. That programme in no way precludes the adoption by the Polish proletariat of the slogan of a free and independent Polish republic, even though the probability of its becoming a reality before socialism is introduced is infinitesimal. The programme merely demands that a genuinely socialist party shall not corrupt proletarian class-consciousness, or slur over the class struggle, or lure working class with bourgeois-democratic phrases, or break the unity of the proletariat's present-day political struggle.

This reservation is the crux of the matter, for only with this reservation do we recognise self-determination. It is useless for the PSP to pretend that it differs from the German or Russian social-democrats in their rejection of the right to self-determination, the right to strive for a free and independent republic. It is not this, but the fact that it loses sight of the class point of view, obscures it by chauvinism and disrupts the unity of the present-day political struggle, that prevents us from regarding the PSP as a genuine social-democratic workers' party.

This, for instance, is how the PSP usually presents the question:

> We can only weaken tsarism by wresting Poland from it; it is the task of the Russian comrades to overthrow it.

Or again:

> After the overthrow of tsarism we would simply decide our fate by seceding from Russia.

See to what monstrous conclusions this monstrous logic leads, even from the viewpoint of the programme's demand for Poland's restoration. *Because* the restoration of Poland is one of the possible (but, whilst the bourgeoisie rules, by no means absolutely certain) consequences of democratic evolution, *therefore* the Polish proletariat must not fight together with the Russian proletariat to overthrow tsarism, but "only" to weaken it by wresting Poland from it. *Because* Russian tsarism is concluding a closer and closer alliance with the bourgeoisie and the governments of Germany, Austria, etc., *therefore* the Polish proletariat must weaken its alliance with the proletariat of Russia, Germany, etc., together with whom it is now fighting against *one and the same* yoke. This is nothing more than sacrificing the most vital interests of the proletariat to the bourgeois-democratic conception of national independence. The disintegration of Russia which the PSP desires, *as distinct from* our aim of overthrowing tsarism, is and will remain an empty phrase, as long as economic development continues to bring the different parts of a political whole more and more closely together, and as long as the bourgeoisie of all countries unite more and more closely against their common enemy, the proletariat, and in support of their common ally, the tsar. But *the division of the forces of the proletariat*, which is now suffering under the yoke of this autocracy, is the sad reality, the direct consequence of the error of the PSP, the direct outcome of its worship of bourgeois-democratic formulas.

To turn a blind eye to this division of the proletariat, the PSP has to stoop to chauvinism and present the views of the Russian social-democrats as follows:

> We [the Poles] must wait for the social revolution, and until then we must patiently endure national oppression.

This is an utter falsehood. The Russian social-democrats have never advised anything of the sort; on the contrary, they themselves fight, and call upon the whole Russian proletariat to fight, against all manifestations of national oppression in Russia; they include in *their* programme not only complete equality of status for all languages, nationalities, etc., but also recognition of every nation's right to determine its own destiny. Recognising this right, we *subordinate* to the interests of the proletarian struggle our support of the demand for national independence, and only a chauvinist can interpret our position as an expression of a Russian's mistrust of a non-Russian, for in reality this position necessarily follows from the class-conscious proletarian's distrust of the bourgeoisie.

The PSP takes the view that the national question is *exhausted* by the contrast: 'we' (Poles) and 'they' (Germans, Russians, etc.). The social-democrat, however, gives first place to the contrast – 'we', the proletarians, and 'they', the bourgeoisie. 'We', the proletarians, have seen dozens of times how the bourgeoisie *betrays* the interests of freedom, motherland, language, and nation, when it is confronted with the revolutionary proletariat. We witnessed the French bourgeoisie's surrender to the Prussians at the moment of the greatest humiliation and suppression of the French nation, the Government of National Defence becoming a 'Government of National Defection', the bourgeoisie of an oppressed nation calling to its aid the troops of the oppressing nation so as to crush its proletarian fellow countrymen, who had dared to assume power.[12] And that is why, undeterred by chauvinist and opportunist heckling, we shall always say to the Polish workers: only the most complete and intimate alliance with the Russian proletariat can meet the requirements of the present political struggle against the autocracy; only such an alliance can guarantee complete political and economic emancipation.

What we have said on the Polish question is wholly applicable to every other national question. The accursed history of autocracy has left us a legacy of tremendous *estrangement* between the working classes of the various nationalities oppressed by that autocracy. This estrangement is a very great evil, a very great obstacle in the struggle against the autocracy, and we must not legitimise this evil or sanctify

---

12 Lenin here is referring to the events of the crushing of the Paris Commune. The Government of National Defence was the provisional government established in September 1870 after the capture of Emperor Napoleon III during the Franco-Prussian War. This government consistently failed to take effective steps to fight off the subsequent siege of Paris by the Prussian army, due to its fear that arming the workers of Paris would result in a revolutionary uprising. This led Marx to dub it the 'Government of National Defection'. Prussian troops continued to surround Paris, even after an armistice was signed in late January 1871. Further, Prussia released thousands of captured French troops to the Versailles government, in return for huge sums of money from the French state. The troops were then used to attack the Paris workers, who were at last overwhelmed and massacred 21-28 May 1871.

this outrageous state of affairs by establishing any such 'principles' as separate parties or a 'federation' of parties. It is, of course, simpler and easier to follow the line of least resistance, and for everyone to make himself comfortable in his own corner following the rule, 'it's none of my business', as the Bund now wants to do. The more we realise the need for unity and the more firmly we are convinced that a concerted offensive against the autocracy is impossible without complete unity, the more obvious becomes the necessity for a centralised organisation of the struggle in the conditions of our political system – the less inclined are we to be satisfied with a 'simple', but specious and, at bottom, profoundly false solution of the problem. So long as the injuriousness of estrangement is not realised, and so long as there is no desire to put an end radically and at all costs to this estrangement in the camp of the proletarian party, there is no need for the fig-leaf of 'federation', and no use in undertaking to solve a problem which one of the 'sides' concerned has no real desire to solve. That being the case, it is better to let the lessons of experience and of the actual movement prove that centralism is essential for success in the struggle waged by the proletarians of all nationalities oppressed by autocracy against that autocracy and against the international bourgeoisie, which is becoming more and more united.

Theses on the National Question

Written June 1913

1. The article of our programme (on the self-determination of nations) cannot be interpreted to mean anything but *political* self-determination, i.e. the right to secede and form a separate state.

2. This article in the social-democratic programme is *absolutely* essential to the social-democrats of Russia:

   a. For the sake of the basic principles of democracy in general;

   b. Also because there are, within the frontiers of Russia and, *what is more, in her frontier areas*, a number of nations with sharply distinctive economic, social and other conditions; furthermore, these nations (like all the nations of Russia except the Great Russians) are unbelievably oppressed by the tsarist monarchy;

   c. Lastly, also in view of the fact that throughout Eastern Europe (Austria and the Balkans) and in Asia – i.e. in countries bordering on Russia – the bourgeois-democratic reform of the state that has everywhere else in the world led, in varying degree, to the creation of independent national states or states with the closest, interrelated national composition, has either not been consummated or has only just begun;

d. At the present moment Russia is a country whose state system is more backward and reactionary than that of *any* of the contiguous countries, beginning – in the West – with Austria where the fundamentals of political liberty and a constitutional regime were consolidated in 1867, and where universal franchise has now been introduced, and ending – in the East – with republican China. In all their propaganda, therefore, the social-democrats of Russia must insist on the right of all nationalities to form separate states or to choose freely the state of which they wish to form part.

3. The Social-Democratic Party's recognition of the right of all nationalities to self-determination requires of social-democrats that they should:

   a. Be unconditionally hostile to the use of force in any form whatsoever by the dominant nation (or the nation which constitutes the majority of the population) in respect of a nation that wishes to secede politically;

   b. Demand the settlement of the question of such secession only on the basis of a universal, direct and equal vote of the population of the given territory by secret ballot;

   c. Conduct an implacable struggle against both the Black Hundred-Octobrist[1] and the liberal-bourgeois (Progressist, Cadet, etc.)[2] parties on every occasion when they defend or sanction national oppression in general or the denial of the right of nations to self-determination in particular.

---

1 The Black Hundreds were ultra-reactionary terrorist bands, loyal to the tsar, responsible for state-sanctioned pogroms of Jewish people and social-democrats. The Octobrists were the party of the big merchants, industrialists and big landowners who ran their estates on capitalist lines.

2 The Constitutional-Democratic Party, who's abbreviated name was the Cadets, were the chief party of the Russian liberal-monarchist bourgeoisie. The Progressists were a political group of the Russian liberal-monarchist bourgeoisie, which, during the elections to the Duma and within the Duma, attempted to unite elements of the various bourgeois-landlord parties and groups under the flag of 'non-partisanship'. Lenin called the Progressists a mixture of the Cadets and the Octobrists.

4. The Social-Democratic Party's recognition of the right of all nationalities to self-determination most certainly does not mean that social-democrats reject an independent appraisal of the advisability of the state secession of any nation in each separate case. Social-Democracy should, on the contrary, give its independent appraisal, taking into consideration the conditions of capitalist development and the oppression of the proletarians of various nations by the united bourgeoisie of all nationalities, as well as the general tasks of democracy, first of all and most of all the interests of the proletarian class struggle for socialism.

From this point of view the following circumstance must be given special attention. There are two nations in Russia that are more civilised and more isolated by virtue of a number of historical and social conditions and that could most easily and most 'naturally' put into effect their right to secession. They are the peoples of Finland and Poland. The experience of the Revolution of 1905 has shown that even in these two nations the ruling classes, the landowners and bourgeoisie, reject the revolutionary struggle for liberty and seek a *rapprochement* with the ruling classes of Russia and with the tsarist monarchy *because of their fear* of the revolutionary proletariat of Finland and Poland.

Social-Democracy, therefore, must give most emphatic warning to the proletariat and other working people of all nationalities against direct deception by the nationalistic slogans of 'their own' bourgeoisie, who with their saccharine or fiery speeches about 'our native land' try to *divide* the proletariat and *divert its attention* from their bourgeois intrigues while they enter into an economic and political alliance with the bourgeoisie of other nations and with the tsarist monarchy.

The proletariat cannot pursue its struggle for socialism and defend its everyday economic interests without the closest and fullest alliance of the workers of all nations in all working-class organisations without exception.

The proletariat cannot achieve freedom other than by revolutionary struggle for the overthrow of the tsarist monarchy and its replacement by a democratic republic. The tsarist monarchy *precludes* liberty and equal rights for nationalities, and is, furthermore, the bulwark of barbarity, brutality and reaction in both Europe and Asia. This monarchy can be overthrown only by the united proletariat of all the nations of Russia, which is giving the lead to consistently democratic elements capable of revolutionary struggle from among the working masses of all nations.

It follows, therefore, that workers who place political unity with 'their own' bourgeoisie above complete unity with the proletariat of all nations, are acting against their own interests, against the interests of socialism and against the interests of democracy.

5. Social-Democrats, in upholding a consistently democratic state system, demand unconditional equality for all nationalities and struggle against absolutely all privileges for one or several nationalities.

In particular, social-democrats reject a 'state' language. It is particularly superfluous in Russia because more than seven-tenths of the population of Russia belong to related Slav nationalities who, given a free school and a free state, could easily achieve intercourse by virtue of the demands of the economic turnover without any 'state' privileges for any one language.

Social-Democrats demand the abolition of the old administrative divisions of Russia established by the feudal landowners and the civil servants of the autocratic feudal state and their replacement by divisions based on the requirements of present-day economic life and in accordance, as far as possible, with the national composition of the population.

All areas of the state that are distinguished by social peculiarities or by the national composition of the population, must enjoy wide self-government and autonomy, with institutions organised on the basis of universal, equal and secret voting.

6. Social-Democrats demand the promulgation of a law, operative throughout the state, protecting the rights of every national minority in no matter what part of the state. This law should declare inoperative any measure by means of which the national majority might attempt to establish privileges for itself or restrict the rights of a national minority (in the sphere of education, in the use of any specific language, in budget affairs, etc.), and forbid the implementation of any such measure by making it a punishable offence.

7. The social-democratic attitude to the slogan of 'cultural-national' (or simply 'national') 'autonomy' or to plans for its implementation is a negative one, since this slogan:

    i. undoubtedly contradicts the internationalism of the class struggle of the proletariat,

    ii. makes it easier for the proletariat and the masses of working people to be drawn into the sphere of influence of bourgeois nationalism, and

    iii. is capable of distracting attention from the task of the consistent democratic transformation of the state as a whole, which transformation alone can ensure (to the extent that this can, in general, be ensured under capitalism) peace between nationalities.

In view of the special acuteness of the question of cultural-national autonomy among social-democrats, we give some explanation of the situation.

    a. It is impermissible, from the standpoint of Social-Democracy, to issue the slogan of *national* culture either directly or indirectly. The slogan is incorrect because already under capitalism, all economic, political and spiritual life is becoming more and more international. Socialism will make it completely international. International culture, which is now already being systematically created by the proletariat of all countries, does not absorb 'national culture' (no matter of what national group) as a whole, but accepts from *each* national culture *exclusively* those of its elements that are consistently democratic and socialist.

b. Probably the one example of an approximation, even though it is a timid one, to the slogan of national culture in social-democratic programmes is Article 3 of the Brünn Programme of the Austrian social-democrats.[3] This Article 3 reads: "All self-governing regions of one and the same nation form a single-national alliance that has complete autonomy in deciding its national affairs."

This is a compromise slogan since it does not contain a shadow of extra-territorial (personal) national autonomy. But this slogan, too, is erroneous and harmful, for it is no business of the social-democrats of Russia to unite into one nation the Germans in Lodz, Riga, St. Petersburg and Saratov. Our business is to struggle for full democracy and the annulment of *all* national privileges and, to unite the German workers in Russia with the workers of all other nations in upholding and developing the international culture of socialism.

Still more erroneous is the slogan of extra-territorial (personal) national autonomy with the setting up (according to a plan drawn up by the consistent supporters of this slogan) of national parliaments and national state secretaries (Otto Bauer and Karl Renner).[4] Such institutions contradict

---

3   This refers to the Congress of the Social Democratic Party of Austria (SDAPÖ) held in Brünn, Austria, from 11-16 September 1899. The national question was the chief item on the agenda. The programme is reproduced in the appendix, see p. 391.

4   Otto Bauer was the most prominent leader of the Austrian Social-Democratic Party. Prior to the First World War, Bauer was the secretary of the parliamentary faction of the SDAPÖ. He was the author of a number of books on the national and colonial questions. During the war, Bauer held a centrist position. In 1919 he became Minister of Foreign Affairs in the coalition government set up after the overthrow of the Habsburgs. Together with Friedrich Adler and others, Bauer participated both in creating the Two-and-a-half International and in fusing it with the Second International in 1923. He was a major theoretician of 'Austro-Marxism'. Karl Renner was also a member of the SDAPÖ.

the economic conditions of the capitalist countries, they have not been tested in any of the world's democratic states and are the opportunist dream of people who despair of setting up consistent democratic institutions and are seeking salvation from the national squabbles of the bourgeoisie in the artificial isolation of the proletariat and the bourgeoisie of each nation on a number of ('cultural') questions.

Circumstances occasionally compel social-democrats to submit for a time to some sort of compromise decisions, but from other countries we must borrow not compromise decisions, but consistently social-democratic decisions. It would be particularly unwise to adopt the unhappy Austrian compromise decision today, when it has been a complete failure in Austria and has led to the separatism and secession of the Czech social-democrats.

c. The history of the 'cultural-national autonomy' slogan in Russia shows that it has been adopted by *all* Jewish bourgeois parties and *only* by Jewish bourgeois parties; and that they have been uncritically followed by the Bund, which has inconsistently rejected the national-Jewish parliament (*sejm*)[5] and national-Jewish state secretaries. Incidentally, even those European social-democrats who accede to or defend the compromise slogan of cultural-national autonomy, admit that the slogan is quite unrealisable for the Jews (Otto Bauer and Karl Kautsky). "The Jews in Galicia and Russia are more of a caste than a nation, and attempts to constitute Jewry as a nation are attempts at preserving a caste" (Karl Kautsky).

d. In civilised countries we observe a fairly full (relatively) approximation to national peace under capitalism *only* in conditions of the *maximum* implementation of democracy throughout the state system and administration (Switzerland). The slogans of consistent democracy (the

---

5 The Polish word *sejm* refers to an assembly, similar to the Russian word *duma*. It is also the name for the modern lower house of the Polish parliament.

republic, a militia, civil servants elected by the people, etc.) unite the proletariat and the working people, and, in general, all progressive elements in each nation in the name of the struggle for conditions that preclude even the slightest national privilege – while the slogan of 'cultural-national autonomy' preaches the isolation of nations in educational affairs (or 'cultural' affairs, in general), an isolation that is quite compatible with the retention of the grounds for all (including national) privileges.

The slogans of consistent democracy *unite* in a single whole the proletariat and the advanced democrats of all nations (elements that demand not isolation but the uniting of democratic elements of the nations in all matters, including educational affairs), while the slogan of cultural-national autonomy *divides* the proletariat of the different nations and links it up with the reactionary and bourgeois elements of the separate nations.

The slogans of consistent democracy are implacably hostile to the reactionaries and to the counter-revolutionary bourgeoisie of all nations, while the slogan of cultural-national autonomy is quite acceptable to the reactionaries and counter-revolutionary bourgeoisie of some nations.

8. The sum-total of economic and political conditions in Russia therefore demands that Social-Democracy should *unite* unconditionally workers of all nationalities in *all* proletarian organisations without exception (political, trade union, co-operative, educational, etc., etc.). The party should not be federative in structure and should not form national social-democratic groups but should unite the proletarians of all nations in the given locality, conduct propaganda and agitation in *all* the languages of the local proletariat, promote the common struggle of the workers of all nations against every kind of national privilege and should recognise the autonomy of local and regional party organisations.

9. More than ten years' experience gained by the RSDLP confirms the correctness of the above thesis. The party was founded in 1898 as a party of all Russia, that is, a party of the proletariat of all the nationalities of Russia. The party remained 'Russian' when the Bund seceded in 1903, after the party congress had rejected the demand to consider the Bund the *only* representative of the Jewish proletariat. In 1906 and 1907 events showed convincingly that there were no grounds for this demand, a large number of Jewish proletarians continued to co-operate in the common social-democratic work in many local organisations, and the Bund re-entered the party. The Stockholm Congress (1906)[6] brought into the party the Polish and Latvian social-democrats, who favoured *territorial* autonomy, and the congress, furthermore, did *not* accept the principle of federation and demanded unity of social-democrats of all nationalities in each locality. This principle has been in operation in the Caucasus for many years, it is in operation in Warsaw (Polish workers and Russian soldiers), in Vilna (Polish, Lettish, Jewish and Lithuanian workers) and in Riga, and in the three last-named places it has been implemented *against* the separatist Bund. In December 1908, the RSDLP, through its conference, adopted a special resolution confirming the demand for the *unity* of workers of all nationalities, *on a principle other than federation*. The splitting activities of the Bund separatists in not fulfilling the party decision led to the collapse of all that "federation of the worst type"[7] and brought about the *rapprochement* of the Bund and the Czech separatists and vice versa (see Kosovsky in *Nasha Zarya*[8] and the organ

---

6   Referring to the Fourth Congress of the RSDLP, held in Stockholm in 1906.

7   See Lenin, 'The Sixth (Prague) All-Russia Conference of the RSDLP', 5-7 January 1912, *Lenin Collected Works* (henceforth referred to as *LCW*), Vol. 17, p. 464.

8   *Nasha Zarya* (*Our Dawn*) was a legal monthly paper of the Menshevik liquidators. Vladimir Kosovsky (born Nokhem Mendel Levinson) was a leading Bundist.
    The Mensheviks were the party which originated at the Second Congress in 1903 as the opposition faction in the Russian Social-Democratic Labour Party (RSDLP). They pursued a policy of class collaboration with the bourgeoisie.

of the Czech separatists, *Der Čechoslavische Sozialdemokrat*[9] No. 3, 1913, on Kosovsky), and, lastly, at the August (1912) Conference of the liquidators it led to an *undercover* attempt by the Bund separatists and liquidators and some of the Caucasian liquidators to insert 'cultural-national autonomy' into the party programme *without any defence of its substance!*

Revolutionary worker social-democrats in Poland, in the Latvian area and in the Caucasus still stand for territorial autonomy and the *unity* of worker social-democrats of *all* nations. The Bund-liquidator secession and the alliance of the Bund with *non*-social-democrats in Warsaw place the *entire* national question, both in its theoretical aspect and in the matter of party structure, *on the order of the day* for all social-democrats.

Compromise decisions have been broken by the very people who introduced them against the will of the party, and the demand for the unity of worker social-democrats of all nationalities is being made more loudly than ever.

10. The crudely militant and Black-Hundred-type nationalism of the tsarist monarchy, and also the revival of *bourgeois* nationalism – Great-Russian (Mr. Struve,[10] *Russkaya Molva*,[11] the Progressists, etc.), the Ukrainian, and Polish (the antisemitism of Narodowa

---

The liquidationists or liquidators were a set of tendencies within the RSDLP after the 1905 Revolution, where the question of the combining of legal and illegal work came under contention. The Liquidators were split between the 'lefts', who fetishised illegal work, and the 'right', chiefly the Mensheviks, who insisted on solely using legal methods of struggle. Lenin for some considerable time waged a ruthless struggle against both of these tendencies.

9 *Der Čechoslavische Sozialdemokrat* (*The Czechoslovak Social-Democrat*) was the German-language paper of the Czech social-democrats.

10 Peter Struve was a Russian political economist, philosopher, historian and editor. He started his career as a Marxist, and exponent of 'legal Marxism' (an academic trend which used Marxism partially, but devoid of its revolutionary content). He later became a liberal and leader of the Cadet party. After the Bolshevik Revolution he joined the counter-revolutionary White movement.

11 *Russkaya Molva* (*Russian Tidings*) was a bourgeois daily paper that was the organ of the Progressists, founded in 1912.

'Demokracja'),[12] and Georgian and Armenian, etc. – all this makes it particularly urgent for social-democratic organisations in all parts of Russia to devote greater attention than before to the national question and to work out consistently Marxist decisions on this subject in the spirit of consistent internationalism and unity of proletarians of all nations.

---

12 Narodowa Demokracja (National Democracy) was a reactionary, chauvinist party of the Polish bourgeoisie, founded in 1897.

The Right of Nations to Self-Determination

Written February-May 1914

Editor's note: As the First World War approached, the national question acquired a renewed importance. The imperialist powers all attempted to justify their drive towards war in terms of the national rights of oppressed nationalities, particularly 'poor little Belgium' and 'poor little Serbia', to better mask their naked imperialist ambitions. The programme of the workers' party towards oppressed nationalities had already been discussed at the 1903 Second Congress of the RSDLP, which had agreed Clause 9, recognising:

> [The] right of self-determination for all nations included within the bounds of the state.

At that time, the representatives of the Polish Social-Democracy had opposed this clause. Subsequently, Rosa Luxemburg wrote a series of articles expressing her point of view in opposition to the recognition of the right of nations to self-determination, which were published under the title 'The National Question and Autonomy' in 1908. Lenin had already partially addressed her arguments in his 'Critical Remarks on the National Question' (Reproduced in this volume, see p. 237) written in October-December 1913. In 'The Right of Nations to Self-Determination', Lenin addresses Luxemburg's arguments in a more comprehensive manner.

* * *

Clause 9 of the Russian Marxists' programme, which deals with the right of nations to self-determination, has (as we have already pointed out in *Prosveshcheniye*)[1] given rise lately to a crusade on the part of the opportunists. The Russian liquidator Semkovsky,[2] in the St. Petersburg liquidationist newspaper, and the Bundist Liebman and the Ukrainian nationalist-socialist Yurkevich[3] in their respective periodicals have violently attacked this clause and treated it with supreme contempt. There is no doubt that this campaign of a motley array of opportunists against our Marxist programme is closely connected with present-day nationalist vacillations in general. Hence we consider a detailed examination of this question timely. We would mention, in passing, that none of the opportunists named above has offered a single argument of his own; they all merely repeat what Rosa Luxemburg[4] said in her lengthy Polish article of 1908-09, 'The National Question and Autonomy'. In our exposition we shall deal mainly with the 'original' arguments of this last-named author.

What is Meant by the Self-Determination of Nations?

Naturally, this is the first question that arises when any attempt is made at a Marxist examination of what is known as self-determination. What should be understood by that term? Should the answer be sought in legal definitions deduced from all sorts of 'general concepts' of law? Or is it rather to be sought in a historico-economic study of the national movements?

It is not surprising that the Semkovskys, Liebmans and Yurkeviches did not even think of raising this question, and shrugged it off by scoffing at the 'obscurity' of the Marxist programme, apparently

---

1   See Lenin, 'Critical Remarks on the National Question', in this volume, p. 237. This article was also published in the legal Bolshevik journal *Prosveshcheniye*.

2   Semen Semkovsky was a Menshevik.

3   Lev Yurkevich was a founding member of the Ukrainian Social-Democratic Workers Party (USDRP), a reformist, nationalist party in the Second International.

4   Rosa Luxemburg was a leading member of the Social-Democratic Party of Germany (SPD) and the Second International. She was a leader of the Left wing of the SPD against the revisionist Right and the Kautskyist group.

unaware, in their simplicity, that the self-determination of nations is dealt with, not only in the Russian Programme of 1903, but in the resolution of the London International Congress of 1896[5] (with which I shall deal in detail in the proper place). Far more surprising is the fact that Rosa Luxemburg, who declaims a great deal about the supposedly abstract and metaphysical nature of the clause in question, should herself succumb to the sin of abstraction and metaphysics. It is Rosa Luxemburg herself who is continually lapsing into generalities about self-determination (to the extent even of philosophising amusingly on the question of how the will of the nation is to be ascertained), without anywhere clearly and precisely asking herself whether the gist of the matter lies in legal definitions or in the experience of the national movements throughout the world.

A precise formulation of this question, which no Marxist can avoid, would at once destroy nine-tenths of Rosa Luxemburg's arguments. This is not the first time that national movements have arisen in Russia, nor are they peculiar to that country alone. Throughout the world, the period of the final victory of capitalism over feudalism has been linked up with national movements. For the complete victory of commodity production, the bourgeoisie must capture the home market, and there must be politically united territories whose population speak a single language, with all obstacles to the development of that language and to its consolidation in literature eliminated. Therein is the economic foundation of national movements. Language is the most important means of human intercourse. Unity and unimpeded development of language are the most important conditions for genuinely free and extensive commerce on a scale commensurate with modern capitalism, for a free and broad grouping of the population in all its various classes and, lastly, for the establishment of a close connection between the

---

5 Lenin is referring to the Fourth Congress of the Second International, where a resolution was discussed on the national and colonial question. See 'Resolutions Adopted at the International Socialist Workers and Trade Union Congress, London, 1896', in this volume, p. 389.

market and each and every proprietor, big or little, and between seller and buyer.

Therefore, the tendency of every national movement is towards the formation of *national states*, under which these requirements of modern capitalism are best satisfied. The most profound economic factors drive towards this goal, and, therefore, for the whole of Western Europe, nay, for the entire civilised world, the national state is *typical* and normal for the capitalist period.

Consequently, if we want to grasp the meaning of self-determination of nations, not by juggling with legal definitions, or 'inventing' abstract definitions, but by examining the historico-economic conditions of the national movements, we must inevitably reach the conclusion that the self-determination of nations means the political separation of these nations from alien national bodies, and the formation of an independent national state.

Later on we shall see still other reasons why it would be wrong to interpret the right to self-determination as meaning anything but the right to existence as a separate state. At present, we must deal with Rosa Luxemburg's efforts to 'dismiss' the inescapable conclusion that profound economic factors underlie the urge towards a national state.

Rosa Luxemburg is quite familiar with Kautsky's pamphlet *Nationality and Internationality* (Supplement to *Die Neue Zeit*, No.11, 1907-08; Russian translation in the journal *Nauchnaya Mysl*,[6] Riga, 1908). She is aware that, after carefully analysing the question of the national state in Section 4 of that pamphlet, Kautsky arrived at the conclusion that Otto Bauer "*underestimates* the strength of the urge towards a national state" (p. 23 of the pamphlet). Rosa Luxemburg herself quotes the following words of Kautsky's:

> The national state is the form *most suited* to present-day conditions [i.e. capitalist, civilised, economically progressive conditions, as distinguished from medieval, pre-capitalist, etc.], it is the form in which the state can best fulfil its tasks [i.e. the tasks of securing the freest, widest and speediest development of capitalism].

---

6   *Nauchnaya Mysl* (*Scientific Thought*) was a journal of a Menshevik trend.

To this we must add Kautsky's still more precise concluding remark that states of mixed national composition (known as multi-national states, as distinct from national states) are "always those whose internal constitution has for some reason or other remained abnormal or underdeveloped" (backward). Needless to say, Kautsky speaks of abnormality exclusively in the sense of lack of conformity with what is best adapted to the requirements of a developing capitalism.

The question now is: How did Rosa Luxemburg treat these historico-economic conclusions of Kautsky's? Are they right or wrong? Is Kautsky right in his historico-economic theory, or is Bauer, whose theory is basically psychological? What is the connection between Bauer's undoubted 'national opportunism', his defence of cultural-national autonomy, his nationalistic infatuation ("an occasional emphasis on the national aspect", as Kautsky put it), his "enormous exaggeration of the national aspect and complete neglect of the international aspect" (Kautsky) – and his underestimation of the strength of the urge to create a national state?

Rosa Luxemburg has not even raised this question. She has not noticed the connection. She has not considered the *sum total* of Bauer's theoretical views. She has not even drawn a line between the historico-economic and the psychological theories of the national question. She confines herself to the following remarks in criticism of Kautsky:

> This 'best' national state is only an abstraction, which can easily be developed and defended theoretically, but which does not correspond to reality. (*Przegląd Socjaldemokratyczny,*[7] 1908, No. 6, p. 499.)

And in corroboration of this emphatic statement there follow arguments to the effect that the 'right to self-determination' of small nations is made illusory by the development of the great capitalist powers and by imperialism.

---

7 *Przegląd Socjaldemokratyczny* (*Social-Democratic Review*), *Przegląd* (abb.) was the monthly journal of the Social-Democratic Party of the Kingdom of Poland and Lithuania (SDKPiL), of which Rosa Luxemburg was a member.

> Can one seriously speak, [Rosa Luxemburg exclaims] about the 'self-determination' of the formally independent Montenegrins, Bulgarians, Rumanians, Serbs, Greeks, partly even the Swiss, whose independence is itself a result of the political struggle and the diplomatic game of the 'concert of Europe'?! (p. 500.)

The state that best suits these conditions is "not a national state, as Kautsky believes, but a predatory one". Some dozens of figures are quoted relating to the size of British, French and other colonial possessions.

After reading such arguments, one cannot help marvelling at the author's ability to misunderstand *the how and the why of things*. To teach Kautsky, with a serious mien, that small states are economically dependent on big ones, that a struggle is raging among the bourgeois states for the predatory suppression of other nations, and that imperialism and colonies exist – all this is a ridiculous and puerile attempt to be clever, for none of this has the slightest bearing on the subject. Not only small states, but even Russia, for example, is entirely dependent, economically, on the power of the imperialist finance capital of the 'rich' bourgeois countries. Not only the miniature Balkan states, but even nineteenth-century America was, economically, a colony of Europe, as Marx pointed out in *Capital*.[8] Kautsky, like any Marxist, is, of course, well aware of this, but that has nothing whatever to do with the question of national movements and the national state.

For the question of the political self-determination of nations and their independence as states in bourgeois society, Rosa Luxemburg has substituted the question of their economic independence. This is just as intelligent as if someone, in discussing the programmatic demand for the supremacy of parliament, i.e. the assembly of people's representatives, in a bourgeois state, were to expound the perfectly correct conviction that big capital dominates in a bourgeois country, whatever the regime in it.

There is no doubt that the greater part of Asia, the most densely populated continent, consists either of colonies of the 'Great

---

8   See Marx, *Capital*, Vol. 1, *MECW*, Vol. 35, p. 7.

Powers', or of states that are extremely dependent and oppressed as nations. But does this commonly-known circumstance in any way shake the undoubted fact that in Asia itself the conditions for the most complete development of commodity production and the freest, widest and speediest growth of capitalism have been created only in Japan, i.e. only in an independent national state? The latter is a bourgeois state, and for that reason has itself begun to oppress other nations and to enslave colonies. We cannot say whether Asia will have had time to develop into a system of independent national states, like Europe, before the collapse of capitalism, but it remains an undisputed fact that capitalism, having awakened Asia, has called forth national movements everywhere in that continent, too; that the tendency of these movements is towards the creation of national states in Asia; that it is such states that ensure the best conditions for the development of capitalism. The example of Asia speaks *in favour* of Kautsky and *against* Rosa Luxemburg.

The example of the Balkan states likewise contradicts her, for anyone can now see that the best conditions for the development of capitalism in the Balkans are created precisely in proportion to the creation of independent national states in that peninsula.

Therefore, Rosa Luxemburg notwithstanding, the example of the whole of progressive and civilised mankind, the example of the Balkans and that of Asia prove that Kautsky's proposition is absolutely correct: the national state is the rule and the 'norm' of capitalism; the multi-national state represents backwardness, or is an exception. From the standpoint of national relations, the best conditions for the development of capitalism are undoubtedly provided by the national state. This does not mean, of course, that such a state, which is based on bourgeois relations, can eliminate the exploitation and oppression of nations. It only means that Marxists cannot lose sight of the powerful *economic* factors that give rise to the urge to create national states. It means that 'self-determination of nations' in the Marxists' programme *cannot*, from a historico-economic point of view, have any other meaning than political self-determination, state independence, and the formation of a national state.

The conditions under which the bourgeois-democratic demand for a 'national state' should be supported from a Marxist, i.e. class-proletarian, point of view will be dealt with in detail below. For the present, we shall confine ourselves to the definition of the *concept* of 'self-determination', and only note that Rosa Luxemburg knows what this concept means ('national state'), whereas her opportunist partisans, the Liebmans, the Semkovskys, the Yurkeviches, *do not even know that!*

The Historically Concrete Presentation of the Question

The categorical requirement of Marxist theory in investigating any social question is that it be examined within *definite* historical limits, and, if it refers to a particular country (e.g. the national programme for a given country), that account be taken of the specific features distinguishing that country from others in the same historical epoch.

What does this categorical requirement of Marxism imply in its application to the question under discussion?

First of all, it implies that a clear distinction must be drawn between the two periods of capitalism, which differ radically from each other as far as the national movement is concerned. On the one hand, there is the period of the collapse of feudalism and absolutism, the period of the formation of the bourgeois-democratic society and state, when the national movements for the first time become mass movements and in one way or another draw *all* classes of the population into politics through the press, participation in representative institutions, etc. On the other hand, there is the period of fully formed capitalist states with a long-established constitutional regime and a highly developed antagonism between the proletariat and the bourgeoisie – a period that may be called the eve of capitalism's downfall.

The typical features of the first period are: the awakening of national movements and the drawing of the peasants, the most numerous and the most sluggish section of the population, into these movements, in connection with the struggle for political liberty in general, and for the rights of the nation in particular. Typical features of the second period are: the absence of mass bourgeois-democratic movements and the fact that developed capitalism, in bringing closer together nations that have already been fully drawn into commercial intercourse, and causing them to intermingle to an increasing degree, brings the antagonism between internationally united capital and the international working-class movement into the forefront.

Of course, the two periods are not walled off from each other; they are connected by numerous transitional links, the various countries differing from each other in the rapidity of their national development, in the national make up and distribution of their population, and so on. There can be no question of the Marxists of any country drawing up their national programme without taking into account all these general historical and concrete state conditions.

It is here that we come up against the weakest point in Rosa Luxemburg's arguments. With extraordinary zeal, she embellishes her article with a collection of hard words directed against Section 9 of our programme, which she declares to be "sweeping", "a platitude", "a metaphysical phrase", and so on without end. It would be natural to expect an author who so admirably condemns metaphysics (in the Marxist sense, i.e. anti-dialectics) and empty abstractions to set us an example of how to make a concrete historical analysis of the question. The question at issue is the national programme of the Marxists of a definite country – Russia, in a definite period – the beginning of the twentieth century. But does Rosa Luxemburg raise the question as to *what historical* period Russia is passing through, or *what are the concrete features* of the national question and the national movements of that *particular* country in that *particular* period?

No, she does not! *She says absolutely nothing about it!* In her work you will not find even the shadow of an analysis of how the national question stands in *Russia* in the present historical period, or of the specific features of *Russia* in this particular respect!

We are told that the national question in the Balkans is presented differently from that in Ireland; that Marx appraised the Polish and

Czech national movements in the concrete conditions of 1848 in such and such a way (a page of excerpts from Marx); that Engels appraised the struggle of the forest cantons of Switzerland against Austria and the Battle of Morgarten which took place in 1315 in such and such a way (a page of quotations from Engels with the appropriate comments from Kautsky); that Lassalle regarded the peasant war in Germany of the sixteenth century as reactionary, etc.

It cannot be said that these remarks and quotations have any novelty about them, but at all events it is interesting for the reader to be occasionally reminded just how Marx, Engels and Lassalle approached the analysis of concrete historical problems in individual countries. And a perusal of these instructive quotations from Marx and Engels reveals most strikingly the ridiculous position Rosa Luxemburg has placed herself in, she preaches eloquently and angrily the need for a concrete historical analysis of the national question in different countries at different times, but she *does not make the least* attempt to determine *what* historical stage in the development of capitalism *Russia* is passing through at the beginning of the twentieth century, or what the *specific features* of the national question in this country are. Rosa Luxemburg gives examples of how *others* have treated the question in a Marxist fashion, as if deliberately stressing how often the road to hell is paved with good intentions and how often good counsel covers up unwillingness or inability to follow such advice in practice.

Here is one of her edifying comparisons. In protesting against the demand for the independence of Poland, Rosa Luxemburg refers to a pamphlet she wrote in 1898, proving the rapid "industrial development of Poland", with the latter's manufactured goods being marketed in Russia. Needless to say, no conclusion whatever can be drawn from this on the question of the *right* to self-determination; it only proves the disappearance of the old Poland of the landed gentry, etc. But Rosa Luxemburg always passes on imperceptibly to the conclusion that among the factors that unite Russia and Poland, the purely economic factors of modern capitalist relations now predominate.

Then our Rosa proceeds to the question of autonomy, and though her article is entitled 'The National Question and Autonomy' *in general*, she begins to argue that the Kingdom of Poland has an *exclusive* right to autonomy (see *Prosveshcheniye*, 1913, No. 12). To support Poland's right to autonomy, Rosa Luxemburg evidently judges the state system of Russia by her economic, political and sociological characteristics and everyday life – a totality of features which, taken together, produce the concept of 'Asiatic despotism' (*Przegląd*, No. 12, p. 137).

It is generally known that this kind of state system possesses great stability whenever completely patriarchal and pre-capitalist features predominate in the economic system and where commodity production and class differentiation are scarcely developed. However, if in a country whose state system is distinctly *pre*-capitalist in character there exists a nationally demarcated region where capitalism is *rapidly* developing, then the more rapidly that capitalism develops, the greater will be the antagonism between it and the *pre*-capitalist state system, and the more likely will be the separation of the progressive region from the whole – with which it is connected, not by 'modern capitalistic', but by 'Asiatically despotic' ties.

Thus, Rosa Luxemburg does not get her arguments to hang together even on the question of the social structure of the government in Russia with regard to bourgeois Poland; as for the concrete, historical, specific features of the national movements in Russia – she does not even raise that question. That is a point we must now deal with.

The Concrete Features of the National Question in Russia, and Russia's Bourgeois-Democratic Reformation

Despite the elasticity of the principle of 'the right of nations to self-determination', which is a mere platitude, and, obviously, equally applicable, not only to the nations inhabiting Russia, but also to the nations inhabiting Germany and Austria, Switzerland and Sweden, America and Australia, we do not find it in the programmes of any of the present-day socialist parties... (*Przegląd*, No. 6, p. 483.)

This is how Rosa Luxemburg opens her attack upon Section 9 of the Marxist programme. In trying to foist on us the conception that this clause in the programme is a "mere platitude", Rosa Luxemburg herself falls victim to this error, alleging with amusing boldness that this point is, "obviously, equally applicable" to Russia, Germany, etc.

Obviously, we shall reply, Rosa Luxemburg has decided to make her article a collection of errors in logic that could be used for schoolboy exercises. For Rosa Luxemburg's tirade is sheer nonsense and a mockery of the historically concrete presentation of the question.

If one interprets the Marxist programme in Marxist fashion, not in a childish way, one will without difficulty grasp the fact that it refers to bourgeois-democratic national movements. That being the case, it is "obvious" that this programme "sweepingly", and as a "mere platitude", etc., covers *all* instances of bourgeois-democratic national movements. No less obvious to Rosa Luxemburg, if she gave the slightest thought to it, is the conclusion that our programme refers *only* to cases where such a movement is actually in existence.

Had she given thought to these obvious considerations, Rosa Luxemburg would have easily perceived what nonsense she was talking. In accusing *us* of uttering a "platitude" she has used *against us* the argument that no mention is made of the right to self-determination in the programmes of countries where there are *no* bourgeois-democratic national movements. A remarkably clever argument!

A comparison of the political and economic development of various countries, as well as of their Marxist programmes, is of tremendous importance from the standpoint of Marxism, for there can be no doubt that all modern states are of a common capitalist nature and are therefore subject to a common law of development. But such a comparison must be drawn in a sensible way. The elementary condition for comparison is to find out whether the historical periods of development of the countries concerned are at all *comparable*. For instance, only absolute ignoramuses (such as Prince Y Trubetskoy in *Russkaya Mysl*) are capable of 'comparing' the Russian Marxists' agrarian programme with the programmes of Western Europe, since our programme replies to questions that concern the *bourgeois-democratic* agrarian reform, whereas in the Western countries no such question arises.[9]

The same applies to the national question. In most Western countries it was settled long ago. It is ridiculous to seek an answer to non-existent questions in the programmes of Western Europe. In this respect Rosa Luxemburg has lost sight of the most important thing – the difference between countries, where bourgeois-democratic reforms have long been completed, and those where they have not.

The crux of the matter lies in this difference. Rosa Luxemburg's complete disregard of it transforms her verbose article into a collection of empty and meaningless platitudes.

The epoch of bourgeois-democratic revolutions in Western, continental Europe embraces a fairly definite period, approximately between 1789 and 1871. This was precisely the period of national movements and the creation of national states. When this period drew to a close, Western Europe had been transformed into a settled system of bourgeois states, which, as a general rule, were nationally uniform states. Therefore, to seek the right to self-determination in the programmes of West-European socialists at this time of day is to betray one's ignorance of the ABC of Marxism.

In Eastern Europe and Asia the period of bourgeois-democratic revolutions did not begin until 1905. The revolutions in Russia, Persia, Turkey and China, the Balkan Wars – such is the chain of world events of *our* period in our 'Orient'. And only a blind man could fail to see in this chain of events the awakening of a *whole series* of bourgeois-democratic national movements which strive to create nationally independent and nationally uniform states. It is precisely and solely because Russia and the neighbouring countries are passing through this period that we must have a clause in our programme on the right of nations to self-determination.

But let us continue the quotation from Rosa Luxemburg's article a little more. She writes:

---

9   Prince Yevgeny Trubetskoy was a Russian nobleman, lawyer and Cadet.
    Russkaya Mysl (*Russian Thought*) was a monthly magazine published by Struve, which while not formally affiliated, argued along the lines of the Cadets.

In particular, the programme of a party which is operating in a state with an extremely varied national composition, and for which the national question is a matter of first-rate importance – the programme of the Austrian Social-Democratic Party – does not contain the principle of the right of nations to self-determination. (Ibid.)

Thus, an attempt is made to convince the reader by the example of Austria 'in particular'. Let us examine this example in the light of concrete historical facts and see just how sound it is.

In the first place, let us pose the fundamental question of the completion of the bourgeois-democratic revolution. In Austria, this revolution began in 1848 and was over in 1867. Since then, a more or less fully established bourgeois constitution has dominated, for nearly half a century, and on its basis a legal workers' party is legally functioning.

Therefore, in the internal conditions of Austria's development (i.e. from the standpoint of the development of capitalism in Austria in general, and among its various nations in particular), there are *no* factors that produce leaps and bounds, a concomitant of which might be the formation of nationally independent states. In assuming, by her comparison, that Russia is in an analogous position in this respect, Rosa Luxemburg not only makes a fundamentally erroneous and anti-historical assumption, but also involuntarily slips into liquidationism.

Secondly, the profound difference in the relations between the nationalities in Austria and those in Russia is particularly important for the question we are concerned with. Not only was Austria for a long time a state in which the Germans preponderated, but the Austrian Germans laid claim to hegemony in the German nation as a whole. This 'claim', as Rosa Luxemburg (who is seemingly so averse to commonplaces, platitudes, abstractions...) will perhaps be kind enough to remember, was shattered in the war of 1866. The German nation predominating in Austria found itself *outside the pale* of the independent German state which finally took shape in 1871. On the other hand, the Hungarians' attempt to create an independent national state collapsed under the blows of the Russian serf army as far back as 1849.

A very peculiar situation was thus created – a striving on the part of the Hungarians and then of the Czechs, not for separation from Austria, but, on the contrary, for the preservation of Austria's integrity, precisely in order to preserve national independence, which might have been completely crushed by more rapacious and powerful neighbours! Owing to this peculiar situation, Austria assumed the form of a dual state, and she is now being transformed into a triple state (Germans, Hungarians, Slavs).

Is there anything like this in Russia? Is there in our country a striving of the 'subject peoples' for unity with the Great Russians in face of the danger of *worse* national oppression?

One need only pose this question in order to see that the comparison between Russia and Austria on the question of self-determination of nations is meaningless, platitudinous and ignorant.

The peculiar conditions in Russia with regard to the national question are just the reverse of those we see in Austria. Russia is a state with a single national centre – Great Russia. The Great-Russians occupy a vast, unbroken stretch of territory, and number about 70 million. The specific features of this national state are: first, that 'subject peoples' (which, on the whole, comprise the majority of the entire population – 57 per cent) inhabit the border regions; secondly, the oppression of these subject peoples is much stronger here than in the neighbouring states (and not even in the European states alone); thirdly, in a number of cases the oppressed nationalities inhabiting the border regions have compatriots across the border, who enjoy greater national independence (suffice it to mention the Finns, the Swedes, the Poles, the Ukrainians and the Rumanians along the western and southern frontiers of the state); fourthly, the development of capitalism and the general level of culture are often higher in the non-Russian border regions than in the centre. Lastly, it is in the neighbouring Asian states that we see the beginning of a phase of bourgeois revolutions and national movements which are spreading to some of the kindred nationalities within the borders of Russia.

Thus, it is precisely the special concrete, historical features of the national question in Russia that make the recognition of the right of nations to self-determination in the present period a matter of special urgency in our country.

Incidentally, even from the purely factual angle, Rosa Luxemburg's assertion that the Austrian social-democrats' programme does not contain any recognition of the right of nations to self-determination is incorrect. We need only open the Minutes of the Brünn Congress, which adopted the national programme, to find the statements by the Ruthenian social-democrat Hankiewicz[10] on behalf of the entire Ukrainian (Ruthenian) delegation (p. 85 of the minutes), and by the Polish social-democrat Reger on behalf of the entire Polish delegation (p. 108), to the effect that one of the aspirations of the Austrian social-democrats of both the above-mentioned nations is to secure national unity, and the freedom and independence of their nations. Hence, while the Austrian social-democrats did not include the right of nations to self-determination directly in their programme, they did nevertheless allow the demand for national independence to be advanced by *sections* of the party. In effect, this means, of course, the recognition of the right of nations to self-determination! Thus, Rosa Luxemburg's reference to Austria speaks *against* Rosa Luxemburg in *all* respects.

'Practicality' in the National Question

Rosa Luxemburg's argument that Section 9 of our programme contains nothing 'practical' has been seized upon by the opportunists. Rosa Luxemburg is so delighted with this argument that in some parts of her article this 'slogan' is repeated eight times on a single page. She writes:

> [Section 9] gives no practical lead on the day-by-day policy of the proletariat, no practical solution of national problems.

Let us examine this argument, which elsewhere is formulated in such a way that it makes Section 9 look quite meaningless, or else commits us to support all national aspirations.

---

10 Mikolaj Hankiewicz was a Ukrainian social-democrat and founder of the Ukrainian Social-Democratic Party.

What does the demand for 'practicality' in the national question mean? It means one of three things: support for all national aspirations; the answer 'yes' or 'no' to the question of secession by any nation; or that national demands are in general immediately 'practicable'.

Let us examine all three possible meanings of the demand for 'practicality'.

The bourgeoisie, which naturally assumes the leadership at the start of every national movement, says that support for all national aspirations is practical. However, the proletariat's policy in the national question (as in all others) supports the bourgeoisie only in a certain direction, but it never coincides with the bourgeoisie's policy. The working class supports the bourgeoisie only in order to secure national peace (which the bourgeoisie cannot bring about completely and which can be achieved only with *complete* democracy), in order to secure equal rights and to create the best conditions for the class struggle. Therefore, it is *in opposition to the practicality* of the bourgeoisie that the proletarians advance their *principles* in the national question; they always give the bourgeoisie *only conditional* support. What every bourgeoisie is out for in the national question is either privileges for its *own* nation, or exceptional advantages for it; this is called being "practical". The proletariat is opposed to all privileges, to all exclusiveness. To demand that it should be "practical" means following the lead of the bourgeoisie, falling into opportunism.

The demand for a 'yes' or 'no' reply to the question of secession in the case of every nation may seem a very "practical" one. In reality it is absurd; it is metaphysical in theory, while in practice it leads to subordinating the proletariat to the bourgeoisie's policy. The bourgeoisie always places its national demands in the forefront, and does so in categorical fashion. With the proletariat, however, these demands are subordinated to the interests of the class struggle. Theoretically, you cannot say in advance whether the bourgeois-democratic revolution will end in a given nation seceding from another nation, or in its equality with the latter; *in either case*, the important thing for the proletariat is to ensure the development of its class. For the bourgeoisie it is important to hamper this development by pushing the aims of its 'own' nation before those of the proletariat. That is why the proletariat confines itself, so to speak, to the negative demand for recognition of the *right* to self-determination, without giving guarantees to any nation, and without undertaking to give *anything at the expense* of another nation.

This may not be "practical", but it is in effect the best guarantee for the achievement of the most democratic of all possible solutions. The proletariat needs *only* such guarantees, whereas the bourgeoisie of every nation requires guarantees for *its own* interest, regardless of the position of (or the possible disadvantages to) other nations.

The bourgeoisie is most of all interested in the 'feasibility' of a given demand – hence the invariable policy of coming to terms with the bourgeoisie of other nations, to the detriment of the proletariat. For the proletariat, however, the important thing is to strengthen its class against the bourgeoisie and to educate the masses in the spirit of consistent democracy and socialism.

This may not be "practical" as far as the opportunists are concerned, but it is the only real guarantee, the guarantee of the greater national equality and peace, despite the feudal landlords and the *nationalist* bourgeoisie.

The whole task of the proletarians in the national question is 'unpractical' from the standpoint of the *nationalist* bourgeoisie of every nation, because the proletarians, opposed as they are to nationalism of every kind, demand 'abstract' equality; they demand, as a matter of principle, that there should be no privileges, however slight. Failing to grasp this, Rosa Luxemburg, by her misguided eulogy of practicality, has opened the door wide for the opportunists, and especially for opportunist concessions to Great-Russian nationalism.

Why Great-Russian? Because the Great Russians in Russia are an oppressor nation, and opportunism in the national question will of course find expression among oppressed nations otherwise than among oppressor nations.

On the plea that its demands are "practical", the bourgeoisie of the oppressed nations will call upon the proletariat to support its aspirations unconditionally. The most practical procedure is to say a plain 'yes' in favour of the secession of a *particular* nation rather than in favour of all nations having the *right* to secede!

The proletariat is opposed to such practicality. While recognising equality and equal rights to a national state, it values above all and places foremost the alliance of the proletarians of all nations, and assesses any national demand, any national separation, *from the angle* of the workers' class struggle. This call for practicality is in fact merely a call for uncritical acceptance of bourgeois aspirations.

By supporting the right to secession, we are told, you are supporting the bourgeois nationalism of the oppressed nations. This is what Rosa Luxemburg says, and she is echoed by Semkovsky, the opportunist, who incidentally is the only representative of liquidationist ideas on this question, in the liquidationist newspaper!

Our reply to this is: No, it is to the bourgeoisie that a "practical" solution of this question is important. To the workers the important thing is to distinguish the *principles* of the two trends. *Insofar* as the bourgeoisie of the oppressed nation fights the oppressor, we are always, in every case, and more strongly than anyone else, *in favour*, for we are the staunchest and the most consistent enemies of oppression. But insofar as the bourgeoisie of the oppressed nation stands for *its own* bourgeois nationalism, we stand against. We fight against the privileges and violence of the oppressor nation, and do not in any way condone strivings for privileges on the part of the oppressed nation.

If, in our political agitation, we fail to advance and advocate the slogan of the *right* to secession, we shall play into the hands, not only of the bourgeoisie, but also of the feudal landlords and the absolutism of the *oppressor* nation. Kautsky long ago used this argument against Rosa Luxemburg, and the argument is indisputable. When, in her anxiety not to 'assist' the nationalist bourgeoisie of Poland, Rosa Luxemburg rejects the *right* to secession in the programme of the Marxists *in Russia*, she is *in fact* assisting the Great-Russian Black Hundreds. She is in fact assisting opportunist tolerance of the privileges (and worse than privileges) of the Great Russians.

Carried away by the struggle against nationalism in Poland, Rosa Luxemburg has forgotten the nationalism of the Great Russians, although it is *this* nationalism that is the most formidable at the present time. It is a nationalism that is more feudal than bourgeois, and is the principal obstacle to democracy and to the proletarian struggle. The bourgeois nationalism of *any* oppressed nation has a general democratic content that is directed *against* oppression, and it is this content that we *unconditionally* support, At the same time we strictly distinguish it from the tendency towards national exclusiveness; we fight against the tendency of the Polish bourgeois to oppress the Jews, etc., etc.

This is 'unpractical' from the standpoint of the bourgeois and the philistine, but it is the only policy in the national question that is practical, based on principles, and really promotes democracy, liberty and proletarian unity.

The recognition of the right to secession for all; the appraisal of each concrete question of secession from the point of view of removing all inequality, all privileges, and all exclusiveness.

Let us consider the position of an oppressor nation. Can a nation be free if it oppresses other nations? It cannot. The interests of the freedom of the Great-Russian population[11] require a struggle against such oppression. The long, centuries-old history of the suppression of the movements of the oppressed nations, and the systematic propaganda in favour of such suppression coming from the 'upper' classes have created enormous obstacles to the cause of freedom of the Great-Russian people itself, in the form of prejudices, etc.

The Great-Russian Black Hundreds deliberately foster these prejudices and encourage them. The Great-Russian bourgeoisie tolerates or condones them. The Great-Russian proletariat cannot achieve *its own* aims or clear the road to its freedom without systematically countering these prejudices.

---

11 A certain L Vl. [abbreviated pseudonym of MK Sheinfinkel, a social-democrat] in Paris considers this word un-Marxist. This L Vl. is amusingly '*superklug*' (too clever by half). And 'this too-clever-by-half' L Vl. apparently intends to write an essay on the deletion of the words 'population', 'nation', etc., from our minimum programme (having in mind the class struggle!). – *Lenin*

In Russia, the creation of an independent national state remains, for the time being, the privilege of the Great-Russian nation alone. We, the Great-Russian proletarians, who defend no privileges whatever, do not defend this privilege either. We are fighting on the ground of a definite state; we unite the workers of all nations living in this state; we cannot vouch for any particular path of national development, for we are marching to our class goal along *all* possible paths.

However, we cannot move towards that goal unless we combat all nationalism, and uphold the equality of the various nations. Whether the Ukraine, for example, is destined to form an independent state is a matter that will be determined by a thousand unpredictable factors. Without attempting idle '*guesses*', we firmly uphold something that is beyond doubt: the right of the Ukraine to form such a state. We respect this right; we do not uphold the privileges of Great Russians with regard to Ukrainians; we *educate* the masses in the spirit of recognition of that right, in the spirit of rejecting *state* privileges for any nation.

In the leaps which all nations have made in the period of bourgeois revolutions, clashes and struggles over the right to a national state are possible and probable. We proletarians declare in advance that we are *opposed* to Great-Russian privileges, and this is what guides our entire propaganda and agitation.

In her quest for 'practicality' Rosa Luxemburg has lost sight of the *principal* practical task both of the Great-Russian proletariat and of the proletariat of other nationalities: that of day-by-day agitation and propaganda against all state and national privileges, and for the right, the equal right of all nations, to their national state. This (at present) is our principal task in the national question, for only in this way can we defend the interests of democracy and the alliance of all proletarians of all nations on an equal footing.

This propaganda may be 'unpractical' from the point of view of the Great-Russian oppressors, as well as from the point of view of the bourgeoisie of the oppressed nations (both demand a *definite* 'yes' or 'no', and accuse the social-democrats of being "vague"). In reality it is this propaganda, and this propaganda alone, that ensures the genuinely democratic, the genuinely socialist education of the masses. This is the only propaganda to ensure the greatest chances of national peace in Russia, should she remain a multi-national state, and the most peaceful (and for the proletarian class struggle, harmless) division into separate national states, should the question of such a division arise.

To explain this policy – the only proletarian policy – in the national question more concretely, we shall examine the attitude of Great-Russian liberalism towards the 'self-determination of nations', and the example of Norway's secession from Sweden.

The Liberal Bourgeoisie and the Socialist Opportunists in the National Question

We have seen that the following argument is one of Rosa Luxemburg's 'trump cards' in her struggle against the programme of the Marxists in Russia: recognition of the right to self-determination is tantamount to supporting the bourgeois nationalism of the oppressed nations. On the other hand, she says, if we take this right to mean no more than combating all violence against other nations, there is no need for a special clause in the programme, for social-democrats are, in general, opposed to all national oppression and inequality.

The first argument, as Kautsky irrefutably proved nearly twenty years ago, is a case of blaming other people for one's own nationalism; in her fear of the nationalism of the bourgeoisie of oppressed nations, Rosa Luxemburg is actually playing into the hands of the Black-Hundred nationalism of the Great Russians! Her second argument is *actually* a timid evasion of the question whether or not recognition of national equality includes recognition of the right to secession. If it does, then Rosa Luxemburg admits that, in principle, Section 9 of our programme is correct. If it does not, then she does not recognise national equality. Shuffling and evasions will not help matters here!

However, the best way to test these and all similar arguments is to study the attitude of the *various classes* of society towards this question. For the Marxist this test is obligatory. We must proceed from what is objective; we must examine the relations between the classes on this point. In failing to do so, Rosa Luxemburg is guilty of those very sins of metaphysics, abstractions, platitudes, and sweeping statements etc., of which she vainly tries to accuse her opponents.

We are discussing the programme of the Marxists *in Russia*, i.e. of the Marxists of all the nationalities in Russia. Should we not examine the position of the *ruling* classes of Russia?

The position of the 'bureaucracy' (we beg pardon for this inaccurate term) and of the feudal landlords of our united-nobility type is well known. They definitely reject both the equality of nationalities and the right to self determination. Theirs is the old motto of the days of serfdom: autocracy, orthodoxy, and the national essence – the last term applying only to the Great-Russian nation. Even the Ukrainians are declared to be an 'alien' people and their very language is being suppressed.

Let us glance at the Russian bourgeoisie, which was 'called upon' to take part – a very modest part, it is true, but nevertheless some part – in the government, under the 'June Third' legislative and administrative system.[12] It will not need many words to prove that the Octobrists are following the Rights in this question. Unfortunately, some Marxists pay much less attention to the stand of the Great-Russian liberal bourgeoisie, the Progressists and the Cadets. Yet he who fails to study that stand and give it careful thought will inevitably flounder in abstractions and groundless statements in discussing the question of the right of nations to self-determination.

Skilled though it is in the art of diplomatically evading direct answers to 'unpleasant' questions, *Rech*,[13] the principal organ of the Constitutional-Democratic Party, was compelled, in its controversy with *Pravda*[14] last year, to make certain valuable admissions. The

---

12 Lenin is referring to the regime formed on 3 June 1907 after the dissolution of the Second State Duma.

13 *Rech* (*Speech*) was a daily paper and the central organ of the Cadet Party. It was published in St. Petersburg from February 1906.

14 *Pravda* was a legal Bolshevik daily newspaper published in St. Petersburg, founded on the initiative of the St. Petersburg workers in April 1912. *Pravda* was repeatedly persecuted by the tsarist authorities, and changed its name eight times.

trouble started over the All-Ukraine Students' Congress held in Lvov in the summer of 1913. Mr. Mogilyansky[15], the 'Ukrainian expert' or Ukrainian correspondent of *Rech*, wrote an article in which he poured vitriolic abuse ("ravings", "adventurism", etc.) on the idea that the Ukraine should secede, an idea which Dontsov,[16] a nationalist-socialist, had advocated and the above-mentioned congress approved.

While in no way identifying itself with Mr. Dontsov, and declaring explicitly that he was a nationalist-socialist and that many Ukrainian Marxists did not agree with him, *Rabochaya Pravda*[17] stated that the *tone* of *Rech*, or, rather, the *way it formulated the question in principle*, was improper and reprehensible for a Great-Russian democrat, or for anyone desiring to pass as a democrat.[18] Let *Rech* repudiate the Dontsovs if it likes, but, *from the standpoint of principle*, a Great-Russian organ of democracy, which it claims to be, cannot be oblivious of the *freedom* to secede, the *right* to secede.

A few months later, *Rech*, No. 331, published an 'explanation' from Mr. Mogilyansky, who had learned from the Ukrainian newspaper *Shlyakhi*,[19] published in Lvov, of Mr. Dontsov's reply, in which, incidentally, Dontsov stated that:

> The chauvinist attacks in *Rech* have been properly sullied [branded?] only in the Russian social-democratic press.

This 'explanation' consisted of the thrice-repeated statement that "criticism of Mr. Dontsov's recipes" "has nothing in common with the repudiation of the right of nations to self-determination".

---

15 Mikhail Mikhailovich Mogilyansky was a leading Cadet, on its Central Committee from 1907-1917. He was a lawyer and journalist who wrote for *Rech*.

16 Dmytro Dontsov was a Ukrainian nationalist and member of the Ukrainian Social-Democratic Worker's Party (USDRP).

17 *Rabochaya Pravda* (*Worker's Truth*) and *Proletarskaya Pravda* (*Proletarian Truth*) were two of the names used by *Pravda* to escape tsarist repression of the Bolshevik paper.

18 See Lenin, 'Cadets on the Question of the Ukraine', *LCW*, Vol. 19, p. 266.

19 *Shlyakhi* (*Paths*) was the organ of the Ukrainian Students' Union, a nationalist organisation, published in Lvov from April 1913 to March 1914.

> It must be said, [wrote Mr. Mogilyansky] that even 'the right of
> nations to self-determination' is not a fetish [mark this!] beyond
> criticism: unwholesome conditions in the life of nations may give rise
> to unwholesome tendencies in national self-determination, and the fact
> that these are brought to light does not mean that the right of nations to
> self-determination has been rejected.

As you see, this liberal's talk of a "fetish" was quite in keeping with
Rosa Luxemburg's. It was obvious that Mr. Mogilyansky was trying
to evade a direct reply to the question whether or not he recognised
the right to political self-determination, i.e. to secession.

The newspaper *Proletarskaya Pravda*, issue No. 4, for 11 December
1913, also put this question *point-blank* to Mr. Mogilyansky and to
the Constitutional-Democratic *Party*.[20]

Thereupon *Rech* (No. 340) published an unsigned, i.e. official,
editorial statement replying to this question. This reply boils down
to the following three points:

1. Section 11 of the Constitutional-Democratic Party's programme
   speaks bluntly, precisely and clearly of the "right of nations to
   free *cultural* self-determination".

2. *Rech* affirms that *Proletarskaya Pravda* "hopelessly confuses" self-
   determination with separatism, with the secession of a given nation.

3. *"Actually, the Cadets have never pledged themselves to advocate the
   right of 'nations to secede' from the Russian state."* (See 'National-
   Liberalism and the Right of Nations to Self-Determination', in
   Proletarskaya Pravda, No. 12, 20 December 1913).[21]

Let us first consider the second point in the *Rech* statement. How
strikingly it shows to the Semkovskys, Liebmans, Yurkeviches and
other opportunists that the hue and cry they have raised about the
alleged 'vagueness', or 'indefiniteness', of the term 'self-determination'
is *in fact*, i.e. from the standpoint of objective class relationships and

---

20 See Lenin, 'The Cadets and 'The Right of Nations to Self-Determination",
   LCW, Vol. 19, p. 525.
21 Reproduced in *LCW*, Vol. 20, p. 56.

the class struggle in Russia, *simply a rehash* of the liberal-monarchist bourgeoisie's utterances!

Proletarskaya Pravda put the following *three* questions to the enlightened 'Constitutional-Democratic' gentlemen of *Rech*:

1. Do they deny that, throughout the entire history of international democracy, and especially since the middle of the nineteenth century, self-determination of nations has been understood to mean precisely political self-determination, the right to form an independent national state?

2. Do they deny that the well-known resolution adopted by the International Socialist Congress in London in 1896 has the same meaning?

3. Do they deny that Plekhanov,[22] in writing about self-determination as far back as 1902, meant precisely political self-determination?

When *Proletarskaya Pravda* posed these three questions, *the Cadets fell silent!* Not a word did they utter in reply, for they had nothing to say. They had to admit tacitly that *Proletarskaya Pravda* was absolutely right.

The liberals' outcries that the term 'self-determination' is vague and that the social-democrats 'hopelessly confuse' it with separatism are nothing more than attempts to *confuse* the issue, and evade recognition of a universally established democratic principle. If the Semkovskys, Liebmans and Yurkeviches were not so ignorant, they would be ashamed to address the workers in a *liberal* vein.

But to proceed. *Proletarskaya Pravda* compelled *Rech* to admit that, in the programme of the Constitutional-Democrats, the term 'cultural' self-determination means in effect the *repudiation of political* self-determination.

---

22 Georgy Plekhanov was the founder of Russian Marxism and a leading member of the RSDLP. After joining the Menshevik faction in 1903, he became extremely hostile to Lenin and the Bolsheviks.

"Actually, the Cadets have never pledged themselves to advocate the right of 'nations to secede' from the Russian state" – it was not without reason that *Proletarskaya Pravda* recommended to *Novoye Vremya*[23] and *Zemshchina*[24] these words from *Rech* as an example of our Cadets' 'loyalty'. In its issue No. 13563, *Novoye Vremya*, which never, of course, misses an opportunity of mentioning 'the Yids' and taking digs at the Cadets, nevertheless stated:

> What, to the social-democrats, is an axiom of political wisdom [i.e. recognition of the right of nations to self-determination, to secede], is today beginning to cause disagreement even among the Cadets.

By declaring that they "have never pledged themselves to advocate the right of nations to secede from the Russian state", the Cadets have, in principle, taken exactly the same stand as *Novoye Vremya*. This is precisely one of the fundamentals of Cadet *national-liberalism*, of their kinship with the Purishkeviches,[25] and of their dependence, political, ideological and practical, on the latter. *Proletarskaya Pravda* wrote:

> The Cadets have studied history and know only too well what – to put it mildly – pogrom-like actions the practice of the ancient right of the Purishkeviches to "grab 'em and hold 'em" has often led to.[26]

Although perfectly aware of the feudalist source and nature of the Purishkeviches' omnipotence; the Cadets are, nevertheless, taking their stand *on the basis* of the relationships and frontiers created by that very class. Knowing full well that there is much in the relationships and frontiers created or fixed by this class that is un-European and anti-European (we would say Asiatic if this did not

---

23 *Novoye Vremya* (*New Times*) was a daily newspaper, published in St. Petersburg from 1868. In 1905 it became an organ of the Black Hundreds.

24 *Zemshchina* was an extremely reactionary bourgeois paper.

25 Vladimir Purishkevich was a far-right extremist, antisemite and a leader of the paramilitary Black Hundreds.

26 "Grab 'em and hold 'em" refers to the duties assigned to Constable Mymretsov, a character from the story *The Booth* by the prominent Narodnik GI Uspensky. In the story, his duties were to 'grab', and to 'hold' those who sought shelter from the elements at his security booth. The phrase in Russian became a metaphor for the bureaucratic, arbitrary tyranny of the tsarist state.

sound undeservedly slighting to the Japanese and Chinese), the Cadets, nevertheless, accept them as the utmost limit.

Thus, they are adjusting themselves to the Purishkeviches, cringing to them, fearing to jeopardise their position, protecting them from the people's movement, from the democracy. As *Proletarskaya Pravda* wrote:

> In effect, this means adapting oneself to the interests of the feudal-minded landlords and to the worst nationalist prejudices of the dominant nation, instead of systematically combating those prejudices.

Being men who are familiar with history and claim to be democrats, the Cadets do not even attempt to assert that the democratic movement, which is today characteristic of both Eastern Europe and Asia and is striving to change both on the model of the civilised capitalist countries, is bound to leave intact the boundaries fixed by the feudal epoch, the epoch of the omnipotence of the Purishkeviches and the disfranchisement of wide strata of the bourgeoisie and petty bourgeoisie.

The fact that the question raised in the controversy between *Proletarskaya Pravda* and *Rech* was not merely a literary question, but one that involved a real political issue of the day, was proved, among other things, by the last conference of the Constitutional-Democratic Party held on 23-25 March 1914; in the official report of this conference in *Rech* (No. 83, of 26 March 1914) we read:

> A particularly lively discussion also took place on national problems. The Kiev deputies, who were supported by NV Nekrasov and AM Kolyubakin,[27] pointed out that the national question was becoming a key issue, which would have to be faced up to more resolutely than hitherto. FF Kokoshkin[28] pointed out, however [this "however" is like Shchedrin's "but" – "the ears never grow higher than the forehead, never!"] that both the programme and past political experience demanded that "elastic formulas" of "political self-determination of nationalities" should be handled very carefully.

---

27 Nikolai Nekrasov and Aleksandr Kolyubakin were Cadets.
28 Fyodor Kokoshkin was a founding member of the Cadets.

This most remarkable line of reasoning at the Cadet conference deserves serious attention from all Marxists and all democrats. (We will note in parentheses that *Kievskaya Mysl*,[29] which is evidently very well informed and no doubt presents Mr. Kokoshkin's ideas correctly, added that, of course, as a warning to his opponents, he laid special stress on the danger of the 'disintegration' of the state.)

The official report in *Rech* is composed with consummate diplomatic skill designed to lift the veil as little as possible and to conceal as much as possible. Yet, in the main, what took place at the Cadet conference is quite clear. The liberal-bourgeois delegates, who were familiar with the state of affairs in the Ukraine, and the 'Left' Cadets raised the question *precisely of the political* self-determination of nations. Otherwise, there would have been no need for Mr. Kokoshkin to urge that this "formula" should be "handled carefully".

The Cadet programme, which was of course known to the delegates at the Cadet conference, speaks of "cultural", *not* of political self-determination. Hence, Mr. Kokoshkin was *defending* the programme *against* the Ukrainian delegates, and against the Left Cadets; he was defending "cultural" self-determination *as opposed to* "political" self-determination. It is perfectly clear that in opposing "political" self-determination, in playing up the danger of the "disintegration of the state", and in calling the formula "political self-determination" an "*elastic*" one (quite in keeping with Rosa Luxemburg!), Mr. Kokoshkin was defending Great-Russian national-liberalism against the more 'Left' or more democratic elements of the Constitutional-Democratic Party and also against the Ukrainian bourgeoisie.

Mr. Kokoshkin won the day at the Cadet conference, as is evident from the treacherous little word "however" in the *Rech* report; Great-Russian national-liberalism has triumphed among the Cadets. Will not this victory help to clear the minds of those misguided individuals among the Marxists in Russia who, like the Cadets, have also begun to fear the "elastic formulas of political self-determination of nationalities"?

---

29 *Kievskaya Mysl* (*Kiev Thought*) was a Russian paper aligned with the intelligentsia.

Let us, "however", examine the substance of Mr. Kokoshkin's line of thought. By referring to "past political experience" (i.e. evidently, the experience of 1905, when the Great-Russian bourgeoisie took alarm for its national privileges and scared the Cadet Party with its fears), and also by playing up the danger of the "disintegration of the state", Mr. Kokoshkin showed that he understood perfectly well that political self-determination can mean nothing else but the right to secede and form an independent national state. The question is – how should Mr. Kokoshkin's fears be appraised in the light of democracy in general, and the proletarian class struggle in particular?

Mr. Kokoshkin would have us believe that recognition of the right to secession increases the danger of the "disintegration of the state". This is the viewpoint of Constable Mymretsov, whose motto was "grab 'em and hold 'em". From the viewpoint of democracy in general, the very opposite is the case: recognition of the right to secession *reduces* the danger of the "disintegration of the state".

Mr. Kokoshkin argues exactly like the nationalists do. At their last congress they attacked the Ukrainian 'Mazeppists'.[30] The Ukrainian movement, Mr. Savenko and co.[31] exclaimed, threatens to weaken the ties between the Ukraine and Russia, since Austrian Ukrainophilism is strengthening the Ukrainians' ties with Austria! It remains unexplained why Russia cannot try to 'strengthen' her ties with the Ukrainians *through the same method* that the Savenkos blame Austria for using, i.e. by granting the Ukrainians freedom to use their own language, self-government and an autonomous Diet.

The arguments of the Savenkos and Kokoshkins are exactly alike, and from the purely logical point of view they are equally ridiculous and absurd. Is it not clear that the more liberty the Ukrainian nationality enjoys in any particular country, the stronger its ties with that country will be? One would think that this truism could not be disputed without totally abandoning all the premises

---

30 The 'Mazeppists' was the moniker for Ukrainian nationalists, named after Ivan Stepanovych Mazepa, who attempted to separate Ukraine from Russia through allying with foreign powers, but was defeated by Tsar Peter I at Poltava.

31 Anatoly Savenko was an ultra-reactionary Russian nationalist. He wrote for *Novoye Vremya*.

of democracy. Can there be greater freedom of nationality, as such, than the freedom to secede, the freedom to form an independent national state?

To clear up this question, which has been so confused by the liberals (and by those who are so misguided, as to echo them), we shall cite a very simple example. Let us take the question of divorce. In her article Rosa Luxemburg writes that the centralised democratic state, while conceding autonomy to its constituent parts, should retain the most important branches of legislation, including legislation on divorce, under the jurisdiction of the central parliament. The concern that the central authority of the democratic state should retain the power to allow divorce can be readily understood. The reactionaries are opposed to freedom of divorce; they say that it must be 'handled carefully', and loudly declare that it means the 'disintegration of the family'. The democrats, however, believe that the reactionaries are hypocrites, and that they are actually defending the omnipotence of the police and the bureaucracy, the privileges of one of the sexes, and the worst kind of oppression of women. They believe that in actual fact freedom of divorce will not cause the 'disintegration' of family ties, but, on the contrary, will strengthen them on a democratic basis, which is the only possible and durable basis in civilised society.

To accuse those who support freedom of self-determination, i.e. freedom to secede, of encouraging separatism, is as foolish and hypocritical as accusing those who advocate freedom of divorce of encouraging the destruction of family ties. Just as in bourgeois society the defenders of privilege and corruption, on which bourgeois marriage rests, oppose freedom of divorce, so, in the capitalist state, repudiation of the right to self-determination, i.e. the right of nations to secede, means nothing more than defence of the privileges of the dominant nation and police methods of administration, to the detriment of democratic methods.

No doubt, the political chicanery arising from all the relationships existing in capitalist society sometimes leads members of parliament and journalists to indulge in frivolous and even nonsensical twaddle about one or another nation seceding. But only reactionaries can allow themselves to be frightened (or pretend to be frightened) by such talk. Those who stand by democratic principles, i.e. who insist that questions of state be decided by the mass of the population, know very well that there is a "tremendous distance"[32] between what the politicians prate about and what the people decide. From their daily experience the masses know perfectly well the value of geographical and economic ties and the advantages of a big market and a big state. They will, therefore, resort to secession only when national oppression and national friction make joint life absolutely intolerable and hinder any and all economic intercourse. In that case, the interests of capitalist development and of the freedom of the class struggle will be best served by secession.

Thus, from whatever angle we approach Mr. Kokoshkin's arguments, they prove to be the height of absurdity and a mockery of the principles of democracy. And yet there is a modicum of logic in these arguments, the logic of the class interests of the Great-Russian bourgeoisie. Like most members of the Constitutional-Democratic Party, Mr. Kokoshkin is a lackey of the money-bags of that bourgeoisie. He defends its privileges in general, and its *state* privileges in particular. He defends them hand in hand and shoulder to shoulder with Purishkevich, the only difference being that Purishkevich puts more faith in the feudalist cudgel, while Kokoshkin and co. realise that this cudgel was badly damaged in 1905, and rely more on bourgeois methods of fooling the masses, such as frightening the petty bourgeoisie and the peasants with the spectre of the "disintegration of the state", and deluding them with phrases about blending "people's freedom" with historical tradition, etc.

The liberals' hostility to the principle of political self-determination of nations can have one, and only one, real class meaning: national-liberalism, defence of the state privileges of the Great-Russian bourgeoisie. And the opportunists among the Marxists in Russia, who today, under the Third of June regime, are against the right of nations to self-determination – the liquidator Semkovsky, the

---

32 Lenin is quoting from Griboyedov's comedy *Wit Works Woe*.

Bundist Liebman, the Ukrainian petty-bourgeois Yurkevich – are *actually* following in the wake of the national-liberals, and corrupting the working class with national-liberal ideas.

The interests of the working class and of its struggle against capitalism demand complete solidarity and the closest unity of the workers of all nations; they demand resistance to the nationalist policy of the bourgeoisie of every nationality. Hence, social-democrats would be deviating from proletarian policy and subordinating the workers to the policy of the bourgeoisie if they were to repudiate the right of nations to self-determination, i.e. the right of an oppressed nation to secede, or if they were to support all the national demands of the bourgeoisie of oppressed nations.

It makes no difference to the hired worker whether he is exploited chiefly by the Great-Russian bourgeoisie rather than the non-Russian bourgeoisie, or by the Polish bourgeoisie rather than the Jewish bourgeoisie, etc. The hired worker who has come to understand his class interests is equally indifferent to the state privileges of the Great-Russian capitalists and to the promises of the Polish or Ukrainian capitalists to set up an earthly paradise when they obtain state privileges. Capitalism is developing and will continue to develop, anyway, both in integral states with a mixed population and in separate national states.

In any case the hired worker will be an object of exploitation. Successful struggle against exploitation requires that the proletariat be free of nationalism, and be absolutely neutral, so to speak, in the fight for supremacy that is going on among the bourgeoisie of the various nations. If the proletariat of any one nation gives the slightest support to the privileges of its 'own' national bourgeoisie, that will inevitably rouse distrust among the proletariat of another nation; it will weaken the international class solidarity of the workers and divide them, to the delight of the bourgeoisie. Repudiation of the right to self-determination or to secession inevitably means, in practice, support for the privileges of the dominant nation.

We will get even more striking confirmation of this if we take the concrete case of Norway's secession from Sweden.

Norway's Secession from Sweden

Rosa Luxemburg cites precisely this example, and discusses it as follows:

> The latest event in the history of federative relations, the secession of
> Norway from Sweden – which at the time was hastily seized upon by the
> social-patriotic Polish press (see the Kraków *Naprzód*)[33] as a gratifying
> sign of the strength and progressive nature of the tendency towards
> state secession – at once provided striking proof that federalism and
> its concomitant, separation, are in no way an expression of progress or
> democracy. After the so-called Norwegian 'revolution', which meant
> that the Swedish king was deposed and compelled to leave Norway,
> the Norwegians coolly proceeded to choose another king, formally
> rejecting, by a national referendum, the proposal to establish a republic.
> That which superficial admirers of all national movements and of all
> semblance of independence proclaimed to be a 'revolution' was simply a
> manifestation of peasant and petty-bourgeois particularism, the desire to
> have a king 'of their own' for their money instead of one imposed upon
> them by the Swedish aristocracy, and was, consequently, a movement
> that had absolutely nothing in common with revolution. At the same
> time, the dissolution of the union between Sweden and Norway showed
> once more to what extent, in this case also, the federation which had
> existed until then was only an expression of purely dynastic interests
> and, therefore, merely a form of monarchism and reaction. (*Przegląd.*)

That is literally all that Rosa Luxemburg has to say on this score!
Admittedly, it would have been difficult for her to have revealed the
hopelessness of her position more saliently than she has done in this
particular instance.

The question was, and is: do the social-democrats in a mixed
national state need a programme that recognises the right to self-
determination or secession?

What does the example of Norway, cited by Rosa Luxemburg, tell
us on this point?

---

33 *Naprzód* (*Forward*) was the central organ of the Social-Democratic Party of
   Galicia and Silesia, published in Kraków beginning in 1892, which peddled
   petty-bourgeois nationalist ideas.

Our author twists and turns, exercises her wit and rails at *Naprzód*, but she does not answer the question! Rosa Luxemburg speaks about everything under the sun so as to *avoid saying a single word* about the actual point at issue!

Undoubtedly, in wishing to have a king of their own for their money, and in rejecting, in a national referendum, the proposal to establish a republic, the Norwegian petty bourgeoisie displayed exceedingly bad philistine qualities. Undoubtedly, *Naprzód* displayed equally bad and equally philistine qualities in failing to notice this.

But what has all this to do with the case?

The question under discussion was the right of nations to self-determination and the attitude to be adopted by the socialist proletariat towards this right! Why, then, does not Rosa Luxemburg answer this question instead of beating about the bush?

To a mouse there is no stronger beast than the cat, it is said. To Rosa Luxemburg there is evidently no stronger beast than the 'Fracy'. 'Fracy' is the popular term for the 'Polish Socialist Party', its so-called revolutionary section, and the Kraków newspaper *Naprzód* shares the views of that 'section'. Rosa Luxemburg is so blinded by her fight against the nationalism of that 'section' that she loses sight of everything except *Naprzód*.

If *Naprzód* says 'yes', Rosa Luxemburg considers it her sacred duty to say an immediate 'no', without stopping to think that by so doing she does not reveal independence of *Naprzód*, but, on the contrary, her ludicrous dependence on the 'Fracy' and her inability to see things from a view point any deeper and broader than that of the Kraków anthill. *Naprzód*, of course, is a wretched and by no means Marxist organ; but that should not prevent us from properly analysing the example of Norway, once we have chosen it.

To analyse this example in Marxist fashion, we must deal, not with the vices of the awfully terrible 'Fracy', but, first, with the concrete historical features of the secession of Norway from Sweden, and secondly, with the tasks which confronted the *proletariat* of both countries in connection with this secession.

The geographic, economic and language ties between Norway and Sweden are as intimate as those between the Great-Russians and many other Slav nations. But the union between Norway and Sweden was not a voluntary one, and in dragging in the question of 'federation' Rosa Luxemburg was talking at random, simply because she did not know what to say. Norway was *ceded* to Sweden by the monarchs during the Napoleonic wars, against the will of the Norwegians; and the Swedes had to bring troops into Norway to subdue her.

Despite the very extensive autonomy which Norway enjoyed (she had her own parliament etc.), there was constant friction between Norway and Sweden for many decades after the union, and the Norwegians strove hard to throw off the yoke of the Swedish aristocracy. At last, in August 1905, they succeeded: the Norwegian parliament resolved that the Swedish king was no longer king of Norway, and in the referendum held later among the Norwegian people, the overwhelming majority (about 200,000 as against a few hundred) voted for complete separation from Sweden. After a short period of indecision, the Swedes resigned themselves to the fact of secession.

This example shows us on what grounds cases of the secession of nations are practicable, and actually occur, under modern economic and political relationships, and the *form* secession sometimes assumes under conditions of political freedom and democracy.

No social-democrat will deny – unless he would profess indifference to questions of political freedom and democracy (in which case he is naturally no longer a social-democrat) – that this example *virtually* proves that it is the *bounden duty* of class-conscious workers to conduct systematic propaganda and prepare the ground for the settlement of conflicts that may arise over the secession of nations, not in the 'Russian way', but *only in the way* they were settled in 1905 between Norway and Sweden. This is exactly what is meant by the demand in the programme for the recognition of the right of nations to self-determination. But Rosa Luxemburg tried to get around a fact that was repugnant to her theory by violently attacking the philistinism of the Norwegian philistines and the Kraków *Naprzód*; for she understood perfectly well that this historical fact *completely refutes* her phrases about the right of nations to self-determination being a "utopia", or like the right "to eat off gold plates", etc. Such phrases only express a smug and opportunist belief in the immutability of the present alignment of forces among the nationalities of Eastern Europe.

To proceed. In the question of the self-determination of nations, as in every other question, we are interested, first and foremost, in the self-determination of the proletariat within a given nation. Rosa Luxemburg modestly evaded this question too, for she realised that an analysis of it on the basis of the example of Norway, which she herself had chosen, would be disastrous to her 'theory'.

What position did the Norwegian and Swedish proletariat take, and indeed had to take, in the conflict over secession? *After* Norway seceded, the class-conscious workers of Norway would naturally have voted for a republic,[34] and if some socialists voted otherwise it only goes to show how much dense, philistine opportunism there sometimes is in the European socialist movement. There can be no two opinions about that, and we mention the point only because Rosa Luxemburg is trying to obscure the issue by speaking *off the mark*. We do not know whether the Norwegian socialist programme made it obligatory for Norwegian social-democrats to hold particular views on the question of secession. We will assume that it did not, and that the Norwegian socialists left it an open question as to what extent the autonomy of Norway gave sufficient scope to wage the class struggle freely, or to what extent the eternal friction and conflicts with the Swedish aristocracy hindered freedom of economic life. But it cannot be disputed that the Norwegian proletariat had to oppose this aristocracy and support Norwegian peasant democracy (with all its philistine limitations).

---

34 Since the majority of the Norwegian nation was in favour of a monarchy while the proletariat wanted a republic, the Norwegian proletariat was, generally speaking, confronted with the alternative: either revolution, if conditions were ripe for it, or submission to the will of the majority and prolonged propaganda and agitational work. – *Lenin*

And the Swedish proletariat? It is common knowledge that the Swedish landed proprietors, abetted by the Swedish clergy, advocated war against Norway. Inasmuch as Norway was much weaker than Sweden, had already experienced a Swedish invasion, and the Swedish aristocracy carries enormous weight in its own country, this advocacy of war presented a grave danger. We may be sure that the Swedish Kokoshkins spent much time and energy in trying to corrupt the minds of the Swedish people by appeals to 'handle' the 'elastic formulas of political self-determination of nations carefully', by painting horrific pictures of the danger of the 'disintegration of the state' and by assuring them that 'people's freedom' was compatible with the traditions of the Swedish aristocracy. There cannot be the slightest doubt that the Swedish social-democrats would have betrayed the cause of socialism and democracy if they had not fought with all their might to combat both the landlord and the 'Kokoshkin' ideology and policy, and if they had failed to demand, *not only* equality of nations in general (to which the Kokoshkins also subscribe), but also the right of nations to self-determination, Norway's freedom to secede.

The close alliance between the Norwegian and Swedish workers, their complete fraternal class solidarity, *gained* from the Swedish workers' recognition of the right of the Norwegians to secede. This convinced the Norwegian workers that the Swedish workers were not infected with Swedish nationalism, and that they placed fraternity with the Norwegian proletarians above the privileges of the Swedish bourgeoisie and aristocracy. The dissolution of the ties imposed upon Norway by the monarchs of Europe and the Swedish aristocracy strengthened the ties between the Norwegian and Swedish workers. The Swedish workers have proved that in spite of *all* the vicissitudes of bourgeois policy – bourgeois relations may quite possibly bring about a repetition of the forcible subjection of the Norwegians to the Swedes! – they will be able to preserve and defend the complete equality and class solidarity of the workers of both nations in the struggle against both the Swedish and the Norwegian bourgeoisie.

Incidentally, this reveals how groundless and even frivolous are the attempts sometimes made by the 'Fracy' to 'use' our disagreements with Rosa Luxemburg against Polish Social-Democracy. The 'Fracy' are not a proletarian or a socialist party, but a petty-bourgeois nationalist party, something like Polish Socialist-Revolutionaries. There never has been, nor could there be, any question of unity between the Russian social-democrats and this party. On the other hand, no Russian social-democrat has ever 'repented' of the close relations and unity that have been established with the Polish social-democrats. The Polish social-democrats have rendered a great historical service by creating the first really Marxist, proletarian party in Poland, a country imbued with nationalist aspirations and passions. Yet the service the Polish social-democrats have rendered is a great one, not because Rosa Luxemburg has talked a lot of nonsense about Section 9 of the Russian Marxists' programme, but despite that sad circumstance.

The question of the 'right to self-determination' is of course not so important to the Polish social-democrats as it is to the Russian. It is quite understandable that in their zeal (sometimes a little excessive, perhaps) to combat the nationalistically blinded petty bourgeoisie of Poland the Polish social-democrats should overdo things. No Russian Marxist has ever thought of blaming the Polish social-democrats for being opposed to the secession of Poland. These social-democrats err only when, like Rosa Luxemburg, they try to deny the necessity of including the recognition of the right to self-determination in the programme of the *Russian* Marxists.

Virtually, this is like attempting to apply relationships, understandable by Kraków standards, to all the peoples and nations inhabiting Russia, including the Great Russians. It means being 'Polish nationalists the wrong way round', not Russian, not international social-democrats.

For international Social-Democracy stands for the recognition of the right of nations to self-determination. This is what we shall now proceed to discuss.

The Resolution of the London International Congress, 1896

This resolution reads:

> This Congress declares that it stands for the full right of all nations to self-determination (*Selbstbestimmungsrecht*) and expresses its sympathy for the workers of every country now suffering under the yoke of military, national or other absolutism. This Congress calls upon the workers of all these countries to join the ranks of the class-conscious (*Klassenbewusste* – those who understand their class interests) workers of the whole world in order jointly to fight for the defeat of international capitalism and for the achievement of the aims of international Social-Democracy.[35]

As we have already pointed out, our opportunists – Semkovsky, Liebman and Yurkevich – are simply unaware of this resolution. But Rosa Luxemburg knows it and quotes the full text, which contains the same expression as that contained in our programme, viz. 'self-determination'.

How does Rosa Luxemburg remove this obstacle from the path of her 'original' theory?

Oh, quite simply … the whole emphasis lies in the second part of the resolution … its declarative character … one can refer to it only by mistake!

The feebleness and utter confusion of our author are simply amazing. Usually it is only the opportunists who talk about the consistent democratic and socialist points in the programme being mere declarations, and cravenly avoid an open debate on them. It is apparently not without reason that Rosa Luxemburg has this time found herself in the deplorable company of the Semkovskys,

---

35 See the official German report of the London Congress: *Verhandlungen und Beschlüsse des internationalen sozialistischen Arbeiter- und Gewerkschafts-Kongresses zu London, vom 27 Juli bis 1 August 1896*, Berlin, 1896, S. 18. A Russian pamphlet has been published containing the decisions of international congresses in which the word 'self-determination' is wrongly translated as 'autonomy'. – *Lenin*
Translated and reproduced in the appendix, see p. 389.

Liebmans and Yurkeviches. Rosa Luxemburg does not venture to state openly whether she regards the above resolution as correct or erroneous. She shifts and shuffles as if counting on the inattentive or ill-informed reader, who forgets the first part of the resolution by the time he has started reading the second, or who has never heard of the discussion that took place in the socialist press *prior* to the London Congress.

Rosa Luxemburg is greatly mistaken, however, if she imagines that, in the sight of the class-conscious workers of Russia, she can get away with trampling upon the resolution of the International on such an important fundamental issue, without even deigning to analyse it critically.

Rosa Luxemburg's point of view was voiced during the discussions which took place prior to the London Congress, mainly in the columns of *Die Neue Zeit*, organ of the German Marxists; *in essence this point of view was defeated in the International!* That is the crux of the matter, which the Russian reader must particularly bear in mind.

The debate turned on the question of Poland's independence. Three points of view were put forward:

1. That of the 'Fracy', in whose name Haecker[36] spoke. They wanted the International to include in *its own* programme a demand for the independence of Poland. The motion was not carried and this point of view was defeated in the International.

2. Rosa Luxemburg's point of view, viz., the Polish socialists should not demand independence for Poland. This point of view entirely precluded the proclamation of the right of nations to self-determination. It was likewise defeated in the International.

3. The point of view which was elaborated at the time by Kautsky, who opposed Rosa Luxemburg and proved that her materialism was extremely 'one-sided'; according to Kautsky,

---

36 Emil Haecker was a Polish historian, member of the Social-Democratic Party of Galicia and Silesia, and Editor-in-Chief of *Naprzód*.

the International could not at the time make the independence of Poland a point in its programme; but the Polish socialists were fully entitled to put forward such a demand. From the socialists' point of view it was undoubtedly a mistake to ignore the tasks of national liberation in a situation where national oppression existed.

The International's resolution reproduces the most essential and fundamental propositions in this point of view: on the one hand, the absolutely direct, unequivocal recognition of the full right of all nations to self-determination; on the other hand, the equally unambiguous appeal to the workers for *international* unity in their class struggle.

We think that this resolution is absolutely correct, and that, to the countries of Eastern Europe and Asia at the beginning of the twentieth century, it is this resolution, with both its parts being taken as an integral whole, that gives the only correct lead to the proletarian class policy in the national question.

Let us deal with the three above-mentioned viewpoints in somewhat greater detail.

As is known, Karl Marx and Frederick Engels considered it the bounden duty of the whole of West-European democracy, and still more of Social-Democracy, to give active support to the demand for Polish independence.[37] For the period of the 1840s and 1860s, the period of the bourgeois revolutions in Austria and Germany, and the period of the 'Peasant Reform' in Russia,[38] this point of view was quite correct and the only one that was consistently democratic and proletarian. So long as the masses of the people in Russia and in most of the Slav countries were still sunk in torpor, so long as *there were no* independent, mass, democratic movements in those countries, the liberation movement of the *gentry* in Poland assumed an immense and paramount importance from the point of view,

---

37 Lenin is referring to the Polish national liberation insurrection of 1863-64 against the yoke of the tsarist autocracy.
38 This refers to the abolition of serfdom in Russia in 1861.

not only of Russian, not only of Slav, but of European democracy as a whole.[39]

But while Marx's standpoint was quite correct for the forties, fifties and sixties or for the third quarter of the nineteenth century, it has ceased to be correct by the twentieth century. Independent democratic movements, and even an independent proletarian movement, have arisen in most Slav countries, even in Russia, one of the most backward Slav countries. Aristocratic Poland has disappeared, yielding place to capitalist Poland. Under such circumstances Poland could not but lose her *exceptional* revolutionary importance.

The attempt of the PSP (the Polish Socialist Party, the present-day 'Fracy') in 1896 to 'establish' for all time the point of view Marx had held in a *different epoch* was an attempt to use the *letter* of Marxism against the *spirit* of Marxism. The Polish social-democrats were therefore quite right in attacking the extreme nationalism of the Polish petty bourgeoisie and pointing out that the national question was of secondary importance to Polish workers, in creating for the first time a purely proletarian party in Poland and proclaiming the extremely important principle that the Polish and the Russian workers must maintain the closest alliance in their class struggle.

But did this mean that at the beginning of the twentieth century the International could regard the principle of political self-determination of nations, or the right to secede, as unnecessary

---

39 It would be a very interesting piece of historical research to compare the position of a noble Polish rebel in 1863 with that of the all-Russia revolutionary democrat, Chernyshevsky, who (like Marx), was able to appreciate the importance of the Polish movement, and with that of the Ukrainian petty bourgeois Dragomanov, who appeared much later and expressed the views of a peasant, so ignorant and sluggish, and so attached to his dung heap, that his legitimate hatred of the Polish gentry blinded him to the significance which their struggle had for all-Russia democracy. (Cf. Dragomanov, *Historical Poland and Great-Russian Democracy*.) Dragomanov richly deserved the fervent kisses which were subsequently bestowed on him by Mr. PB Struve, who by that time had become a national-liberal. – *Lenin*

Mykhailo Dragomanov was a Ukrainian historian, ethnographer and publicist. He was an exponent of Ukrainian bourgeois national-liberalism.

to Eastern Europe and Asia? This would have been the height of absurdity, and (theoretically) tantamount to admitting that the bourgeois-democratic reform of the Turkish, Russian and Chinese states had been consummated; indeed it would have been tantamount (in practice) to opportunism, towards absolutism.

No. At a time when bourgeois-democratic revolutions in Eastern Europe and Asia have begun, in this period of the awakening and intensification of national movements and of the formation of independent proletarian parties, the task of these parties with regard to national policy must be twofold: recognition of the right of all nations to self-determination, since bourgeois-democratic reform is not yet completed and since working-class democracy consistently, seriously and sincerely (and not in a liberal, Kokoshkin fashion) fights for equal rights for nations; then, a close, unbreakable alliance in the class struggle of the proletarians of all nations in a given state, throughout all the changes in its history, irrespective of any reshaping of the frontiers of the individual states by the bourgeoisie.

It is this twofold task of the proletariat that the 1896 resolution of the International formulates. That is the substance, the underlying principle, of the resolution adopted by the Conference of Russian Marxists held in the summer of 1913. Some people profess to see a 'contradiction' in the fact that while Point 4 of this resolution, which recognises the right to self-determination and secession, seems to 'concede' the maximum to nationalism (in reality, the recognition of the *right of all* nations to self-determination implies the maximum of *democracy* and the minimum of nationalism), Point 5 warns the workers against the nationalist slogans of the bourgeoisie of any nation and demands the unity and amalgamation of the workers of all nations in internationally united proletarian organisations. But this is a 'contradiction' only for extremely shallow minds, which, for instance, cannot grasp why the unity and class solidarity of the Swedish and the Norwegian proletariat *gained* when the Swedish workers upheld Norway's freedom to secede and form an independent state.

The Utopian Karl Marx and the Practical Rosa Luxemburg

Calling Polish independence a 'utopia' and repeating this *ad nauseam*, Rosa Luxemburg exclaims ironically: "Why not raise the demand for the independence of Ireland?"

The 'practical' Rosa Luxemburg evidently does not know what Karl Marx's attitude to the question of Irish independence was. It is worthwhile dwelling upon this, so as to show how a *concrete* demand for national independence was analysed from a genuinely Marxist, not opportunist, standpoint.

It was Marx's custom to 'sound out' his socialist acquaintances, as he expressed it, to test their intelligence and the strength of their convictions.[40] After making the acquaintance of Lopatin,[41] Marx wrote to Engels on 5 July 1870, expressing a highly flattering opinion of the young Russian socialist but adding at the same time:

> *Poland* is his weak point. On this point he speaks quite like an Englishman
> – say, an English Chartist[42] of the old school – about Ireland.[43]

Marx questions a socialist belonging to an oppressor nation about his attitude to the oppressed nation and at once reveals a defect *common* to the socialists of the dominant nations (the English and the Russian): failure to understand their socialist duties towards the downtrodden nations, their echoing of the prejudices acquired from the bourgeoisie of the 'dominant nation'.

Before passing on to Marx's positive declarations on Ireland, we must point out that in general the attitude of Marx and Engels to the national question was strictly critical, and that they recognised its historically conditioned importance. Thus, Engels wrote to Marx on 23 May 1851, that the study of history was leading him to pessimistic conclusions in regard to Poland, that the importance of Poland was

---

40 Lenin refers to Wilhelm Liebknecht's reminiscences of Marx. (See Liebknecht, *Reminiscences of Marx and Engels*, Progress Publishers, 1957, p. 98.)

41 German Lopatin was an early Russian Marxist and friend of Marx and Engels.

42 Chartism was a mass revolutionary movement in Britain in the 1840s.

43 See Marx, 'Letter to Engels', 5 July 1870, *MECW*, Vol. 43, p. 530.

temporary – only until the agrarian revolution in Russia. The role of the Poles in history was one of "bold (hotheaded) foolishness".

> And one cannot point to a single instance in which Poland has successfully represented progress, even in relation to Russia, or done anything at all of historical importance.

Russia contains more of civilisation, education, industry and the bourgeoisie than 'the Poland of the indolent gentry'. "What are Warsaw and Kraków compared to St. Petersburg, Moscow, Odessa!" Engels had no faith in the success of the Polish gentry's insurrections.

But all these thoughts, showing the deep insight of genius, by no means prevented Engels and Marx from treating the Polish movement with the most profound and ardent sympathy twelve years later, when Russia was still dormant and Poland was seething.

When drafting the Address of the International in 1864, Marx wrote to Engels (on 4 November 1864) that he had to combat Mazzini's nationalism,[44] and went on to say:

> Inasmuch as international politics occurred in the Address, I spoke of countries, not of nationalities, and denounced Russia, not the *minores gentium* [minor nations].

Marx had no doubt as to the subordinate position of the national question as compared with the 'labour question'. But his theory is as far from ignoring national movements as heaven is from earth.

Then came 1866. Marx wrote to Engels about the "Proudhonist [45]clique" in Paris which:

> … declares nationalities to be an absurdity, attacks Bismarck and Garibaldi. As polemics against chauvinism their doings are useful and explicable. But as believers in Proudhon (Lafargue and Longuet, two very good friends of mine here, also belong to them), who think all Europe must and will sit quietly on their hindquarters until the gentlemen in France abolish poverty and ignorance – they are grotesque. (Letter of 7 June 1866.)

---

44 Giuseppe Mazzini was an Italian nationalist and republican who played a leading role in the bourgeois revolutionary movement.
45 Pierre-Joseph Proudhon was a petty-bourgeois French anarchist.

Yesterday [Marx wrote on 20 June 1866] there was a discussion in the International Council on the present war [...] The discussion wound up, as was to be foreseen, with 'the question of nationality' in general and the attitude we take towards it [...] The representatives of 'Young France' (*non-workers*) came out with the announcement that all nationalities and even nations were 'antiquated prejudices'. Proudhonised Stirnerism...[46] The whole world waits until the French are ripe for a social revolution... The English laughed very much when I began my speech by saying that our friend Lafargue and others, who had done away with nationalities, had spoken 'French' to us, i.e. a language which nine-tenths of the audience did not understand. I also suggested that by the negation of nationalities he appeared, quite unconsciously, to understand their absorption by the model French nation.

The conclusion that follows from all these critical remarks of Marx's is clear: the working class should be the last to make a fetish of the national question, since the development of capitalism does not necessarily awaken *all* nations to independent life. But to brush aside the mass national movements once they have started, and to refuse to support what is progressive in them means, in effect, pandering to *nationalistic* prejudices, that is, recognising 'one's own nation' as a model nation (or, we would add, one possessing the exclusive privilege of forming a state).[47]

But let us return to the question of Ireland. Marx's position on this question is most clearly expressed in the following extracts from his letters:

I have done my best to bring about this demonstration of the English workers in favour of Fenianism[48] [...] I used to think the separation of

---

46 Max Stirner was a German anarchist philosopher, close to the Young Hegelians, of which Marx, Engels and Ludwig Feuerbach were members.
47 Cf. also Marx's letter to Engels of 3 June 1867:

> ... I have learned with real pleasure from the Paris letters to *The Times* about the pro-Polish exclamations of the Parisians against Russia [...] Mr. Proudhon and his little doctrinaire clique are not the French people. – *Lenin*

48 Fenianism refers to the revolutionary movement for Irish independence.

Ireland from England impossible. I now think it inevitable, although after the separation there may come federation.

This is what Marx wrote to Engels on 2 November 1867.

In his letter of 30 November of the same year, he added:

… what shall we advise the *English* workers? In my opinion they must make the *Repeal of the Union* [Ireland with England, i.e. the separation of Ireland from England] (in short, the affair of 1783, only democratised and adapted to the conditions of the time) an article of their *pronunziamento* [manifesto]. This is the only legal and therefore only possible form of Irish emancipation which can be admitted in the programme of an *English* party. Experience must show later whether a mere personal union can continue to subsist between the two countries [...]

What the Irish need is:

1.   Self-government and independence from England;

2.   An agrarian revolution…

Marx attached great importance to the Irish question and delivered hour-and-a-half lectures on this subject at the German Workers' Union (letter of 17 December 1867).

In a letter dated 20 November 1868, Engels spoke of "the hatred towards the Irish found among the English workers", and almost a year later (24 October 1869), returning to this subject, he wrote:

Il n'y a qu'un pas [it is only one step] from Ireland to Russia… Irish history shows what a misfortune it is for one nation to have subjugated another. All the abominations of the English have their origin in the Irish Pale. I have still to plough my way through the Cromwellian period, but this much seems certain to me, that things would have taken another turn in England, too, but for the necessity of military rule in Ireland and the creation of a new aristocracy there.

Let us note, in passing, Marx's letter to Engels of 18 August 1869:

The Polish workers in Posen have brought a strike to a victorious end with the help of their colleagues in Berlin. This struggle against Monsieur le Capital – even in the lower form of the strike – is a more serious way of getting rid of national prejudices than peace declamations from the lips of bourgeois gentlemen.

The policy on the Irish question pursued by Marx in the International may be seen from the following:

On 18 November 1869, Marx wrote to Engels that he had spoken for an hour and a quarter at the Council of the International on the question of the attitude of the British Ministry to the Irish Amnesty, and had proposed the following resolution:

Resolved,

– that in his reply to the Irish demands for the release of the imprisoned Irish patriots [...] Mr. Gladstone deliberately insults the Irish nation;

– that he clogs political amnesty with conditions alike degrading to the victims of misgovernment and the people they belong to;

– that having, in the teeth of his responsible position, publicly and enthusiastically cheered on the American slave-holders' rebellion, he now steps in to preach to the Irish people the doctrine of passive obedience;

– that his whole proceedings with reference to the Irish amnesty question are the true and genuine offspring of that '*policy of conquest*', by the fiery denunciation of which Mr. Gladstone ousted his Tory rivals from office;

– that the General Council of the International Workingmen's Association express their admiration of the spirited, firm and high-souled manner in which the Irish people carry on their amnesty movement;

– that this resolution be communicated to all branches of, and workingmen's bodies connected with, the International Workingmen's Association in Europe and America.

On 10 December 1869, Marx wrote that his paper on the Irish question to be read at the Council of the International would be couched as follows:

Quite apart from all phrases about 'international' and 'humane' justice for Ireland – which are taken for granted in the International Council – *it is in the direct and absolute interest of the English working class to get rid of their present connection with Ireland.* And this is my fullest conviction; and for reasons which in part I can *not* tell the English workers themselves. For a long time I believed that it would be possible to overthrow the Irish regime by English working-class ascendancy. I always expressed this point of view in the *New York Tribune*[49] [an American paper to which Marx contributed for a long time]. Deeper study has now convinced me of the opposite. The English working class will *never accomplish anything* until it has got rid of Ireland [...] The English reaction in England had its roots in the subjugation of Ireland. (Marx's italics.)

Marx's policy on the Irish question should now be quite clear to our readers. Marx, the 'utopian', was so 'unpractical' that he stood for the separation of Ireland, which half a century later has not yet been achieved.

What gave rise to Marx's policy, and was it not mistaken?

At first Marx thought that Ireland would not be liberated by the national movement of the oppressed nation, but by the working-class movement of the oppressor nation. Marx did not make an absolute of the national movement, knowing, as he did, that only the victory of the working class can bring about the complete liberation of all nationalities. It is impossible to estimate beforehand all the possible relations between the bourgeois liberation movements of the oppressed nations and the proletarian emancipation movement

---

49 *The New York Daily Tribune* was an American newspaper published from 1841 to 1924. Until the 1850s it was the organ of the Left wing of the American Whigs, and thereafter the organ of the Republican Party. Karl Marx contributed to the paper from August 1851 to March 1862, and at his request Friedrich Engels wrote numerous articles for it. During the period of reaction that set in in Europe, Karl Marx and Frederick Engels used this widely circulated and at that time progressive newspaper to publish concrete material exposing the evils of capitalist society. During the American Civil War Marx's contributions to the newspaper stopped. His break with *The New York Daily Tribune* was largely due to the growing influence on the editorial board of the advocates of compromise with the slaveowners, and the paper's departure from progressive positions.

of the oppressor nation (the very problem which today makes the national question in Russia so difficult).

However, it so happened that the English working class fell under the influence of the liberals for a fairly long time, became an appendage to the liberals, and by adopting a liberal-labour policy left itself leaderless. The bourgeois liberation movement in Ireland grew stronger and assumed revolutionary forms. Marx reconsidered his view and corrected it. "What a misfortune it is for a nation to have subjugated another." The English working class will never be free until Ireland is freed from the English yoke. Reaction in England is strengthened and fostered by the enslavement of Ireland (just as reaction in Russia is fostered by her enslavement of a number of nations!).

And, in proposing in the International a resolution of sympathy with "the Irish nation", "the Irish people" (the clever L Vl. would probably have berated poor Marx for forgetting about the class struggle!), Marx advocated the *separation* of Ireland from England, "although after the separation there may come federation".

What were the theoretical grounds for Marx's conclusion? In England the bourgeois revolution had been consummated long ago. But it had not yet been consummated in Ireland; it is being consummated only now, after the lapse of half a century, by the reforms of the English Liberals. If capitalism had been overthrown in England as quickly as Marx had at first expected, there would have been no room for a bourgeois-democratic and general national movement in Ireland. But since it had arisen, Marx advised the English workers to support it, give it a revolutionary impetus and see it through in the interests of *their own* liberty.

The economic ties between Ireland and England in the 1860s were of course, even closer than Russia's present ties with Poland, the Ukraine, etc. The 'unpracticality' and 'impracticability' of the separation of Ireland (if only owing to geographical conditions and England's immense colonial power) were quite obvious. Though, in principle, an enemy of federalism, Marx in this instance granted the possibility of federation, as well,[50] *if only* the emancipation of Ireland was achieved in a revolutionary, not reformist way, through a movement of the mass of the people of Ireland supported by the working class of England. There can be no doubt that only such a solution of the historical problem would have been in the best interests of the proletariat and most conducive to rapid social progress.

Things turned out differently. Both the Irish people and the English proletariat proved weak. Only now, through the sordid deals between the English Liberals and the Irish bourgeoisie, is the Irish problem *being solved* (the example of Ulster shows with what difficulty) through the land reform (with compensation) and Home Rule (not yet introduced). Well then? Does it follow that Marx and Engels were 'utopians', that they put forward 'impracticable' national demands, or that they allowed themselves to be influenced by the Irish petty-bourgeois nationalists (for there is no doubt about the petty-bourgeois nature of the Fenian movement), etc.?

No. In the Irish question, too, Marx and Engels pursued a consistently proletarian policy, which really educated the masses in a spirit of democracy and socialism. Only such a policy could have saved both Ireland and England half a century of delay in introducing the necessary reforms, and prevented these reforms from being mutilated by the liberals to please the reactionaries.

The policy of Marx and Engels on the Irish question serves as a splendid example of the attitude the proletariat of the oppressor nations should adopt towards national movements, an example which has lost none of its immense *practical* importance. It serves as

---

50 By the way, it is not difficult to see why, from a social-democratic point of view, the right to 'self-determination' means neither federation nor autonomy (although, speaking in the abstract, both come under the category of 'self-determination'). The right to federation is simply meaningless, since federation implies a bilateral contract. It goes without saying that Marxists cannot include the defence of federalism in general in their programme. As far as autonomy is concerned, Marxists defend, not the 'right' to autonomy, but autonomy itself, as a general universal principle of a democratic state with a mixed national composition, and a great variety of geographical and other conditions. Consequently, the recognition of the 'right of nations to autonomy' is as absurd as that of the 'right of nations to federation'. – *Lenin*

a warning against that 'servile haste' with which the philistines of all countries, colours and languages hurry to label as 'utopian' the idea of altering the frontiers of states that were established by the violence and privileges of the landlords and bourgeoisie of one nation.

If the Irish and English proletariat had not accepted Marx's policy and had not made the secession of Ireland their slogan, this would have been the worst sort of opportunism, a neglect of their duties as democrats and socialists, and a concession to *English* reaction and the *English* bourgeoisie.

The 1903 Programme and its Liquidators

The minutes of the 1903 Congress, at which the programme of the Russian Marxists was adopted, have become a great rarity, and the vast majority of the active members of the working-class movement today are unacquainted with the motives underlying the various points (the more so since not all the literature relating to it enjoys the blessings of legality…). It is therefore necessary to analyse the debate that took place at the 1903 Congress on the question under discussion.

Let us state first of all that however meagre the Russian social-democratic literature on the 'right of nations to self-determination' may be, it nevertheless shows clearly that this right has always been understood to mean the right to secession. The Semkovskys, Liebmans and Yurkeviches who doubt this and declare that Section 9 is 'vague', etc., do so only because of their sheer ignorance or carelessness. As far back as 1902, Plekhanov, in *Zarya*,[51] defended 'the right to self-determination' in the draft programme, and wrote that this demand, while not obligatory upon bourgeois democrats, was "obligatory upon social-democrats".

> If we were to forget it or hesitate to advance it, [Plekhanov wrote] for fear of offending the national prejudices of our fellow-countrymen of Great-Russian nationality, the call […] 'workers of all countries, unite!' would be a shameful lie on our lips…

---

51 *Zarya* (*Dawn*) was a Marxist scientific and political journal, published in Stuttgart in 1901-02 by the editors of *Iskra*.

This is a very apt description of the fundamental argument in favour of the point under consideration; so apt that it is not surprising that the 'anythingarian' critics of our programme have been timidly avoiding it. The abandonment of this point, no matter for what motives, is *actually* a "shameful" concession to *Great-Russian* nationalism. But why Great-Russian, when it is a question of the right of *all* nations to self-determination? Because it refers to secession *from* the Great Russians. The interests of the *unity of the proletarians*, the interests of their class solidarity call for recognition of the right of *nations to secede* – that is what Plekhanov admitted twelve years ago in the words quoted above. Had our opportunists given thought to this they would probably not have talked so much nonsense about self-determination.

At the 1903 Congress, which adopted the draft programme that Plekhanov advocated, the main work was done by the *Programme Commission*. Unfortunately no minutes of its proceedings were kept; they would have been particularly interesting on this point, for it was *only* in the Commission that the representatives of the Polish social-democrats, Warszawski and Hanecki,[52] tried to defend their views and to dispute "recognition of the right to self-determination". Any reader who goes to the trouble of comparing their arguments (set forth in the speech by Warszawski and the statement by him and Hanecki, pp. 134-36 and 388-90 of the Congress minutes) with those which Rosa Luxemburg advanced in her Polish article, which we have analysed, will find them identical.

How were these arguments treated by the Programme Commission of the Second Congress, where Plekhanov, more than anyone else, spoke against the Polish Marxists? They were mercilessly ridiculed! The absurdity of proposing to the Marxists of *Russia* that they should reject the recognition of the right of nations to self-determination was demonstrated so plainly and clearly that the Polish Marxists *did not even venture to repeat their arguments at the plenary meeting of the Congress!* They left the Congress, convinced of the hopelessness

---

52 Adolf Warszawski and Yakov Hanecki were Polish Marxists and members of the SDKPiL.

of their case at the supreme assembly of Marxists – Great-Russian, Jewish, Georgian, and Armenian.

Needless to say, this historic episode is of very great importance to everyone seriously interested in *his own* programme. The fact that the Polish Marxists' arguments were completely defeated at the Programme Commission of the Congress, and that the Polish Marxists gave up the attempt to defend their views at the plenary meeting of the Congress is very significant. No wonder Rosa Luxemburg maintained a 'modest' silence about it in her article in 1908 – the recollection of the Congress must have been too unpleasant! She also kept quiet about the ridiculously inept proposal made by Warszawski and Hanecki in 1903, on behalf of all Polish Marxists, to 'amend' Section 9 of the programme, a proposal which neither Rosa Luxemburg nor the other Polish social-democrats have ventured (or will ever venture) to repeat.

But although Rosa Luxemburg, concealing her defeat in 1903, has maintained silence over these facts, those who take an interest in the history of their party will make it their business to ascertain them and give thought to their significance.

On leaving the 1903 Congress, Rosa Luxemburg's friends submitted the following statement:

> We propose that Clause 7 [now Clause 9] of the draft programme read as follows: 'Section 7. *Institutions guaranteeing full freedom of cultural development to all nations incorporated in the state.*' (p. 390 of the minutes.)

Thus, the Polish Marxists at that time put forward views on the national question that were so vague that *instead of* self-determination they practically proposed the notorious 'cultural-national autonomy', only under another name!

This sounds almost incredible, but unfortunately it is a fact. At the Congress itself, attended though it was by five Bundists with five votes and three Caucasians with six votes, without counting Kostrov's consultative voice, *not a single* vote was cast for the *rejection* of the clause about self-determination. Three votes were cast for the proposal to add 'cultural-national autonomy' to this clause (in favour of Goldblatt's formula: "the establishment of institutions guaranteeing the nations full freedom of cultural development") and four votes for Lieber's formula ("the right of nations to freedom in their cultural development").

Now that a Russian liberal party – the Constitutional-Democratic Party – has appeared on the scene, we know that in *its* programme the political self-determination of nations has been replaced by 'cultural self-determination'. Rosa Luxemburg's Polish friends, therefore, were '*combating*' the nationalism of the PSP, and, did it so successfully that they proposed the substitution of a *liberal* programme for the Marxist programme! And in the same breath they accused our programme of being opportunist; no wonder this accusation was received with laughter by the Programme Commission of the Second Congress!

How was 'self-determination' understood by the delegates to the Second Congress, of whom, as we have seen, *not one* was opposed to 'self-determination of nations'?

The following three extracts from the minutes provide the answer:

> *Martynov*[53] is of the opinion that the term 'self-determination' should not be given a broad interpretation; it merely means the right of a nation to establish itself as a separate polity, not regional self-government. (p. 171)

Martynov was a member of the Programme Commission, in which the arguments of Rosa Luxemburg's friends were repudiated and ridiculed. Martynov was then an Economist[54] in his views, and a violent opponent of *Iskra*; had he expressed an opinion that was not

---

53 Alexandr Martynov was a leading Menshevik and a member of the Economists. He was a strong advocate of the two stage theory, arguing that a fully capitalistic government needed to run its course in Russia before socialism was possible. He joined the Communist Party in 1923, and became an opponent of the Left Opposition. He was a chief architect of the Stalinist theories used to justify subordinating the workers to the 'progressive' bourgeoisie, including the concept of the 'bloc of four classes'.

54 Economism was an opportunist trend in Russian Social-Democracy at the turn of the century. The Economists limited the tasks of the working-class movement to the economic struggle for higher wages, better working conditions etc., maintaining that the political struggle should be left to the liberal bourgeoisie.

shared by the majority of the Programme Commission he would certainly have been repudiated.

Bundist Goldblatt was the first to speak when the Congress, after the Commission had finished its work, discussed Section 8 (the present Clause 9) of the programme. He said:

> No objections can be raised to the 'right to self-determination'. When a nation is fighting for independence, that should not be opposed. If Poland refuses to enter into lawful marriage with Russia, she should not be interfered with, as Plekhanov put it. I agree with this opinion within these limits. (pp. 175-76)

Plekhanov had not spoken on this subject at all at the plenary meeting of the Congress. Goldblatt was referring to what Plekhanov had said at the Programme Commission, where the "right to self-determination" had been explained in a simple yet detailed manner to mean the right to secession. Lieber, who spoke after Goldblatt, remarked:

> Of course, if any nationality finds that it cannot live within the frontiers of Russia, the party will not place any obstacles in its way (p. 176).

The reader will see that at the Second Congress of the party, which adopted the programme, it was unanimously understood that self-determination meant 'only' the right to secession. Even the Bundists grasped this truth at the time, and it is only in our own deplorable times of continued counter-revolution and all sorts of 'apostasy' that we can find people who, bold in their ignorance, declare that the programme is 'vague'. But before devoting time to these sorry would-be social-democrats, let us first finish with the attitude of the Poles to the programme.

They came to the Second Congress (1903) declaring that unity was necessary and imperative. But they left the Congress after their 'reverses' in the Programme Commission, and their *last word* was a written statement, printed in the minutes of the congress, containing the above-mentioned proposal to *substitute* cultural-national autonomy for self-determination.

In 1906 the Polish Marxists joined the party; *neither* upon joining *nor* afterwards (at the Congress of 1907, the conferences of 1907 and 1908, or the plenum of 1910) *did they introduce* a single proposal to amend Section 9 of the Russian Programme! That is a fact.

And, despite all utterances and assurances, this fact definitely proves that Rosa Luxemburg's friends regarded the question as having been settled by the debate at the Programme Commission of the Second Congress, as well as by the decision of that Congress, and that they tacitly acknowledged their mistake and corrected it by joining the party in 1906, after they had left the Congress in 1903, without a single attempt to raise the question of amending Section 9 of the programme through *party* channels.

Rosa Luxemburg's article appeared over her signature in 1908 – of course, it never entered anyone's head to deny party publicists the right to criticise the programme – and, *since* the writing of this article, *not a single* official body of the Polish Marxists has raised the question of revising Section 9.

Trotsky was therefore rendering a great disservice to certain admirers of Rosa Luxemburg when he wrote, on behalf of the editors of *Borba*, in issue No. 2 of that publication (March 1914):

> The Polish Marxists consider that 'the right to national self-determination' is entirely devoid of political content and should be deleted from the programme (p. 25).

The obliging Trotsky is more dangerous than an enemy! Trotsky could produce *no* proof, except 'private conversations' (i.e. simply gossip, on which Trotsky always subsists), for classifying "Polish Marxists" in general as supporters of every article by Rosa Luxemburg. Trotsky presented the "Polish Marxists" as people devoid of honour and conscience, incapable of respecting even their own convictions and the programme of their party. How obliging Trotsky is![55]

---

55 At this time, Lenin is sharply critical of Trotsky due to his role in creating the 'August bloc' in 1912. In January 1912, Lenin had pushed for a decisive break with the Mensheviks at the Prague Conference in February 1912, with the creation, in effect, of a separate party. Trotsky thought it was possible to unite

When, in 1903, the representatives of the Polish Marxists walked out of the Second Congress *over* the right to self-determination, Trotsky could have said *at the time* that they regarded this right as devoid of content and subject to deletion from the programme.

But after that the Polish Marxists *joined* the party whose programme this was, and they have never introduced a motion to amend it.[56]

---

the party and took the initiative of convening a conference in Vienna in August 1912. Trotsky explains :

> I participated actively in this bloc. In a certain sense I created it. Politically I differed with the Mensheviks on all fundamental questions. I also differed with the ultra-left Bolsheviks, the Vperyodists. In the general tendency of politics I stood far more closely to the Bolsheviks. But I was against the Leninist 'regime' because I had not yet learned to understand that, in order to realise the revolutionary goal, a firmly welded centralised party is indispensable. And so I formed this episodic bloc consisting of heterogeneous elements which was directed against the proletarian wing of the party. [...]

> Lenin subjected the August Bloc to merciless criticism and the harshest blows fell to my lot. Lenin proved that inasmuch as I did not agree politically with either the Mensheviks or the Vperyodists my policy was adventurism. *This was severe but it was true.* [...]

> I had not freed myself at that period, especially in the organisational sphere from the traits of a petty-bourgeois revolutionist. I was sick with the disease of conciliationism toward Menshevism and with a distrustful attitude toward Leninist centralism. Immediately after the August conference the bloc began to disintegrate into its component parts. Within a few months I was not only in principle but organisationally outside the bloc. (Trotsky, Leon, *In Defence of Marxism*, Wellred Books, 2024, pp. 184-185)

This episode and Lenin's comments in this text would later be fished out of the archives and used by the Stalinists for unprincipled factional purposes in the struggle to discredit Trotsky after Lenin's death, despite the explicit instructions in Lenin's Testament that "Trotsky's non-Bolshevik past should not be used against him."

In relation to the national question, Trotsky defended the right of nations to self-determination and had argued against the position of the Bund at the Second Congress in 1903. The August bloc on the other hand included the Bund and the Mensheviks. The Mensheviks by this time had adopted the Bund's position in favour of 'cultural-national autonomy'.

56 We are informed that the Polish Marxists attended the Summer Conference of the Russian Marxists in 1913 with only a consultative voice and did not vote at all on the right to self-determination (secession), declaring their opposition to this right in general. Of course, they had a perfect right to act the way they did,

Why did Trotsky withhold these facts from the readers of his journal? Only because it pays him to speculate on fomenting differences between the Polish and the Russian opponents of liquidationism and to deceive the Russian workers on the question of the programme.

Trotsky has never yet held a firm opinion on any important question of Marxism. He always contrives to worm his way into the cracks of any given difference of opinion, and desert one side for the other. At the present moment he is in the company of the Bundists and the liquidators. And these gentlemen do not stand on ceremony where the party is concerned.

Listen to the Bundist Liebman:

> When, fifteen years ago, the Russian social-democrats included the point about the right of every nationality to 'self-determination' in their programme, everyone [!] asked himself: What does this fashionable [!] term really mean? No answer was forthcoming [!]. This word was left [!] wrapped in mist. And indeed, at the time, it was difficult to dispel that mist. The moment had not come when this point could be made concrete – it was said – so let it remain wrapped in mist [!] for the time being and practice will show what content should he put into it.

Isn't it magnificent, the way this "ragamuffin"[57] mocks at the party programme? And why does he mock at it?

Because he is an absolute ignoramus, who has never learnt anything or even read any party history, but merely happened to land in liquidationist circles where going about in the nude is considered the 'right' thing to do as far as knowledge of the party and everything it stands for is concerned.

Pomyalovsky's seminary student boasts of having "spat into a barrel of sauerkraut".[58] The Bundist gentlemen have gone one better.

------

and, as hitherto, to agitate in Poland against secession. But this is not quite what Trotsky said; for the Polish Marxists did not demand the "deletion" of Section 9 "from the programme". – *Lenin*

57 A quotation from the sketch '*Abroad*' by the Russian satirist Saltykov-Shchedrin.
58 Lenin is quoting '*Seminary Sketches*' by the Russian writer NG Pomyalovsky.

They let the Liebmans loose to spit publicly into their own barrel. What do the Liebmans care about the fact that the International Congress has passed a decision, that at the Congress of their own party the representatives of their own Bund proved that they were quite able (and what 'severe' critics and determined enemies of *Iskra* they were!) to understand the meaning of 'self-determination' and were even in agreement with it? And will it not be easier to liquidate the party if the 'party publicists' (no jokes, please!) treat its history and programme after the fashion of the seminary student?

Here is a second "ragamuffin", Mr. Yurkevich of *Dzvin*.[59] Mr. Yurkevich must have had the minutes of the Second Congress before him, because he quotes Plekhanov, as repeated by Goldblatt, and shows that he is aware of the fact that self-determination can only mean the right to secession. This, however, does not prevent him from spreading slander about the Russian Marxists among the Ukrainian petty bourgeoisie, alleging that they stand for the "state integrity" of Russia. (No. 7-8, 1913, p. 83, etc.) Of course, the Yurkeviches could not have invented a better method than such slander to alienate the Ukrainian democrats from the Great-Russian democrats. And such alienation is in line with the entire policy of the group of *Dzvin* publicists who advocate the *separation* of the Ukrainian workers *in a special* national organisation![60]

It is quite appropriate, of course, that a group of nationalist philistines, who are engaged in splitting the ranks of the proletariat – and objectively this is the role of *Dzvin* – should disseminate such hopeless confusion on the national question. Needless to say, the Yurkeviches and Liebmans, who are 'terribly' offended when they are called 'near party-men', do not say a word, not a single word, as to how *they* would like the problem of the right to secede to be settled in the programme.

---

59 *Dzvin* (*The Bell*) was a Ukrainian language nationalist journal with a Menshevik trend, published in Kiev from January 1913 to the middle of 1914.

60 See particularly Mr. Yurkevich's preface to Mr. Levinsky's book (written in Ukrainian) *Outline of the Development of the Ukrainian Working-Class Movement in Galicia*, Kiev, 1914. – *Lenin*

But here is the third and principal "ragamuffin", Mr. Semkovsky, who, addressing a Great-Russian audience through the columns of a liquidationist newspaper, lashes at Section 9 of the programme and at the same time declares that "for certain reasons he does not approve of the proposal" to delete this clause!

This is incredible, but it is a fact.

In August 1912, the liquidators' conference raised the national question officially. For eighteen months not a single article has appeared on the question of Section 9, except the one written by Mr. Semkovsky. And in this article the author *repudiates* the programme, "without approving", however, "for *certain* reasons" (is this a secrecy disease?) the proposal to amend it! We may be sure that it would be difficult to find anywhere in the world similar examples of opportunism, or even worse – renunciation of the party, and a desire to liquidate it.

A single example will suffice to show what Semkovsky's arguments are like:

> What are we to do [he writes] if the Polish proletariat wants to fight side by side with the proletariat of all Russia within the framework of a single state, while the reactionary classes of Polish society, on the contrary, want to separate Poland from Russia and obtain a majority of votes in favour of secession by referendum? Should we, Russian social-democrats in the central parliament, vote together with our Polish comrades *against* secession, or – in order not to violate the 'right to self-determination' – vote *for* secession? (*Novaya Rabochaya Gazeta*, No. 71.)[61]

From this it is evident that Mr. Semkovsky does not even understand the *point at issue*! It did not occur to him that the right to secession presupposes the settlement of the question by a parliament (Diet, referendum, etc.) of the *seceding* region, *not* by a central parliament.

The childish perplexity over the question "what are we to do", if under democracy the majority are for reaction, serves to screen the real and live issue when *both* the Purishkeviches and the Kokoshkins consider the very idea of secession criminal! Perhaps

---

61 *Novaya Rabochaya Gazeta* (*New Workers' Paper*) was a legal daily newspaper of the Menshevik-liquidators, published after 1913.

the proletarians of *all* Russia ought not to fight the Purishkeviches and the Kokoshkins today, but should bypass them and fight the reactionary classes of Poland!

Such is the sheer rubbish published in the liquidators' organ of which Mr. L Martov is one of the ideological leaders, the selfsame L Martov who drafted the programme and spoke in favour of its adoption in 1903, and even subsequently wrote in favour of the right to secede. Apparently L Martov is now arguing according to the rule:

> No clever man is needed there;
>
> Better send Read,
>
> And I shall wait and see.[62]

He sends 'Read-Semkovsky' along and allows our programme to be distorted, and endlessly muddled up in a daily paper whose new readers are unacquainted with it!

Yes. Liquidationism has gone a long way – there are even very many prominent ex-social-democrats who have not a trace of party spirit left in them.

Rosa Luxemburg cannot, of course, be classed with the Liebmans, Yurkeviches and Semkovskys, but the fact that it was this kind of people who seized upon her error shows with particular clarity the opportunism she has lapsed into.

Conclusion

To sum up. As far as the theory of Marxism in general is concerned, the question of the right to self-determination presents no difficulty. No one can seriously question the London resolution of 1896, or the fact that self-determination implies only the right to secede, or that the formation of independent national states is the tendency in all bourgeois-democratic revolutions.

---

62 Lenin quotes the words of a Sevastopol soldiers' song written by Leo Tolstoy. The song is about the unsuccessful operation of the Russian troops at the river Chornaya on 4 August 1855, during the Crimean War. In that action General Read commanded two divisions, which suffered heavy losses and were forced to retreat, where Read himself was killed.

A difficulty is to some extent created by the fact that in Russia the proletariat of both the oppressed and oppressor nations are fighting, and must fight, side by side. The task is to preserve the unity of the proletariat's class struggle for socialism, and to resist all bourgeois and Black-Hundred nationalist influences. Where the oppressed nations are concerned, the separate organisation of the proletariat as an independent party sometimes leads to such a bitter struggle against local nationalism that the perspective becomes distorted and the nationalism of the oppressor nation is lost sight of.

But this distortion of perspective cannot last long. The experience of the joint struggle waged by the proletarians of various nations has demonstrated all too clearly that we must formulate political issues from the all-Russia, not the 'Kraków' point of view. And in all-Russia politics it is the Purishkeviches and the Kokoshkins who are in the saddle. Their ideas predominate, and their persecution of non-Russians for 'separatism', for *thinking* about secession, is being preached, and practised in the Duma, in the schools, in the churches, in the barracks, and in hundreds and thousands of newspapers. It is this Great-Russian nationalist poison that is polluting the entire all-Russia political atmosphere. This is the misfortune of one nation, which, by subjugating other nations, is strengthening reaction throughout Russia. The memories of 1849 and 1863 form a living political tradition, which, unless great storms arise, threatens to hamper every democratic and *especially* every social-democratic movement for decades to come.

There can be no doubt that however natural the point of view of certain Marxists belonging to the oppressed nations (whose 'misfortune' is sometimes that the masses of the population are blinded by the idea of their 'own' national liberation) may appear at times, *in reality* the objective alignment of class forces in Russia makes refusal to advocate the right to self-determination tantamount to the worst opportunism, to the infection of the proletariat with the ideas of the Kokoshkins. And these ideas are, essentially, the ideas and the policy of the Purishkeviches.

Therefore, although Rosa Luxemburg's point of view could at first have been excused as being specifically Polish, 'Kraków' narrow-mindedness,[63] it is inexcusable today, when nationalism and, above all, governmental Great-Russian nationalism, has everywhere gained ground, and when policy is being shaped by this *Great-Russian nationalism*. In actual fact; it is being seized upon by the opportunists of *all* nations, who fight shy of the idea of 'storms' and 'leaps', believe that the bourgeois-democratic revolution is over, and follow in the wake of the liberalism of the Kokoshkins.

Like any other nationalism, Great-Russian nationalism passes through various phases, according to the classes that are dominant in the bourgeois country at any given time. Up to 1905, we almost exclusively knew national-reactionaries. After the revolution, *national-liberals* arose in our country.

In our country this is virtually the stand adopted both by the Octobrists and by the Cadets (Kokoshkin), i.e. by the whole of the present-day bourgeoisie.

Great-Russian national-democrats will *inevitably* appear later on. Mr. Peshekhonov, one of the founders of the 'Popular Socialist' Party, already expressed this point of view (in the issue of *Russkoye Bogatstvo*[64] for August 1906) when he called for caution in regard to the peasants' nationalist prejudices. However much others may slander us Bolsheviks and accuse us of 'idealising' the peasant, we always have made and always will make a clear distinction between peasant intelligence and peasant prejudice, between peasant strivings for democracy and opposition to Purishkevich, and the peasant desire to make peace with the priest and the landlord.

---

63 It is not difficult to understand that the recognition by the Marxists of the whole of Russia, and first and foremost by the Great-Russians, of the right of nations to secede in no way precludes agitation against secession by Marxists of a particular oppressed nation, just as the recognition of the right to divorce does not preclude agitation against divorce in a particular case. We think, therefore, that there will be an inevitable increase in the number of Polish Marxists who laugh at the non-existent 'contradiction' now being 'encouraged' by Semkovsky and Trotsky. – *Lenin*

64 *Russkoye Bogatstvo* (*Russian Wealth*) was a monthly magazine of the liberal Narodniks.

Even now, and probably for a fairly long time to come, proletarian democracy must reckon with the nationalism of the Great-Russian peasants (not with the object of making concessions to it, but in order to combat it).[65] The awakening of nationalism among the oppressed nations, which became so pronounced after 1905 (let us recall, say, the group of 'Federalist-Autonomists' in the First Duma, the growth of the Ukrainian movement, of the Moslem movement, etc.), will inevitably lead to greater nationalism among the Great-Russian petty bourgeoisie in town and countryside. The slower the democratisation of Russia, the more persistent, brutal and bitter will be the national persecution and bickering among the bourgeoisie of the various nations. The particularly reactionary nature of the Russian Purishkeviches will simultaneously give rise to (and strengthen) 'separatist' tendencies among the various oppressed nationalities, which sometimes enjoy far greater freedom in neighbouring states.

In this situation, the proletariat, of Russia is faced with a twofold or, rather, a two-sided task: to combat nationalism of every kind, above all, Great-Russian nationalism; to recognise, not only fully equal rights, for all nations in general, but also equality of rights as regards polity, i.e. the right of nations to self-determination, to secession. And at the same time, it is their task, in the interests of a successful struggle against all and every kind, of nationalism among all nations, to preserve the unity of the proletarian struggle and the proletarian organisations,

---

65 It would be interesting to trace the changes that take place in Polish nationalism, for example, in the process of its transformation from gentry nationalism into bourgeois nationalism, and then into peasant nationalism. In his book *Das polnische Gemeinwesen im preussischen Staat* (*The Polish Community in the Prussian State;* there is a Russian translation), Ludwig Bernhard, who shares the view of a German Kokoshkin, describes a very typical phenomenon: the formation of a sort of 'peasant republic' by the Poles in Germany in the form of a close alliance of the various co-operatives and other associations of Polish peasants in their struggle for nationality, religion, and 'Polish' land. German oppression has welded the Poles together lend segregated them, after first awakening the nationalism of the gentry, then of the bourgeoisie, and finally of the peasant masses (especially after the campaign the Germans launched in 1873 against the use of the Polish language in schools). Things are moving in the same direction in Russia, and not only with regard to Poland. – *Lenin*

amalgamating these organisations into a close-knit international association, despite bourgeois strivings for national exclusiveness.

Complete equality of rights for all nations; the right of nations to self-determination; the unity of the workers of all nations – such is the national programme that Marxism, the experience of the whole world, and the experience of Russia, teach the workers.

* * *

This article had been set up when I received No. 3 of *Nasha Rabochaya Gazeta*, in which Mr. V Kosovsky writes the following about the recognition of the right of all nations to self-determination:

> Taken mechanically from the resolution of the First Congress of the party (1898), which in turn had borrowed it from the decisions of international socialist congresses, it was given, as is evident from the debate, the same meaning at the 1903 Congress as was ascribed to it by the Socialist International, i.e. political self-determination, the self-determination of nations in the field of political independence. Thus the formula: national self-determination, which implies the right to territorial separation, does not in any way affect the question of how national relations *within* a given state organism should be regulated for nationalities that cannot or have no desire to leave the existing state.

It is evident from this that Mr. V Kosovsky has seen the minutes of the Second Congress of 1903 and understands perfectly well the real (and only) meaning of the term self-determination. Compare this with the fact that the editors of the Bund newspaper *Zeit*[66] let Mr. Liebman loose to scoff at the programme and to declare that it is vague! Queer 'party' ethics among these Bundists... The Lord alone knows why Kosovsky should declare that the Congress took over the principle of self-determination *mechanically*. Some people want to 'object', but how, why, and for what reason – they do not know.

V Ilyin[67]

---

66 *Zeit* (*Time*) was a weekly newspaper and organ of the Bund, published in Yiddish in St. Petersburg from December 1912 to May 1914.

67 Pseudonym of Vladimir Ilyich Ulyanov (Lenin).

Is a Compulsory Official Language Needed?

Published 18 January 1914

The liberals differ from the reactionaries in that they recognise the right to have instruction conducted in the native language, at least in the *elementary* schools. But they are completely at one with the reactionaries on the point that a compulsory official language is necessary.

What does a compulsory official language mean? In practice, it means that the language of the Great Russians, who are a *minority* of the population of Russia, is imposed upon all the rest of the population of Russia. In every school the teaching of the official language must be *obligatory*. All official correspondence must be conducted in the official language, not in the language of the local population.

On what grounds do the parties who advocate a compulsory official language justify its necessity?

The 'arguments' of the Black Hundreds are curt, of course. They say: All non-Russians should be ruled with a rod of iron to keep them from 'getting out of hand'. Russia must be indivisible, and all the peoples must submit to Great-Russian rule, for it was the Great Russians who built up and united the land of Russia. Hence, the language of the ruling class must be the compulsory official language. The Purishkeviches would not mind having the 'local lingoes' banned altogether; although they are spoken by about 60 per cent of Russia's total population.

The attitude of the liberals is much more 'cultured' and 'refined'. They are for permitting the use of the native languages within certain limits (for example, in the elementary schools). At the same time they advocate an obligatory official language, which, they say, is necessary in the interests of 'culture', in the interests of a 'united' and 'indivisible' Russia, and so forth.

> Statehood is the affirmation of cultural unity […] An official language is an essential constituent of state culture […] Statehood is based on unity of authority, the official language being an instrument of that unity. The official language possesses the same compulsory and universally coercive power as all other forms of statehood […]

> If Russia is to remain united and indivisible, we must firmly insist on the political expediency of the Russian literary language.

This is the typical philosophy of a liberal on the necessity of an official language.

We have quoted the above passage from an article by Mr. S Patrashkin in the liberal newspaper *Dyen*[1] (No. 7). For quite understandable reasons, the Black-Hundred *Novoye Vremya* rewarded the author of these ideas with a resounding kiss. Mr. Patrashkin expresses "very sound ideas", Menshikov's newspaper stated (No. 13588). Another paper the Black Hundreds are constantly praising for such very "sound" ideas is the national-liberal *Russkaya Mysl*. And how can they help praising them when the liberals, with the aid of 'cultured' arguments, are advocating things that please the *Novoye Vremya* people so much?

Russian is a great and mighty language, the liberals tell us. Don't you want everybody who lives in the border regions of Russia to know this great and mighty language? Don't you see that the Russian language will enrich the literature of the non-Russians, put great treasures of culture within their reach, and so forth?

---

1   *Dyen* (*Day*) was a daily newspaper of a liberal-bourgeois trend, published in St. Petersburg from 1912. Among its contributors were Menshevik liquidators, who took over complete control of the paper after February 1917.

That is all true, gentlemen, we say in reply to the liberals. We know better than you do that the language of Turgenev, Tolstoy, Dobrolyubov and Chernyshevsky is a great and mighty one. We desire more than you do that the closest possible intercourse and fraternal unity should be established between the oppressed classes of all the nations that inhabit Russia, without any discrimination. And we, of course, are in favour of every inhabitant of Russia having the opportunity to learn the great Russian language.

What we do not want is the element of *coercion*. We do not want to have people driven into paradise with a cudgel; for no matter how many fine phrases about 'culture' you may utter, a *compulsory* official language involves coercion, the use of the cudgel. We do not think that the great and mighty Russian language needs anyone having to study it by *sheer compulsion*. We are convinced that the development of capitalism in Russia, and the whole course of social life in general, are tending to bring all nations closer together. Hundreds of thousands of people are moving from one end of Russia to another; the different national populations are intermingling; exclusiveness and national conservatism must disappear. People whose conditions of life and work make it necessary for them to know the Russian language will learn it without being forced to do so. But coercion (the cudgel) will have only one result: it will hinder the great and mighty Russian language from spreading to other national groups, and, most important of all, it will sharpen antagonism, cause friction in a million new forms, increase resentment, mutual misunderstanding, and so on.

Who wants that sort of thing? Not the Russian people, not the Russian democrats. They do not recognise national oppression *in any form*, even in "the interests of Russian culture and statehood".

That is why Russian Marxists say that there must be no compulsory official language, that the population must be provided with schools where teaching will be carried on in all the local languages, that a fundamental law must be introduced in the constitution declaring invalid all privileges of any one nation and all violations of the rights of national minorities.

Bill on the Equality of Nations and the Safeguarding of the Rights of National Minorities

Written after 6 May 1914

Editor's note: The 'Bill on the Equality of Nations and the Safeguarding of the Rights of National Minorities' was drafted by Lenin for introduction to the Fourth Duma by the Bolshevik group.

Lenin outlined the plan of the bill in a letter, dated 6 May 1914, to the Armenian Bolshevik SG Shahumyan. Lenin attached special importance to the introduction of this bill in the Duma. He wrote:

> In this way, I believe we can popularly explain the stupidity of cultural-national autonomy and crush the votaries of this folly once for all.

The bill was not introduced.

* * *

1. The boundaries of Russia's administrative divisions, rural and urban (villages, volosts, uyezds, gubernias,[1] parts and sections of

---

1 A gubernia (governorate) refers to one of the chief administrative divisions of tsarist Russia. Gubernias were divided into uyezds, similar to the English concept of counties, then further into volosts, similar to districts.

towns, suburbs, etc.), shall be revised on the basis of a register of present-day economic conditions and the national composition of the population.

2.　This register shall be made by commissions elected by the local population on the basis of universal, direct and equal suffrage by secret ballot with proportional representation; national minorities too small (under proportional representation) to elect one commission member shall elect a commission member with a consultative voice.

3.　The new boundaries shall be endorsed by the central parliament of the country.

4.　Local self-government shall be introduced in all areas of the country without exception, on the basis of universal, direct and equal suffrage by secret ballot with proportional representation; areas with specific geographical, living or economic conditions or a special national composition of the population shall have the right to form autonomous regions with autonomous regional Diets.

5.　The limits of jurisdiction exercised by the autonomous Diets and local self-governing bodies shall be determined by the central parliament of the country.

6.　All nations in the state are absolutely equal, and all privileges enjoyed by any one nation or any one language are held to be inadmissible and anti-constitutional.

7.　The local self-governing bodies and autonomous Diets shall determine the language in which business is to be conducted by state and public establishments in a given area or region, all national minorities having the right to demand absolute safeguards for their language on the basis of the principle of equality, for example, the right to receive replies from state and public establishments in the language in which they are addressed, etc. Measures by zemstvos,[2] towns, etc., which infringe the equality of languages enjoyed by the national minorities in financial, administrative, legal and all other fields, shall be considered non-valid and subject to repeal on a protest filed by any citizen of the state, regardless of domicile.

8. Each self-governing unit of the state, rural and urban, shall elect, on the basis of universal, direct and equal suffrage by secret ballot with proportional representation, boards of education to take care, wholly and autonomously, of expenditures on all the cultural and educational needs of the population subject to the control and management of the town and zemstvo bodies.

9. In territorial units with a mixed population the number of members on the boards of education shall not be less than twenty. This number may be increased by order of the self-governing bodies and autonomous Diets. Areas shall be considered as having a mixed population where a national minority constitutes up to 5 per cent of the population.

10. Every national minority of a given self-governing unit that is too small to elect, under proportional representation, one member of the board of education shall be entitled to elect a member with a consultative voice.

11. The proportional share of the funds expended on the cultural and educational needs of the national minorities in a given area shall not be less than the proportional share of the national minorities in the whole population of the given area.

12. A census of the population, with due account of the native language of citizens, shall be carried out every ten years throughout the state, and every five years in regions and areas with a mixed population.

---

2   Zemstvos were rural self-government bodies set up in the central gubernias of tsarist Russia in 1864. They were dominated by the nobility, and their jurisdiction was limited to purely local economic and welfare matters: hospital and road building, statistics, insurance, etc.

13. All measures by boards of education which in any way infringe the complete equality of nations and languages of the local population or the proportionality of expenditures on cultural and educational needs in conformity with the share of the national minorities in the population, shall be considered non-valid and subject to repeal on a protest of any citizen of the state, regardless of domicile.

The Socialist Revolution and the Right of Nations to Self-Determination

Written January-February 1916

Editor's note: In the context of the First World War, the discussion on the attitude of Marxists to the national question resurfaced. Lenin wrote this document as a series of theses summarising the position of the Bolsheviks.

* * *

Imperialism, socialism, and the liberation of oppressed nations

Imperialism is the highest stage in the development of capitalism. In the foremost countries capital has outgrown the bounds of national states, has replaced competition by monopoly and has created all the objective conditions for the achievement of socialism. In Western Europe and in the United States, therefore, the revolutionary struggle of the proletariat for the overthrow of capitalist governments and the expropriation of the bourgeoisie is on the order of the day. Imperialism forces the masses into this struggle by sharpening class contradictions on a tremendous scale, by worsening the conditions of the masses both economically – trusts, high cost of living – and politically – the growth of militarism, more frequent wars, more powerful reaction, the intensification and expansion of national oppression and colonial plunder. Victorious socialism must necessarily establish a full democracy and, consequently, not only introduce full equality of nations but also realise the right of the oppressed nations to self-determination, i.e. the right to free political separation. Socialist parties which did not show by all their activity, both now, during the revolution, and after its victory, that they would liberate the enslaved nations and build up relations with them on the basis of a free union – and free union is a false phrase without the right to secede – these parties would be betraying socialism.

Democracy, of course, is also a form of state which must disappear when the state disappears, but that will only take place in the transition from conclusively victorious and consolidated socialism to full communism.

The socialist revolution and the struggle for democracy

The socialist revolution is not a single act, it is not one battle on one front, but a whole epoch of acute class conflicts, a long series of battles on all fronts, i.e. on all questions of economics and politics, battles that can only end in the expropriation of the bourgeoisie. It would be a radical mistake to think that the struggle for democracy was capable of diverting the proletariat from the socialist revolution or of hiding, overshadowing it, etc. On the contrary, in the same way as there can be no victorious socialism that does not practice full democracy, so the proletariat cannot prepare for its victory over the bourgeoisie without an all-round, consistent and revolutionary struggle for democracy.

It would be no less a mistake to remove one of the points of the democratic programme, for example, the point on the self-determination of nations, on the grounds of it being 'impracticable' or 'illusory' under imperialism. The contention that the right of nations to self-determination is impracticable within the bounds of capitalism can be understood either in the absolute, economic sense, or in the conditional, political sense.

In the first case it is radically incorrect from the standpoint of theory. First, in that sense, such things as, for example, labour money, or the abolition of crises etc., are impracticable under capitalism. It is absolutely untrue that the self-determination of nations is *equally* impracticable. Secondly, even the one example of the secession of Norway from Sweden in 1905 is sufficient to refute 'impracticability' in that sense. Thirdly, it would be absurd to deny that some slight change in the political and strategic relations of, say, Germany and Britain, might today or tomorrow make the formation of a new Polish, Indian and other similar state fully 'practicable'. Fourthly, finance capital, in its drive to expand, can 'freely' buy or bribe the freest democratic or republican government and the elective officials of any, even an 'independent', country. The domination of finance capital and of capital in general is not to be abolished by *any* reforms in the sphere of political democracy; and self-determination belongs wholly and exclusively to this sphere. This domination of finance capital, however, does not in the least nullify the significance of political democracy as a freer, wider and clearer *form* of class oppression and class struggle. Therefore all arguments about the 'impracticability', in the economic sense, of one of the demands of political democracy under capitalism are reduced to a theoretically incorrect definition of the general and basic relationships of capitalism and of political democracy as a whole.

In the second case the assertion is incomplete and inaccurate. This is because not only the right of nations to self-determination, but *all* the fundamental demands of political democracy are only partially 'practicable' under imperialism, and then in a distorted form and by way of exception (for example, the secession of Norway from Sweden in 1905). The demand for the immediate liberation of the colonies that is put forward by all revolutionary social-democrats is also 'impracticable' under capitalism without a series of revolutions. But from this it does not by any means follow that Social-Democracy should reject the immediate and most determined struggle for *all* these demands – such a rejection would only play into the hands of the bourgeoisie and reaction – but, on the contrary, it follows that these demands must be formulated and put through in a revolutionary and not a reformist manner, going beyond the bounds of bourgeois legality, breaking them down, going beyond speeches in parliament and verbal protests, and drawing the masses into decisive action, extending and intensifying the struggle for every fundamental democratic demand up to a direct proletarian onslaught on the bourgeoisie, i.e. up to the socialist revolution that expropriates the bourgeoisie. The socialist revolution may flare up not only through some big strike, street demonstration or hunger riot or a military insurrection or colonial revolt, but also as a result of a political crisis such as the Dreyfus case[1] or the Zabern incident,[2] or in connection with a referendum on the secession of an oppressed nation, etc.

Increased national oppression under imperialism does not mean that Social-Democracy should reject what the bourgeoisie call the 'utopian' struggle for the freedom of nations to secede but, on the contrary, it should make greater use of the conflicts that arise in this sphere, *too*, as grounds for mass action and for revolutionary attacks on the bourgeoisie.

The meaning of the right to self-determination and its relation to federation

The right of nations to self-determination implies exclusively the right to independence in the political sense, the right to free political separation from the oppressor nation. Specifically, this demand for

---

1   The Dreyfus Affair began in 1894 when Captain Alfred Dreyfus, a Jewish officer, was convicted in a secret court-martial of selling secrets to a foreign power, and sentenced to life on Devil's Island. This was a frame-up to protect another officer – a non-Jewish aristocrat – involving the General Staff. A scandal erupted that shook French society. Dreyfus was finally released from prison in 1899 and fully vindicated in 1906.

2   The incident was caused by the brutality of a Prussian officer towards Alsatians in Zabern, Alsace, in November 1913, and resulted in a burst of indignation among the local, mainly French, population against the Prussian militarists.

political democracy implies complete freedom to agitate for secession and for a referendum on secession by the seceding nation. This demand, therefore, is not the equivalent of a demand for separation, fragmentation and the formation of small states. It implies only a consistent expression of struggle against all national oppression. The closer a democratic state system is to complete freedom to secede the less frequent and less ardent will the desire for separation be in practice, because big states afford indisputable advantages, both from the standpoint of economic progress and from that of the interests of the masses and, furthermore, these advantages increase with the growth of capitalism. Recognition of self-determination is not synonymous with recognition of federation as a principle. One may be a determined opponent of that principle and a champion of democratic centralism but still prefer federation to national inequality as the only way to full democratic centralism. It was from this standpoint that Marx, who was a centralist, preferred even the federation of Ireland and England to the forcible subordination of Ireland to the English.

The aim of socialism is not only to end the division of mankind into tiny states and the isolation of nations in any form, it is not only to bring the nations closer together but to integrate them. And it is precisely in order to achieve this aim that we must, on the one hand, explain to the masses the reactionary nature of Renner and Otto Bauer's idea of so-called 'cultural and national autonomy' and, on the other, demand the liberation of oppressed nations in a clearly and precisely formulated political programme that takes special account of the hypocrisy and cowardice of socialists in the oppressor nations, and not in general nebulous phrases, not in empty declamations and not by way of 'relegating' the question until socialism has been achieved. In the same way as mankind can arrive at the abolition of classes only through a transition period of the dictatorship of the oppressed class, it can arrive at the inevitable integration of nations only through a transition period of the complete emancipation of all oppressed nations, i.e. their freedom to secede.

The proletarian-revolutionary presentation of the question of the self-determination of nations

The petty bourgeoisie had put forward not only the demand for the self-determination of nations but *all* the points of our democratic minimum programme long *before*, as far back as the seventeenth and eighteenth centuries. They are still putting them *all* forward in a utopian manner because they fail to see the class struggle and its increased intensity under democracy, and because they believe in 'peaceful' capitalism. That is the exact nature of the utopia of a peaceful union of equal nations under imperialism which deceives the people and which is defended by Kautsky's followers. The programme of Social-Democracy, as a counter-balance to this petty-bourgeois, opportunist utopia, must postulate the division of nations into oppressor and oppressed as basic, significant and inevitable under imperialism.

The proletariat of the oppressor nations must not confine themselves to general, stereotyped phrases against annexation and in favour of the equality of nations in general, such as any pacifist bourgeois will repeat. The proletariat cannot remain silent on the question of the *frontiers* of a state founded on national oppression, a question so 'unpleasant' for the imperialist bourgeoisie. The proletariat must struggle against the enforced retention of oppressed nations within the bounds of the given state, which means that they must fight for the right to self-determination. The proletariat must demand freedom of political separation for the colonies and nations oppressed by 'their own' nation. Otherwise, the internationalism of the proletariat would be nothing but empty words; neither confidence nor class solidarity would be possible between the workers of the oppressed and the oppressor nations, the hypocrisy of the reformists and Kautskyites, who defend self-determination but remain silent about the nations oppressed by 'their own' nation and kept in 'their own' state by force, would remain unexposed.

On the other hand, the socialists of the oppressed nations must, in particular, defend and implement the full and unconditional unity, including organisational unity, of the workers of the oppressed nation and those of the oppressor nation. Without this it is impossible to defend the independent policy of the proletariat and their class solidarity with the proletariat of other countries in face of all manner of intrigues, treachery and trickery on the part of the bourgeoisie. The bourgeoisie of the oppressed nations persistently utilise the slogans of national liberation to deceive the workers; in their internal policy they use these slogans for reactionary agreements with the bourgeoisie of the dominant nation (for example, the Poles in Austria and Russia who come to terms with reactionaries for the oppression of the Jews and Ukrainians); in their foreign policy they strive to come to terms with one of the rival imperialist powers for the sake of implementing their predatory plans (the policy of the small Balkan states, etc.).

The fact that the struggle for national liberation against one imperialist power may, under certain conditions, be utilised by another 'great' power for its own, equally imperialist, aims, is just as unlikely to make the social-democrats refuse to recognise the right of nations to self-determination as the numerous cases of bourgeois utilisation of republican slogans for the purpose of political deception and financial plunder (as in the Romance countries, for example) are unlikely to make the social-democrats reject their republicanism.[3]

Marxism and Proudhonism on the national question

In contrast to the petty-bourgeois democrats, Marx regarded every democratic demand without exception not as an absolute, but as

---

3 It would, needless to say, be quite ridiculous to reject the right to self-determination on the grounds that it implies 'defence of the fatherland'. With equal right, i.e. with equal lack of seriousness, the social-chauvinists of 1914-16 refer to any of the demands of democracy (to its republicanism, for example) and to any formulation of the struggle against national oppression in order to justify 'defence of the fatherland'. Marxism deduces the defence of the fatherland in wars, for example, in the great French Revolution or the wars of Garibaldi, in Europe, and the renunciation of defence of the fatherland in the imperialist war of 1914-16, from an analysis of the concrete historical peculiarities of each individual war and never from any 'general principle', or any one point of a programme. – *Lenin*

an historical expression of the struggle of the masses of the people, led by the bourgeoisie, against feudalism. There is not one of these demands which could not serve and has not served, under certain circumstances, as an instrument in the hands of the bourgeoisie for deceiving the workers. To single out, in this respect, one of the demands of political democracy, specifically, the self-determination of nations, and to oppose it to the rest, is fundamentally wrong in theory. In practice, the proletariat can retain its independence only by subordinating its struggle for all democratic demands, not excluding the demand for a republic, to its revolutionary struggle for the overthrow of the bourgeoisie.

On the other hand, in contrast to the Proudhonists who 'denied' the national problem 'in the name of social revolution', Marx, mindful in the first place of the interests of the proletarian class struggle in the advanced countries, put the fundamental principle of internationalism and socialism in the foreground – namely, that no nation can be free if it oppresses other nations. It was from the standpoint of the interests of the German workers' revolutionary movement that Marx in 1848 demanded that victorious democracy in Germany should proclaim and grant freedom to the nations oppressed by the Germans. It was from the standpoint of the revolutionary struggle of the English workers that Marx, in 1869, demanded the separation of Ireland from England, and added: "… even if federation should follow upon separation." Only by putting forward this demand was Marx really educating the English workers in the spirit of internationalism. Only in this way could he counterpose the opportunists and bourgeois reformism – which even to this day, half a century later, has not carried out the Irish 'reform' – with a revolutionary solution of the given historical task. Only in this way could Marx maintain – in contradiction to the apologists of capital who shout that the freedom of small nations to secede is utopian and impracticable and that not only economic but also political concentration is progressive – that this concentration is progressive when it is *non*-imperialist, and that nations should not be brought together by force, but by a free union of the proletarians of all countries. Only in this way could Marx, in opposition to the merely verbal, and often hypocritical, recognition of the equality and self-determination of nations, advocate the revolutionary action of the masses in the settlement of national questions *as well.* The imperialist war of 1914-16, and the Augean stables of hypocrisy on the part of the opportunists and Kautskyites that it has exposed, have strikingly confirmed the correctness of Marx's policy, which should serve as a model for all advanced countries, for all of them are now oppressing other nations.[4]

Three types of countries in relation to self-determination of nations

In this respect, countries must be divided into three main types:

First, the advanced capitalist countries of Western Europe and the United States. In these countries progressive bourgeois national movements came to an end long ago. Every one of these 'great' nations oppresses other nations both in the colonies and at home. The tasks of the proletariat of these ruling nations are the same as those of the proletariat in England in the nineteenth century in relation to Ireland.[5]

---

4   Reference is often made – e.g. recently by the German chauvinist Lensch in *Die Glocke* Nos. 8 and 9 – to the fact that Marx's objection to the national movement of certain peoples, to that of the Czechs in 1848, for example, refutes the necessity of recognising the self-determination of nations from the Marxist standpoint. But this is incorrect, for in 1848 there were historical and political grounds for drawing a distinction between 'reactionary' and revolutionary-democratic nations. Marx was right to condemn the former and defend the latter. The right to self-determination is one of the demands of democracy which must naturally be subordinated to its general interests. In 1848 and the following years these general interests consisted primarily in combating tsarism. – *Lenin*
Paul Lensch was an SPD Reichstag member elected in 1912.
Die Glocke (*The Bell*) was a magazine published by Alexander Lvovich Parvus (born Israel Lazarevich Gelfand) who was a member of the SPD. Lensch was an editor. The magazine put forward a social-chauvinist position, arguing that socialists should support the German war effort in the First World War.

5   In some small states which have kept out of the war of 1914-16 – Holland and Switzerland, for example – the bourgeoisie makes extensive use of the 'self-determination of nations' slogan to justify participation in the imperialist war.

Secondly, Eastern Europe: Austria, the Balkans and particularly Russia. Here it was the twentieth century that particularly developed the bourgeois-democratic national movements and intensified the national struggle. The tasks of the proletariat in these countries, both in completing their bourgeois-democratic reforms, and rendering assistance to the socialist revolution in other countries, cannot be carried out without championing the right of nations to self-determination. The most difficult and most important task in this is to unite the class struggle of the workers of the oppressor nations with that of the workers of the oppressed nations.

Thirdly, the semi-colonial countries, such as China, Persia and Turkey, and all the colonies, which have a combined population of 1 billion. In these countries the bourgeois-democratic movements either have hardly begun, or have still a long way to go. Socialists must not only demand the unconditional and immediate liberation of the colonies without compensation – and this demand in its political expression signifies nothing else than the recognition of the right to self-determination; they must also render determined support to the more revolutionary elements in the bourgeois-democratic movements for national liberation in these countries and assist their uprising – or revolutionary war, in the event of one – *against* the imperialist powers that oppress them.

This is a motive inducing the social-democrats in such countries to repudiate self-determination. Wrong arguments are being used to defend a correct proletarian policy, the repudiation of 'defence of the fatherland' in an *imperialist* war. This results in a distortion of Marxism in theory, and in practice leads to a peculiar small-nation narrow-mindedness, neglect of the *hundreds of millions* of people in nations that are enslaved by the 'dominant' nations. Comrade Gorter, in his excellent pamphlet 'Imperialism, War and Social-Democracy' wrongly rejects the principle of self-determination of nations, but correctly *applies* it, when he demands the *immediate* granting of 'political and *national* independence' to the Dutch Indies and exposes the Dutch opportunists who refuse to put forward this demand and to fight for it. – *Lenin*

Herman Gorter was a Dutch poet and social-democrat. He fought revisionism and took an internationalist position during the First World War. He later joined the Comintern where he held an ultra-left position.

Social-chauvinism and self-determination of nations

The imperialist epoch and the war of 1914-16 has laid special emphasis on the struggle against chauvinism and nationalism in the leading countries. There are two main trends on the self-determination of nations among the social-chauvinists, that is, among the opportunists and Kautskyites, who hide the imperialist, reactionary nature of the war by applying to it the 'defence of the fatherland' concept.

On the one hand, we see quite undisguised servants of the bourgeoisie who defend annexation on the plea that imperialism and political concentration are progressive, and who deny what they call the utopian, illusory, petty-bourgeois, etc., right to self-determination. This includes Cunow, Parvus and the extreme opportunists in Germany,[6] some of the Fabians[7] and trade union leaders in England, and the opportunists in Russia: Semkovsky, Liebman, Yurkevich, etc.

On the other hand, we see the Kautskyites, among whom are Vandervelde, Renaudel, many pacifists in Britain and France, and others.[8] They favour unity with the former and in practice are completely identified with them; they defend the right to self-determination hypocritically and by words alone; they consider "excessive" ("*zu viel verlangt*"; Kautsky in *Die Neue Zeit*, 21 May 1915) the demand for free political separation, they do not defend the necessity for revolutionary tactics on the part of the socialists of the oppressor nations in particular but, on the contrary, obscure their revolutionary obligations, justify their opportunism, make easy for them their deception of the people, and avoid the very question of the *frontiers* of a state forcefully retaining underprivileged nations within its bounds, etc.

---

6   Heinrich Cunow was a member of the SPD and a social-chauvinist, who argued that backward nations should be denied the right to self-determination in the face of more advanced, 'progressive' imperialist nations.

7   The Fabian Society is a British reformist organisation founded in 1884.

8   Pierre Renaudel was a founder and leader of the Socialist Party of France, on its right wing.

Emile Vandervelde was a Belgian social-democrat and president of the Second International.

Both are equally opportunist, they prostitute Marxism, having lost all ability to understand the theoretical significance and practical urgency of the tactics which Marx explained with Ireland as an example.

As for annexations, the question has become particularly urgent in connection with the war. But what is annexation? It is quite easy to see that a protest against annexations either boils down to recognition of the self-determination of nations or is based on the pacifist phrase that defends the *status quo* and is hostile to *any*, even revolutionary, violence. Such a phrase is fundamentally false and incompatible with Marxism.

The concrete tasks of the proletariat in the immediate future

The socialist revolution may begin in the very near future. In this case the proletariat will be faced with the immediate task of winning power, expropriating the banks and effecting other dictatorial measures. The bourgeoisie – and especially the intellectuals of the Fabian and Kautskyite type – will, at such a moment, strive to split and check the revolution by foisting limited, democratic aims on it. Whereas *any* purely democratic demands are in a certain sense liable to act as a hindrance to the revolution, provided the proletarian attack on the pillars of bourgeois power has begun, the necessity to proclaim and grant liberty to *all* oppressed peoples (i.e. their right to self-determination) will be as urgent in the socialist revolution as it was for the victory of the bourgeois-democratic revolution in, say, Germany in 1848, or Russia in 1905.

It is possible, however, that five, ten or more years will elapse before the socialist revolution begins. This will be the time for the revolutionary education of the masses in a spirit that will make it impossible for socialist-chauvinists and opportunists to belong to the working-class party and gain a victory, as was the case in 1914-16. The socialists must explain to the masses that British socialists who do not demand freedom to separate for the colonies and Ireland, German socialists who do not demand freedom to separate for the colonies, the Alsatians, Danes and Poles, and who do not extend their revolutionary propaganda and revolutionary mass activity directly to the sphere of struggle against national oppression, or who do not make use of such incidents as that at Zabern for the broadest illegal propaganda among the proletariat of the oppressor nation, for street demonstrations and revolutionary mass action – Russian socialists who do not demand freedom to separate for Finland, Poland, the Ukraine, etc., etc. – that such socialists act as chauvinists and lackeys of bloodstained and filthy imperialist monarchies and the imperialist bourgeoisie.

The attitude of Russian and Polish Social-Democracy and of the Second International to self-determination

The differences between the revolutionary social-democrats of Russia and the Polish social-democrats on the question of self-determination came out into the open as early as 1903, at the congress which adopted the Programme of the RSDLP, and which, despite the protest by the Polish social-democrat delegation, inserted Clause 9, recognising the right of nations to self-determination. Since then the Polish social-democrats have on no occasion repeated, in the name of their party, the proposal to remove Clause 9 from our party's programme, or to replace it by some other formula.

In Russia, where the oppressed nations account for no less than 57 per cent of the population, or over 100 million, where they occupy mostly the border regions, where some of them are more highly cultured than the Great Russians, where the political system is especially barbarous and medieval, where the bourgeois-democratic revolution has not been consummated – there, in Russia, recognition of the right of nations oppressed by tsarism to free secession from Russia is absolutely obligatory for social-democrats, for the furtherance of their democratic and socialist aims. Our party, re-established in January 1912, adopted a resolution in 1913 reaffirming the right to self-determination and explaining it in precisely the above concrete sense. The rampage of Great-Russian chauvinism in 1914-16 both among the bourgeoisie and among the opportunist socialists (Rubanovich, Plekhanov, *Nashe Dyelo*, etc.)[9] has given us even more reason to insist on this demand and to regard those who deny it as actual supporters of Great-Russian chauvinism and tsarism. Our party declares that it most emphatically declines to accept any responsibility for such actions against the right to self-determination.

The latest formulation of the position of the Polish social-democrats on the national question (the declaration of the Polish social-democrats at the Zimmerwald Conference) contains the following ideas:

The declaration condemns the German and other governments that regard the 'Polish regions' as a pawn in the forthcoming compensation game, "*depriving the Polish people of the opportunity of deciding their own fate themselves*". "Polish social-democrats resolutely and solemnly protest against the *carving up and parcelling out of a whole country*" … They flay the socialists who left it to the Hohenzollerns[10] "*to liberate the oppressed peoples*". They express the conviction that only participation in the approaching struggle of the international revolutionary proletariat, the struggle for socialism, "*will break the fetters of national oppression* and destroy *all forms of foreign* rule, will ensure for *the Polish people* the possibility of free all-round development as an *equal* member of a concord of nations". The declaration recognises that "*for the Poles*" the war is "*doubly fratricidal*". (*Bulletin of the International Socialist Committee*,[11] No. 2, 27 September 1915, p. 15. Russian translation in the symposium *The International and the War*, p. 97.)

---

9   Ilya Rubanovich was a Narodnik.
    Nashe Dyelo was a journal of the Mensheviks, which succeeded *Nasha Zarya*.

10 The House of Hohenzollern was the royal dynasty which ruled Germany. It was overthrown in the November Revolution of 1918 where Kaiser Wilhelm II was forced to abdicate.

11 The *Bulletin of the International Socialist Committee in Berne* was published by the executive of the Zimmerwald organisation, an organisation of socialists who took a revolutionary, anti-imperialist and anti-war stance after the majority of the Second International lent its support to their own nation's bourgeoisie in the First World War. It was, Lenin said, the first step in the development of the internationalist movement against the war.

These propositions do not differ in substance from recognition of the right of nations to self-determination, although their political formulations are even vaguer and more indeterminate than those of most programmes and resolutions of the Second International. Any attempt to express these ideas as precise political formulations and to define their applicability to the capitalist system or only to the socialist system will show even more clearly the mistake the Polish social-democrats make in denying the self-determination of nations.

The decision of the London International Socialist Congress of 1896, which recognised the self-determination of nations, should be supplemented on the basis of the above theses by specifying:

1. The particular urgency of this demand under imperialism,

2. The political conventionalism and class content of all the demands of political democracy, the one under discussion included,

3. The necessity to distinguish the concrete tasks of the social-democrats of the oppressor nations from those of the social-democrats of the oppressed nations,

4. The inconsistent, purely verbal recognition of self-determination by the opportunists and the Kautskyites, which is, therefore, hypocritical in its political significance,

5. The actual identity of the chauvinists and those social-democrats, especially those of the Great Powers (Great Russians, Anglo-Americans, Germans, French, Italians, Japanese, etc.), who do not uphold the freedom to secede for colonies and nations oppressed by 'their own' nations,

6. The necessity to subordinate the struggle for the demand under discussion and for all the basic demands of political democracy directly to the revolutionary mass struggle for the overthrow of the bourgeois governments and for the achievement of socialism.

The introduction into the International of the viewpoint of certain small nations, especially that of the Polish social-democrats, who have been led by their struggle against the Polish bourgeoisie, which deceives the people with its nationalist slogans, to the incorrect denial of self-determination, would be a theoretical mistake, a substitution of Proudhonism for Marxism implying in practice involuntary support for the most dangerous chauvinism and opportunism of the Great-Power nations.

Editorial Board of *Sotsial-Demokrat*,[12]
Central Organ of the RSDLP

* * *

Postscript

In *Die Neue Zeit* for 3 March 1916, which has just appeared, Kautsky openly holds out the hand of Christian reconciliation to Austerlitz,[13] a representative of the foulest German chauvinism, rejecting freedom of separation for the oppressed nations of Habsburg Austria but recognising it for *Russian* Poland, as a menial service to Hindenburg and Wilhelm II.[14] One could not have wished for a better self-exposure of Kautskyism!

---

12 *Sotsial-Demokrat* (*The Social-Democrat*) was an illegal paper published from 1908 to January 1917. The paper was run by Lenin and was the central organ of the RSDLP as a whole.

13 Friedrich Austerlitz was an Austrian social-democratic journalist and politician.

14 Paul von Hindenburg was a prominent General who spent nearly fifty years in the Imperial German Army. He served in the Franco-Prussian war, was present at the crushing of the Paris Commune, and came out of retirement to lead the army during the First World War, becoming the Chief of the General Staff in 1916. He would later go on to be the last President of Germany, until his death and Hitler's rise to power in 1933.

Kaiser Wilhelm II was the last German Emperor and King of Prussia from 1888 until his abdication in 1918 after the November Revolution.

The Nascent Trend of Imperialist Economism

Written August-September 1916

Editor's note: This article was directed against the Baugy Group, named after the town in Switzerland where they were based, which began to take shape in the spring of 1915, when preparations were being made for publication of the magazine *Kommunist* by Nikolai Bukharin, Georgy Pyatakov and Yevgenia Bosch.

In their theses 'On the Self-Determination Slogan', which they sent to *Sotsial-Demokrat*, Bukharin, Pyatakov and Bosch opposed Lenin's theory of socialist revolution, rejected the struggle for democracy in the imperialist era and insisted on the party withdrawing its demand for national self-determination.

The group did not confine itself to theoretical differences and openly attacked the party's policy and slogans. It sought to use *Kommunist* in furtherance of its factional aims and tried to dictate terms to the editors of *Sotsial-Demokrat*. Pyatakov and Bosh insisted on the Central Committee Bureau Abroad recognising them as a separate group not accountable to it and authorised to maintain independent connections with Central Committee members in Russia and publish leaflets and other literature. Though this demand was turned down, the group attempted to establish contact with the Central Committee Bureau in Russia.

Lenin was sharply opposed to the Baugy Group's theses, saying:

> ... we can take no responsibility for them – either direct or indirect – even for harbouring them in the party, let alone granting them equality.

In letters to Bukharin, Pyatakov, Zinoviev and Shlyapnikov, Lenin trenchantly criticised the group's views and anti-party, factional actions and condemned the conciliatory attitude of Zinoviev and Shlyapnikov. On his proposal, joint publication of *Kommunist* by the *Sotsial-Demokrat* editors and the group was discontinued.

The 'Nascent Trend of Imperialist Economism' was written when the *Sotsial-Demokrat* editors had received Bukharin's comments on the theses 'The Socialist Revolution and the Right of Nations to Self-Determination'. The article was not published at the time.

* * *

The old Economism of 1894-1902 reasoned thus: the Narodniks have been refuted; capitalism has triumphed in Russia. Consequently, there can be no question of political revolution. The practical conclusion: either "economic struggle be left to the workers and political struggle to the liberals" – that is a leap to the right – or, instead of political revolution, a general strike for socialist revolution. That leap to the left was advocated in a pamphlet, now forgotten, of a Russian Economist of the late nineties.

Now a new Economism is being born. Its reasoning is similarly based on the two leaps: 'Right': we are against the 'right to self-determination' (i.e. against the liberation of oppressed peoples, the struggle against annexations – that has not yet been fully thought out or clearly stated). 'Left': we are opposed to a minimum programme (i.e. opposed to struggle for reforms and democracy) as 'contradictory' to socialist revolution.

It is more than a year now since this nascent trend was revealed to several comrades at the Berne Conference in the spring of 1915. At that time, happily, only one comrade, who met with *universal* disapproval, insisted on these ideas of imperialist Economism right up to the end of the Conference and formulated them in writing in special 'theses'.[1] *No one* associated himself with these theses.

Subsequently two others associated themselves with this comrade's theses against self-determination (unaware that the question was inextricably linked with the general line of the aforementioned 'theses').[2] But the appearance of the 'Dutch programme' in February 1916, published in No. 3 of the *Bulletin of the International Socialist Committee*, *immediately* brought out this 'misunderstanding' and *again* compelled the author of the original theses to *restate* his imperialist Economism, this time, too, as a whole, and not merely in application to one allegedly 'partial' issue.

It is absolutely necessary again and again to *warn* the comrades concerned that they have *landed themselves* in a quagmire, that their 'ideas' have *nothing in common either with Marxism or revolutionary Social-Democracy*. We can no longer leave the matter 'in the dark': that would only encourage ideological confusion and direct it into the *worst possible channel* of equivocation, 'private' conflicts, incessant 'friction', etc. Our duty, on the contrary, is to insist, in the most emphatic and categorical manner, on the *obligation* thoroughly to think out and analyse questions raised for discussion.

In its theses on self-determination[3] (which appeared in German as a reprint from No. 2 of *Vorbote*),[4] the *Sotsial-Demokrat* editorial board purposely brought the matter into the press in an *impersonal*, but

---

1   Lenin is referring to Nikolai Bukharin, who vehemently defended his resolutions at the Berne Conference of Bolshevik Groups Abroad in 1915. Bukharin's errors are discussed in the third section of this volume, see pp. 273-329.

     Georgy Pyatakov was a Ukrainian revolutionary and member of the Bolsheviks. He supported Lenin in opposing the First World War but joined Bukharin in opposing Lenin's defence of the right of nations to self-determination. He became chairman of the provisional Ukrainian workers and peasants' government formed at Kursk in November 1918, but was replaced by Christian Rakovsky, a Bolshevik, in the Kharkov-based Ukrainian Soviet government.

2   Pyatakov Trend Bosch signed the theses prepared by Bukharin.

3   See 'The Socialist Revolution and the Right of Nations to Self-Determination', in this volume, p. 109.

4   *Der Vorbote* (*The Herald*) was a German-language paper published in the Netherlands by Anton Pannekoek, a Dutch socialist and member of the German SPD.

most detailed, form, emphasising in particular the *link* between self-determination and the *general* question of the struggle for reforms, for democracy, the impermissibility of ignoring the *political* aspect, etc. In his comments on the editorial board's theses, the author of the original theses (imperialist Economism) comes out in *solidarity with the Dutch programme*, thereby clearly demonstrating that self-determination is by no means a 'partial' question, as exponents of the nascent trend maintain, but a general and basic one.

The Dutch programme was laid before representatives of the Zimmerwald Left on 5-8 February 1916, at the Berne meeting of the International Socialist Committee. Not a single member of the Zimmerwald Left, *not even Radek*,[5] spoke in favour of the programme, for it combines, indiscriminately, such points as "expropriation of the banks" and "repeal of customs tariffs", "abolition of the first Senate chamber", etc. The Zimmerwald Left unanimously, with practically no comment, in fact merely with a shrug of the shoulders, dismissed the Dutch programme as patently and wholly unsuitable.

However, the author of the original theses, written in the spring of 1915, was so fond of the programme that he declared:

> Substantially, that is all I said, too (in the spring of 1915), the Dutch have *thought things out*: *with them the economic aspect is expropriation of the banks and large-scale production* (enterprises), *the political aspect is a republic and so on. Absolutely correct!*

The fact, however, is that the Dutch did not "think things out", but produced an *un-thought-out* programme. It is the sad fate of Russia that some among us grasp at precisely what is not thought out in the newest novelty...

The author of the 1915 theses believes that the *Sotsial-Demokrat* editors lapsed into a contradiction when they 'themselves' urged "expropriation of the banks", and even added the word "immediately" (plus "dictatorial measures") in Section 8 ('Concrete Measures').

---

5 Karl Radek was a social-democrat and member of the SDKPiL and SPD. He helped establish the KPD and played a leading role in the Communist International.

"And how I was reproached for this very thing in Berne!", the author of the 1915 theses exclaims indignantly, recalling the Berne debates in the spring of 1915.

He forgets or fails to see this 'minor' point: in Section 8 the *Sotsial-Demokrat* editors clearly distinguish *two* eventualities:

1. The socialist revolution has *begun*. In that event, they say: "immediate expropriation of the banks", etc.

2. The socialist revolution has *not* begun, and in that event we shall have to postpone talking about these good things.

Since the socialist revolution, in the above-mentioned sense, has obviously not *yet* begun, the Dutch programme is incongruous. And the author of the theses adds his bit of *'profundity'* by reverting (he always seems to slip on the same spot!) to his old mistake of turning political demands (like "abolition of the first chamber"?) into a *"political formula for social revolution"*.

Having marked time for a whole year, the author returned to his old mistake. That is the 'crux' of his misadventures: he cannot solve the problem of *how to link the advent of imperialism with the struggle for reforms and democracy* – just as the Economism of blessed memory could not link the advent of capitalism with the struggle for democracy.

Hence: complete confusion concerning the 'unachievability' of democratic demands under imperialism.

Hence: ignoring of the political struggle now, at present, immediately, and at all times, which is impermissible for a Marxist (and permissible only for a *Rabochaya Mysl*[6] Economist).

Hence: the knack of persistently 'sliding' from *recognition* of imperialism to *apology* for imperialism (just as the Economists of blessed memory slid from recognition of capitalism to apology for capitalism).

And so on, and so forth.

---

6 *Rabochaya Mysl* (*Workers' Thought*) was a newspaper published by a group of Economists in Russia from October 1897 to December 1902.

A detailed examination of the errors the author of the 1915 theses commits in his comments on the *Sotsial-Demokrat* self-determination theses is impossible, for *every line is wrong!* After all, you cannot write pamphlets or books in reply to 'comments' if the initiators of imperialist Economism spend a whole year marking time and stubbornly refuse to concern themselves with what ought to be their direct party duty if they want to take a serious attitude to political, issues, namely: a considered and articulate statement of what they designate as "our differences".

I am therefore obliged to confine myself to a brief review of how the author applies his basic error and how he 'supplements' it.

He believes that I contradict myself: in 1914 (in *Prosveshcheniye*) I wrote that it was absurd to look for self-determination "in the programmes of West-European socialists",[7] but in 1916 I proclaim self-determination to be especially urgent.

It did not occur (!!!) to the author that these "programmes" were drawn up in 1875, 1880, 1891!

Now let us take his objections (to the *Sotsial-Demokrat* self-determination theses) point by point.

1. The same Economist refusal to see and pose *political* questions. *Since* socialism creates the economic basis for the abolition of national oppression in the political sphere, *therefore* our author refuses to formulate our *political* tasks in this sphere! That's ridiculous!

    Since the victorious proletariat does not negate wars against the bourgeoisie of other countries, *therefore* the author refuses to formulate our political tasks in relation to national oppression!! These are all examples of downright violation of Marxism and logic, or, if you like, manifestations of the *logic* of the fundamental errors of imperialist Economism.

2. The opponents of self-determination are hopelessly confused in their references to its being "unachievable".

---

7   See Lenin, 'The Right of Nations to Self-Determination', in this volume, p. 45.

The *Sotsial-Demokrat* editors explain to them *two* possible interpretations of unachievability and their error in *both* cases.

Yet the author of the 1915 theses, without even trying to give *his* interpretation of 'unachievability', i.e. *accepting* our explanation that two different things are confused here, *persists in that confusion!!!*

He ties crises to "imperialist" "policy": our expert on political economy *has forgotten* that there were crises *before* imperialism!

To maintain that self-determination is unachievable economically is to confuse the issue, the editors explain. The author does *not* reply, does *not* state that he considers self-determination unachievable *economically*; he abandons his dubious position and jumps over to politics (unachievable "all the same") though he has been told with the utmost clarity that *politically* a republic is just as "unachievable" under imperialism as self-determination.

Cornered, the author 'jumps' again: he accepts a republic and the whole minimum programme only as a "political formula for social revolution"!!!

He refuses to defend the "economic" unachievability of self-determination and jumps to politics, maintaining that political unachievability applies to the minimum programme as a whole. Here again there is not a grain of Marxism, not a grain of logic, save the *logic of imperialist Economism.*

The author wants *imperceptibly* (without stopping to think, without producing anything articulate, without making any effort to work out his programme) to jettison the Social-Democratic Party minimum programme! No wonder he has been marking time for a whole year!!

The question of combating *Kautskyism* is again not a partial, but a *general* and *basic* question of modern times: the author does *not understand* this struggle. Just as the Economists turned the struggle against the Narodniks into an apology for capitalism, so the author turns the struggle against Kautskyism into an apology for imperialism (that applies also to Section 3).

The mistake of the Kautskyites lies in the fact that they present in a reformist manner such demands, and at such a time, that can be presented only in a revolutionary manner (but the author lapses into the position that their mistake is to advance these demands altogether, just as the Economists 'understood' the struggle against Narodnism to mean that the slogan "Down with the autocracy" was Narodnism).

The mistake of Kautskyism lies in projecting *correct* democratic demands into the past, to peaceful capitalism, and not into the future, to the social revolution (the author, however, falls into the position of regarding these demands as incorrect).

3. See above. The author bypasses *also* the question of "federation". The same old fundamental mistake of the same old Economism: inability to pose *political* questions.[8]

4. "From self-determination follows defence of the fatherland", the author obstinately repeats. His mistake here is to make negation of defence of the fatherland a *shibboleth*, deduce it *not* from the concrete historical features of a *given* war, but apply it "in general". That is not Marxism.

The author has been told long ago – try to think up a formula of struggle against national oppression or inequality which (formula) does *not* justify "defence of the fatherland". You cannot devise such a formula, and the author has not challenged that.

Does that mean that we reject the fight against national oppression if it *could* be interpreted to imply defence of the fatherland?

No, for we are opposed not to "defence of the fatherland" "in general" (see our party resolutions),[9] but to using this fraudulent slogan to *embellish* the present *imperialist* war.

---

8 "We are not afraid of disintegration", the author writes, "we do not defend national boundaries". Now, just try to give that a precise political formulation!! You simply cannot do it and that's where the trouble lies; you are hampered by Economist blindness on questions of political democracy. – *Lenin*

9 See Lenin, 'Conference of RSDLP Groups Abroad', *LCW*, Vol. 20, p. 159.

The author *wants* to pose the question of "defence of the fatherland" in a *basically incorrect* and *unhistorical* way (but he cannot; he has been trying in vain for a whole year…).

His reference to "dualism" shows that he does *not understand* the difference between monism and dualism.

If I "unite" a shoe brush and a mammal, will that be "monism"?

$$(c) \rightarrow a \leftarrow (b)$$

If I say that to reach goal *a* we must travel to the left from point (b) and to the right from point (c), will that be "dualism"?

Is the position of the proletariat with regard to national oppression the same in oppressing and oppressed nations? No, it is not the same, not the same *economically*, *politically*, *ideologically*, *spiritually*, etc.

Meaning?

Meaning that some will approach in *one* way, others in *another* way, *the same* goal (the merger of nations) from *different* starting-points. Denial of that is the "monism" that unites a shoe brush and a mammal.

"It is *not* proper to say this [i.e. to *urge* self-determination] to the proletarians of an oppressed nation" – that is how the author 'interprets' the editors' theses.

That's amusing!! There is *nothing of the kind* in the theses. The author has either not read them to the end or has not given them any thought at all.

5. See above on Kautskyism.

6. The author is told there are three *types* of countries in the world. He 'objects' and snatches out 'cases'. That is casuistry, not politics. You want a concrete 'case': "How about Belgium"?

See the Lenin and Zinoviev pamphlet: it says that we would be *for* the defence of Belgium (even *by war*) if this concrete war were different.[10]

---

10 See Lenin, 'Socialism and War', *LCW*, Vol. 21, pp. 305-6. Reproduced in *Lenin Selected Writings: On Imperialist War*, pp. 69-70.

You do not agree with that?

Then say so!!

You have *not properly thought out* the question of *why* social-democrats are against "defence of the fatherland".

We are not against it for the reasons you believe, because your presentation of the question (vain efforts, not really a presentation) goes against history. That is my reply to the author.

To describe as "sophistry" the fact that while *justifying wars for the elimination of national oppression*, we do not justify the present imperialist war, which on *both* sides is being waged to *increase* national oppression – is to use 'strong' words without giving the matter *the least bit of thought*.

The author *wants* to pose the question of "defence of the fatherland" from a more 'Left' position, but the result (for a whole year now) is utter confusion!

7. The author *criticises*: "The question of 'peace terms' is not touched upon at all."

Strange criticism: failure to deal with a question we did not even raise!!

But what is 'touched upon' and discussed is the question of *annexations*, on which the imperialist Economists are utterly confused, this time *together* with the Dutch and Radek.

Either you reject the immediate slogan *against old and new annexations* – (no less "unachievable" under imperialism than self-determination, in Europe as well as in the colonies) – and in that case you pass from concealed to open apology for imperialism.

Or you accept the slogan (as Radek has done in the press) – and in that case you accept self-determination of nations under a different name!!

8. The author proclaims "Bolshevism on a West-European scale" ("not your position", he adds).

I attach no importance to this desire to cling to the word 'Bolshevism', for I know such 'old Bolsheviks' from whom God save us. I can only say that the author's proclamation of "Bolshevism on a West-European scale" is, I am deeply convinced, neither Bolshevism nor Marxism, but a minor variant of the same old Economism.

In my view it is highly intolerable, flippant and non-party to proclaim for a whole year the *new Bolshevism* and leave things at that. Is it not time to *think* matters out and give the comrades an articulate and integrated *exposé* of "Bolshevism on a West-European scale"?

The author has not proved and will not prove the difference between colonies and oppressed nations in Europe (as applied to the question under discussion).

* * *

The Dutch and the Polish Social Democrats' rejection of self-determination is *not only*, and even not so much, the result of confusion, for Gorter factually accepts it, and so does the Zimmerwald statement of the Poles, but rather the result of the *special* position of their *nations* (small nations with *centuries-old* traditions and pretentions to *Great-Power status*).

It is extremely thoughtless and naive to take over and mechanically and uncritically repeat what in others has developed over decades of struggle against the nationalist bourgeoisie and its deception of the people. Here we have a case of people taking over *precisely* what should not be taken over.

The Discussion on
Self-Determination Summed Up

Written in July 1916

Issue No. 2 of the *Herald* (*Vorbote*, No. 2, April 1916), the Marxist journal of the Zimmerwald Left, published theses for and against the self-determination of nations, signed by the Editorial Board of our Central Organ, *Sotsial-Demokrat*, and by the Editorial Board of the organ of the Polish social-democratic opposition, *Gazeta Robotnicza*.[1] Above the reader will find a reprint of the former and a translation of the latter theses.[2] This is practically the first time that the question has been presented so extensively in the international field: it was raised only in respect of Poland in the discussion carried on in the German Marxist journal *Neue Zeit*[3] twenty years ago, 1895-96, before the London International Socialist Congress of 1896, by Rosa Luxemburg, Karl Kautsky and the Polish 'independents' (champions of the independence of Poland, the Polish Socialist

---

1 *Gazeta Robotnicza* (*Workers' Gazette*) was the illegal paper of the Warsaw committee of the Polish Social Democrats (SDKPiL).

2 See Lenin, 'The Socialist Revolution and the Right of Nations to Self-Determination', in this volume, p. 109.

3 *Neue Zeit* (*New Times*) was the theoretical journal of the German Social-Democratic Party, published in Stuttgart from 1883 to 1923; edited until October 1917 by Karl Kautsky.

Party), who represented three different views. Since then, as far as we know, the question of self-determination has been discussed at all systematically only by the Dutch and the Poles. Let us hope that the *Herald* will succeed in promoting the discussion of this question, so urgent today, among the British, Americans, French, Germans and Italians. Official socialism, represented both by direct supporters of 'their own' governments, the Plekhanovs, Davids[4] and co., and the undercover defenders of opportunism, the Kautskyites (among them Axelrod, Martov, Chkheidze and others),[5] has told so many lies on this question that for a long time there will inevitably be efforts, on the one hand, to maintain silence and evade the issue, and, on the other, workers' demands for 'direct answers' to these 'accursed questions'. We shall try to keep our readers informed of the struggle between the trends among socialists abroad.

This question is of specific importance to us Russian social-democrats; the present discussion is a continuation of the one that took place in 1903 and 1913; during the war this question has been the cause of some wavering in the thinking of party members: it has been made more acute by the trickery of such prominent leaders of the Gvozdev[6] or chauvinist workers' party as Martov and Chkheidze, in their efforts to evade the substance of the problem. It is essential, therefore, to sum up at least the initial results of the discussion that has been started in the international field.

It will be seen from the theses that our Polish comrades provide us with a direct answer to some of our arguments, for example, on Marxism and Proudhonism. In most cases, however, they do not answer us directly but indirectly, by opposing *their* assertions to ours. Let us examine both their direct and indirect answers.

Socialism and the self-determination of nations

We have affirmed that it would be a betrayal of socialism to refuse to implement the self-determination of nations under socialism. We

---

4   Eduard David was a Reichstag deputy for the SPD and on its right wing.
5   Pavel Axelrod, Yuri Martov and Nikolai Chkheidze were leading Mensheviks.
6   Kuzma Gvozdev was a Menshevik.

are told in reply that 'the right of self-determination is not applicable to a socialist society'. The difference is a radical one. Where does it stem from?

> We know [runs our opponents' reasoning] that socialism will abolish every kind of national oppression since it abolishes the class interests that lead to it…

What has this argument about the *economic* prerequisites for the abolition of national oppression, which are very well known and undisputed, to do with a discussion of *one* of the forms of *political* oppression, namely, the forcible retention of one nation within the state frontiers of another? This is nothing but an attempt to evade political questions! And subsequent arguments further convince us that our judgement is right:

> We have no reason to believe that in a socialist society, the nation will exist as an economic and political unit. It will in all probability assume the character of a cultural and linguistic unit only, because the territorial division of a socialist cultural zone, if practised at all, can be made only according to the needs of production and, furthermore, the question of such a division will naturally not be decided by individual nations alone and in possession of full sovereignty [as is required by 'the right to self-determination'], but will be *determined jointly* by all the citizens concerned…

Our Polish comrades like this last argument, on *joint* determination instead of self-determination, so much that they repeat it *three times* in their theses! Frequency of repetition, however, does not turn this Octobrist and reactionary argument into a social-democratic argument. All reactionaries and bourgeois grant to nations forcibly retained within the frontiers of a given state the right to "determine jointly" their fate in a common parliament. Wilhelm II also gives the Belgians the right to "determine jointly" the fate of the German Empire in a common German parliament.

Our opponents try to evade precisely the point at issue – the only one that is up for discussion – the right to secede. This would be funny if it were not so tragic!

Our very first thesis said that the liberation of oppressed nations implies a dual transformation in the political sphere: (1) the full equality of nations. This is not disputed and applies only to what takes place within the state; (2) freedom of political separation. This refers to the demarcation of state frontiers. This *only* is disputed. But it is precisely this that our opponents remain silent about. They do not want to think either about state frontiers or even about the state as such. This is a sort of 'imperialist Economism' like the old Economism of 1894-1902, which argued in this way: capitalism is victorious, *therefore* political questions are a waste of time. Imperialism is victorious, *therefore* political questions are a waste of time! Such an apolitical theory is extremely harmful to Marxism.

In his *Critique of the Gotha Programme*, Marx wrote:

> Between capitalist and communist society lies the period of the revolutionary transformation of the one into the other. There corresponds to this also a political transition period in which the state can be nothing but the revolutionary dictatorship of the proletariat.[7]

Up to now this truth has been indisputable for socialists and it includes the recognition of the fact that the *state* will exist until victorious socialism develops into full communism. Engels' dictum about the *withering away* of the state is well known. We deliberately stressed, in the first thesis, that democracy is a form of state that will also wither away when the state withers away. And until our opponents replace Marxism by some sort of 'non-state' viewpoint their arguments will constitute one big mistake.

Instead of speaking about the state (which *means*, about the demarcation of its *frontiers!*), they speak of a "socialist cultural zone", i.e. they deliberately choose an expression that is indefinite in the sense that all state questions are obliterated! Thus we get a ridiculous tautology: if there is no state there can, of course, be no question of frontiers. In that case the whole democratic-political programme is unnecessary. Nor will there be any republic, when the state 'withers away'.

7	See *MECW*, Vol. 3, p.13.

The German chauvinist Lensch, in the articles we mentioned in Thesis 5, quoted an interesting passage from Engels' article 'The Po and the Rhine'. Amongst other things, Engels says in this article that in the course of historical development, which swallowed up a number of small and non-viable nations, the "frontiers of great and viable European nations" were being increasingly determined by the "language and sympathies" of the population. Engels calls these frontiers "natural". Such was the case in the period of progressive capitalism in Europe, roughly from 1848 to 1871. Today, these democratically determined frontiers are more and more often being *broken down* by reactionary, imperialist capitalism. There is every sign that imperialism will leave its successor, socialism, a heritage of *less* democratic frontiers, a number of annexations in Europe and all other parts of the world. Is it to be supposed that victorious socialism, restoring and implementing full democracy all along the line, will refrain from *democratically* demarcating state frontiers and ignore the 'sympathies' of the population? Those questions need only be stated to make it quite clear that our Polish colleagues are sliding down from Marxism towards imperialist Economism.

The old Economists, who made a caricature of Marxism, told the workers that 'only the economic' was of importance to Marxists. The new Economists seem to think either that the democratic state of victorious socialism will exist without frontiers (like a 'complex of sensations' without matter) or that frontiers will be delineated 'only' in accordance with the needs of production. In actual fact its frontiers will be delineated democratically, i.e. in accordance with the will and 'sympathies' of the population. Capitalism rides roughshod over these sympathies, adding more obstacles to the rapprochement of nations. Socialism, by organising production *without* class oppression, by ensuring the well-being of *all* members of the state, gives *full play* to the 'sympathies' of the population, thereby promoting and greatly accelerating the drawing together and fusion of the nations.

To give the reader a rest from the heavy and clumsy Economism let us quote the reasoning of a socialist writer who is outside our dispute. That writer is Otto Bauer, who also has his own 'pet little point' – 'cultural and national autonomy' – but who argues quite correctly on a large number of most important questions. For example, in Chapter 29 of his book *The National Question and Social-Democracy*, he was doubly right in noting the use of national ideology to cover up *imperialist* policies. In Chapter 30, 'Socialism and the Principle of Nationality', he says:

> The socialist community will never be able to include whole nations within its make-up by the use of force. Imagine the masses of the people, enjoying the blessings of national culture, taking a full and active part in legislation and government, and, finally, supplied with arms – would it be possible to subordinate such a nation to the rule of an alien social organism by force? All state power rests on the force of arms. The present-day people's army, thanks to an ingenious mechanism, still constitutes a tool in the hands of a definite person, family or class exactly like the knightly and mercenary armies of the past. The army of the democratic community of a socialist society is nothing but the people armed, since it consists of highly cultured persons, working without compulsion in socialised workshops and taking full part in all spheres of political life. In such conditions any possibility of alien rule disappears.

This is true. It is *impossible* to abolish national (or any other political) oppression under capitalism, since this *requires* the abolition of classes, i.e. the introduction of socialism. But while being based on economics, socialism cannot be reduced to economics alone. A foundation – socialist production – is essential for the abolition of national oppression, but this foundation must *also* carry a democratically organised state, a democratic army, etc. By transforming capitalism into socialism the proletariat creates the *possibility* of abolishing national oppression; the possibility becomes *reality* 'only' – 'only'! – with the establishment of full democracy in all spheres, including the delineation of state frontiers in accordance with the 'sympathies' of the population, including complete freedom to secede. And this, in turn, will serve as a basis for developing the *practical* elimination of even the slightest national friction and the least national mistrust, for an accelerated drawing together and fusion of nations that will be completed when the state *withers away*. This is the Marxist theory, the theory from which our Polish colleagues have mistakenly departed.

Is democracy 'practicable' under imperialism?

The old polemic conducted by Polish social-democrats against the self-determination of nations is based entirely on the argument that it is 'impracticable' under capitalism. As long ago as 1903 we, the *Iskra* supporters, laughed at this argument in the Programme Commission of the Second Congress of the RSDLP and said that it was a repetition of the distortion of Marxism preached by the (late lamented) Economists. In our theses we dealt with this error in particular detail and it is precisely on this point, which contains the theoretical kernel of the whole dispute, that the Polish comrades did not wish to (or could not?) answer *any* of our arguments.

To prove the economic impossibility of self-determination would require an economic analysis such as that used to prove the impracticability of prohibiting machines or introducing labour money, etc. No one has even attempted to make such an analysis. No one will maintain that it has been possible to introduce 'labour money' under capitalism 'by way of exception' in even one country, in the way it was possible for one small country to realise this impracticable self-determination, even without war or revolution, 'by way of exception', in the era of the most rabid imperialism (Norway, 1905).

In general, political democracy is merely one of the possible *forms* of superstructure *above* capitalism (although it is theoretically the normal one for 'pure' capitalism). The facts show that both capitalism and imperialism develop within the framework of *any* political form and subordinate them *all*. It is, therefore, a basic theoretical error to speak of the 'impracticability' of *one* of the forms and of *one* of the demands of democracy.

The absence of an answer to these arguments from our Polish colleagues compels us to consider the discussion closed on this point. To make it graphic, so to say, we made the very concrete assertion that it would be 'ridiculous' to deny the 'practicability' of the restoration of Poland today, making it dependent on the strategic and other aspects of the present war. No reply was forthcoming!

The Polish comrades simply *repeated* an obviously incorrect assertion (Section 2, 1), saying that:

> … in questions of the annexation of foreign territories, forms of political democracy are pushed aside; sheer force is decisive [...] Capital will never allow the people to decide the question of their state frontiers.

As though "capital" could "allow the people" to select *its* civil servants, the servants of imperialism! Or as though weighty decisions on important democratic questions, such as the establishment of a republic in place of a monarchy, or a militia in place of a regular army, were, *in general*, conceivable without "sheer force". Subjectively, the Polish comrades want to make Marxism 'more profound' but they are doing it altogether unsuccessfully. *Objectively*, their phrases about impracticability are opportunism, because their tacit assumption is: this is 'impracticable' without a series of revolutions, in the same way as democracy *as a whole*, *all* its demands taken together, is impracticable under imperialism.

Once only, at the very end of Section 2.1, in the discussion on Alsace, our Polish colleagues abandoned the position of imperialist Economism and approached the question of one of the forms of democracy with a concrete answer and not with general references to the 'economic'. And it was precisely this approach that was wrong! It would, they wrote, be "particularist, undemocratic" if *some* Alsatians, without asking the French, were to "impose" on them a union with Alsace, although part of Alsace was German-oriented and this threatened war!!! The confusion is amusing: self-determination presumes (this is in itself clear, and we have given it special emphasis in our theses) freedom to *separate* from the oppressor state; but the fact that *union* with a state presumes the consent of *that state* is something that is 'not customarily' mentioned in politics any more than the 'consent' of a capitalist to receive profit or of a worker to receive wages is mentioned in economics! It is ridiculous even to speak of such a thing.

If one wants to be a Marxist politician, one should, in speaking of Alsace, attack the German socialist scoundrels for not fighting for Alsace's freedom to secede and attack the French socialist scoundrels for making their peace with the French bourgeoisie who want to annex the whole of Alsace by force – and both of them for serving the imperialism of 'their own' country and for fearing a separate state, even if only a little one – the thing is to show *how* the socialists who recognize self-determination would solve the problem in a few weeks without going against the will of the Alsatians. To argue, instead, about the horrible danger of the French Alsatians 'forcing' themselves on France is a real pearl.

What is annexation?

We raised this question in a most definite manner in our theses (Section 7). The Polish comrades did *not* reply to it: they evaded it, insisting (1) that they are against annexations and explaining (2) why they are against them. It is true that these are very important questions. But they are questions of *another kind*. If we want our principles to be theoretically sound at all, if we want them to be clearly and precisely formulated, we cannot *evade* the question of what an annexation is, since this concept is used in our political propaganda and agitation. The evasion of the question in a discussion between colleagues cannot be interpreted as anything but desertion of one's position.

Why have we raised this question? We explained this when we raised it. It is because "a protest against annexations is nothing but recognition of the right to self-determination". The concept of annexation usually includes: (1) the concept of force (joining by means of force); (2) the concept of oppression by another nation (the joining of *'alien'* regions, etc.), and, sometimes (3) the concept of violation of the *status quo*. We pointed this out in the theses and this did not meet with any criticism.

Can social-democrats be against the use of force in general, it may be asked? Obviously not. This means that we are against annexations not because they constitute force, but for some other reason. Nor can the social-democrats be for the *status quo*. However you may twist and turn, annexation is *violation of the self-determination* of a nation, it is the establishment of state *frontiers contrary to the will of the population.*

To be against annexations *means* to be in favour of the right to self-determination. To be "against the forcible retention of any nation within the frontiers of a given state" (we deliberately employed this slightly changed formulation of the same idea in Section 4 of our theses, and the Polish comrades *answered* us with *complete* clarity at the beginning of their section I, 4, that they "are against the forcible retention of oppressed nations within the frontiers of the annexing state") — is *the same* as being in favour of the self-determination of nations.

We do not want to haggle over words. If there is a party that says in its programme (or in a resolution binding on all, the form does not matter) that it is against annexations,[8] against the forcible retention of oppressed nations within the frontiers of *its* state, we declare our complete agreement in principle with that party. It would be absurd to insist on the *word* 'self-determination'. And if there are people in our party who want to change words in this spirit, who want to amend Clause 9 of our party programme, we should consider our differences with such comrades to be anything but a matter of principle!

The only thing that matters is political clarity and theoretical soundness of our slogans.

In verbal discussions on this question — the importance of which nobody will deny, especially now, in view of the war — we have met the following argument (we have not come across it in the press): *a protest against* a known evil does not necessarily mean recognition of a positive concept that precludes the evil. This is obviously an unfounded argument and, apparently, as such has not been

---

8   Karl Radek formulated this as "against old and new annexations" in one of his articles in *Berner Tagwacht. — Lenin*
    Berner Tagwacht (*Berne Reveille*) was the organ of the Social-Democratic Party of Switzerland, published in Berne from 1893.

reproduced in the press. If a socialist party declares that it is "against the forcible retention of an oppressed nation within the frontiers of the annexing state", it is *thereby committed to renounce retention by force* when it comes to power.

We do not for one moment doubt that if Hindenburg were to accomplish the semi-conquest of Russia tomorrow and this semi-conquest were to be expressed by the appearance of a new Polish state (in connection with the desire of Britain and France to weaken tsarism somewhat), something that is quite 'practicable' from the standpoint of the economic laws of capitalism and imperialism, and if, the day after tomorrow, the socialist revolution were to be victorious in Petrograd, Berlin and Warsaw, the Polish socialist government, like the Russian and German socialist governments, would renounce the 'forcible retention' of, say, the Ukrainians, 'within the frontiers of the Polish state'. If there were members of the *Gazeta Robotnicza* editorial board in that government they would no doubt sacrifice their 'theses', thereby disproving the 'theory' that "the right of self-determination is not applicable to a socialist society". If we thought otherwise we should not put a comradely discussion with the Polish social-democrats on the agenda but would rather conduct a ruthless struggle against them as chauvinists.

Suppose I were to go out into the streets of any European city and make a public 'protest', which I then published in the press, against my not being permitted to purchase a man as a slave. There is no doubt that people would have the right to regard me as a slave-owner, a champion of the principle, or system, if you like, of slavery. No one would be fooled by the fact that my sympathies with slavery were expressed in the negative form of a protest and not in a positive form ('I am for slavery'). A political 'protest' is *quite* the equivalent of a political programme; this is so obvious that one feels rather awkward at having to explain it. In any case, we are firmly convinced that on the part of the Zimmerwald Left, at any rate – we do not speak of the Zimmerwald group as a whole since it contains Martov and other Kautskyites – we shall not meet with any 'protest' if we say that in the Third International there will be no place for people capable of separating a political protest from a political programme, of counterposing the one to the other, etc.

Not wishing to haggle over words, we take the liberty of expressing the sincere hope that the Polish social-democrats will try soon to formulate, officially, their proposal to delete Clause 9 from our party programme (which is also *theirs*) and also from the programme of the International (the resolution of the 1896 London Congress), as well as *their own* definition of the relevant political concepts of "old and new annexations" and of "the forcible retention of an oppressed nation within the frontiers of the annexing state".

Let us now turn to the next question.

For or against annexations?

In Section 3 of Part 1 of their theses the Polish comrades declare very definitely that they are against any kind of annexation. Unfortunately, in Section 4 of the same part we find an assertion that must be considered annexationist. It opens with the following... how can it be put more delicately?... the following strange phrase:

> The starting-point of Social-Democracy's struggle against annexations, against the forcible retention of oppressed nations within the frontiers of the annexing state is *renunciation of any defence of the fatherland* [the authors' italics], which, in the era of imperialism, is defence of the rights of one's own bourgeoisie to oppress and plunder foreign peoples...

What's this? How is it put?

"The starting-point of the struggle against annexations is renunciation of *any* defence of the fatherland..." But any national war and any national revolt can be called "defence of the fatherland" and, until now, has been *generally* recognised as such! We are against annexations, but... we mean by this that we are against the annexed waging a war *for* their liberation from those who have annexed them, that we are against the annexed revolting to liberate themselves from those who have annexed them! Isn't that an annexationist declaration?

The authors of the theses motivate their... strange assertion by saying that "in the era of imperialism" defence of the fatherland amounts to defence of the right of one's own bourgeoisie to oppress foreign peoples. This, however, is true *only* in respect of all imperialist war, i.e. in respect of a war *between* imperialist powers or groups of powers, when *both* belligerents not only oppress "foreign peoples" but are fighting a war *to decide* who shall have a *greater share* in oppressing foreign peoples!

The authors seem to present the question of "defence of the fatherland" very differently from the way it is presented by our party. We renounce "defence of the fatherland" in an imperialist war. This is said as clearly as it can be in the manifesto of our party's Central Committee and in the Berne resolutions reprinted in the pamphlet *Socialism and War*, which has been published both in German and French. We stressed this *twice* in our theses (footnotes to Sections 4 and 6). The authors of the Polish theses seem to renounce defence of the fatherland *in general*, i.e. *for a national war as well*, believing, perhaps, that in the "era of imperialism" national wars *are impossible*. We say "perhaps" because the Polish comrades have *not* expressed this view in their theses.

Such a view is clearly expressed in the theses of the German *Internationale* group and in the Junius pamphlet which is dealt with in a special article.[9] In addition to what is said there, let us note that the national revolt of an annexed region or country against the annexing country may be called precisely a revolt and not a war (we have heard this objection made and, therefore, cite it here, although we do not think this terminological dispute a serious one). In any case, hardly anybody would risk denying that annexed Belgium, Serbia, Galicia and Armenia would call their 'revolt' against those who annexed them "defence of the fatherland" *and would do so in all justice*. It looks as if the Polish comrades are *against* this type of revolt on the grounds that there is *also* a bourgeoisie in these annexed countries which *also* oppresses foreign peoples or, more

---

9 Lenin is referring to 'The Junius Pamphlet', written by Rosa Luxemburg in 1915. Lenin's response to Luxemburg was published also under the name 'The Junius Pamphlet'. See *LCW*, Vol. 22, p. 305. Reproduced in *Lenin Selected Writings Volume 1: On Imperialist War*, Wellred Books, 2024, p. 173.

exactly, could oppress them, since the question is one of the '*right* to oppress'. Consequently, the given war or revolt is not assessed on the strength of its *real* social content (the struggle of an oppressed nation for its liberation from the oppressor nation) but the possible exercise of the '*right* to oppress' by a bourgeoisie which is at present itself oppressed. If Belgium, let us say, is annexed by Germany in 1917, and in 1918 revolts to secure her liberation, the Polish comrades will be against her revolt on the grounds that the Belgian bourgeoisie possess "the right to oppress foreign peoples"!

There is nothing Marxist or even revolutionary in this argument. If we do not want to betray socialism we *must* support *every* revolt against our chief enemy, the bourgeoisie of the big states, provided it is not the revolt of a reactionary class. By refusing to support the revolt of annexed regions we become, objectively, annexationists. It is precisely in the "era of imperialism", which is the era of nascent social revolution, that the proletariat will today give especially vigorous support to any revolt of the annexed regions so that tomorrow, or simultaneously, it may attack the bourgeoisie of the "great" power that is weakened by the revolt.

The Polish comrades, however, go further in their annexationism. They are not only against any revolt by the annexed regions; they are against *any* restoration of their independence, even a peaceful one! Listen to this:

> Social-Democracy, rejecting all responsibility for the consequences of the policy of oppression pursued by imperialism, and conducting the sharpest struggle against them, *does not by any means favour the erection of new frontier posts in Europe or the re-erection of those swept away by imperialism* (the authors' italics).

Today "imperialism has swept away the frontier posts" between Germany and Belgium and between Russia and Galicia. International Social-Democracy, if you please, ought to be against their re-erection in general, whatever the means. In 1905, "in the era of imperialism", when Norway's autonomous Diet proclaimed her secession from Sweden, and Sweden's war against Norway, as preached by the Swedish reactionaries, did not take place, what with the resistance of the Swedish workers and the international imperialist situation – Social-Democracy ought to have been against Norway's secession, since it undoubtedly meant "the erection of now frontier posts in Europe"!!

This is downright annexationism. There is no need to refute it because it refutes itself. No socialist party would risk taking this stand: "We oppose annexations in general but we sanction annexations for Europe or tolerate them once they have been made…"

We need deal only with the theoretical sources of the error that has led our Polish comrades to such a patent… 'impossibility'. We shall say further on why there is no reason to make exceptions for "Europe". The following two phrases from the theses will explain the other sources of the error:

> Wherever the wheel of imperialism has rolled over and crushed an already formed capitalist state, the political and economic concentration of the capitalist world, paving the way for socialism, takes place in the brutal form of imperialist oppression…

This justification of annexations is not Marxism but Struveism. Russian social-democrats who remember the 1890s in Russia have a good knowledge of this manner of distorting Marxism, which is common to Struve, Cunow, Legien[10] and co. In another of the theses (II, 3) of the Polish comrades we read the following, specifically about the German Struveists, the so-called 'social-imperialists':

> [The slogan of self-determination] provides the social-imperialists with an opportunity, by demonstrating the illusory nature of that slogan, to represent our struggle against national oppression as historically unfounded sentimentality, thereby undermining the faith of the proletariat in the scientific validity of the social-democratic programme…

This means that the authors consider the position of the German Struveists "scientific"! Our congratulations.

---

10 Carl Legien was a Reichstag member of the German SPD. He was the leader of the right wing of the SPD.

One 'trifle', however, brings down this amazing argument which threatens to show that the Lensches, Cunows and Parvuses are *right* in comparison to us: it is that the Lensches are consistent people in their own way and in issue No. 8-9 of the chauvinist German *Glocke* – we deliberately quoted it in our theses – Lensch demonstrates *simultaneously* both the 'scientific invalidity' of the self-determination slogan (the Polish social-democrats apparently believe that *this* argument of Lensch's is irrefutable, as can be seen from their arguments in the theses we have quoted) *and* the 'scientific invalidity' of the slogan against annexations!!!

For Lensch had an excellent understanding of that simple truth which we pointed out to those Polish colleagues who showed no desire to reply to our statement: there is no difference "either political or economic", or even logical, between the 'recognition' of self-determination and the 'protest' against annexations. If the Polish comrades regard the arguments of the Lensches against self-determination to be irrefutable, there is one *fact* that has to be accepted: the Lensches also use *all* these arguments to oppose the struggle against annexations.

The theoretical error that underlies all the arguments of our Polish colleagues has led them to the point of becoming *inconsistent annexationists.*

Why are social-democrats against annexations?

In our view the answer is obvious: because annexation violates the self-determination of nations, or, in other words, is a form of national oppression.

In the view of the Polish social-democrats there have to be *special* explanations of why we are against annexations, and it is these (I, 3 in the theses) that inevitably enmesh the authors in a further series of contradictions.

They produce two reasons to 'justify' our opposition to annexations (the "scientifically valid" arguments of the Lensches notwithstanding). First:

To the assertion that annexations in Europe are essential for the military security of a victorious imperialist state, the social-democrats counterpose the fact that annexations only serve to sharpen antagonisms, thereby increasing the danger of war...

This is an inadequate reply to the Lensches because their chief argument is not that annexations are a military necessity but that they are *economically* progressive and under imperialism mean concentration. Where is the logic if the Polish social-democrats in the same breath recognise the progressive nature of *such* a concentration, refusing to re-erect frontier posts in Europe that have been swept away by imperialism, and protest *against* annexations?

Furthermore, the danger of *what* wars is increased by annexations? Not imperialist wars, because they have other causes: the chief antagonisms in the present imperialist war are undoubtedly those between Germany and Britain, and between Germany and Russia. These antagonisms have nothing to do with annexations. It is the danger of *national* wars and national revolts that is increased. But how can one declare national wars to be *impossible* in "the era of imperialism", on the one hand, and then speak of the "danger" of national wars, on the other? This is not logical.

The second argument:

[Annexations] create a gulf between the proletariat of the ruling nation and that of the oppressed nation [...] the proletariat of the oppressed nation would unite with its bourgeoisie and regard the proletariat of the ruling nation as its enemy. Instead of the proletariat waging an international class struggle against the international bourgeoisie it would be split and ideologically corrupted...

We fully agree with these arguments. But is it logical to put forward simultaneously two arguments on the same question which cancel each other out? In Section 3 of the first part of the theses we find the above arguments that regard annexations as causing a *split* in the proletariat, and next to it, in Section 4, we are told that we must oppose the annulment of annexations already effected in Europe and favour "the education of the working masses of the oppressed and the oppressor nations in a spirit of solidarity in struggle". If the annulment of annexations is reactionary "sentimentality", annexations *must not* be said to create a "gulf" between sections of the "proletariat" and cause a "split", but should, on the contrary, be regarded as a condition for the *bringing together* of the proletariat of different nations.

We say: In order that we may have the strength to accomplish the socialist revolution and overthrow the bourgeoisie, the workers must unite more closely and this close union is promoted by the struggle for self-determination, i.e. the struggle against annexations. We are consistent. But the Polish comrades who say that European annexations are 'non-annullable' and national wars, 'impossible', defeat themselves by contending 'against' annexations with the use of arguments *about* national wars! These arguments are to the effect that annexations *hamper* the drawing together and fusion of workers of different nations!

In other words, the Polish social-democrats, in order to contend against annexations, have to draw for arguments on the theoretical stock they themselves reject in principle.

The question of colonies makes this even more obvious.

Is it right to contrast 'Europe' with the colonies in the present question?

Our theses say that the demand for the immediate liberation of the colonies is as 'impracticable' (that is, it cannot be effected without a number of revolutions and is not stable without socialism) under capitalism as the self-determination of nations, the election of civil servants by the people, the democratic republic, and so on – and, furthermore, that the demand for the liberation of the colonies is nothing more than "the recognition of the right of nations to self-determination".

The Polish comrades have not answered a single one of these arguments. They have tried to differentiate between 'Europe' and the colonies. For Europe alone they become inconsistent annexationists by refusing to annul any annexations once these have been made. As for the colonies, they demand unconditionally: 'Get out of the colonies!'

Russian socialists must put forward the demand: 'Get out of Turkestan, Khiva, Bukhara, etc.', but, it is alleged, they would be guilty of 'utopianism', 'unscientific sentimentality' and so on if they demanded a similar freedom of secession for Poland, Finland, the Ukraine, etc. British socialists must demand: 'Get out of Africa, India, Australia', but not out of Ireland. What are the theoretical grounds for a distinction that is so patently false? This question cannot be evaded.

The chief 'ground' of those opposed to self-determination is its 'impracticability'. The same idea, with a nuance, is expressed in the reference to 'economic and political concentration'.

Obviously, concentration *also* comes about with the annexation of colonies. There was formerly an economic distinction between the colonies and the European peoples – at least, the majority of the latter – the colonies having been drawn into *commodity* exchange but not into capitalist *production*. Imperialism changed this. Imperialism is, among other things, the export of *capital*. Capitalist production is being transplanted to the colonies at an ever increasing rate. They cannot be extricated from dependence on European finance capital. From the military standpoint, as well as from the standpoint of expansion, the separation of the colonies is practicable, as a general rule, only under socialism; under capitalism it is practicable only by way of exception or at the cost of a series of revolts and revolutions both in the colonies and the metropolitan countries.

The greater part of the dependent nations in Europe are capitalistically more developed than the colonies (though not all, the exceptions being the Albanians and many non-Russian peoples in Russia.) But it is just this that generates greater resistance to national oppression and annexations! Precisely because of this, the development of capitalism is *more secure* in Europe under any political conditions, including those of separation, than in the colonies...

> There [the Polish comrades say about the colonies (I, 4)] capitalism
> is still confronted with the task of developing the productive forces
> independently...

This is even more noticeable in Europe: capitalism is undoubtedly developing the productive forces more vigorously, rapidly and independently in Poland, Finland, the Ukraine and Alsace than in India, Turkestan, Egypt and other straightforward colonies. In a commodity producing society, no independent development, or development of any sort whatsoever, is possible without capital. In Europe the dependent nations have both *their own* capital and easy access to it on a wide range of terms. The colonies have no capital of *their own*, or none to speak of, and under finance capital no colony can obtain any except on terms of political submission. What then, in face of all this, is the significance of the demand to liberate the colonies immediately and unconditionally? Is it not clear that it is more 'utopian' in the vulgar, caricature-'Marxist' sense of the word, 'utopian', in the sense in which it is used by the Struves, Lenches, Cunows, with the Polish comrades unfortunately following in their footsteps? Any deviation from the ordinary, the commonplace, as well as everything that is revolutionary, is here labelled 'utopianism'. But revolutionary movements of *all* kinds – including national movements – are more possible, more practicable, more stubborn, more conscious and more difficult to defeat in Europe than they are in the colonies.

Socialism, say the Polish comrades (I, 3), "will be able to give the underdeveloped peoples of the colonies *unselfish, cultural aid without ruling over them*". This is perfectly true. But what grounds are there for supposing that a great nation, a great state that goes over to socialism, will not be able to attract a small, oppressed European nation by means of "unselfish cultural aid"? It is the freedom to secede *'granted'* to the colonies by the Polish social-democrats that will attract the small but cultured and politically *exacting* oppressed nations of Europe to union with great socialist states, because under socialism a great state will mean so many hours *less* work a day and so much more *pay* a day. The masses of working people, as they liberate themselves from the bourgeois yoke, *will gravitate* irresistibly towards union and integration with the great, advanced socialist nations for the sake of that "cultural aid", provided yesterday's oppressors do not infringe on the long-oppressed nations' highly developed democratic feeling of self-respect, and provided they are granted equality in everything, including state construction, that is, experience in organising 'their own' state. Under capitalism this 'experience' means war, isolation, seclusion, and the narrow egoism of the small privileged nations (Holland, Switzerland). Under socialism the working people themselves will nowhere consent to seclusion merely for the above-mentioned purely economic motives, while the variety of political forms, freedom to secede, and experience in state organisation – there will be all this until the state in all its forms withers away – will be the basis of a prosperous cultured life and an earnest that the nations will draw closer together and integrate at an ever faster pace.

By setting the colonies aside and contrasting them to Europe the Polish comrades step into a contradiction which immediately brings down the whole of their fallacious argument.

Marxism or Proudhonism?

By way of an exception, our Polish comrades parry our reference to Marx's attitude towards the separation of Ireland directly and not indirectly. What is their objection? References to Marx's position from 1848 to 1871, they say, are "not of the slightest value". The argument advanced in support of this unusually irate and peremptory assertion is that "at one and the same time" Marx opposed the strivings for independence of the "Czechs, South Slavs, etc.".

The argument is so very irate because it is so very unsound. According to the Polish Marxists, Marx was simply a muddlehead who "in one breath" said contradictory things! This is altogether untrue, and it is certainly not Marxism. It is precisely the demand for "concrete" analysis, which our Polish comrades insist on, but do not themselves apply, that makes it necessary for us to investigate whether

Marx's different attitudes towards different concrete "national" movements did not spring from *one and the same* socialist outlook.

Marx is known to have favoured Polish independence in the interests of *European* democracy in its struggle against the power and influence – or, it might be said, against the omnipotence and predominating reactionary influence – of tsarism. That this attitude was correct was most clearly and practically demonstrated in 1849, when the Russian serf army crushed the national liberation and revolutionary-democratic rebellion in Hungary. From that time until Marx's death, and even later, until 1890, when there was a danger that tsarism, allied with France, would wage a reactionary war against a *non-imperialist* and nationally independent Germany, Engels stood first and foremost for a struggle against tsarism. It was for this reason, and exclusively for this reason, that Marx and Engels were opposed to the national movement of the Czechs and South Slavs. A simple reference to what Marx and Engels wrote in 1848 and 1841 will prove to anyone who is interested in Marxism in real earnest and not merely for the purpose of brushing Marxism aside, that Marx and Engels at that time drew a clear and definite *distinction* between "whole reactionary nations" serving as "Russian outposts" in Europe, and "revolutionary nations" namely, the Germans, Poles and Magyars. This is a fact. And it was indicated *at the time with incontrovertible* truth: in 1848 revolutionary nations fought for liberty, whose principal enemy was tsarism, whereas the Czechs, etc., were in fact reactionary nations, and outposts of tsarism.

What is the lesson to be drawn from this concrete example which must be analysed *concretely* if there is any desire to be true to Marxism? Only this: (1) that the interests of the liberation of a number of big and very big nations in Europe rate higher than the interests of the movement for liberation of small nations; (2) that the demand for democracy must not be considered in isolation but on a European – today we should say a world – scale.

That is all there is to it. There is no hint of any repudiation of that elementary socialist principle which the Poles forget but to which Marx was *always* faithful – that no nation can be free if it oppresses other nations. If the concrete situation which confronted Marx when tsarism dominated international politics were to repeat itself, for instance, in the form of a few nations starting a socialist revolution (as a bourgeois-democratic revolution was started in Europe in 1848), and *other* nations serving as the chief bulwarks of bourgeois reaction – then we too would have to be in favour of a revolutionary war against the latter, in favour of 'crushing' them, in favour of destroying all their outposts, no matter what small-nation movements arose in them. Consequently, instead of rejecting any examples of Marx's tactics – this would mean professing Marxism while abandoning it in practice – we must analyse them concretely and draw invaluable lessons for the future. The several demands of democracy, including self-determination, are not an absolute, but only a *small part* of the general-democratic (now: general-socialist) *world* movement. In individual concrete cases, the part may contradict the whole; if so, it must be rejected. It is possible that the republican movement in one country may be merely an instrument of the clerical or financial-monarchist intrigues of other countries; if so, we must *not* support this particular, concrete movement, but it would be ridiculous to delete the demand for a republic from the programme of international Social-Democracy on these grounds.

In what way has the concrete situation changed between the periods of 1848-71 and 1898-1916 (I take the most important landmarks of imperialism as a period: from the Spanish-American imperialist war to the European imperialist war)? Tsarism has manifestly and indisputably ceased to be the chief mainstay of reaction, first, because it is supported by international finance capital, particularly French, and, secondly, because of 1905. At that time the system of big national states – the democracies of Europe – was bringing democracy and socialism to the world in spite of tsarism.[11] Marx and Engels did not live to see the period of imperialism. The system now

---

11 Riazanov has published in Grünberg's *Archives of the History of Socialism* (1916, I) a very interesting article by Engels on the Polish question, written in 1866. Engels emphasises that the proletariat must recognise the political independence and "self-determination" ("right to dispose of itself" [These words are in English in the original]) of the great, major nations of Europe, and points to the absurdity

is a handful of imperialist 'Great' Powers (five or six in number), each oppressing other nations: and this oppression is a source for artificially retarding the collapse of capitalism, and artificially supporting opportunism and social-chauvinism in the imperialist nations which dominate the world. At that time, West-European democracy, liberating the big nations, was opposed to tsarism, which used certain small-nation movements for reactionary ends. Today, the socialist proletariat, split into chauvinists, 'social-imperialists', on the one hand, and revolutionaries, on the other, is confronted by an *alliance* of tsarist imperialism and advanced capitalist, European, imperialism, which is based on their common oppression of a number of nations.

Such are the concrete changes that have taken place in the situation, and it is just these that the Polish social-democrats ignore, in spite of their promise to be concrete! Hence the concrete change in the *application* of the same socialist principles: *formerly* the main thing was to fight 'against tsarism' (and against certain small-nation movements that *it* was using for undemocratic ends), and for the greater revolutionary peoples of the West; the main thing *today* is to stand against the united, aligned front of the imperialist powers, the imperialist bourgeoisie and the social-imperialists, and *for* the utilisation of *all* national movements against imperialism for the purposes of the socialist revolution. The *more purely* proletarian the struggle against the general imperialist front now is, the more vital, obviously, is the internationalist principle: "No nation can be free if it oppresses other nations".

In the name of their doctrinaire concept of social revolution, the Proudhonists ignored the international role of Poland and brushed

---

of the "principle of nationalities" (particularly in its Bonapartist application), i.e. of placing any small nation on the same level as these big ones.

And as to Russia, [says Engels] she could only be mentioned as the detainer of an immense amount of stolen property [i.e. oppressed nations] which would have to be disgorged on the day of reckoning.

Both Bonapartism and tsarism utilise the small-nation movements for their own benefit, against European democracy. – *Lenin* aside the national movements. Equally doctrinaire is the attitude of the Polish social-democrats, who *break up* the international front of struggle against the social-imperialists, and (objectively) help the latter by their vacillations on the question of annexations. For it is precisely the international front of proletarian struggle that has changed in relation to the concrete position of the small nations: at that time (1848-71) the small nations were important as the potential allies either of 'Western democracy' and the revolutionary nations, or of tsarism; now (1898-1914) that is no longer so; today they are important as one of the nutritive media of the parasitism and, consequently, the social-imperialism of the 'dominant nations'. The important thing is not whether one-fiftieth or one-hundredth of the small nations are liberated before the socialist revolution, but the fact that in the epoch of imperialism, owing to objective causes, the proletariat has been split into two international camps, one of which has been corrupted by the crumbs that fall from the table of the dominant-nation bourgeoisie – obtained, among other things, from the double or triple exploitation of small nations – while the other cannot liberate itself without liberating the small nations, without educating the masses in an anti-chauvinist, i.e. anti-annexationist, i.e. 'self-determinationist', spirit.

This, the most important aspect of the question, is ignored by our Polish comrades, who do *not* view things from the key position in the epoch of imperialism, the standpoint of the division of the international proletariat into two camps.

Here are some other concrete examples of their Proudhonism: (1) their attitude to the Irish rebellion of 1916, of which later: (2) the declaration in the theses (11.3, end of Section 3) that the slogan of socialist revolution "must not be overshadowed by anything". The idea that the slogan of socialist revolution can be "overshadowed" by *linking* it up with a consistently revolutionary position on all questions, including the national question, is certainly profoundly anti-Marxist.

The Polish social-democrats consider our programme "national-reformist". Compare these two practical proposals: (1) for autonomy (Polish theses, III, 4), and (2) for freedom to secede. It is in this, and in this alone, that our programmes differ! And is it not clear that it is precisely the first programme that is reformist and not the second. A reformist change is one which leaves intact the foundations of the power of the ruling class and is merely a concession leaving its power unimpaired. A revolutionary change undermines the foundations of power. A reformist national programme does *not* abolish *all* the privileges of the ruling nation; it does *not* establish complete equality; it does *not* abolish national oppression *in all its forms.* An 'autonomous' nation does not enjoy rights equal to those of the 'ruling' nation; our Polish comrades could not have failed to notice this had they not (like our old Economists) obstinately avoided making an analysis of *political* concepts and categories. Until 1905 autonomous Norway, as a part of Sweden, enjoyed the widest autonomy, but she was not Sweden's equal. Only by her free secession was her equality manifested *in practice* and proved (and let us add in parenthesis that: it was this free secession that created the basis for a more intimate and more democratic association, founded on equality of rights). As long as Norway was merely autonomous, the Swedish aristocracy had *one* additional privilege; and secession did not 'mitigate' this privilege (the essence of reformism lies in *mitigating* an evil and not in destroying it), but *eliminated* it *altogether* (the principal criterion of the revolutionary character of a programme).

Incidentally, autonomy, as a reform, differs in principle from freedom to secede, as a revolutionary measure. This is unquestionable. But as everyone knows, in practice a reform is often merely a step towards revolution. It is autonomy that enables a nation forcibly retained within the boundaries of a given state to crystallise into a nation, to gather, assess and organise its forces, and to select the most opportune moment for a *declaration* ... in the 'Norwegian' spirit: We, the autonomous diet of such-and-such a nation, or of such-and-such a territory, declare that the Emperor of all the Russias has ceased to be King of Poland, etc. The usual 'objection' to this is that such questions are decided by wars and not by declarations. True: in the vast majority of cases they are decided by wars (just as questions of the form of government of big states are decided, in the vast majority of cases, only by wars and revolutions). However, it would do no harm to reflect whether *such* an 'objection' to the political programme of a revolutionary party is logical. Are we opposed to wars and revolutions for what is just and beneficial to the proletariat, *for* democracy and socialism?

'But we cannot be in favour of a war between great nations, in favour of the slaughter of twenty million people for the sake of the problematical liberation of a small nation with a population of perhaps ten or twenty millions!' Of course not! And it does not mean that we throw complete national equality out of our programme; it means that the democratic interests of *one* country must be subordinated to the democratic interests of *several and all* countries. Let us assume that between two great monarchies there is a little monarchy whose kinglet is 'bound' by blood and other ties to the monarchs of both neighbouring countries. Let us further assume that the declaration of a republic in the little country and the expulsion of *its* monarch would in practice lead to a war between the two neighbouring big countries for the restoration of that or another monarch in the little country. There is no doubt that all international Social-Democracy, as well as the really internationalist section of Social-Democracy in the little country, *would be against substituting a republic for the monarchy* in this case. The substitution of a republic for a monarchy is not an absolute, but one of the democratic demands, subordinate to the interests of democracy (and still more, of course, to those of the socialist proletariat) as a whole. A case like this would in all probability not give rise to the slightest disagreement among social-democrats in any country. But if any social-democrat were to propose on *these* grounds that the demand for a republic be deleted altogether from the programme of international Social-Democracy, he would certainly be regarded as quite mad. He would be told that after all one must not forget the elementary logical difference between the *general* and the *particular*.

This example brings us, from a somewhat different angle, to the question of the *internationalist* education of the working class. Can such education – on the necessity and urgent importance of which differences of opinion among the Zimmerwald Left are inconceivable – be *concretely identical* in great, oppressor nations and in small, oppressed nations, in annexing nations and in annexed nations?

Obviously not. The way to the common goal – complete equality, the closest association and the eventual *amalgamation of all* nations – obviously runs along different routes in each concrete case, as, let us say, the way to a point in the centre of this page runs left from one edge and right, from the opposite edge. If a social-democrat from a great, oppressing, annexing nation, while advocating the amalgamation of nations in general, were for one moment to forget that 'his' Nicholas II, 'his' Wilhelm, George, Poincaré, etc.,[12] *also stand for amalgamation* with small nations (by means of annexations) – Nicholas II for 'amalgamation' with Galicia, Wilhelm II for 'amalgamation' with Belgium, etc. – such a social-democrat would be a ridiculous doctrinaire in theory and an abettor of imperialism in practice.

In the internationalist education of the workers of the oppressor countries, emphasis must necessarily be laid on their advocating freedom for the oppressed countries to secede and their fighting for it. Without this there can be no internationalism. It is our right and duty to treat every social-democrat of an oppressor nation who *fails* to conduct such propaganda as a scoundrel and an imperialist. This is an absolute demand, even where the *chance* of secession being possible and 'practicable' before the introduction of socialism is only one in a thousand.

It is our duty to teach the workers to be 'indifferent' to national distinctions. There is no doubt about that. But it must not be the indifference of the *annexationists*. A member of an oppressor nation must be 'indifferent' to whether small nations belong to *his* state or to a neighbouring state, or to themselves, according to where

---

12 Referring to the Kaiser of Germany, King George V of England and Raymond Poincaré, President of France.

their sympathies lie: without such 'indifference' he is *not* a social-democrat. To be an internationalist social-democrat one must *not* think only of one's own nation, but place *above it* the interests of all nations, their common liberty and equality. Everyone accepts this in 'theory' but displays an annexationist indifference in practice. There is the root of the evil.

On the other hand, a social-democrat from a small nation must emphasise in his agitation the second word of our general formula: 'voluntary *integration*' of nations. He may, without failing in his duties as an internationalist, be in favour of *both* the political independence of his nation and its integration with the neighbouring state of X, Y, Z etc. But in all cases he must fight *against* small-nation narrow-mindedness, seclusion and isolation, consider the whole and the general, subordinate the particular to the general interest.

People who have not gone into the question thoroughly think that it is 'contradictory' for the social-democrats of oppressor nations to insist on the 'freedom to *secede*', while social-democrats of oppressed nations insist on the 'freedom to *integrate*'. However, a little reflection will show that there is not, and cannot be, any *other* road to internationalism and the amalgamation of nations, any other road *from the given* situation to this goal.

And now we come to the *specific* position of Dutch and Polish social-democrats.

The specific and the general in the position of the Dutch and Polish social-democrat internationalists

There is not the slightest doubt that the Dutch and Polish Marxists who oppose self-determination are among the best revolutionary and internationalist elements in international Social-Democracy. How *can* it be then that their theoretical arguments as we have seen, are a mass of errors? There is not a single correct general argument, nothing but imperialist Economism!

It is not at all due to the especially bad subjective qualities of the Dutch and Polish comrades but to the *specific* objective conditions in their countries. Both countries are:

1. Small and helpless in the present-day 'system' of great powers;

2. Both are geographically situated between tremendously powerful imperialist plunderers engaged in the most bitter rivalry with each other (Britain and Germany; Germany and Russia);

3. In both there are terribly strong memories and traditions of the times when they *themselves* were great powers: Holland was once a colonial power greater than England, Poland was more cultured and was a stronger great power than Russia and Prussia;

4. To this day both retain their privileges consisting in the oppression of other peoples: the Dutch bourgeois owns the very wealthy Dutch East Indies; the Polish landed proprietor oppresses the Ukrainian and Byelorussian peasant; the Polish bourgeois, the Jew, etc.

The particularity comprised in the combination of these four points is not to be found in Ireland, Portugal (she was at one time annexed to Spain), Alsace, Norway, Finland, the Ukraine, the Lettish and Byelorussian territories or many others. And it is this very peculiarity that is the *real essence* of the matter! When the Dutch and Polish social-democrats reason against self-determination, using general arguments, i.e. those that concern imperialism in general, socialism in general, democracy in general, national oppression in general, we may truly say that they wallow in mistakes. But one has only to discard this obviously erroneous *shell* of general arguments and examine the *essence* of the question from the standpoint of the *specific* conditions obtaining in Holland and Poland for their particular position to become *comprehensible* and quite legitimate. It may be said, without any fear of sounding paradoxical, that when the Dutch and Polish Marxists battle against self-determination they do not say quite what they mean, or, to put it another way, mean quite what they say.[13]

---

13 Let us recall that *all* the Polish social-democrats *recognised* self-determination *in general* in their Zimmerwald declaration, although their formulation was slightly different. – *Lenin*

We have already quoted one example in our theses.[14] Gorter is against the self-determination of *his own* country but *in favour* of self-determination for the Dutch East Indies, oppressed as they are by 'his' nation! Is it any wonder that we see in him a more sincere internationalist and a fellow-thinker who is closer to us than those who recognise self-determination *as* verbally and hypocritically as Kautsky in Germany, and Trotsky and Martov in Russia? The general and fundamental principles of Marxism undoubtedly imply the duty to struggle for the freedom to secede for nations that are oppressed by 'one's own' nation, but they certainly do not require the independence specifically of Holland to be made a matter of paramount importance – Holland, which suffers most from her narrow, callous, selfish and stultifying seclusion: let the whole world burn, we stand aside from it all, 'we' are satisfied with our old spoils and the rich 'left-overs', the Indies, 'we' are not concerned with anything else!

Here is another example. Karl Radek, a Polish social-democrat, who has done particularly great service by his determined struggle for internationalism in German Social-Democracy since the outbreak of war, made a furious attack on self-determination in an article entitled 'The Right of Nations to Self-Determination' (*Lichtstrahlen*,[15] No. 3, 5 December 1915). He quotes, incidentally, *only* Dutch and Polish authorities in his support and propounds, amongst others, the argument that self-determination fosters the idea that "it is allegedly the duty of social-democrats to support any struggle for independence".

From the standpoint of *general* theory this argument is outrageous, because it is clearly illogical: first, no democratic demand can fail to give rise to abuses, unless the specific is subordinated to the general; we are not obliged to support either "any" struggle for independence or "any" republican or anti-clerical movement. Secondly, *no* formula

---

14 See Lenin, 'The Socialist Revolution and the Right of Nations to Self-Determination', in this volume, p. 109.

15 *Lichtstrahlen* (*Rays of Light*) was an irregularly published paper, and served as the organ of the left-wing Social-Democrats of Germany.

for the struggle against national oppression can fail to suffer from the same 'shortcoming'. Radek himself in *Berner Tagwacht* used the formula (1915, Issue 253): "Against old and new annexations." Any Polish nationalist will legitimately 'deduce' from this formula: 'Poland is an annexment, I am against annexations, *i.e.* I am for the independence of Poland.' Or I recall Rosa Luxemburg saying in an article written in 1908, that the formula: "against national oppression" was quite adequate. But any Polish nationalist would say – and quite justly – that annexation is one of the forms of national oppression, *consequently*, etc.

However, take Poland's *specific* conditions in place of these general arguments: her independence *today* is 'impracticable' without wars or revolutions. To be in favour of an all-European war merely for the sake of restoring Poland is to be a nationalist of the worst sort, and to place the interests of a small number of Poles above those of the hundreds of millions of people who suffer from war. Such, indeed, are the 'Fracy' (the right wing of the PSP) who are socialists only in word, and compared with whom the Polish social-democrats are a thousand times right. To raise the question of Poland's independence *today*, with the *existing* alignment of the *neighbouring* imperialist powers, is really to run after a will-o'-the-wisp, plunge into narrow-minded nationalism and forget the necessary premise of an all-European or at least a Russian and a German revolution. To have put forward in 1908-14 freedom of coalition in Russia as an independent slogan would also have meant running after a will-o'-the-wisp, and would, objectively, have helped the Stolypin labour party (now the Potresov-Gvozdev party, which, incidentally, is the same thing).[16] But it would be madness to remove freedom of coalition in general from the programme of Social-Democracy!

A third and, perhaps, the most important example. We read in the Polish theses (III, end of 82) that the idea of an independent Polish buffer state is opposed on the grounds that it is an:

---

16 Lenin is referring ironically to the Mensheviks, comparing their policy to that of arch-reactionary Pyotr Stolypin.

… inane utopia of small impotent groups. Put into effect, it would mean the creation of a tiny fragment of a Polish state that would be a military colony of one or another group of Great Powers, a plaything of their military or economic interests, an area exploited by foreign capital, and a battlefield in future war.

This is all very *true* when used as an argument *against* the slogan of Polish independence *today*, because even a revolution in Poland alone would change nothing and would only divert the attention of the masses in Poland from *the main thing* – the connection between their struggle and that of the Russian and German proletariat. It is not a paradox but a fact that today the Polish proletariat as such can help the cause of socialism and freedom, including the freedom of Poland, only by *joint* struggle with the proletariat of the neighbouring countries, against the *narrow Polish* nationalists. The great historical service rendered by the Polish social-democrats in the struggle against the nationalists cannot possibly be denied.

But these same arguments, which are true from the standpoint of Poland's *specific* conditions in the *present* epoch, are manifestly untrue in the *general* form in which they are presented. So long as there are wars, Poland will always remain a battlefield in wars between Germany and Russia, but this is no argument against greater political liberty (and, therefore, against political independence) in the periods between wars. The same applies to the arguments about exploitation by foreign capital and Poland's role as a plaything of foreign interests. The Polish social-democrats cannot, at the moment, raise the slogan of Poland's independence, for the Poles, as proletarian internationalists, can do *nothing* about it without stooping, like the 'Fracy', to humble servitude to *one* of the imperialist monarchies. But it is *not* indifferent to the Russian and German workers whether Poland is independent, or they take part in annexing her (and that would mean educating the Russian and German workers and peasants in the basest turpitude and their consent to play the part of executioner of other peoples).

The situation is, indeed, bewildering, but there is a way out in which *all* participants would remain internationalists: the

Russian and German social-democrats by demanding for Poland unconditional '*freedom* to secede'; the Polish social-democrats by working for the unity of the proletarian struggle in both small and big countries without putting forward the slogan of Polish independence for the given epoch or the given period.

Engels' letter to Kautsky

In his pamphlet *Socialism and Colonial Politics* (Berlin, 1907), Kautsky, who was then still a Marxist, published a letter written to him by Engels, dated 12 September 1882, which is extremely interesting in relation to the question under discussion. Here is the principal part of the letter.

> In my opinion the colonies proper, i.e. the countries occupied by a European population – Canada, the Cape, Australia – will all become independent; on the other hand, the countries inhabited by a native population, which are simply subjugated – India, Algeria, the Dutch, Portuguese and Spanish possessions – must be taken over for the time being by the proletariat and led as rapidly as possible towards independence. How this process will develop is difficult to say. India will perhaps, indeed very probably, make a revolution, and as a proletariat in process of self-emancipation cannot conduct any colonial wars, it would have to be allowed to run its course; it would not pass off without all sorts of destruction, of course, but that sort of thing is inseparable from all revolutions. The same might also take place elsewhere, e.g. in Algeria and Egypt, and would certainly be the best thing *for us*. We shall have enough to do at home. Once Europe is reorganised, and North America, that will furnish such colossal power and such an example that the semi-civilised countries will of themselves follow in their wake; economic needs, if anything, will see to that. But as to what social and political phases these countries will then have to pass through before they likewise arrive at socialist organisation, I think we today can advance only rather idle hypotheses. One thing alone is certain: *the victorious proletariat can force no blessings of any kind upon any foreign nation without undermining*

its own victory by so doing. Which of course by no means excludes defensive wars of various kinds...[17]

Engels does not at all suppose that the 'economic' alone will directly remove all difficulties. An economic revolution will be a stimulus to *all* peoples to *strive* for socialism; but at the same time revolutions – against the socialist state – and wars are possible. Politics will inevitably adapt themselves to the economy, but not immediately or smoothly, not simply, not directly. Engels mentions as "certain" only one, absolutely internationalist, principle, and this he applies to *all* "foreign nations", i.e. not to colonial nations only: to force blessings upon them would mean to undermine the victory of the proletariat.

Just because the proletariat has carried out a social revolution it will not become holy and immune from errors and weaknesses. But it will be inevitably led to realise this truth by possible errors (and selfish interest – attempts to saddle others).

We of the Zimmerwald Left all hold the same conviction as Kautsky, for example, held before his desertion of Marxism for the defence of chauvinism in 1914, namely, that the socialist revolution is quite possible *in the very near* future – "any day", as Kautsky himself once put it. National antipathies will not disappear so quickly: the hatred – and perfectly legitimate hatred – of an oppressed nation for its oppressor will last for a while; it will evaporate only *after* the victory of socialism and *after* the final establishment of completely democratic relations between nations. If we are to be faithful to socialism we must even now educate the masses in the spirit of internationalism, which is impossible in oppressor nations without advocating freedom of secession for oppressed nations.

The Irish Rebellion of 1916

Our theses were written before the outbreak of this rebellion, which must be the touchstone of our theoretical views.

The views of the opponents of self-determination lead to the conclusion that the vitality of small nations oppressed by imperialism

---

17 Engels, 'Letter to Karl Kautsky', 12 September 1882, *MECW*, Vol. 46, p. 320.

has already been sapped, that they cannot play any role against imperialism, that support of their purely national aspirations will lead to nothing, etc. The imperialist war of 1914-16 has provided *facts* which refute such conclusions.

The war proved to be an epoch of crisis for the West-European nations, and for imperialism as a whole. Every crisis discards the conventionalities, tears away the outer wrappings, sweeps away the obsolete and reveals the underlying springs and forces. What has it revealed from the standpoint of the movement of oppressed nations? In the colonies there have been a number of attempts at rebellion, which the oppressor nations, naturally, did all they could to hide by means of a military censorship. Nevertheless, it is known that in Singapore the British brutally suppressed a mutiny among their Indian troops; that there were attempts at rebellion in French Annam (see *Nashe Slovo*)[18] and in the German Cameroons (see the Junius pamphlet); that in Europe, on the one hand, there was a rebellion in Ireland, which the 'freedom-loving' English, who did not dare to extend conscription to Ireland, suppressed by executions, and, on the other, the Austrian Government passed the death sentence on the deputies of the Czech Diet 'for treason', and shot whole Czech regiments for the same 'crime'.

This list is, of course, far from complete. Nevertheless, it proves that, *owing* to the crisis of imperialism, the flames of national revolt have flared up *both* in the colonies and in Europe, and that national sympathies and antipathies have manifested themselves in spite of the Draconian threats and measures of repression. All this before the crisis of imperialism hit its peak; the power of the imperialist bourgeoisie was yet to be undermined (this may be brought about by a war of 'attrition' but has not yet happened) and the proletarian movements in the imperialist countries were still very feeble. What

---

18 *Nashe Slovo* (*Our Word*) was an Internationalist daily paper published in Paris from January 1915 to September 1916. Trotsky was the main editor and attended the Zimmerwald Conference as a representative of *Nashe Slovo*. The paper was banned by the French authorities on 15 September 1916 and Trotsky was ordered to leave France.

will happen when the war has caused complete exhaustion, or when, in one state at least, the power of the bourgeoisie has been shaken under the blows of proletarian struggle, as that of tsarism in 1905?

On 9 May 1916, there appeared in *Berner Tagwacht* the organ of the Zimmerwald group, including some of the Leftists, an article on the Irish rebellion entitled 'Their Song Is Over' and signed with the initials KR [Karl Radek]. It described the Irish rebellion as being nothing more nor less than a "putsch", for, as the author argued, "the Irish question was an agrarian one", the peasants had been pacified by reforms, and the nationalist movement remained only a "purely urban, petty-bourgeois movement, which, notwithstanding the sensation it caused, had not much social backing".

It is not surprising that this monstrously doctrinaire and pedantic assessment coincided with that of a Russian national-liberal Cadet, Mr. A Kulischer[19] (*Rech*, No. 102, 15 April 1916), who also labelled the rebellion "the Dublin putsch".

It is to be hoped that, in accordance with the adage, "it's an ill wind that blows nobody any good", many comrades, who were not aware of the morass they were sinking into by repudiating 'self-determination' and by treating the national movements of small nations with disdain, will have their eyes opened by the 'accidental' coincidence of opinion held by a social-democrat and a representative of the imperialist bourgeoisie!!

The term 'putsch', in its scientific sense, may be employed only when the attempt at insurrection has revealed nothing but a circle of conspirators or stupid maniacs, and has aroused no sympathy among the masses. The centuries-old Irish national movement, having passed through various stages and combinations of class interest, manifested itself, in particular, in a mass Irish National Congress in America (*Vorwärts*,[20] 20 March 1916) which called for Irish independence; it also manifested itself in street fighting conducted by a section of the urban petty bourgeoisie *and a section*

---

19 Alexander Kulischer was a lawyer and Cadet.
20 *Vorwärts* (*Forwards*) was the central organ of the German Social-Democratic Party, published daily in Berlin from 1891 to 1933.

of the workers after a long period of mass agitation, demonstrations, suppression of newspapers, etc. Whoever calls *such* a rebellion a "putsch" is either a hardened reactionary, or a doctrinaire hopelessly incapable of envisaging a social revolution as a living phenomenon.

To imagine that social revolution is *conceivable* without revolts by small nations in the colonies and in Europe, without revolutionary outbursts by a section of the petty bourgeoisie *with all its prejudices*, without a movement of the politically non-conscious proletarian and semi-proletarian masses against oppression by the landowners, the church, and the monarchy, against national oppression, etc. – to imagine all this is to *repudiate social revolution*. So one army lines up in one place and says, 'We are for socialism', and another, somewhere else and says, 'We are for imperialism', and that will be a social revolution! Only those who hold such a ridiculously pedantic view could vilify the Irish rebellion by calling it a "putsch".

Whoever expects a 'pure' social revolution will *never* live to see it. Such a person pays lip-service to revolution without understanding what revolution is.

The Russian Revolution of 1905 was a bourgeois-democratic revolution. It consisted of a series of battles in which *all* the discontented classes, groups and elements of the population participated. Among these there were masses imbued with the crudest prejudices, with the vaguest and most fantastic aims of struggle; there were small groups which accepted Japanese money, there were speculators and adventurers, etc. But *objectively*, the mass movement was breaking the back of tsarism and paving the way for democracy; for this reason the class-conscious workers led it.

The socialist revolution in Europe *cannot be* anything other than an outburst of mass struggle on the part of all and sundry oppressed and discontented elements. Inevitably, sections of the petty bourgeoisie and of the backward workers will participate in it – without such participation, *mass* struggle is *impossible*, without it *no* revolution is possible – and just as inevitably will they bring into the movement their prejudices, their reactionary fantasies, their weaknesses and errors. But *objectively* they will attack *capital*, and the class-conscious vanguard of the revolution, the advanced proletariat, expressing this objective truth of a variegated and discordant, motley and outwardly fragmented, mass struggle, will be able to unite and direct it, capture power, seize the banks, expropriate the trusts which all hate (though for different reasons!), and introduce other dictatorial measures which in their totality will amount to the overthrow of the bourgeoisie and the victory of socialism, which, however, will by no means immediately 'purge' itself of petty-bourgeois slag.

Social-Democracy, we read in the Polish theses (I, 4):

> ... must utilise the struggle of the young colonial bourgeoisie against European imperialism *in order to sharpen the revolutionary crisis in Europe*. (Authors' italics. – *Lenin*)

Is it not clear that it is least of all permissible to contrast Europe to the colonies in *this* respect? The struggle of the oppressed nations *in Europe*, a struggle capable of going all the way to insurrection and street fighting, capable of breaking down the iron discipline of the army and martial law, will "sharpen the revolutionary crisis in Europe" to an infinitely greater degree than a much more developed rebellion in a remote colony. A blow delivered against the power of the English imperialist bourgeoisie by a rebellion in Ireland is a hundred times more significant politically than a blow of equal force delivered in Asia or in Africa.

The French chauvinist press recently reported the publication in Belgium of the eightieth issue of an illegal journal, *Free Belgium*.[21] Of course, the chauvinist press of France very often lies, but this piece of news seems to be true. Whereas chauvinist and Kautskyite German Social-Democracy has failed to establish a free press for itself during the two years of war, and has meekly borne the yoke of military censorship (only the Left Radical elements, to their credit be it said, have published pamphlets and manifestos, in spite of the censorship) – an oppressed civilised nation has reacted to a military oppression unparalleled in ferocity by establishing an organ

---

21 *Libre Belgique* (*Free Belgium*) was an illegal journal of the Belgian Labour Party, Brussels (1915-18).

of revolutionary protest! The dialectics of history are such that small nations, powerless as an *independent* factor in the struggle against imperialism, play a part as one of the ferments, one of the bacilli, which help the *real* anti-imperialist force, the socialist proletariat, to make its appearance on the scene.

The general staffs in the current war are doing their utmost to utilise any national and revolutionary movement in the enemy camp: the Germans utilise the Irish rebellion, the French – the Czech movement, etc. They are acting quite correctly from their own point of view. A serious war would not be treated seriously if advantage were not taken of the enemy's slightest weakness and if every opportunity that presented itself were not seized upon, the more so since it is impossible to know beforehand at what moment, where, and with what force some powder magazine will 'explode'. We would be very poor revolutionaries if, in the proletariat's great war of liberation for socialism, we did not know how to utilise *every* popular movement against every single disaster imperialism brings in order to intensify and extend the crisis. If we were, on the one hand, to repeat in a thousand keys the declaration that we are 'opposed' to all national oppression and, on the other, to describe the heroic revolt of the most mobile and enlightened section of certain classes in an oppressed nation against its oppressors as a 'putsch', we should be sinking to the same level of stupidity as the Kautskyites.

It is the misfortune of the Irish that they rose prematurely, before the European revolt of the proletariat had *had time* to mature. Capitalism is not so harmoniously built that the various sources of rebellion can immediately merge of their own accord, without reverses and defeats. On the other hand, the very fact that revolts do break out at different times, in different places, and are of different kinds, guarantees wide scope and depth to the general movement; but it is only in premature, individual, sporadic and therefore unsuccessful revolutionary movements that the masses gain experience, acquire knowledge, gather strength, and get to know their real leaders: the socialist proletarians, and in this way prepare for the general onslaught, just as certain strikes, demonstrations, local and national, mutinies in the army, outbreaks among the peasantry etc., prepared the way for the general onslaught in 1905.

Conclusion

Contrary to the erroneous assertions of the Polish social-democrats, the demand for the self-determination of nations has played no less a role in our party agitation than, for example, the arming of the people, the separation of the church from the state, the election of civil servants by the people and other points the philistines have called 'utopian'. On the contrary, the strengthening of the national movements after 1905 naturally prompted more vigorous agitation by our party, including a number of articles in 1912-13,[22] and the resolution of our party in 1913 giving a precise 'anti-Kautskian' definition (i.e. one that does not tolerate purely verbal 'recognition') of the content of the point.

It will not do to overlook a fact which was revealed at that early date: opportunists of various nationalities, the Ukrainian Yurkevich, the Bundist Liebmann, Semkovsky, the Russian myrmidon of Potresov and co., all spoke *in favour* of Rosa Luxemburg's arguments *against* self-determination! What for Rosa Luxemburg, the Polish social-democrat, had been merely an incorrect theoretical generalisation of the *specific* conditions of the movement in Poland, became *objective* opportunist support for Great-Russian imperialism when actually applied to more extensive circumstances, to conditions obtaining in a big state instead of a small one, when applied on an international scale instead of the narrow Polish scale. The history of *trends* in political thought (as distinct from the views of individuals) has proved the correctness of our programme.

Outspoken social-imperialists, such as Lensch still rail both against self-determination and the renunciation of annexations. As for the Kautskyites, they hypocritically recognise self-determination – Trotsky and Martov are going the same way here in Russia. *Both of them*, like Kautsky, say they favour self-determination. What

---

22　See Lenin, 'Resolution on the National Question', in this volume, p. 221.

happens in practice? Take Trotsky's articles 'The Nation and the Economy' in *Nashe Slovo*, and you will find his usual eclecticism: on the one hand, the economy unites nations and, on the other, national oppression divides them. The conclusion? The conclusion is that the prevailing hypocrisy remains unexposed, agitation is dull and does not touch upon what is most important, basic, significant and closely connected with practice – one's attitude to the nation that is oppressed by 'one's own' nation. Martov and other secretaries abroad simply preferred to forgot – a profitable lapse of memory! – the struggle of their colleague and fellow-member Semkovsky against self-determination. In the legal press of the Gvozdevites (*Nash Golos*)[23] Martov spoke *in favour* of self-determination, pointing out the indisputable truth that during the imperialist war it does not *yet* imply participation etc., but evading the main thing – he also evades it in the illegal, free press! – which is that *even in peace time* Russia set a world record for the oppression of nations with an imperialism that is much more crude, medieval, economically backward and militarily bureaucratic. The Russian social-democrat who 'recognises' the self-determination of nations more or less as it is recognised by Messrs. Plekhanov, Potresov and co., that is, without bothering to fight for the freedom of secession for nations oppressed by tsarism, is *in fact* an imperialist and a lackey of tsarism.

No matter what the subjective 'good' intentions of Trotsky and Martov may be, their evasiveness objectively supports Russian social-imperialism. The epoch of imperialism has turned all the 'great' powers into the oppressors of a number of nations, and the development of imperialism will inevitably lead to a more definite division of trends in this question in international Social-Democracy as well.

---

23 *Nash Golos* (*Our Voice*) was a Menshevik social-chauvinist newspaper.

*Part 2:
Lenin, the Bund and
'Cultural-National'
Autonomy*

Does the Jewish Proletariat Need an 'Independent Political Party'?

Published 15 February 1903

Editor's note: The General Jewish Workers' Union of Lithuania, Poland, and Russia, known as the Bund, was a secular Jewish socialist party initially formed in the Russian Empire and active between 1897 and 1920.

It was among the largest constituent groups to found the Russian Social-Democratic Labour Party in 1898, to which it joined with autonomous structures. Lenin wrote this polemic in the debate over the Bund's demand for a new 'federated' relationship that preceded the RSDLP's 1903 Congress. At that congress, federation was rejected by both Menshevik and Bolshevik delegates. In response, the Bund withdrew from the RSDLP.

However, events would change things, and under the influence of the 1905 Revolution – and the mass pogroms that accompanied it – the Bund would rejoin the party in 1906, where it would remain. In 1912's formal split of the RSDLP, the Bund allied with the Mensheviks, who had come to support federation. In 1917, the Bund opposed the October Revolution. However, the revolution, civil war, and (again) mass pogroms had a powerful impact on the ranks of the Bund, finally leading to a majority within it agreeing to join the Communist Party in 1920-21.

* * *

No. 105 of *Posledniye Izvestia*[1] (15 January 1903), published by the Foreign Committee of the General Jewish Workers' Union of Lithuania, Poland, and Russia, carries a brief article entitled 'Concerning a Certain Manifesto' (viz. the manifesto issued by the Ekaterinoslav Committee of the Russian Social-Democratic Labour Party) containing the following statement, which is as extraordinary as it is significant and indeed "fraught with consequences":

> The Jewish proletariat has formed itself [sic!] into an independent [sic!] political party, the Bund.

We did not know this before. This is something new.

Hitherto the Bund has been a constituent part of the Russian Social-Democratic Labour Party, and in No. 106 of *Posledniye Izvestia* we still (still!) find a statement of the Central Committee of the Bund, bearing the heading "Russian Social-Democratic Labour Party". It is true that at its latest congress, the Fourth, the Bund decided to change its name (without stipulating that it would like to hear the Russian comrades' opinion on the name a section of the Russian Social-Democratic Labour Party should bear) and to 'introduce' new *federal* relations into the rules of the Russian party. The Bund's Foreign Committee has even 'introduced' these relations, if that word can be used to describe the fact that it has withdrawn from the Union of Russian Social-Democrats Abroad and has concluded a federal agreement with the latter.

On the other hand, when *Iskra* polemicised with the decisions of the Bund's Fourth Congress, the Bund itself stated very definitely that it only wanted to *secure the acceptance of its wishes and decisions* by the RSDLP; in other words, it flatly and categorically acknowledged that until the RSDLP adopted new rules and settled new forms of its attitude towards the Bund, the latter would remain a section of the RSDLP.

But now, suddenly, we are told that the Jewish proletariat has already *formed itself* into an *independent* political party! We repeat – this is something new.

---

1 *Posledniye Izvestia* (*Latest News*) was a periodical bulletin issued by the Foreign Committee of the Bund from 1901 to 1906.

Equally new is the furious and foolish onslaught of the Bund's Foreign Committee upon the Ekaterinoslav Committee. We have at last (*though unfortunately after much delay*) received a copy of this manifesto, and we do not hesitate to say that in attacking a manifesto *like this* the Bund has *undoubtedly* taken a serious political step.[2] This step fully accords with the Bund's proclamation as an independent political party and throws much light on the physiognomy and behaviour of this new party.

We regret that lack of space prevents us from reprinting the Ekaterinoslav manifesto in full (it would take up about two columns in *Iskra*),[3] and shall confine ourselves to remarking that this admirable manifesto excellently explains to the Jewish workers of the *city of Ekaterinoslav* (we shall presently explain why we have emphasised these words) the social-democratic attitude towards Zionism and antisemitism. Moreover, the manifesto treats the sentiments, moods, and desires of the Jewish workers so considerately, with such comradely consideration, that it specially refers to and emphasises the necessity of fighting under the banner of the RSDLP:

> ... *even for the preservation and further development of your* [the manifesto addresses the Jewish workers] *national culture,* [...] *even from the standpoint of purely national interests.* [Underlined and italicised in the manifesto itself. – *Lenin*]

Nevertheless, the Bund's Foreign Committee (we almost said the new party's Central Committee) has fallen upon the manifesto for *making no mention of the Bund.* That is the manifesto's only crime, but one that is terrible and unpardonable. It is for this that the Ekaterinoslav Committee is accused of lacking in "political sense". The Ekaterinoslav comrades are chastised for not "yet having digested the idea of the necessity for a separate organisation [a profound and significant idea!] of the forces [!!!] of the Jewish proletariat",

---

2 That is, of course, if the Bund's Foreign Committee expresses the views of the Bund as a whole on this question. – *Lenin*

3 We intend to reprint in full the manifesto and the attack of the Bund's Foreign Committee in a pamphlet which we are preparing for the press. – *Lenin*

for "still harbouring the absurd hope of somehow getting rid of it" (the Bund), for spreading the "no less dangerous fable" (no less dangerous than the Zionist fable) that antisemitism is connected with the bourgeois strata and with their interests, and not with those of the working class. That is why the Ekaterinoslav Committee is advised to "abandon the harmful habit of keeping silent about the independent Jewish working-class movement" and to "reconcile itself to the fact that the Bund exists."

Now, let us consider whether the Ekaterinoslav Committee is actually guilty of a crime, and whether it really should have mentioned the Bund without fail. Both questions can be answered only in the negative, for the simple reason that the manifesto is not addressed to the "Jewish workers" in general (as the Bund's Foreign Committee quite wrongly stated), but to "the Jewish workers of *the city of Ekaterinoslav*" (the Bund's Foreign Committee forgot to quote these last words!). *The Bund has no organisation* in Ekaterinoslav. (And, in general, regarding the south of Russia, the Fourth Congress of the Bund passed a resolution *not to organise separate committees of the Bund* in cities where the Jewish organisations are included in the party committees and where their needs can be fully satisfied without separation from the committees.) Since the Jewish workers in Ekaterinoslav are not organised in a separate committee, it follows that their movement (inseparably from the entire working-class movement in that area) is wholly guided by the Ekaterinoslav Committee, which subordinates them *directly* to the RSDLP, which *must* call upon them to work *for the whole party*, and not for its individual sections. It is clear that under these circumstances the Ekaterinoslav Committee was not obliged to mention the Bund; on the contrary, if it had presumed to advocate "the necessity for a separate organisation of the forces [it would rather and more probably have been an organisation of *impotence*][4] of the

---

4 It is this task of "organising impotence" that the Bund serves when, for example, it uses such a phrase as "our comrades of the 'Christian working-class organisation.'" The phrase is as preposterous as is the whole attack on the Ekaterinoslav Committee. We have no knowledge of any "Christian" working-class organisations. Organisations belonging to the RSDLP have never distinguished their members according to religion, never asked them about their

Jewish proletariat" (which is what the Bundists want), it would have made a very grave error and committed a direct breach, not only of the party rules, but of the unity of the proletarian class struggle.

Further, the Ekaterinoslav Committee is accused of lack of 'orientation' in the question of antisemitism. The Bund's Foreign Committee betrays truly infantile views on important social movements. The Ekaterinoslav Committee speaks of the *international* antisemitic movement of the *last decades* and remarks that:

> From Germany this movement spread to other countries and everywhere found adherents among the bourgeois, and not among the working-class sections of the population.

"This is a no less dangerous fable" (than the Zionist fables), cries the thoroughly aroused Bund's Foreign Committee. Antisemitism "has struck roots in the mass of the workers", and to prove this the 'well-oriented' Bund cites two facts: (1) workers' participation in a pogrom in Częstochowa and (2) the behaviour of twelve (*twelve!*) Christian workers in Zhitomir, who scabbed on the strikers and threatened to "kill off all the Yids". Very weighty proofs indeed, especially the latter! The editors of *Posledniye Izvestia* are so accustomed to dealing with big strikes involving five or ten workers that the behaviour of twelve ignorant Zhitomir workers is dragged out as evidence of the link between international antisemitism and one "section" or another "of the population". This is, indeed, magnificent! If, instead of flying into a foolish and comical rage at the Ekaterinoslav Committee, the Bundists had pondered a bit over this question and had consulted, let us say, Kautsky's pamphlet on the social revolution,[5] a Yiddish edition of which they themselves published recently, they would have understood the link that *undoubtedly* exists between antisemitism and the interests of the bourgeois, and not of the working-class sections of the population. If they had given it a little more thought they might have realised that the social character of antisemitism

---

religion and never will — even when the Bund will in actual fact "have formed itself into an independent political party". – *Lenin*

5　The reference is to Karl Kautsky's 1902 pamphlet, *The Social Revolution*.

today is not changed by the fact that dozens or even hundreds of unorganised workers, nine-tenths of whom are still quite ignorant, take part in a pogrom.

The Ekaterinoslav Committee has risen up (and rightly so) against the Zionist fable about antisemitism being eternal; by making its angry comment the Bund has only confused the issue and planted in the minds of the Jewish workers ideas which tend to *blunt* their class-consciousness.

From the viewpoint of the struggle for political liberty and for socialism being waged by the whole working class of Russia, the Bund's attack on the Ekaterinoslav Committee is the height of folly. From the viewpoint of the Bund as "an independent political party", this attack becomes understandable: don't dare anywhere organise 'Jewish' workers together with, and inseparably from, 'Christian' workers! If you would address the Jewish workers in the name of the Russian Social-Democratic Labour Party or its committees, don't dare do so directly, over our heads, ignoring the Bund or making no mention of it.

And this profoundly regrettable fact is not accidental. Having once demanded 'federation' instead of autonomy in matters concerning the Jewish proletariat, you were *compelled* to proclaim the Bund an "independent political party" in order to carry out this principle of federation *at all costs*. However, your declaring the Bund an independent political party is just that reduction to an absurdity of your fundamental error in the national question which will inescapably and inevitably be the starting-point of a change in the views of the Jewish proletariat and of the Jewish social-democrats in general. 'Autonomy' under the rules adopted in 1898 provides the Jewish working-class movement with all it needs: propaganda and agitation in Yiddish, its own literature and congresses, the right to advance separate demands to supplement a single general social-democratic programme and to satisfy local needs and requirements arising out of the special features of Jewish life. In everything else there must be complete fusion with the Russian proletariat, in the interests of the struggle waged by the entire proletariat of Russia.

As for the fear of being 'steam-rollered' in the event of such fusion, the very nature of the case makes it groundless, since it is autonomy that is a guarantee against all 'steam-rollering' in matters pertaining specifically to the *Jewish* movement, while in matters pertaining to the struggle against the autocracy, the struggle against the bourgeoisie of Russia as a whole, we must act as a single and centralised militant organisation, have behind us the whole of the proletariat, without distinction of language or nationality, a proletariat whose unity is cemented by the continual joint solution of problems of theory and practice, of tactics and organisation; and we must not set up organisations that would march separately, each along its own track; we must not weaken the force of our offensive by breaking up into numerous independent political parties; we must not introduce estrangement and isolation and then have to heal an artificially implanted disease with the aid of these notorious 'federation' plasters.

Second Congress of the RSDLP

17 July – 10 August 1903

Resolution Adopted On the Place of the Bund in the Party

Considering:

— that the closest unity of the Jewish proletariat with the proletariat of those races amidst which it lives is absolutely necessary in the interests of its struggle for political and economic liberation;

— that only such very close unity guarantees success for the social-democrats in the struggle against all forms of chauvinism and antisemitism; and

— that such unity in no way rules out independence for the Jewish workers' movement in all matters concerned with special tasks of agitation among the Jewish population which arise from differences in language and living conditions;

The Second Congress of the RSDLP expresses its profound conviction that restructuring the organisational relations between the Jewish proletariat and the Russian proletariat on federal lines would constitute a substantial obstacle in the way of fuller organisational rapprochement between conscious proletarians of different races, and would inevitably do enormous harm to the interests of the proletariat generally and of the Jewish proletariat of Russia in particular; and, therefore, emphatically rejecting as absolutely inadmissible in principle any possibility of federal relations between the RSDLP and the Bund, as a component section of the party, the Congress resolves that the Bund occupies, within the united RSDLP, the position of an autonomous component, the limits to its autonomy to be defined when the general party rules are elaborated. In view of the above, the Congress, regarding the 'rules' proposed by the Bund delegates as a draft for a section of the general party rules, defers discussion of this draft until Point 6 of the agenda, and proceeds to next business.

* * *

Draft Resolution on the Withdrawal of the Bund

Not Submitted to the Congress

The Congress considers the refusal of the Bund delegates to submit to the decision adopted by the majority of the Congress as the Bund's withdrawal from the RSDLP.

The Congress deeply regrets this step, which, it is convinced, is a major political mistake on the part of the leaders of the 'Jewish Workers' Union', a mistake which must inevitably injure the interests of the Jewish proletariat and working-class movement. The Congress considers that the arguments cited by the Bund delegates in justification of their step amount in practice to entirely unfounded apprehensions and suspicion that the social-democratic convictions of the Russian social-democrats are insincere and inconsistent; in respect of theory they are the result of the unfortunate penetration of nationalism into the social-democratic movement of the Bund.

The Congress voices its desire for, and firm conviction of, the need for complete and closest unity of the Jewish and Russian working-class movement in Russia, unity not only in principle but also in organisation, and resolves to take all measures in order to acquaint the Jewish proletariat in detail both with this resolution of the Congress and with the general attitude of the Russian social-democrats towards every national movement.

* * *

First Speech on the Agenda of the Congress

18 July 1903

I should like to make a remark. It would be wrong, it is claimed, to make the question of the Bund the first item on the agenda, since the reports should be the first item, the programme the second, and the Bund the third. The arguments in favour of this order will not stand criticism. They amount to the presumption that the party as a whole has not yet reached agreement on the programme, and that it is possible that precisely on this question we may part company. I am surprised at that.

It is true that we have not yet adopted a programme, but the surmise that a rupture may take place over the programme is conjectural in the highest degree. No such tendencies have been discernible in the party, at least as far as its literature is concerned, which of late has given the fullest reflection of party opinion. There are both formal and moral reasons for making the question of the Bund the first item on the agenda. Formally, we stand by the Manifesto of 1898, but the Bund has expressed a desire for a radical change in our party's organisation. Morally, many other organisations have expressed their disagreement with the Bund over this question; that has caused sharp differences leading even to polemics. The Congress therefore cannot begin harmonious work until these differences have been removed. As to the delegates' reports, it is possible that they may not be heard *in pleno* [in full] at all. I therefore second the agenda in the order approved by the Organising Committee.

* * *

Speech on the Place of the Bund in the RSDLP

20 July 1903

I shall first deal with Hofman's[1] speech and his expression "a compact majority". Comrade Hofman uses these words by way of reproach. In my opinion we should be proud, not ashamed, of the fact that there is a compact majority at the Congress. And we shall be prouder still if our whole party proves to be a compact, a highly compact, 90 per cent, majority. (*Applause.*) The majority were right in making the position of the Bund in the party the first item on the agenda, and the Bundists at once proved this by submitting their so-called Rules, but in essence proposing *federation*. Once there are members in the party who propose federation and others who reject it, there could be no other course open but to make the question of the Bund the first item on the agenda. It is no use forcing your favours on anybody, and the internal affairs of the party cannot be discussed until we have firmly and uncompromisingly settled whether or not we want to march together.

The crux of the issue has not always been presented quite correctly in the debate. The point of the matter is that, in the opinion of many party members, federation is *harmful* and runs counter to the principles of social-democracy as applied to existing Russian conditions. Federation is harmful because it *sanctions* segregation and alienation, elevates them to a principle, to a law. Complete alienation does indeed prevail among us, and we ought not to sanction it, or cover it with a fig leaf, but combat it and resolutely acknowledge and proclaim the necessity of firmly and unswervingly advancing towards the *closest* unity. That is why we reject federation in principle, *in limine*[2] (as the Latin phrase has it); that is why we reject *all* obligatory partitions that serve to divide us. As it is, there will always be different groupings in the party, groupings of comrades who do not think quite alike on questions of programme,

---

1 Hofman was the pseudonym of Bundist V Kosovsky.
2 "At the beginning", before anything else.

tactics or organisation; but let there be only *one* division into groups throughout the party, that is, let all like-minded members join in a single group, instead of groups first being formed in *one section* of the party, separately from the groups in another section of the party, and then having a union not of groups holding different views or different shades of opinion, but of sections of the party, each containing different groups. I repeat, we recognise no *obligatory* partitions, and that is why we reject federation in principle.

I shall now pass to the question of autonomy. Comrade Liber[3] has said that federation means centralism, while autonomy means decentralism. Can it be that Comrade Liber takes the Congress members for six-year-old children, who may be regaled with such sophistries? Is it not clear that centralism demands the *absence* of all partitions between the central body and even the most remote and out-of-the-way sections of the party? Our central body will be given the absolute right to communicate directly with every party member. The Bundists would only laugh if someone would propose to them a form of "centralism" *within* the Bund, under which its Central Committee could not communicate with all the Kovno groups and comrades *otherwise than* through the Kovno Committee. Incidentally, as regards the committees, Comrade Liber has exclaimed with feeling: "What is the good of talking about the Bund's autonomy if it is to be an organisation subordinated to one central body? After all, you would not grant autonomy to some Tula Committee!" You are mistaken, Comrade Liber; we will certainly and most decidedly grant autonomy to "some" Tula Committee, too, autonomy in the sense of freedom from petty interference by the central body, although the duty of obeying that body will, of course, remain. I have taken the words "petty interference" from the Bund leaflet, 'Autonomy or Federation?' The Bund has advanced this freedom from "petty interference" as a *condition*, as a *demand* to the party. The mere fact that it advances such ridiculous demands shows how muddled the Bund is on the question at issue. Does

---

3   Mikhail Liber was a leader of the Bund and a leading Menshevik.

the Bund really think that the party would tolerate the existence of a central body that indulged in "*petty*" interference in the affairs of *any* party organisation or group? Is this not, in effect, precisely that "organised distrust" which has already been mentioned at this Congress? Such distrust runs through all the proposals and arguments of the Bundists. Is it not, in fact, the *duty* of our entire party to fight, for example, for *full* equality and even for *recognition* of the right of nations to self-determination? Consequently, if any section of our party failed in this duty, it would unquestionably be liable to condemnation by virtue of our principles; it would unquestionably be liable to *correction* on the part of the central institutions of the party. And if the neglect of that duty were conscious and deliberate, despite full opportunity to carry out that duty, then that would be *treachery*.

Further, Comrade Liber has asked us in moving tones *how it can be proved* that autonomy is able to guarantee to the Jewish workers' movement that independence which is absolutely essential to it. A strange question, indeed! How can it be proved that one of the several paths suggested is the right one? The only way is to try it and see. My reply to Comrade Liber's question is: *March with us*, and we undertake to prove to you in practice that all legitimate demands for independence are gratified in full.

When I hear disputes about the place of the Bund, I always recollect the British miners. They are excellently organised, better than any other workers. And *because of that* they want to thwart the general demand for an eight-hour day put forward by all proletarians.[4] These miners have the same narrow idea of the unity of the proletariat as our Bundists. Let the sad example of the miners serve as a warning to our comrades of the Bund.

---

4   This refers to the Northumberland and Durham miners who, in the 1880s, secured a seven-hour working day for skilled underground workers – through a deal with the coal-owners – but later for a number of years opposed the legal enactment of an eight-hour working day for all workers in Britain.

The Position of the Bund in the Party

Published 22 October 1903

Under this title the Bund has published a translation of an article from No. 34 of the *Arbeiterstimme*.[1] This article, accompanying the decisions of the Fifth Bund Congress, represents as it were an official commentary on those decisions. It attempts to give a systematic exposition of all the arguments which lead to the conclusion that the Bund "must be a federated component of the party". It will be interesting to examine these arguments.

The author begins by stating that the most burning question facing the Russian social-democratic movement is the question of unity. On what basis can it be effected? The Manifesto of 1898[2] took the principle of autonomy as the basis. The author examines this principle and finds it to be logically false and inherently contradictory. If by questions which specifically concern the Jewish proletariat are meant only such as relate to methods of agitation (with reference to the specific language, mentality and culture of

---

1 The *Arbeiterstimme* (*Worker's Voice*) was the central organ of the Bund; it appeared from 1897 to 1905.

2 The reference is to the decision of the First Congress of the RSDLP that the Bund "is affiliated to the party as an autonomous organisation independent only in regard to questions specifically concerning the Jewish proletariat".

the Jews), that will be technical (?) autonomy. But such autonomy will mean the destruction of all independence, for it is an autonomy enjoyed by every party committee, and to put the Bund on a par with the committees will be a denial of autonomy. If, on the other hand, autonomy is understood to mean autonomy in some questions of the programme, it is unreasonable to deprive the Bund of all independence in the other questions of the programme; and independence in questions of programme necessarily involves representation of the Bund, as such, on the central bodies of the party – that is, not autonomy, but federation. A sound basis for the position of the Bund in the party must be sought in the history of the Jewish revolutionary movement in Russia, and what that history shows is that all organisations active among the Jewish workers joined to form a single union – the Bund – and that its activities spread from Lithuania to Poland and then to the South of Russia. Consequently, history broke down all regional barriers and brought forward the Bund as the sole representative of the Jewish proletariat. And there you have a principle which is not the fruit of an idle brain (?) but follows from the whole history of the Jewish working-class movement: the Bund is the sole representative of the interests of the Jewish proletariat. And, naturally, the organisation of the proletariat of a whole nationality can enter the party only if the latter has a federal structure: the Jewish proletariat is not only part of the world family of proletarians, but also part of the Jewish nation, which occupies a special position among the nations. Lastly, it is federation that denotes close unity between the component elements of the party, for its chief feature is direct participation by each of them in party affairs, and they all feel they have equal rights. Under autonomy, on the other hand, the components of the party have no rights, and there is indifference to its common affairs, and mutual distrust, friction and conflict.

Such is the author's line of argument, which we have presented almost entirely in his own words. It boils down to three things: considerations of a general nature as to the inherent contradictoriness of autonomy and its unsuitability from the standpoint of close unity between the components of the party; lessons from history, which has made the Bund the sole representative of the Jewish proletariat; and, lastly, the affirmation that the Jewish proletariat is the proletariat of a whole nationality, a nationality occupying a special position. Thus the author endeavours to build his case on general principles of organisation, on the lessons of history, and on the idea of nationality. He tries – we must give him his due – to examine the matter from all angles. And for that very reason his statement of the case brings out so saliently the attitude of the Bund on this question which is of deep concern to all of us.

Under federation, we are told, the components of the party have equal rights and share directly in its common affairs; under autonomy they have no rights, and as such do not share in the general life of the party. This argument belongs entirely to the realm of obvious fallacies; it is as like as two peas to those arguments which mathematicians call mathematical sophistries, and which prove – quite logically, at first glance – that twice two are five, that the part is greater than the whole, and so on. There are collections of such mathematical sophistries, and they are of some value to school children. But it is even embarrassing to have to explain to people who claim to be the sole representatives of the Jewish proletariat so elementary a sophistry as the attribution of different meanings to the term "component of the party" in two parts of one and the same argument. When they speak of federation, they mean by a component of the party a sum-total of organisations in different localities; but when they speak of autonomy, they mean by it each local organisation separately. Put these supposedly identical concepts side by side in the same syllogism, and you will arrive inevitably at the conclusion that twice two are five. And if the Bundists are still unclear as to the nature of their sophistry, let them consult their own maximum rules and they will see that it is under federation that the local organisations communicate with the party centre *in*directly, and under autonomy – directly. No, our federalists would do better not to talk about "close unity"! By trying to disprove that federation means the *isolation*, and autonomy the *fusion* of the different components of the party, they only provoke hilarity.

Hardly more successful is the attempt to prove the 'logical falsity' of autonomy by dividing the latter into programme autonomy and technical autonomy. The division itself is utterly absurd. Why should the specific methods of agitation among Jewish workers be classed under technical questions? What has technique to do with it, when it is a matter of peculiarities of language, mentality, conditions of life? How can you talk of independence in questions of programme in connection, for example, with the demand for civil equality for the Jews? The social-democratic programme only sets forth the basic demands, common to the entire proletariat, irrespective of occupational, local, national, or racial distinctions.

The effect of these distinctions is that one and the same demand for complete equality of citizens before the law gives rise to agitation against one form of inequality in one locality and against another form of inequality in another locality or in relation to other groups of the proletariat, and so on. One and the same point in the programme will be applied differently depending on differences in conditions of life, differences of culture, differences in the relation of social forces in different parts of the country, and so forth. Agitation on behalf of one and the same demand in the programme will be carried on in different ways and in different languages taking into account all these differences.

Consequently, autonomy in questions specifically concerning the proletariat of a given race, nation, or district implies that it is left to the discretion of the organisation concerned to determine the specific demands to be advanced in pursuance of the common programme, and the methods of agitation to be employed. The party as a whole, its central institutions, lay down the common fundamental principles of programme and tactics; as to the different methods of carrying out these principles in practice and agitating for them, they are laid down by the various party organisations subordinate to the centre, depending on local, racial, national, cultural, and other differences.

Is there anything unclear about this conception of autonomy? And is it not the sheerest scholasticism to make a division into programme autonomy and technical autonomy?

Just see how the concept autonomy is 'logically analysed' in the pamphlet we are examining:

> From the total body of questions with which the social-democrats have to deal, [the pamphlet says in connection with the autonomy principle taken as the basis in the 1898 Manifesto] there are singled out [*sic!!!*] some questions, which, it is recognised, specifically concern the Jewish proletariat [...] Where the realm of general questions begins, the autonomy of the Bund ends [...] This gives rise to a duality in the position of the Bund in the party: in specific questions it acts as the Bund [...] in general questions it loses its distinctive character and is put on a par with an ordinary committee of the party...

The social-democratic programme demands complete equality of all citizens before the law. *In pursuance* of that programme the Jewish worker in Vilna puts forward one specific demand, and the Bashkir worker in Ufa an entirely different specific demand. Does that mean that "from the total body of questions" "*some are singled out*"? If the general demand for equality is embodied in a number of specific demands for the abolition of specific forms of inequality, is that a *singling out* of the specific from the general questions?

The specific demands are not singled out from the general demands of the programme, but are advanced in pursuance of them. What is singled out is what specifically concerns the Jew in Vilna as distinct from what specifically concerns the Bashkir in Ufa. The generalisation of their demands, the representation of their *common class interests* (and not of their specific occupational, racial, local, national, or other interests) is the affair of the whole party, of the party centre. That would surely seem clear enough! The reason the Bundists have muddled it is that, instead of logical analysis, they have again and again given us specimens of logical fallacies. They have entirely failed to grasp the relation between the social-democrats' general and specific demands. They imagine that "from the total body of questions with which the social-democrats have to deal, some questions are singled out", when actually *every* question dealt with in our programme is a generalisation of a number of specific questions and demands; *every* point in the programme is common to the *entire* proletariat, while at the same time it is subdivided into specific questions depending on the proletarians' different occupations, their different conditions of life, differences of language, and so on and so forth.

The Bundists are disturbed by the contradictoriness and duality of the position of the Bund, consisting, don't you see, in the fact that in specific questions it acts as the Bund, while in general questions it loses its distinctive character. A little reflection would show them that such a "duality" exists in the position of *absolutely every* social-democratic worker, who in specific questions acts as a worker in a particular trade, a member of a particular nation, an inhabitant of a particular locality, while in general questions he "loses his distinctive character" and is put on a par with every other social-democrat.

The autonomy of the Bund, under the rules of 1898, is of exactly the same nature as the autonomy of the Tula Committee; only the limits of this autonomy are somewhat different and somewhat wider in the former case than in the latter. And there is nothing but a crying logical fallacy in the following argument, by which the Bund tries to refute this conclusion: "If the Bund is allowed independence in some questions of the *programme*, on what grounds is it deprived of *all* independence in the other questions of the programme?"

This contrasting of specific and general questions as "some" and "*the others*" is an inimitable specimen of Bundist 'logical analysis'! These people simply cannot understand that it is like contrasting the different colours, tastes, and fragrances of particular apples to the *number* of 'other' apples. We make bold to inform you, gentlemen, that not only some, but every apple has its special taste, colour, and fragrance. Not only in "some" questions of the programme, *but in all without exception*, you are allowed independence, gentlemen, but only as far as concerns their application to the specific features of the Jewish proletariat. *"Mein teuerer Freund, ich rat' Euch drum zuerst Collegium logicum!"*[3]

The second argument of the Bundists is an appeal to history, which is supposed to have brought forward the Bund as the sole representative of the Jewish proletariat.

In the first place, this is not true. The author of the pamphlet himself says that:

> ... the work of other organisations [besides the Bund] in this direction [i.e. among the Jewish proletariat] either yielded no results at all, or results too insignificant to merit attention.

Hence, on his own admission, there was such work, and consequently the Bund *was not* the *sole* representative of the Jewish proletariat; as regards the results of this work, no one, of course, will rely on the Bund's opinion; and, lastly, it is a known fact that the Bund *interfered* with the work of other organisations among the Jewish proletariat (we have only to mention the well-known incident of its campaign against the Ekaterinoslav Party Committee for daring to issue a proclamation to the Jewish workers),[4] so that even if the results did indeed merit no attention, the Bund itself would be partly to blame.

Further, the measure of truth contained in the Bund's historical reference does not in the least prove the soundness of its arguments. The facts which did take place and which the Bund has in mind speak against it, not for it. These facts are that the Bund existed and developed – during the five years since the First Congress – quite separately and independently from the other organisations of the party. In general, the actual ties between all party organisations during this period were very weak, but the ties between the Bund and the rest of the party were not only far weaker than those between the other organisations, but they kept growing weaker all the time. That the Bund itself *weakened* these ties is directly proved by the history of our party's organisations

---

3　"My dear friend, I would advise you to begin with college logic!" Mephistopheles' to the Student in Goethe's *Faust*.

4　See Lenin, 'Does the Jewish Proletariat Need an 'Independent Political Party'?', 15 February 1903, in this volume, p. 183.

abroad. In 1898, the Bund members abroad belonged to the one common party organisation; but by 1903 they had left it to form a completely separate and independent organisation. The separateness and independence of the Bund is beyond question, as is also the fact that it has steadily become more pronounced.

What follows from this unquestionable fact? What follows in the opinion of the Bundists is that one must bow to this fact, slavishly submit to it, turn it into a principle, into the sole principle providing a sound basis for the position of the Bund, and legitimise this principle in the rules, which should recognise the Bund as the sole representative of the Jewish proletariat in the party. In our opinion, on the other hand, such a conclusion is the sheerest opportunism, 'tail-ism'[5] of the worst kind. The conclusion to be drawn from the five years of disunity is not that this disunity should be legitimised, but that an end should be put to it once and for all. And will anybody still venture to deny that it really was disunity? *All* component parts of the party developed separately and independently during this period – are we perhaps to deduce from this the "principle" of federation between Siberia, the Caucasus, the Urals, the South, and the rest?? The Bundists themselves say that, as regards organisational unity of its components, the party virtually did not exist – and how can what evolved when the party did not exist be taken as a pattern for the *restoration* of organisational unity? No, gentlemen, your reference to the history of the disunity that gave rise to isolation proves nothing whatever except that this isolation is abnormal. To deduce a "principle" of *organisation* from several years of *disorganisation* in the party is to act like those representatives of the historical school who, as Marx sarcastically observed, were prepared to defend the knout on the grounds that it was historical.

Hence, neither the 'logical analysis' of autonomy nor the appeals to history can provide even the shadow of a 'principle' justifying

---

5   "Tail-ism" – expression originally coined by Lenin to describe the Economists, who denied the leading role of the party and the importance of theory in the working-class movement; their position implied that the party should trail after the spontaneously developing movement, follow in the tail of events.

the isolation of the Bund. But the Bund's third argument, which invokes the idea of a Jewish nation, is undoubtedly of the nature of a principle. Unfortunately, however, this Zionist idea is absolutely false and essentially reactionary. "The Jews have ceased to be a nation, for a nation without a territory is unthinkable", says one of the most prominent of Marxist theoreticians, Karl Kautsky (see No. 42 of *Iskra* and the separate reprint from it 'The Kishinev Massacre and the Jewish Question', p. 3). And quite recently, examining the problem of nationalities in Austria, the same writer endeavoured to give a scientific definition of the concept nationality and established two principal criteria of a nationality: language and territory (*Neue Zeit*, 1903, No. 2). A French Jew, the radical Alfred Naquet, says practically the same thing, word for word, in his controversy with the antisemites and the Zionists.[6]

> If it pleased Bernard Lazare, [he writes of the well-known Zionist] to consider himself a citizen of a separate nation, that is his affair; but I declare that, although I was born a Jew... I do not recognise Jewish nationality... I belong to no other nation but the French... Are the Jews a nation? Although they were one in the remote past, my reply is a categorical *negative*. The concept 'nation' implies certain conditions which do not exist in this case. A nation must have a territory on which to develop, and, in our time at least, until a world confederation has extended this basis, a nation must have a common language. And the Jews no longer have either a territory or a common language... Like myself, Bernard Lazare probably did not know a word of Hebrew, and would have found it no easy matter, if Zionism had achieved its purpose, to make himself understood to his co-racials [*congénères*] from other parts of the world.

> German and French Jews are quite unlike Polish and Russian Jews. The characteristic features of the Jews include nothing that bears the imprint [*empreinte*] of nationality. If it were permissible to recognise the Jews as a nation, as Drumont does, it would be an artificial nation. The modern Jew

---

6   The quotations are from Alfred Naquet's article 'Drumont and Bernard Lazare', published on 24 September 1903, in the Paris *La Petite République*, at that time the organ of the French reformist socialists.

is a product of the unnatural selection to which his forebears were subjected for nearly eighteen centuries. (*La Petite République*, 24 September 1903.)

All that remains for the Bundists is to develop the theory of a separate Russian-Jewish nation, whose language is Yiddish and their territory the Pale of Settlement.[7]

Absolutely untenable scientifically,[8] the idea that the Jews form a separate nation is reactionary politically. Irrefutable practical proof of that is furnished by generally known facts of recent history and of present-day political realities. All over Europe, the decline of medievalism and the development of political liberty went hand in hand with the political emancipation of the Jews, their abandonment of Yiddish for the language of the people among whom they lived, and, in general, their undeniable progressive assimilation with the surrounding population. Are we again to revert to the exceptionalist theories and proclaim that Russia will be the one exception, although the Jewish emancipation movement is far broader and deeper-rooted here, thanks to the awakening of a heroic class-consciousness among the Jewish proletariat? Can we possibly attribute to chance the fact that it is the reactionary forces all over Europe, and especially in Russia, who *oppose* the assimilation of the Jews and try to perpetuate their isolation?

That is precisely what the Jewish problem *amounts to*: assimilation or isolation? – and the idea of a Jewish 'nationality' is definitely

---

7   The Pale of Settlement was the territory in tsarist Russia outside which Jewish people were not allowed to live.

8   Not only national, but even racial peculiarities are denied to the Jews by modern scientific investigators, who give prime prominence to the peculiarities of the *history* of the Jews. "Do the peculiarities of Jewry spring from its racial character?" Karl Kautsky asks, and replies that we do not even know with precision what race means.

> There is no need to bring in the concept race, which provides no real answer but only poses new problems. It is enough to trace the history of the Jews to ascertain the reasons for their characteristics.

> And such an expert in this history as Renan says: "The characteristic features of the Jews and their manner of life are far more a product of the social conditions [*nécessités sociales*] by which they have been influenced for centuries than a racial distinction [*phénomène de race*]." – *Lenin*

reactionary not only when expounded by its consistent advocates (the Zionists), but likewise on the lips of those who try to combine it with the ideas of Social-Democracy (the Bundists). The idea of a Jewish nationality runs counter to the interests of the Jewish proletariat, for it fosters among them, directly or indirectly, a spirit hostile to assimilation, the spirit of the 'ghetto'. Renan writes:

> When the National Assembly of 1791 decreed the emancipation of the Jews,[9] it was very little concerned with the question of race... It is the business of the nineteenth century to abolish all 'ghettos', and I cannot compliment those who seek to restore them. The Jewish race has rendered the world the greatest services. Assimilated with the various nations, harmoniously blended with the various national units, it will render no lesser services in the future than in the past.

And Karl Kautsky, in particular reference to the Russian Jews, expresses himself even more vigorously. Hostility towards non-native sections of the population can only be eliminated:

> ... when the non-native sections of the population cease to be alien and blend with the general mass of the population. *That is the only possible solution of the Jewish problem, and we should support everything that makes for the ending of Jewish isolation.*

Yet the Bund is resisting this only possible solution, for it is helping, not to end but to increase and legitimise Jewish isolation, by propagating the idea of a Jewish 'nation' and a plan of federating Jewish and non-Jewish proletarians. That is the basic mistake of 'Bundism', which consistent Jewish social-democrats must and will correct. This mistake drives the Bundists to actions unheard-of in the international social-democratic movement, such as stirring up distrust among Jewish towards non-Jewish proletarians, fostering suspicion of the latter and disseminating falsehoods about them. Here is proof, taken from this same pamphlet:

---

9 The National Constituent Assembly of the Kingdom of France was the parliament under the constitutional monarchy established after 1789. Before its dissolution in September, it passed a decree giving equal rights to Jewish people.

Such an absurdity (as that the organisation of the proletariat of a whole nationality should be denied representation on the central party bodies) could be openly advocated only [mark that!] in regard to the Jewish proletariat, which, owing to the peculiar historical fortunes of the Jewish people, still has to fight for equality [!!!] in the world family of the proletariat.

We recently came across just such a trick in a Zionist leaflet, whose authors raved and fumed against *Iskra*, purporting to detect in its struggle with the Bund a refusal to recognise the 'equality' of Jew and non-Jew. And now we find the Bundists repeating the tricks of the Zionists! This is disseminating an outright falsehood, for we have "advocated" "denying representation" not "only" to the Jews, but also to the Armenians, the Georgians and so on, and in the case of the Poles, too, we called for the closest union and fusion of the entire proletariat fighting against the tsarist autocracy. It was not for nothing that the PSP (Polish Socialist Party) raged and fulminated against us! To call a fight for the Zionist *idea* of a Jewish nation, for the federal *principle* of party organisation, a "fight for the equality of the Jews *in the world family of the proletariat*" is to degrade the struggle from the plane of ideas and principles to that of suspicion, incitement and fanning of historically-evolved prejudices. It glaringly reveals a lack of real ideas and principles as weapons of struggle.

* * *

We thus arrive at the conclusion that neither the logical, nor the historical, nor yet the nationalist arguments of the Bund will stand criticism. The period of disunity, which aggravated waverings among the Russian social-democrats and the isolation of the various organisations, had the same effect, to an even more marked degree, in the case of the Bundists. Instead of proclaiming war on this historically evolved isolation (further increased by the general disunity), they elevated it to a principle, seizing for this purpose on the sophistry that autonomy is inherently contradictory, and on the Zionist idea of a Jewish nation. Only if it frankly and resolutely admits its mistake and sets out to *move towards fusion* can the Bund turn away from the false path it has taken. And we are convinced that the finest adherents of social-democratic ideas among the Jewish proletariat will sooner or later compel the Bund to turn from the path of isolation to that of fusion.

To the Jewish Workers

Written at the end of May 1905

Editor's note: After the withdrawal of the Bund from the
RSDLP at the Second Congress, the party made an effort
to reach Jewish workers in order to win them over, thus the
publication of the pamphlet 'Report on the Third Congress
of the RSDLP', published in Yiddish in 1905, with an this
document acting as an editorial introduction explaining the
position of the party and the reasons for its differences with
the Bund.

* * *

In publishing the 'Report on the Third Congress of the RSDLP' in
Yiddish, the Editorial Board of the party central organ considers it
necessary to say a few words in connection with this publication.

The conditions under which the class-conscious proletariat of the
whole world lives tend to create the closest bonds and increasing unity
in the systematic social-democratic struggle of the workers of the various
nationalities. The great slogan "Workers of all countries, unite!",[1]
which was proclaimed for the first time more than half a century ago,
has now become more than the slogan of just the Social-Democratic
parties of the different countries. This slogan is being increasingly
embodied both in the unification of the tactics of international Social-

---

1   Karl Marx and Friedrich Engels, *The Communist Manifesto*, MECW, Vol. 6, p. 519.

Democracy and in the building of organisational unity among the proletarians of the various nationalities who are struggling under the yoke of one and the same despotic state for freedom and socialism.

In Russia the workers of all nationalities, especially those of non-Russian nationality, endure an economic and political oppression such as obtains in no other country. The Jewish workers, as a disfranchised nationality, not only suffer general economic and political oppression, but they also suffer under the yoke which deprives them of elementary civic rights. The heavier this yoke, the greater the need for the closest possible unity among the proletarians of the different nationalities; for without such unity a victorious struggle against the general oppression is impossible. The more the predatory tsarist autocracy strives to sow the seeds of discord, distrust and enmity among the nationalities it oppresses, the more abominable its policy of inciting the ignorant masses to savage pogroms becomes, the more does the duty devolve upon us, the social-democrats, to rally the isolated Social-Democratic parties of the different nationalities into a single Russian Social-Democratic Labour Party.

The First Congress of our party, held in the spring of 1898, set itself the aim of establishing such unity. To dispel any idea of its being national in character, the party called itself *'Rossiyskaya'* and not *'Russkaya'*.[2] The organisation of Jewish workers – the Bund – affiliated with the party as an autonomous section. Unfortunately, from that moment the unity of the Jewish and non-Jewish social-democrats within the single party was destroyed. Nationalist ideas began to spread among the leading members of the Bund, ideas which are in sharp contradiction to the entire world view of Social-Democracy. Instead of trying to draw the Jewish and the non-Jewish workers closer together, the Bund embarked upon a policy of weaning the former away from the latter; at its congresses it claimed a separate existence for the Jews as a nation. Instead of carrying on the work begun by the First Congress of the Russian Social-Democratic

---

2 The adjective *Russkaya* (Russian) pertains to nationality, *Rossiyskaya* (Russian) pertains to Russia as a country.

Labour Party towards still closer unity between the Bund and the party, the Bund moved a step away from the party. First, it withdrew from the united organisation of the RSDLP abroad and set up an independent organisation abroad; later, it withdrew from the RSDLP as well, when the Second Congress of our party in 1903 refused by a considerable majority to recognise the Bund as sole representative of the Jewish proletariat. The Bund held to its position, claiming not only that it was the sole representative of the Jewish proletariat, but that no territorial limits were set to its activities. Naturally, the Second Congress of the RSDLP could not accept such conditions, since in a number of regions, as, for instance, in South Russia, the organised Jewish proletariat constitutes part of the general party organisation. Ignoring that stand, the Bund withdrew from the party and thereby broke the unity of the social-democratic proletariat, despite the work that had been carried out in common at the Second Congress, and despite the party programme and rules.

At its Second and Third Congresses the Russian Social-Democratic Labour Party expressed its firm conviction that the Bund's withdrawal from the party was a grave and deplorable mistake on its part. The Bund's mistake is a result of its basically untenable nationalist views; the result of its groundless claim to be the sole, monopolistic representative of the Jewish proletariat, from which the federalist principle of organisation necessarily derives; the result of its long-standing policy of keeping aloof and separate from the party. We are convinced that this mistake must be rectified and that it will be rectified as the movement continues to grow. We consider ourselves ideologically at one with the Jewish social-democratic proletariat. After the Second Congress our Central Committee pursued a non-nationalist policy; it took pains that such committees should be set up (Polesye, North-Western) as would unite all the local workers, Jewish as well as non-Jewish, into a single whole. At the Third Congress of the RSDLP a resolution was adopted providing for the publication of literature in Yiddish. In fulfilment of that resolution we are now issuing a complete translation into Yiddish of the 'Report on the Third Congress of the RSDLP', which has appeared in Russian. The report will show the Jewish workers – both those who are now in our party and those who are temporarily out of it – how our party is progressing. The report will show the Jewish workers that our party is already emerging from the internal crisis from which it has been suffering since the Second Congress. It will show them what the actual aspirations of our party are and what its attitude is towards the social-democratic parties and organisations of the other nationalities, as well as the attitude of the entire party and its central body to its component parts. Finally, it will show them – and this is most important – the tactical directives that were drawn up by the Third Congress of the RSDLP with regard to the policy of the entire class-conscious proletariat in the present revolutionary situation.

Comrades! The hour of political struggle against the tsarist autocracy is drawing near – the struggle of the proletariat for the freedom of all classes and peoples in Russia, for the freedom of the proletarian drive towards socialism. Terrible trials are in store for us. The outcome of the revolution in Russia depends on our class-consciousness and preparedness, on our unity and determination. Let us set to work then with greater boldness and greater unity, let us do all in our power for the proletarians of the different nationalities to march to freedom under the leadership of a really united Russian Social-Democratic Labour Party.

Editorial Board of the Central Organ of the
Russian Social-Democratic Labour Party

'Cultural-National' Autonomy

Published 28 November 1913

The essence of the plan, or programme, of what is called 'cultural-national' autonomy (or: 'the establishment of institutions that will guarantee freedom of national development') is *separate schools for each nationality*.

The more often all avowed and tacit nationalists (including the Bundists) attempt to obscure this fact the more we must insist on it.

Every nation, irrespective of place of domicile of its individual members (irrespective of territory, hence the term 'extra-territorial' autonomy) is a united, officially recognised association conducting national-cultural affairs. The most important of these affairs is education. The determination of the composition of the nations by allowing every citizen to register freely, irrespective of place of domicile, as belonging to any national association, ensures absolute precision and absolute consistency in segregating the schools according to nationality.

Is such a division, be it asked, permissible from the point of view of democracy in general, and from the point of view of the interests of the proletarian class struggle in particular?

A clear grasp of the essence of the 'cultural-national autonomy' programme is sufficient to enable one to reply without hesitation – it is absolutely impermissible.

As long as different nations live in a single state they are bound to one another by millions and thousands of millions of economic, legal and social bonds. How can education be extricated from these bonds? Can it be "taken out of the jurisdiction" of the state, to quote the Bund formula, classical in its striking absurdity? If the various nations living in a single state are bound by economic ties, then any attempt to divide them permanently in 'cultural' and particularly educational matters would be absurd and reactionary. On the contrary, efforts should be made to *unite* the nations in educational matters, so that the schools should be a preparation for what is actually done in real life. At the present time we see that the different nations are unequal in the rights they possess and in their level of development. Under these circumstances, segregating the schools according to nationality would *actually* and inevitably *worsen* the conditions of the more backward nations. In the Southern, former slave states of America, Negro children are still segregated in separate schools, whereas in the North, white and Negro children attend the same schools. In Russia a plan was recently proposed for the 'nationalisation of Jewish schools', i.e. the segregation of Jewish children from the children of other nationalities in separate schools. It is needless to add that this plan originated in the most reactionary, Purishkevich circles.

One cannot be a democrat and at the same time advocate the principle of segregating the schools according to nationality. Note: we are arguing at present from the general democratic (i.e. bourgeois-democratic) point of view.

From the point of view of the proletarian class struggle we must oppose segregating the schools according to nationality far more emphatically. Who does not know that the capitalists of all the nations in a given state are most closely and intimately united in joint-stock companies, cartels and trusts, in manufacturers' associations, etc., which are directed *against* the workers irrespective of their nationality? Who does not know that in *any* capitalist undertaking – from huge works, mines and factories and commercial enterprises down to capitalist farms – we *always*, without exception, see a larger variety of nationalities among the workers than in remote, peaceful and sleepy villages?

The urban workers, who are best acquainted with developed capitalism and perceive more profoundly the psychology of the class struggle – their whole life teaches them, or they perhaps imbibe it with their mothers' milk – such workers instinctively and inevitably realise that segregating the schools according to nationality is not only a *harmful* scheme, but a downright fraudulent swindle on the part *of the capitalists*. The workers *can* be split up, divided and weakened by the advocacy of such an idea, and still more by the segregation, of the ordinary peoples' schools according to nationality; while the capitalists, whose children are well provided with rich private schools and specially engaged tutors, *cannot in any way* be threatened by any division or weakening through 'cultural-national autonomy'.

As a matter of fact, 'cultural-national autonomy', i.e. the absolutely pure and consistent segregating of education according to nationality, was invented not by the capitalists (*for the time being* they resort to cruder methods to divide the workers) but by the opportunist, philistine intelligentsia of Austria. There is *not a trace* of this brilliantly philistine and brilliantly nationalist idea in any of the democratic West-European countries with mixed populations. This idea of the despairing petty bourgeois could arise only in Eastern Europe, in backward, feudal, clerical, bureaucratic Austria, where *all* public and political life is hampered by wretched, petty squabbling (worse still: cursing and brawling) over the question of languages. Since cat and dog can't agree, let us at least segregate all the nations once and for all absolutely clearly and consistently in 'national curias' for educational purposes! – such is the psychology that engendered this foolish idea of 'cultural-national autonomy'. The proletariat, which is conscious of and cherishes its internationalism, will never accept this nonsense of refined nationalism.

It is no accident that in Russia this idea of 'cultural-national autonomy' was accepted *only by all* the Jewish bourgeois parties then (in 1907) by the conference of the *petty-bourgeois* Left-Narodnik[1] parties of different nationalities, and lastly by the petty-bourgeois, opportunist elements of the *near-Marxist* groups, i.e. the Bundists and the liquidators (the latter were even too timid to do so straightforwardly and definitely). It is no accident that in the State Duma[2] *only* the semi-liquidator Chkhenkeli, who is infected with nationalism, and the petty-bourgeois Kerensky,[3] spoke in favour of 'cultural-national autonomy'.

In general, it is quite funny to read the liquidator and Bundist references to Austria on this question. First of all, why should the most backward of the multinational countries be taken as the *model*? Why not take the most advanced? This is very much in the style of the bad Russian liberals, the Cadets, who for models of a constitution turn mainly to such backward countries as Prussia and Austria, and not to advanced countries like France, Switzerland and America!

Secondly, after taking the Austrian model, the Russian nationalist philistines, i.e. the Bundists, liquidators, Left Narodniks, and so forth, have themselves changed it *for the worse*. In this country it is the Bundists (plus *all* the Jewish bourgeois parties, in whose wake the Bundists follow without always realising it) that mainly and primarily use this plan for 'cultural-national autonomy' in their propaganda and agitation; and yet in Austria, the country where this idea of 'cultural-national autonomy' originated, Otto Bauer, the father of the idea, devoted a special chapter of his book to proving that 'cultural-national autonomy' *cannot* be applied to the Jews!

This proves more conclusively than lengthy speeches how inconsistent Otto Bauer is and how little he believes in his own idea,

---

1 The Narodniks were the members of the *Narodnaya Volya*, a revolutionary movement active in the 1860s and 70s, led by students and the intelligentsia, who believed the peasantry was the revolutionary class that would overthrow the monarchy. They regarded the village commune as the embryo of socialism.

2 During the reign of Nicholas II, the State Duma was the name given to the national parliament, which only had an advisory role.

3 Akaki Chkhenkeli was a leading Menshevik.
Alexander Kerensky was a lawyer who would go on to lead the Provisional Government in 1917. He was a nominal member of the SRs.

for he excludes the *only* extra-territorial (not having its own territory) nation from his plan for extra-territorial national autonomy.

This shows how Bundists borrow *old-fashioned* plans from Europe, multiply the mistakes of Europe tenfold and 'develop' them to the point of absurdity.

The fact is – and this is the third point – that at their congress in Brünn (in 1899) the Austrian social-democrats *rejected* the programme of 'cultural-national autonomy' that was proposed to them. They merely adopted a compromise in the form of a proposal for a union of the nationally delimited *regions* of the country. This compromise did *not* provide either for extra-territoriality or for segregating education according to nationality. In accordance with this compromise, in the most advanced (capitalistically) populated centres, towns, factory and mining districts, large country estates, etc., there are no separate schools for each nationality!

The Russian working class has been combating this reactionary, pernicious, petty-bourgeois nationalist idea of 'cultural-national autonomy', and will continue to do so.

Resolutions of the Summer 1913 Joint Conference of the Central Committee of the RSDLP and Party Officials

Written September 1913

Editor's note: The Joint Conference of the Central Committee of the RSDLP and Party Officials (for purposes of secrecy it was known as 'the summer' or 'August' Conference), was held from 23 September to 1 October 1913 in the village of Poronin (near Kraków) where Lenin spent the summer months. The Conference decided in favour of united All-Russia party work to guide the actions of the working class on a country-wide scale.

* * *

Resolution on the National Question

The orgy of Black-Hundred nationalism, the growth of nationalist tendencies among the liberal bourgeoisie and the growth of nationalist tendencies among the upper classes of the oppressed nationalities, give prominence at the present time to the national question.

The state of affairs in the social-democratic movement (the attempts of the Caucasian social-democrats, the Bund and the liquidators to annul the party programme,[1] etc.) compels the party to devote more attention than ever to this question.

This Conference, taking its stand on the Programme of the RSDLP, and in order to organise correctly social-democratic agitation on the national question, advances the following propositions:

1. Insofar as national peace is in any way possible in a capitalist society based on exploitation, profit-making and strife, it is attainable only under a consistently and thoroughly democratic republican system of government which guarantees full equality of all nations and languages, which recognises no compulsory official language, which provides the people with schools where instruction is given in all the native languages, and the constitution of which contains a fundamental law that prohibits any privileges whatsoever to any one nation and any encroachment whatsoever upon the rights of a national minority. This particularly calls for wide regional autonomy and fully democratic local self-government, with the boundaries of the self-governing and autonomous regions determined by the local inhabitants themselves on the basis of their economic and social conditions, national make-up of the population, etc.

2. The division of the educational affairs of a single state according to nationalities is undoubtedly harmful from the standpoint of democracy in general, and of the interests of the proletarian class struggle in particular. It is precisely this division that is implied in the plan for 'cultural-national' autonomy, or for 'the creation of institutions that will guarantee freedom for national development' adopted in Russia by all the Jewish bourgeois parties and by the petty-bourgeois, opportunist elements among the different nations.

3. The interests of the working class demand the amalgamation of the workers of all the nationalities in a given state in united

---

1   The resolution refers here to the decision adopted by the liquidators' August Conference in 1912 claiming that 'cultural-national autonomy' was compatible with the programme of the RSDLP.

proletarian organisations – political, trade union, co-operative, educational, etc. This amalgamation of the workers of different nationalities in single organisations will alone enable the proletariat to wage a victorious struggle against international capital and reaction, and combat the propaganda and aspirations of the landowners, clergy and bourgeois nationalists of all nations, who usually cover up their anti-proletarian aspirations with the slogan of 'national culture'. The world working-class movement is creating and daily developing more and more an international proletarian culture.

4. As regards the right of the nations oppressed by the tsarist monarchy to self-determination, i.e. the right to secede and form independent states, the Social-Democratic Party must unquestionably champion this right. This is dictated by the fundamental principles of international democracy in general, and specifically by the unprecedented national oppression of the majority of the inhabitants of Russia by the tsarist monarchy, which is a most reactionary and barbarous state compared with its neighbouring states in Europe and Asia. Furthermore, this is dictated by the struggle of the Great-Russian inhabitants themselves for freedom, for it will be impossible for them to create a democratic state if they do not eradicate Black-Hundred, Great-Russian nationalism, which is backed by the traditions of a number of bloody suppressions of national movements and systematically fostered not only by the tsarist monarchy and all the reactionary parties, but also by the Great-Russian bourgeois liberals, who toady to the monarchy, particularly in the period of counter-revolution.

5. The right of nations to self-determination (i.e. the constitutional guarantee of an absolutely free and democratic method of deciding the question of secession) must under no circumstances be confused with the expediency of a given nation's secession. The Social-Democratic Party must decide the latter question exclusively on its merits in each particular case in conformity

with the interests of social development as a whole and with the interests of the proletarian class struggle for socialism.

Social-Democrats must moreover bear in mind that the landowners, the clergy and the bourgeoisie of the oppressed nations often cover up with nationalist slogans their efforts to divide the workers and dupe them by doing deals behind their backs with the landowners and bourgeoisie of the ruling nation to the detriment of the masses of the working people of all nations.

* * *

This Conference places on the agenda of the party congress the question of the national programme. It invites the Central Committee, the party press and the local organisations to discuss (in pamphlets, debates, etc.) the national question in fullest detail.

The Nationality of Pupils in Russian Schools

Published 14 December 1913

To obtain a more precise idea of the plan for 'cultural national autonomy', which boils down to segregating the schools according to nationality, it is useful to take the concrete data which show the nationality of the pupils attending Russian schools. For the St. Petersburg educational area such data are provided by the returns of the school census taken on 18 January 1911.

The following are the data on the distribution of pupils attending elementary schools under the Ministry of Public Education according to the *native languages* of the pupils. The data covers the whole of the St. Petersburg educational area, but *in brackets* we give the *figures* for the city of St. Petersburg. Under the term 'Russian language' the officials constantly lump together Great-Russian, Byelorussian and Ukrainian ('Little Russian', according to official terminology).

Total pupils: 265,660 (48,076).

Russian: 232,618 (44,223); Polish: 1,737 (780); Czech: 3 (2); Lithuanian: 84 (35); Lettish: 1,371 (113); Zhmud: 1 (0); French: 14 (13); Italian: 4 (4); Rumanian: 2 (2); German: 2,408 (845); Swedish: 228 (217); Norwegian: 31 (0); Danish: 1 (1); Dutch: 1 (0); English: 8 (7); Armenian: 3 (3); Gipsy: 4 (0); Jewish: 1,196

(396); Georgian: 2 (1); Ossetian: 1 (0); Finnish: 10,750 (874); Karelian: 3,998 (2); Chud: 247 (0); Estonian: 4,723 (536); Lapp: 9 (0); Zyryan: 6,008 (0); Samoyed: 5 (0); Tatar: 63 (13); Persian: 1 (1); Chinese: 1 (1); not ascertained: 138 (7).

These are comparatively accurate figures. They show that the national composition of the population is extremely mixed, although they apply to one of the basically Great-Russian districts of Russia. The extremely mixed national composition of the population of the large city of St. Petersburg is at once evident. This is no accident, but results from a law of capitalism that operates in all countries and in all parts of the world. Large cities, factory, metallurgical, railway and commercial and industrial centres generally, are certain, more than any other, to have very mixed populations, and it is precisely these centres that grow faster than all others and constantly attract larger and larger numbers of the inhabitants of the backward rural areas.

Now try to apply to these real-life data the lifeless utopia of the nationalist philistines called 'cultural-national autonomy' or (in the language of the Bundists) "taking out of the jurisdiction of the state" questions of national culture, i.e. primarily educational affairs.

Educational affairs "shall be taken out of the jurisdiction of the state" and transferred to twenty-three (in St. Petersburg) "national associations" each developing "its own" "national culture"!

It would be ridiculous to waste words to prove the absurdity and reactionary nature of a 'national programme' of this sort.

It is as clear as daylight that the advocacy of such a plan means, *in fact*, pursuing or supporting the ideas of bourgeois nationalism, chauvinism and clericalism. The interests of democracy in general, and the interests of the working class in particular, demand the very opposite. We must strive to secure the *mixing* of the children of *all* nationalities in *uniform* schools in each locality; the workers of all nationalities must *jointly* pursue the proletarian educational policy which Samoilov, the deputy of the Vladimir workers, so ably formulated on behalf of the Russian social-democratic workers' group in the State Duma.[1] We must most emphatically oppose segregating the schools according to nationality, no matter what form it may take.

It is not our business to segregate the nations in matters of education in any way; on the contrary, we must strive to create the fundamental democratic conditions for the peaceful coexistence of the nations on the basis of equal rights. We must not champion 'national culture', but expose the clerical and bourgeois character of this slogan in the name of the international culture of the world working-class movement.

But we may be asked whether it is possible to safeguard the interests of the *one* Georgian child among the 48,076 schoolchildren in St. Petersburg on the basis of equal rights. And we should reply that it is impossible to establish a special Georgian school in St. Petersburg on the basis of Georgian 'national culture', and that to advocate such a plan means sowing *pernicious* ideas among the masses of the people.

But we shall not be defending anything harmful, or be striving after anything that is impossible, if we demand for this child free government premises for lectures on the Georgian language, Georgian history, etc., the provision of Georgian books from the Central Library for this child, a state contribution towards the fees of the Georgian teacher, and so forth. Under real democracy, when bureaucracy and 'Peredonovism'[2] are completely eliminated from the schools, the people can quite easily achieve this. But this real democracy can be achieved *only* when the workers of *all* nationalities are united.

To preach the establishment of special national schools for every 'national culture' is reactionary. But under real democracy it is quite possible to ensure instruction in the native language, in native history, and so forth, *without* splitting up the schools according

---

1 Fyodor Samoilov was a Bolshevik deputy in the Fourth State Duma. Lenin is referring to his statement on 26 November 1913, during a discussion on a bill to increase the salaries of teachers of religion in agrarian schools.

2 Peredonov is a character from Fyodor Sologub's novel, *The Petty Demon*. A sadistic, hateful and nihilistic schoolteacher, his name became symbolic of this mentality. Lenin describes Peredonov as "a type of teacher-spy and dull lout".

to nationality. And complete local self-government will make it impossible for anything to be forced upon the people, as for example, upon the 713 Karelian children in Kem Uyezd (where there are only 514 Russian children) or upon the 681 Zyryan children in Pechora Uyezd (153 Russian), or upon the 267 Lettish children in Novgorod Uyezd (over 7,000 Russian), and so on and so forth.

Advocacy of impracticable cultural-national autonomy is an absurdity, which now already is only disuniting the workers ideologically. To advocate the amalgamation of the workers of all nationalities means facilitating the success of proletarian class solidarity, which will guarantee equal rights for, and maximum peaceful coexistence of, all nationalities.

The National Programme
of the RSDLP

Published 15 December 1913

The Conference of the Central Committee has adopted a resolution on the national question,[1] which has been printed in the 'Notification', and has placed the question of a national programme on the agenda of the Congress.

Why and how the national question has, at the present time, been brought to the fore – in the entire policy of the counter-revolution, in the class-consciousness of the bourgeoisie and in the proletarian Social-Democratic Party of Russia – is shown in detail in the resolution itself. There is hardly any need to dwell on this in view of the clarity of the situation. This situation and the fundamentals of a national programme for Social-Democracy have recently been dealt with in Marxist theoretical literature (the most prominent place being taken by Stalin's article).[2] We therefore consider that it will be to the point if, in this article, we confine ourselves to the

---

1 See 'Resolution on the National Question', in this volume p. 221.
2 The work referred to is Joseph Stalin's 'Marxism and the National Question'. For years it was regarded as the standard party text on the national question. In spite of a somewhat formalistic presentation, it remains a valuable work. This, however, was not a result of Stalin's theoretical genius. In fact, this article was not Stalin's work at all. As EH Carr points out:

presentation of the problem from a purely party standpoint and to explanations that cannot be made in the legal press, crushed as it is by the Stolypin-Maklakov oppression.[3]

Social-Democracy in Russia is taking shape by drawing exclusively on the experience of older countries, i.e. of Europe, and on the theoretical expression of that experience, Marxism. The specific feature of our country and the specific features of the historical period of the establishment of Social-Democracy in our country are: first, in our country, as distinct from Europe, Social-Democracy began to take shape *before* the bourgeois revolution and continued taking shape *during* that revolution. Secondly, in our country the inevitable struggle to separate proletarian from general bourgeois and petty-bourgeois democracy – a struggle that is fundamentally the same as that experienced by every country – is being conducted under the conditions of a complete theoretical victory of Marxism in the West and in our country. The form taken by this struggle, therefore, is not so much that of a struggle for Marxism as a struggle for or against petty-bourgeois theories that are hidden behind 'almost Marxist' phrases.

That is how the matter stands, beginning with Economism (1895-1901) and 'legal Marxism' (1895-1901, 1902). Only those who shrink from historical truth can forget the close, intimate connection and relationship between these trends and Menshevism (1903-07) and liquidationism (1908-13).

On the national question the old *Iskra*, which in 1901-03 worked on and completed a programme for the RSDLP as well as laying the first and fundamental basis of Marxism in the theory and

External and internal evidence shows it to have been written under Lenin's inspiration. (EH Carr, *The Bolshevik Revolution*, Vol. 1, WW Norton and Co., 1985, p. 420.)

The ideas in the article are entirely those of Lenin, who oversaw and edited the work.

3 After the 1905 Revolution, a period of reaction and counter-revolution set in, led by Pyotr Stolypin, one of the largest feudal landowners in Russia and Primer Minister until his assassination in 1911.

Vasily Maklakov was a Moscow landowner, leading lawyer, right-wing Cadet, and deputy in the Fourth Duma.

practice of the Russian working-class movement, had to struggle, in the same way as on other questions, against petty-bourgeois opportunism. This opportunism was expressed, first and foremost, in the nationalist tendencies and waverings of the Bund. The old *Iskra* conducted a stubborn struggle against Bund nationalism, and to forget this is tantamount to becoming a Forgetful John again, and cutting oneself off from the historical and ideological roots of the whole social-democratic workers' movement in Russia.

On the other hand, when the Programme of the RSDLP was finally adopted at the Second Congress in August 1903, there was a struggle, unrecorded in the Minutes of the Congress because it took place in the *Programme Commission*, which was visited by almost the entire Congress – a struggle against the clumsy attempts of several Polish social-democrats to cast doubts on "the right of nations to self-determination", i.e. attempts to deviate towards opportunism and nationalism from a quite different angle.

And today, ten years later, the struggle goes on along those same two basic *lines*, which shows equally that there is a profound connection between this struggle and all the objective conditions affecting the national question in Russia.

At the Brünn Congress in Austria (1899) the programme of 'cultural-national autonomy' (defended by Kristan, Ellenbogen and others and expressed in the draft of the Southern Slavs) was *rejected*. *Territorial* national autonomy was adopted, and social-democratic propaganda for the obligatory union of all national regions was only a *compromise* with the idea of 'cultural-national autonomy'. The chief theoreticians of this unfortunate idea themselves lay particular emphasis on its *inapplicability* to Jewry.

In Russia – *as usual* – people have been found who have made it their business to enlarge on a little opportunist error and develop it into a system of opportunist policy. In the same way as Bernstein[4] in

---

4 Eduard Bernstein was a German social-democrat who tried to revise Marx's revolutionary theory on the lines of bourgeois liberalism. Bernsteinism, the opportunist trend in German and International Social-Democracy, hostile to Marxism, derived its name from his ideas.

Germany brought into being the Right Constitutional-Democrats in Russia – Struve, Bulgakov, Tugan and co. – so Otto Bauer's "forgetfulness of internationalism" (as the super-cautious Kautsky calls it!) *gave rise* in Russia to the *complete* acceptance of 'cultural national autonomy' *by all* the Jewish bourgeois parties and a large number of petty-bourgeois trends (the Bund and a *conference* of Socialist-Revolutionary national parties in 1907). Backward Russia serves, one might say, as an example of how the microbes of West-European opportunism produce whole *epidemics* on our savage soil.

In Russia people are fond of saying that Bernstein is 'tolerated' in Europe, but they forget to add that nowhere in the world, with the exception of 'holy' Mother Russia, has Bernsteinism engendered Struvism,[5] or has 'Bauerism' led to the justification, by social-democrats, of the refined nationalism of the Jewish bourgeoisie.

'Cultural-national autonomy' implies precisely the most refined and, therefore, the most harmful nationalism, it implies the corruption of the workers by means of the slogan of national culture and the propaganda of the profoundly harmful and even anti-democratic segregating of schools according to nationality. In short, this programme undoubtedly contradicts the internationalism of the proletariat and is in accordance only with the ideals of the nationalist petty bourgeoisie.

But there is *one case* in which the Marxists are duty bound, if they do not want to betray democracy and the proletariat, to defend one special demand in the national question; that is, the right of nations to self-determination (Section 9 of the RSDLP Programme), i.e. the right to political secession. The Conference resolution explains and motivates this demand in such detail that there is no place left for misunderstanding.

We shall, therefore, give only a brief description of those amazingly ignorant and opportunist objections that have been raised against this section of the programme. In connection with this let us mention that *in the course of the ten years'* existence of the programme *not one single unit* of the RSDLP, not one single national organisation, not

---

5   Struvism refers to the liberal-bourgeois distortion of Marxism by Peter Struve.

one single regional conference, not one local committee and not one delegate to a congress or conference, has attempted to raise the question of changing or annulling Section 9!

It is necessary to bear this in mind. It shows us at once whether there is a grain of seriousness or party spirit in the objections raised to this point.

Take Mr. Semkovsky of the liquidators' newspaper. With the casual air of a man who has liquidated a party, he announces:

> For certain reasons we do not share Rosa Luxemburg's proposal to remove Section 9 from the programme altogether (*Novaya Rabochaya Gazeta*, No. 71).

So the reasons are a secret! But then, how can secrecy be avoided in face of such ignorance of the history of our programme? Or when that same Mr. Semkovsky, incomparably casual (what do the party and the programme matter!) makes an exception for Finland?

> What are we to do […] if the Polish proletariat wants to carry on a joint struggle together with the whole proletariat of Russia within the framework of one state, and the reactionary classes of Polish society, on the contrary, want to separate Poland from Russia and, through a referendum, obtain a majority of votes in favour of separation; are we, Russian social-democrats, to vote in a central parliament together with our Polish comrades *against* secession, or, in order not to infringe on the 'right to self-determination', vote *in favour* of secession?

What, indeed, are we to do when such naive and so hopelessly confused questions are raised?

The *right* to self-determination, my dear Mr. Liquidator, certainly does *not* imply the solution of the problem by a central parliament, but by a parliament, a diet, or a referendum of the *seceding minority*. When Norway seceded from Sweden (1905) it was decided by Norway *alone* (a country half the size of Sweden).

Even a child could see that Mr. Semkovsky is hopelessly mixed up.

"The right to self-determination" implies a democratic system *of a type* in which there is not only democracy in general, but specifically one in which there *could not be an undemocratic* solution of the question of secession. Democracy, speaking generally, is compatible with militant and tyrannical nationalism. The proletariat demands a democracy that *rules out* the forcible retention of any one of the nations within the bounds of the state. "In order not to infringe on the right to self-determination", therefore, we are duty bound *not* "to vote for secession", as the wily Mr. Semkovsky assumes, but to vote for the right of the seceding region to decide the question *itself.*

It would seem that even with Mr. Semkovsky's mental abilities it is not difficult to deduce that "the *right* to divorce" does not require that one should *vote* for divorce! But such is the fate of those who criticise Section 9 – they forget the ABC of logic.

At the time of Norway's secession from Sweden, the Swedish proletariat, if they did not want to follow the nationalist petty bourgeoisie, were *duty bound to vote* and agitate against the annexation of Norway by force, as the Swedish priesthood and landed proprietors desired. This is obvious and not too difficult to understand. Swedish nationalist democrats could refrain from a type of agitation that the principle of the *right* to self-determination demands of the proletariat of *ruling, oppressor nations.*

"What are we to do if the reactionaries are in the majority?" asks Mr. Semkovsky. This is a question worthy of a third-form schoolboy. What is to be done about the *Russian* constitution if democratic voting gives the reactionaries a majority? Mr. Semkovsky asks idle, empty questions that have nothing to do with the matter in hand – they are the kind of questions that, as it is said, seven fools can ask more of than seventy wise men can answer.

When a democratic vote gives the reactionaries a majority, one of two things may, and usually does occur: either the decision of the reactionaries is implemented and its harmful consequences send the masses more or less speedily over to the side of democracy and against the reactionaries; or the conflict between democracy and reaction is decided by a civil or other war, which is also quite possible (and no doubt even the Semkovskys have heard of this) under a democracy.

The recognition of the right to self-determination is, Mr. Semkovsky assures us, "playing into the hands of the most thorough-paced bourgeois nationalism". This is childish nonsense since the recognition of the *right* does not exclude either propaganda and agitation *against* separation or the exposure of bourgeois nationalism. But it is absolutely indisputable that the denial of the *right* to secede is "playing into the hands" of the *most thorough-paced reactionary Great-Russian* nationalism!

This is the essence of Rosa Luxemburg's amusing error for which she was ridiculed a long time ago by German and Russian (August 1903) social-democrats; in their fear of playing into the hands of the bourgeois nationalism of oppressed nations, people play into the hands not merely of the bourgeois but of the reactionary nationalism of the *oppressor* nation.

If Mr. Semkovsky had not been so virginally innocent in matters concerning party history and the party programme he would have understood that it was his duty to refute Plekhanov, who, *eleven years ago*, in defending the draft programme (which became the programme in 1903) of the RSDLP in *Zarya*,[6] made a *special point* (p. 38) of the recognition of the right to self-determination and wrote the following about it:

> This demand, which is not obligatory for bourgeois democrats, even in theory, is obligatory for us as social-democrats. If we were to forget about it or were afraid to put it forward for fear of impinging on the national prejudices of our compatriots of Great-Russian origin, the battle-cry of world Social-Democracy, 'Workers of all countries, unite!' would be a shameful lie upon our lips.

As long ago as the *Zarya* days, Plekhanov put forward the basic argument which was developed in detail in the conference resolution, an argument to which the Semkovskys have not attempted to draw attention for eleven years. In Russia there are 43 per cent Great Russians, but Great-Russian nationalism rules over the other 57

---

6   Lenin is referring to Plekhanov's article 'Draft Programme of the Russian Social-Democratic Party', published in *Zarya*.

per cent of the population and oppresses all nations. The National-Liberals (Struve and co., the Progressists, etc.) have already joined forces with our national-reactionaries and the 'first swallows' of *national* democracy have appeared (remember Mr. Peshekhonov's appeal in August 1906 to be cautious in our attitude to the nationalist prejudices of the muzhik).

In Russia only the liquidators consider the bourgeois-democratic revolution to be over, and the concomitant of *such* a revolution all over the world always has been and still is national movements. In Russia in particular there are oppressed nations in many of the border regions, which in neighbouring states enjoy greater liberty. Tsarism is more reactionary than the neighbouring states, constitutes the *greatest* barrier to free economic development, and does its utmost to foster Great-Russian nationalism. For a Marxist, of course, *all other conditions being equal,* big states are always preferable to small ones. But it would be ridiculous and reactionary even to suppose that conditions under the tsarist monarchy might be equal to those in any European country or any but a minority of Asian countries.

The denial of the right of nations to self-determination in present-day Russia is, therefore, undoubted opportunism and a refusal to fight against the reactionary Great-Russian nationalism that is still all-powerful.

Critical Remarks on the National Question

Written October-December 1913

It is obvious that the national question has now become prominent among the problems of Russian public life. The aggressive nationalism of the reactionaries, the transition of counter-revolutionary bourgeois liberalism to nationalism (particularly Great-Russian, but also Polish, Jewish, Ukrainian, etc.), and lastly, the increase of nationalist vacillations among the different 'national' (i.e. non-Great-Russian) social-democrats, who have gone to the length of violating the party programme – all these make it incumbent on us to give more attention to the national question than we have done so far.

This article pursues a special object, namely, to examine, in their general bearing, precisely these programme vacillations of Marxists and would-be Marxists, on the national question. In *Severnaya Pravda*[1] No. 29 (for 5 September 1913, 'Liberals and Democrats on the Language Question') I had occasion to speak of the opportunism of the liberals on the national question; this article of mine was attacked by the opportunist Jewish newspaper *Zeit*, in an article

---

1 *Severnaya Pravda* (*Northern Truth*) was one of the names used for *Pravda* to escape the tsarist authorities.

by Mr. F Liebman. From the other side, the programme of the Russian Marxists on the national question has been criticised by the Ukrainian opportunist Mr. Lev Yurkevich (*Dzvin*, 1913, Nos. 7-8). Both these writers touched upon so many questions that to reply to them we are obliged to deal with the most diverse aspects of the subject. I think the most convenient thing would be to start with a reprint of the article from *Severnaya Pravda*.

Liberals and democrats on the language question

On several occasions the newspapers have mentioned the report of the Governor of the Caucasus, a report that is noteworthy, not for its Black-Hundred spirit, but for its timid 'liberalism'. Among other things, the Governor objects to artificial Russification of non-Russian nationalities. Representatives of non-Russian nationalities in the Caucasus are *themselves* striving to teach their children Russian; an example of this is the Armenian church schools, in which the teaching of Russian is not obligatory.

Russkoye Slovo[2] (No. 198), one of the most widely circulating liberal newspapers in Russia, points to this fact and draws the correct conclusion that the hostility towards the Russian language in Russia "stems exclusively from" the "artificial" (it should have said 'forced') implanting of that language.

"There is no reason to worry about the fate of the Russian language. It will itself win recognition throughout Russia", says the newspaper. This is perfectly true, because the requirements of economic exchange will always compel the nationalities living in one state (as long as they wish to live together) to study the language of the majority. The more democratic the political system in Russia becomes, the more powerfully, rapidly and extensively capitalism will develop, the more urgently will the requirements of economic exchange impel various nationalities to study the language most convenient for general commercial relations.

------

2   *Russkoye Slovo* (*Russian Word*) was a daily newspaper, published in Moscow from 1895 to 1918. The paper defended the interests of the Russian bourgeoisie from a liberal platform.

The liberal newspaper, however, hastens to slap itself in the face and demonstrate its liberal inconsistency.

> Even those who oppose Russification [it says] would hardly be likely to deny that in a country as huge as Russia there must be one single official language, and that this language can be only Russian.

Logic turned inside out! Tiny Switzerland has not lost anything, but has gained from having not *one single* official language, but three – German, French and Italian. In Switzerland, 70 per cent of the population are Germans (in Russia 43 per cent are Great Russians), 22 per cent French (in Russia 17 per cent are Ukrainians) and 7 per cent Italians (in Russia 6 per cent are Poles and 4.5 per cent Byelorussians). If Italians in Switzerland often speak French in their common parliament they do not do so because they are menaced by some savage police law (there are none such in Switzerland), but because the civilised citizens of a democratic state themselves prefer a language that is understood by a majority. The French language does not instill hatred in Italians because it is the language of a free civilised nation, a language that is not imposed by disgusting police measures.

Why should 'huge' Russia, a much more varied and terribly backward country, *inhibit* her development by the retention of any kind of privilege for any one language? Should not the contrary be true, liberal gentlemen? Should not Russia, if she wants to overtake Europe, put an end to every kind of privilege as quickly as possible, as completely as possible and as vigorously as possible?

If all privileges disappear, if the imposition of any one language ceases, all Slavs will easily and rapidly learn to understand each other and will not be frightened by the 'horrible' thought that speeches in different languages will be heard in the common parliament. The requirements of economic exchange will themselves *decide* which language of the given country it is to the *advantage* of the majority to know in the interests of commercial relations. This decision will be all the firmer because it is adopted voluntarily by a population of various nationalities, and its adoption will be the more rapid and extensive the more consistent the democracy and, as a consequence of it, the more rapid the development of capitalism.

The liberals approach the language question in the same way as they approach all political questions – like hypocritical hucksters, holding out one hand (openly) to democracy and the other (behind their backs) to the feudalists and police. 'We are against privileges', shout the liberals, and under cover they haggle with the feudalists for first one, then another, privilege.

Such is the nature of *all* liberal-bourgeois nationalism – not only Great-Russian (it is the worst of them all because of its violent character and its kinship with the Purishkeviches), but Polish, Jewish, Ukrainian, Georgian and every other nationalism. Under the slogan of 'national culture' the bourgeoisie of *all* nations, both in Austria and in Russia, are *in fact* pursuing the policy of splitting the workers, emasculating democracy and haggling with the feudalists over the sale of the people's rights and the people's liberty.

The slogan of working-class democracy is not 'national culture' but the international culture of democracy and the world-wide working-class movement. Let the bourgeoisie deceive the people with various 'positive' national programmes. The class-conscious worker will answer the bourgeoisie – there is only one solution to the national problem (insofar as it can, in general, be solved in the capitalist world, the world of profit, squabbling and exploitation), and that solution is consistent democracy.

The proof – Switzerland in Western Europe, a country with an old culture and Finland in Eastern Europe, a country with a young culture.

The national programme of working-class democracy is: absolutely no privileges for any one nation or any one language; the solution of the problem of the political self-determination of nations, that is, their separation as states by completely free, democratic methods; the promulgation of a law for the whole state by virtue of which any measure (rural, urban or communal, etc., etc.) introducing any privilege of any kind for one of the nations and militating against the equality of nations or the rights of a national minority, shall be declared illegal and ineffective, and any citizen of the state shall have the right to demand that such a measure be annulled as unconstitutional, and that those who attempt to put it into effect be punished.

Working-class democracy contraposes to the nationalist wrangling of the various bourgeois parties over questions of language, etc., the demand for the unconditional unity and complete amalgamation of workers of *all* nationalities in *all* working-class organisations – trade union, co-operative, consumers', educational and all others – in contradistinction to any kind of bourgeois nationalism. Only this type of unity and amalgamation can uphold democracy and defend the interests of the workers against capital – which is already international and is becoming more so – and promote the development of mankind towards a new way of life that is alien to all privileges and all exploitation.

'National culture'

As the reader will see, the article in *Severnaya Pravda* made use of a particular example, i.e. the problem of the official language, to illustrate the inconsistency and opportunism of the liberal bourgeoisie, which, in the national question, extends a hand to the feudalists and the police. Everybody will understand that, apart from the problem of an official language, the liberal bourgeoisie behaves just as treacherously, hypocritically and stupidly (even from the standpoint of the interests of liberalism) in a number of other related issues.

The conclusion to be drawn from this? It is that *all* liberal-bourgeois nationalism sows the greatest corruption among the workers and does immense harm to the cause of freedom and the proletarian class struggle. This bourgeois (and bourgeois-feudalist) tendency is all the more dangerous for its *being concealed* behind the slogan of 'national culture'. It is under the guise of national culture – Great-Russian, Polish, Jewish, Ukrainian, and so forth – that the Black-Hundreds and the clericals, and also the bourgeoisie of *all* nations, are doing their dirty and reactionary work.

Such are the facts of the national life of today, if viewed from the Marxist angle, i.e. from the standpoint of the class struggle, and if the slogans are compared with the interests and policies of classes, and not with meaningless 'general principles', declamations and phrases.

The slogan of national culture is a bourgeois (and often also a Black-Hundred, and clerical) fraud. Our slogan is: the international culture of democracy and of the world working-class movement.

Here the Bundist Mr. Liebman rushes into the fray and annihilates me with the following deadly tirade:

> Anyone in the least familiar with the national question knows that international culture is not non-national culture (culture without a national form); non-national culture, which must not be Russian, Jewish, or Polish, but only pure culture, is nonsense; international ideas can appeal to the working class only when they are adapted to the language spoken by the worker, and to the concrete national conditions under which he lives; the worker should not be indifferent to the condition and development of his national culture, because it is through it, and only through it, that he is able to participate in the 'international culture of democracy and of the world working-class movement'. This is well known, but VI turns a deaf ear to it all…

Ponder over this typically Bundist argument, designed, if you please, to demolish the Marxist thesis that I advanced. With the air of supreme self-confidence of one who is "familiar with the national question", this Bundist passes off ordinary bourgeois views as "well-known" axioms.

It is true, my dear Bundist, that international culture is not non-national. Nobody said that it was. Nobody has proclaimed a "pure" culture, either Polish, Jewish, or Russian etc., and your jumble of empty words is simply an attempt to distract the reader's attention and to obscure the issue with tinkling words.

The *elements* of democratic and socialist culture are present, if only in rudimentary form, in *every* national culture, since in *every* nation there are toiling and exploited masses, whose conditions of life inevitably give rise to the ideology of democracy and socialism. But *every* nation also possesses a bourgeois culture (and most nations a reactionary and clerical culture as well) in the form, not merely of 'elements', but of the *dominant* culture. Therefore, the general "national culture" is the culture of the landlords, the clergy and the bourgeoisie. This fundamental and, for a Marxist, elementary truth was kept in the background by the Bundist, who 'drowned' it in his jumble of words, i.e. *instead* of revealing and clarifying the class gulf to the reader, he in fact obscured it. *In fact*, the Bundist acted like a bourgeois, whose every interest requires the spreading of a belief in a non-class national culture.

In advancing the slogan of "the international culture of democracy and of the world working-class movement", we take *from each* national culture *only* its democratic and socialist elements; we take them *only* and *absolutely* in opposition to the bourgeois culture and the bourgeois nationalism of *each* nation. No democrat, and certainly no Marxist, denies that all languages should have equal status, or that it is necessary to polemise with one's 'native' bourgeoisie in one's native language and to advocate anti-clerical or anti-bourgeois ideas among one's 'native' peasantry and petty bourgeoisie. That goes without saying, but the Bundist uses these indisputable truths to obscure the point in dispute, i.e. the real issue.

The question is whether it is permissible for a Marxist, directly or indirectly, to advance the slogan of national culture, or whether he should *oppose* it by advocating, in all languages, the slogan of workers' *internationalism* while 'adapting' himself to all local and national features.

The significance of the 'national culture' slogan is not determined by some petty intellectual's promise, or good intention, to 'interpret' it as 'meaning the development through it of an international culture'. It would be puerile subjectivism to look at it in that way. The significance of the slogan of national culture is determined by the objective alignment of all classes in a given country, and in all countries of the world. The national culture of the bourgeoisie is a *fact* (and, I repeat, the bourgeoisie everywhere enters into deals with the landed proprietors and the clergy). Aggressive bourgeois nationalism, which drugs the minds of the workers, stultifies and disunites them in order that the bourgeoisie may lead them by the halter – such is the fundamental fact of the times.

Those who seek to serve the proletariat must unite the workers of all nations, and unswervingly fight bourgeois nationalism, *domestic* and foreign. The place of those who advocate the slogan of national culture is among the nationalist petty bourgeois, not among the Marxists.

Take a concrete example. Can a Great-Russian Marxist accept the slogan of national, Great-Russian, culture? No, he cannot. Anyone who does that should stand in the ranks of the nationalists, not of the Marxists. Our task is to fight the dominant, Black-Hundred and bourgeois national culture of the Great Russians, and to develop, exclusively in the internationalist spirit and in the closest alliance with the workers of other countries, the rudiments also existing in the history of our democratic and working-class movement. Fight your own Great-Russian landlords and bourgeoisie, fight their 'culture' in the name of internationalism, and, in so fighting, 'adapt' yourself to the special features of the Purishkeviches and Struves – that is your task, not preaching or tolerating the slogan of national culture.

The same applies to the most oppressed and persecuted nation – the Jews. Jewish national culture is the slogan of the rabbis and the bourgeoisie, the slogan of our enemies. But there are other elements in Jewish culture and in Jewish history as a whole. Of the ten and a half million Jews in the world, somewhat over a half live in Galicia and Russia, backward and semi-barbarous countries, where the Jews are *forcibly* kept in the status of a caste. The other half lives in the civilised world, and there the Jews do not live as a segregated caste. There the great world-progressive features of Jewish culture stand clearly revealed: its internationalism, its identification with the advanced movements of the epoch (the percentage of Jews in the democratic and proletarian movements is everywhere higher than the percentage of Jews among the population).

Whoever, directly or indirectly, puts forward the slogan of Jewish 'national culture' is (whatever his good intentions may be) an enemy of the proletariat, a supporter of all that is *outmoded* and connected with *caste* among the Jewish people; he is an accomplice of the rabbis and the bourgeoisie. On the other hand, those Jewish Marxists who mingle with the Russian, Lithuanian, Ukrainian and other workers in international Marxist organisations, and make their contribution (both in Russian and in Yiddish) towards creating the international culture of the working-class movement – those Jews, despite the separatism of the Bund, uphold the best traditions of Jewry by fighting the slogan of 'national culture'.

Bourgeois nationalism and proletarian internationalism – these are the two irreconcilably hostile slogans that correspond to the two great class camps throughout the capitalist world, and express the *two* policies (nay, the two world outlooks) in the national question. In advocating the slogan of national culture and building upon it an entire plan and practical programme of what they call 'cultural-national autonomy', the Bundists are *in effect* instruments of bourgeois nationalism among the workers.

The nationalist bogey of 'assimilation'

The question of assimilation, i.e. of the shedding of national features, and absorption by another nation, strikingly illustrates the consequences of the nationalist vacillations of the Bundists and their fellow-thinkers.

Mr. Liebman, who faithfully conveys and repeats the stock arguments, or rather, tricks, of the Bundists, has qualified as "the *old assimilation story*" the demand for the unity and amalgamation of the workers of all nationalities in a given country in united workers' organisations (see the concluding part of the article in *Severnaya Pravda*).

> Consequently, [says Mr. F Liebman, commenting on the concluding part of the article in *Severnaya Pravda*] if asked what nationality he belongs to, the worker must answer: "I am a social-democrat."

Our Bundist considers this the acme of wit. As a matter of fact, he gives himself away completely by *such* witticisms and outcries about 'assimilation', *levelled against* a consistently democratic and Marxist slogan.

Developing capitalism knows two historical tendencies in the national question. The first is the awakening of national life and national movements, the struggle against all national oppression, and the creation of national states. The second is the development and growing frequency of international intercourse in every form, the break-down of national barriers, the creation of the international unity of capital, of economic life in general, of politics, science, etc.

Both tendencies are a universal law of capitalism. The former predominates in the beginning of its development, the latter characterises a mature capitalism that is moving towards its transformation into socialist society. The Marxists' national programme takes both tendencies into account, and advocates, firstly, the equality of nations and languages and the impermissibility of all *privileges* in this respect (and also the right of nations to self-determination with which we shall deal separately later); secondly, the principle of internationalism and uncompromising struggle against contamination of the proletariat with bourgeois nationalism, even of the most refined kind.

The question arises: what does our Bundist mean when he cries out to heaven against 'assimilation'? He *could not* have meant the oppression of nations, or the *privileges* enjoyed by a particular nation, because the word 'assimilation' here does not fit at all, because all Marxists, individually, and as an official, united whole, have quite definitely and unambiguously condemned the slightest violence against and oppression and inequality of nations, and finally because this general Marxist idea, which the Bundist has attacked, is expressed in the *Severnaya Pravda* article in the most emphatic manner.

No, evasion is impossible here. In condemning 'assimilation' Mr. Liebman had in mind, *not* violence, *not* inequality, and *not* privileges. Is there anything real left in the concept of assimilation, after all violence and all inequality have been eliminated?

Yes, there undoubtedly is. What is left is capitalism's world-historical tendency to break down national barriers, obliterate national distinctions, and to *assimilate* nations – a tendency which manifests itself more and more powerfully with every passing decade, and is one of the greatest driving forces transforming capitalism into socialism.

Whoever does not recognise and champion the equality of nations and languages, and does not fight against all national oppression or inequality, is not a Marxist; he is not even a democrat. That is beyond doubt. But it is also beyond doubt that the pseudo-Marxist who heaps abuse upon a Marxist of another nation for being an 'assimilator' is simply a *nationalist philistine*. In this unhandsome category of people are all the Bundists and (as we shall shortly see) Ukrainian nationalist-socialists such as L Yurkevich, Dontsov and co.

To show concretely how reactionary the views held by these nationalist philistines are, we shall cite facts of three kinds.

It is the Jewish nationalists in Russia in general, and the Bundists in particular, who vociferate most about Russian orthodox Marxists being 'assimilators'. And yet, as the aforementioned figures show, out of the ten and a half million Jews all over the world, *about half* that number live in the *civilised* world, where conditions favouring 'assimilation' are *strongest*, whereas the unhappy, downtrodden, disfranchised Jews in Russia and Galicia, who are crushed under the heel of the Purishkeviches (Russian and Polish), live where conditions for 'assimilation' *least* prevail, where there is most segregation, and even a 'Pale of Settlement', a *numerus clausus*[3] and other charming features of the Purishkevich regime.

The Jews in the civilised world are not a nation, they have in the main become assimilated, say Karl Kautsky and Otto Bauer. The Jews in Galicia and in Russia are not a nation; unfortunately (through *no* fault of their own but through that of the Purishkeviches), they are still a *caste* here. Such is the incontrovertible judgement of people who are undoubtedly familiar with the history of Jewry and take the above-cited facts into consideration.

What do these facts prove? It is that only Jewish reactionary philistines, who want to turn back the wheel of history, and make it

---

3 *Numerus clausus* ('closed number' in Latin) refers to the numerical restriction imposed on the admission of Jewish people to state secondary and higher educational establishments, employment at factories, offices, and the professions.

proceed, not from the conditions prevailing in Russia and Galicia to those prevailing in Paris and New York, but in the reverse direction – only they can clamour against 'assimilation'.

The best Jews, those who are celebrated in world history, and have given the world foremost leaders of democracy and socialism, have never clamoured against assimilation. It is only those who contemplate the 'rear aspect' of Jewry with reverential awe that clamour against assimilation.

A rough idea of the scale which the general process of assimilation of nations is assuming under the present conditions of advanced capitalism may be obtained, for example, from the immigration statistics of the United States of America. During the decade between 1891-1900, Europe sent 3,700,000 people there, and during the nine years between 1901 and 1909, 7,200,000. The 1900 census in the United States recorded over 10,000,000 foreigners. New York State, in which, according to the same census, there were over 78,000 Austrians, 136,000 Englishmen, 20,000 Frenchmen, 480,000 Germans, 37,000 Hungarians, 425,000 Irish, 182,000 Italians, 70,000 Poles, 166,000 people from Russia (mostly Jews), 43,000 Swedes, etc., grinds down national distinctions. And what is taking place on a grand, international scale in New York is also to be seen in *every* big city and industrial township.

No one unobsessed by nationalist prejudices can fail to perceive that this process of assimilation of nations by capitalism means the greatest historical progress, the break down of hidebound national conservatism in the various backwoods, especially in backward countries like Russia.

Take Russia and the attitude of Great-Russians towards the Ukrainians. Naturally, every democrat, not to mention Marxists, will strongly oppose the incredible humiliation of Ukrainians, and demand complete equality for them. But it would be a downright betrayal of socialism and a silly policy *even* from the standpoint of the bourgeois 'national aims' of the Ukrainians to *weaken* the ties and the alliance between the Ukrainian and Great-Russian proletariat that now exist within the confines of a single state.

Mr. Lev Yurkevich, who calls himself a 'Marxist' (poor Marx!), is an example of that silly policy. In 1906, Sokolovsky (Basok) and Lukashevich (Tuchapsky) asserted, Mr. Yurkevich writes, that the Ukrainian proletariat had become completely Russified and needed no separate organisation. Without quoting a single fact *bearing on the direct issue*, Mr. Yurkevich falls upon both for saying this and cries out hysterically – quite in the spirit of the basest, most stupid and most reactionary nationalism – that this is 'national passivity', 'national renunciation', that these men have "split [!!!] the Ukrainian Marxists", and so forth. Today, despite the "growth of Ukrainian national consciousness among the workers", the *minority* of the workers are "nationally conscious", while the majority, Mr. Yurkevich assures us, "are still under, the influence of Russian culture". And it is our duty, this nationalist philistine exclaims, "not to follow the masses, but to lead them, to explain to them their national aims (*natsionalna sprava*)" (*Dzvin*, p. 89).

This argument of Mr. Yurkevich's is wholly bourgeois-nationalistic. But even from the point of view of the bourgeois nationalists, some of whom stand for complete equality and autonomy for the Ukraine, while others stand for an independent Ukrainian state, this argument will not wash. The Ukrainians' striving for liberation is opposed by the Great-Russian and Polish landlord class and by the bourgeoisie of these two nations. What social force is capable of standing up to these classes? The first decade of the twentieth century provided an actual reply to this question: that force is none other than the working class, which rallies the democratic peasantry behind it. By striving to divide, and thereby weaken, the genuinely democratic force, whose victory would make national oppression impossible, Mr. Yurkevich is betraying not only the interests of democracy in general, but also the interests of his own country, the Ukraine. Given united action by the Great-Russian and Ukrainian proletarians, a free Ukraine is *possible*; without such unity, it is out of the question.

But Marxists do not confine themselves to the bourgeois-national standpoint. For several decades a well-defined process of accelerated economic development has been going on in the South, i.e. the Ukraine, attracting hundreds of thousands of peasants and workers from Great Russia to the capitalist farms, mines, and cities. The 'assimilation' – within these limits – of the Great-Russian and Ukrainian proletariat is an indisputable fact. *And this fact is undoubtedly* progressive. Capitalism is replacing the ignorant, conservative, settled muzhik of the Great-Russian or Ukrainian backwoods with a mobile proletarian whose conditions of life break down specifically national narrow-mindedness, both Great-Russian and Ukrainian. Even if we assume that, in time, there will be a state frontier between Great Russia and the Ukraine, the historically progressive nature of the 'assimilation' of the Great-Russian and Ukrainian workers will be as undoubted as the progressive nature of the grinding down of nations in America. The freer the Ukraine and Great Russia become, the *more extensive and more rapid* will be the development of capitalism, which will still more powerfully attract the workers, the working masses of *all* nations from all regions of the state and from all the neighbouring states (should Russia become a neighbouring state in relation to the Ukraine) to the cities, the mines, and the factories.

Mr. Lev Yurkevich acts like a real bourgeois, and a short-sighted, narrow-minded, obtuse bourgeois at that, i.e. like a philistine, when he dismisses the benefits to be gained from, the intercourse, amalgamation and assimilation of the *proletariat* of the two nations, for the sake of the momentary success of the Ukrainian national cause (*sprava*). The national cause comes first and the proletarian cause second, the bourgeois nationalists say, with the Yurkeviches, Dontsovs and similar would-be Marxists repeating it after them. The proletarian cause must come first, we say, because it not only protects the lasting and fundamental interests of labour and of humanity, but also those of democracy; and without democracy neither an autonomous nor an independent Ukraine is conceivable.

Another point to be noted in Mr. Yurkevich's argument, which is so extraordinarily rich in nationalist gems, is this: the minority of

Ukrainian workers are nationally conscious, he says: "the majority are still under the influence of Russian culture" (*bilshist perebuvaye shche pid vplyvom rosiiskoi kultury*).

Contraposing Ukrainian culture as a whole to Great-Russian culture as a whole, when speaking of the proletariat, is a gross betrayal of the proletariat's interests for the benefit of bourgeois nationalism.

There are two nations in every modern nation – we say to all nationalist-socialists. There are two national cultures in every national culture. There is the Great-Russian culture of the Purishkeviches, Guchkovs and Struves – but there is also the Great-Russian culture typified in the names of Chernyshevsky and Plekhanov. There are *the same two* cultures in the Ukraine as there are in Germany, in France, in England, among the Jews, and so forth. If the majority of the Ukrainian workers are under the influence of Great-Russian culture, we also know definitely that the ideas of Great-Russian democracy and Social-Democracy operate parallel with the Great-Russian clerical and bourgeois culture. In fighting the latter kind of 'culture', the Ukrainian *Marxist* will always bring the former into focus, and say to his workers:

> 'We must snatch at, make use of, and develop to the utmost every opportunity for intercourse with the Great-Russian class-conscious workers, with their literature and with their range of ideas; the fundamental interests of *both* the Ukrainian and the Great-Russian working-class movements demand it.'

If a Ukrainian Marxist allows himself to he swayed by his *quite legitimate and natural* hatred of the Great-Russian oppressors *to such a degree* that he transfers even a particle of this hatred, even if it be only estrangement, to the proletarian culture and proletarian cause of the Great-Russian workers, then such a Marxist will get bogged down in bourgeois nationalism. Similarly, the Great-Russian Marxist will be bogged down, not only in bourgeois, but also in Black-Hundred nationalism, if he loses sight, even for a moment, of the demand for complete equality for the Ukrainians, or of their *right* to form an independent state.

The Great-Russian and Ukrainian workers must work together, and, as long as they live in a single state, act in the closest organisational unity and concert, towards a common or international culture of the proletarian movement, displaying absolute tolerance in the question of the language in which propaganda is conducted, and in the purely local or purely national *details* of that propaganda. This is the imperative demand of Marxism. All advocacy of the segregation of the workers of one nation from those of another, all attacks upon Marxist 'assimilation', or attempts, where the proletariat is concerned, to contrapose one national culture as a whole to another allegedly integral national culture, and so forth, is *bourgeois* nationalism, against which it is essential to wage a ruthless struggle.

'Cultural-national' autonomy

The question of the 'national culture' slogan is of enormous importance to Marxists, not only because it determines the ideological content of all our propaganda and agitation on the national question, as distinct from bourgeois propaganda, but also because the entire programme of the much-discussed cultural-national autonomy is based on this slogan.

The main and fundamental flaw in this programme is that it aims at introducing the most refined, most absolute and most extreme nationalism. The gist of this programme is that every citizen registers as belonging to a particular nation, and every nation constitutes a legal entity with the right to impose compulsory taxation on its members, with national parliaments (Diets) and national secretaries of state (ministers).

Such an idea, applied to the national question, resembles Proudhon's idea, as applied to capitalism. Not abolishing capitalism and its basis – commodity production – but *purging* that basis of abuses, of excrescences, and so forth; not abolishing exchange and exchange value, but, on the contrary, making it 'constitutional', universal, absolute, '*fair*', and free of fluctuations, crises and abuses – such was Proudhon's idea.

Just as Proudhon was petty-bourgeois, and his theory converted exchange and commodity production into an absolute category and exalted them as the acme of perfection, so is the theory and programme of 'cultural-national autonomy' petty bourgeois, for it converts bourgeois nationalism into an absolute category, exalts it as the acme of perfection, and purges it of violence, injustice, etc.

Marxism cannot be reconciled with nationalism, be it even of the 'most just', 'purest', most refined and civilised brand. In place of all forms of nationalism Marxism advances internationalism, the amalgamation of all nations in the higher unity, a unity that is growing before our eyes with every mile of railway line that is built, with every international trust, and every workers' association that is formed (an association that is international in its economic activities as well as in its ideas and aims).

The principle of nationality is historically inevitable in bourgeois society and, taking this society into due account, the Marxist fully recognises the historical legitimacy of national movements. But to prevent this recognition from becoming an apologia of nationalism, it must be strictly limited to what is progressive in such movements, in order that this recognition may not lead to bourgeois ideology obscuring proletarian consciousness.

The awakening of the masses from feudal lethargy, and their struggle against all national oppression, for the sovereignty of the people, of the nation, are progressive. Hence, it is the Marxist's *bounden* duty to stand for the most resolute and consistent democratism on all aspects of the national question. This task is largely a negative one. But this is the limit the proletariat can go to in supporting nationalism, for beyond that begins the 'positive' activity of the *bourgeoisie* striving to *fortify* nationalism.

To throw off the feudal yoke, all national oppression, and all privileges enjoyed by any particular nation or language, is the imperative duty of the proletariat as a democratic force, and is certainly in the interests of the proletarian class struggle, which is obscured and retarded by bickering on the national question. But to go *beyond* these strictly limited and definite historical limits in helping bourgeois nationalism means betraying the proletariat and siding with the bourgeoisie. There is a borderline here, which is often very slight and which the Bundists and Ukrainian nationalist-socialists completely lose sight of.

Combat all national oppression? Yes, of course! Fight *for* any kind of national development, *for* 'national culture' in general? – Of course not. The economic development of capitalist society presents us with examples of immature national movements all over the world, examples of the formation of big nations out of a number of small ones, or to the detriment of some of the small ones, and also examples of the assimilation of nations. The development of nationality in general is the principle of bourgeois nationalism; hence the exclusiveness of bourgeois nationalism, hence the endless national bickering. The proletariat, however, far from undertaking to uphold the national development of every nation, on the contrary, warns the masses against such illusions, stands for the fullest freedom of capitalist intercourse and welcomes every kind of assimilation of nations, except that which is founded on force or privilege.

Consolidating nationalism within a certain 'justly' delimited sphere, 'constitutionalising' nationalism, and securing the separation of all nations from one another by means of a special state institution – such is the ideological foundation and content of cultural-national autonomy. This idea is thoroughly bourgeois and thoroughly false. The proletariat cannot support any consecration of nationalism; on the contrary, it supports everything that helps to obliterate national distinctions and remove national barriers; it supports everything that makes the ties between nationalities closer and closer, or tends to merge nations. To act differently means siding with reactionary nationalist philistinism.

When, at their Congress in Brünn (in 1899), the Austrian social-democrats discussed the plan for 'cultural-national autonomy', practically no attention was paid to a theoretical appraisal of that plan. It is, however, noteworthy that the following two arguments were levelled against this programme: (1) it would tend to strengthen clericalism; (2) "its result would be the perpetuation of chauvinism, its introduction into every small community, into every small group" (p. 92 of the official report of the Brünn Congress, in German. A Russian translation was published by the Jewish nationalist party, the JSLP).[4]

There can be no doubt that 'national culture', in the ordinary sense of the term, i.e. schools etc., is at present under the predominant influence of the clergy and the bourgeois chauvinists in all countries in the world. When the Bundists, in advocating 'cultural-national' autonomy, say that the constituting of nations will keep the class struggle within them *clean* of all extraneous considerations, then that is manifest and ridiculous sophistry. It is primarily in the economic and political sphere that a serious class struggle is waged in any capitalist society. To separate the sphere of education *from this* is, firstly, absurdly utopian, because schools (like 'national culture' in general) cannot be separated from economics and politics; secondly, it is the economic and political life of a capitalist country that *necessitates* at every step the smashing of the absurd and outmoded national barriers and prejudices, whereas separation of the school system and the like, would only perpetuate, intensify and strengthen 'pure' clericalism and 'pure' bourgeois chauvinism.

On the boards of joint-stock companies we find capitalists of different nations sitting together in complete harmony. At the factories workers of different nations work side by side. In any really serious and profound political issue sides are taken according to classes, not nations. Withdrawing school education and the like from state control and placing it under the control of the nations is in effect an attempt to *separate* from economics, which unites the nations, the most highly, so to speak, ideological sphere of social life, the sphere in which 'pure' national culture or the national cultivation of clericalism and chauvinism has the freest play.

In practice, the plan for 'extra-territorial' or 'cultural-national' autonomy could mean only one thing: *the division of educational*

---

4   The JSLP (Jewish Socialist Labour Party) was a petty-bourgeois nationalist organisation, founded in 1906. In 1907, it became a sub-section of the Party of Socialist-Revolutionaries.

affairs according to nationality, i.e. the introduction of national curias in school affairs. Sufficient thought to the real significance of the famous Bund plan will enable one to realise how utterly reactionary it is even from the standpoint of democracy, let alone from that of the proletarian class struggle for socialism.

A single instance and a single scheme for the 'nationalisation' of the school system will make this point abundantly clear. In the United States of America the division of the States into Northern and Southern holds to this day in all departments of life; the former possess the greatest traditions of freedom and of struggle against the slave-owners; the latter possess the greatest traditions of slave ownership, survivals of persecution of the Negroes, who are economically oppressed and culturally backward (44 per cent of Negroes are illiterate, and 6 per cent of whites), and so forth. In the Northern States, Negro children attend the same schools as white children do. In the South there are separate 'national', or racial, whichever you please, schools for Negro children. I think that this is the sole instance of actual 'nationalisation' of schools.

In Eastern Europe there exists a country where things like the Beilis case[5] are still possible, and Jews are condemned by the Purishkeviches to a condition worse than that of the Negroes. In that country a scheme for *nationalising Jewish schools* was recently mooted in the ministry. Happily, this reactionary utopia is no more likely to be realised than the utopia of the Austrian petty bourgeoisie, who have despaired of achieving consistent democracy or of putting an end to national bickering, and have invented for the nation's school-education *compartments* to keep them from bickering *over the distribution* of schools ... but have 'constituted' themselves for an *eternal* bickering of one 'national culture' with another.

---

5   In 1913 the tsar's government staged a trial of Menahem Beilis, a Jewish man falsely accused of the ritual murder of a Christian boy. The murder was actually committed by the Black Hundreds. The government's aim was to stir up antisemitism and take advantage of anti-Jewish pogroms to divert the people's attention from the revolutionary movement growing throughout the country. The trial aroused public indignation. In a number of towns, workers held protest demonstrations. Beilis was eventually acquitted.

In Austria, the idea of cultural-national autonomy has remained largely a flight of literary fancy, which the Austrian social-democrats themselves have not taken seriously. In Russia, however, it has been incorporated in the programmes of all the Jewish bourgeois parties, and of several petty-bourgeois, opportunist elements in the different nations – for example, the Bundists, the liquidators in the Caucasus, and the conference of Russian national parties of the Left-Narodnik trend. (This conference, we will mention parenthetically, took place in 1907, its decision being adopted *with abstention* on the part of the Russian Socialist-Revolutionaries and the PSP, the Polish social-patriots. Abstention from voting is a method surprisingly characteristic of the Socialist-Revolutionaries and PSP, when they want to show their attitude towards a most important question of principle in the sphere of the national programme!)

In Austria it was Otto Bauer, the principal theoretician of 'cultural-national autonomy', who devoted a special chapter of his book to prove that such a programme cannot possibly be proposed for the Jews. In Russia, however, it is precisely among the Jews that all the bourgeois parties – and the Bund which echoes them – have adopted this programme.[6] What does this go to show? It goes to show that history, through the political practice of another state, has exposed the absurdity of Bauer's invention, in exactly the same way as the Russian Bernsteinians (Struve, Tugan-Baranovsky, Berdayev and

---

6 That the Bundists often vehemently deny that all the Jewish bourgeois parties have accepted 'cultural-national autonomy' is understandable. This fact only too glaringly exposes the actual role being played by the Bund. When Mr. Manin, a Bundist, tried, in *Luch* to repeat his denial, he was fully exposed by N Skop (see *Prosveshcheniye* No. 3). But when Mr. Lev Yurkevich, in *Dzvin* (1913, Nos. 7-8, p. 92), quotes from *Prosveshcheniye* (No. 3, p. 78) N Skop's statement that "the Bundists together with all the Jewish bourgeois parties and groups have long been advocating cultural-national autonomy" and distorts this statement by dropping the word "Bundists", and substituting the words "national rights" for the words "cultural national autonomy", one can only raise one's hands in amazement! Mr. Lev Yurkevich is not only a nationalist, not only an astonishing ignoramus in matters concerning the history of the social-democrats and their programme, but a downright falsifier of quotations for the benefit of the Bund. The affairs of the Bund and the Yurkeviches must be in a bad way indeed! – *Lenin*

co.), through their rapid evolution from Marxism to liberalism, have exposed the real ideological content of the German Bernsteinism.

Neither the Austrian nor the Russian social-democrats have incorporated 'cultural-national' autonomy in their programme. However, the Jewish bourgeois parties in a most backward country, and a number of petty-bourgeois, so-called socialist groups *have adopted it* in order to spread ideas of bourgeois nationalism among the working class in a refined form. This fact speaks for itself.

* * *

Since we have had to touch upon the Austrian programme on the national question, we must reassert a truth which is often distorted by the Bundists. At the Brünn Congress a *pure* programme of 'cultural-national autonomy' *was* presented. This was the programme of the South-Slav Social Democrats, Section 2 of which reads:

> Every nation living in Austria, irrespective of the territory occupied by its members, constitutes an autonomous group which manages all its national (language and cultural) affairs quite independently.

This programme was supported, not only by Kristan but by the influential Ellenbogen. But it was withdrawn; not a single vote was cast for it. A *territorialist* programme was adopted, i.e. one that did *not* create *any* national groups "irrespective of the territory occupied by the members of the nation". Clause 3 of the adopted programme reads:

> The self governing *regions* of one and the same nation shall jointly form a nationally united association, which shall manage its national affairs on an absolutely autonomous basis. (cf. *Prosveshcheniye*, 1913, No. 4, p. 28.)[7]

Clearly, this compromise programme is wrong too. An example will illustrate this. The German colonists' community in Saratov Gubernia, plus the German working-class suburb of Riga or Lodz, plus the German housing estate near St. Petersburg, etc., would

---

7   Lenin is referring to Stalin's article 'Marxism and the National Question', published in the legal Bolshevik journal *Prosveshcheniye*. See footnote 2 on p. 229.

constitute a 'nationally united association' of Germans in Russia. Obviously the social-democrats cannot *demand* such a thing or *enforce* such an association, although of course they do not in the least deny *freedom* of every kind of association, including associations of any communities of any nationality in a given state. The segregation, by a law of the state, of Germans, etc., in different localities and of different classes in Russia into a single German-national association may be practised by anybody – priests, bourgeois or philistines, but not by social-democrats.

The equality of nations and the rights of national minorities

When they discuss the national question, opportunists in Russia are given to citing the example of Austria. In my article in *Severnaya Pravda* (No. 10, *Prosveshcheniye*, pp. 96-98),[8] which the opportunists have attacked (Mr. Semkovsky in *Novaya Rabochaya Gazeta*, and Mr. Liebman in *Zeit*), I asserted that, insofar as that is at all possible under capitalism, there was only one solution of the national question, viz., through consistent democracy. In proof of this, I referred, among other things, to Switzerland.

This has not been to the liking of the two opportunists mentioned above, who are trying to refute it or belittle its significance. Kautsky, we are told, said that Switzerland is an exception; Switzerland, if you please, has a special kind of decentralisation, a special history, special geographical conditions, unique distribution of a population that speak different languages, etc., etc.

All these are nothing more than attempts to *evade* the issue. To be sure, Switzerland is an exception in that she is not a single-nation state. But Austria and Russia are also exceptions (or are backward, as Kautsky adds). To be sure, it was only her special, unique historical and social conditions that ensured Switzerland *greater* democracy than most of her European neighbours.

---

8   See Lenin, 'Liberals and Democrats on the Language Question', reproduced at the start of this text, p. 238. It was also published as a separate article in *Severnaya Pravda* and *Prosveshcheniye*.

But where does all this come in, if we are speaking of the *model* to be adopted? In the whole world, under present-day conditions, countries in which any particular institution has been founded on *consistent* democratic principles are the exception. Does this prevent us, in our programme, from upholding consistent democracy in all institutions?

Switzerland's special features lie in her history, her geographical and other conditions. Russia's special features lie in the strength of her proletariat, which has no precedent in the epoch of bourgeois revolutions, and in her shocking general backwardness, which objectively necessitates an exceptionally rapid and resolute advance, under the threat of all sorts of drawbacks and reverses.

We are evolving a national programme from the proletarian standpoint; since when has it been recommended that the worst examples, rather than the best, be taken as a model?

At all events, does it not remain an indisputable and undisputed fact that national peace under capitalism has been achieved (insofar as it is achievable) *exclusively* in countries where consistent democracy prevails?

Since this is indisputable, the opportunists' persistent references to Austria instead of Switzerland are nothing but a typical Cadet device, for the Cadets always copy the worst European constitutions rather than the best.

In Switzerland there are *three* official languages, but bills submitted to a referendum are printed in *five* languages, that is to say, in two Romansh dialects, in addition to the three official languages. According to the 1900 census, these two dialects are spoken by 38,651 out of the 3,315,443 inhabitants of Switzerland, i.e. by a little over *one per cent*. In the army, commissioned and non-commissioned officers "are given the fullest freedom to speak to the men in their native language". In the cantons of Graubünden and Wallis (each with a population of a little over a hundred thousand) both dialects enjoy complete equality.

The question is: should we advocate and support this, the living *experience* of an advanced country, or borrow from the Austrians *inventions* like 'extra-territorial autonomy', which have not yet been tried out anywhere in the world (and not yet been adopted by the Austrians themselves)?

To advocate this invention is to advocate the division of school education according to nationality, and that is a downright harmful idea. The experience of Switzerland proves, however, that the greatest (relative) degree of national peace *can be, and has been, ensured in practice* where you have a consistent (again relative) democracy throughout the state.

> In Switzerland, [say people who have studied this question] there is no national question in the East-European sense of the term. The very phrase (national question) is unknown there…
>
> Switzerland left the struggle between nationalities a long way behind, in 1797-1803.

This means that the epoch of the great French Revolution, which provided the most democratic solution of the current problems of the transition from feudalism to capitalism, *succeeded* incidentally, *en passant* [in passing], in '*solving*' the national question.

Let the Semkovskys, Liebmans, and other opportunists now try to assert that this 'exclusively Swiss' solution is *inapplicable* to any uyezd or even part of an uyezd in Russia, where out of a population of only 200,000, 40,000 speak *two dialects* and want to have *complete equality* of language in their area!

Advocacy of complete equality of nations and languages distinguishes only the consistently democratic elements in each nation (i.e. only the proletarians), and *unites* them, not according to nationality, but in a profound and earnest desire to improve the entire system of state. On the contrary, advocacy of 'cultural-national autonomy', despite the pious wishes of individuals and groups, *divides the nations* and in fact draws the workers and the bourgeoisie of any one nation closer together (the adoption of this 'cultural-national autonomy' by all the Jewish bourgeois parties).

Guaranteeing the rights of a national minority is inseparably linked up with the principle of complete equality. In my article in

Severnaya Pravda this principle was expressed in almost the same terms as in the later, official and more accurate decision of the conference of Marxists. That decision demands:

> ... the incorporation in the constitution of a fundamental law which shall declare null and void all privileges enjoyed by any one nation and all infringements of the rights of a national minority.

Mr. Liebman tries to ridicule this formula and asks: "Who knows what the rights of a national minority are?" Do these rights, he wants to know, include the right of the minority to have "its own programme" for the national schools? How large must the national minority be to have the right to have its own judges, officials, and schools with instruction in its own language? Mr. Liebman wants it to be inferred from these questions that a *'positive'* national programme is essential.

Actually, these questions clearly show what reactionary ideas our Bundist tries to smuggle through under cover of a dispute on supposedly minor details and particulars.

"Its own programme" in its national schools! ... Marxists, my dear nationalist-socialist, have a *general* school programme which demands, for example, an absolutely secular school. As far as Marxists are concerned, no *departure* from this general programme is anywhere or at any time permissible in a democratic state (the question of introducing any 'local' subjects, languages, and so forth into it being decided by the local inhabitants). However, from the principle of "taking educational affairs out of the hands of the state" and placing them under the control of the nations, it ensues that we, the workers, must allow the 'nations' in our democratic state to spend the people's money on clerical schools! Without being aware of the fact, Mr. Liebman has clearly demonstrated the reactionary nature of 'cultural-national autonomy'!

"How large must a national minority be?" This is not defined even in the Austrian programme, of which the Bundists are enamoured. It says (more briefly and less clearly than our programme does):

> The rights of the national minorities are protected by a special law to be passed by the Imperial Parliament. (Section 4 of the Brünn programme.)

Why has nobody asked the Austrian social-democrats the question: what exactly is that law, and exactly which rights and of which minority is it to protect?

That is because all sensible people understand that it is inappropriate and impossible to define particulars in a programme. A programme lays down only fundamental principles. In this case the fundamental principle is implied with the Austrians, and directly expressed in the decision of the latest conference of Russian Marxists. That principle is: no national privileges and no national inequality.

Let us take a concrete example to make the point clear to the Bundist. According to the school census of 18 January 1911, St. Petersburg elementary schools under the Ministry of Public 'Education' were attended by 48,076 pupils. Of these, 396, i.e. less than 1 per cent, were Jews. The other figures are: Rumanian pupils: 2; Georgians: 1; Armenians: 3; etc. Is it possible to draw up a 'positive' national programme that will cover this diversity of relationships and conditions? (And St. Petersburg is, of course, far from being the city with the most mixed population in Russia.) Even such specialists in national 'subtleties' as the Bundists would hardly be able to draw up such a programme.

And yet, if the constitution of the country contained a fundamental law rendering null and void every measure that infringed the rights of a minority, any citizen would be able to demand the rescinding of orders prohibiting, for example, the hiring, at state expense, of special teachers of Hebrew, Jewish history, and the like, or the provision of state-owned premises for lectures for Jewish, Armenian, or Rumanian children, or even for the one Georgian child. At all events, it is by no means impossible to meet, on the basis of equality, all the reasonable and just wishes of the national minorities, and nobody will say that advocacy of equality is harmful. On the other hand, it would certainly be harmful to advocate division of schools according to nationality, to advocate, for example, special schools for

Jewish children in St. Petersburg, and it would be utterly impossible to set up national schools for *every* national minority, for one, two or three children.

Furthermore, it is impossible, in any country-wide law, to define how large a national minority must be to be entitled to special schools, or to special teachers for supplementary subjects, etc.

On the other hand, a country-wide law establishing equality can be worked out in detail and developed through special regulations and the decisions of regional Diets, and town, Zemstvo, village commune and other authorities.

Centralisation and autonomy

In his rejoinder, Mr. Liebman writes:

> Take our Lithuania, the Baltic province, Poland, Volhynia, South Russia, etc – everywhere you will find a *mixed* population; there is not a single city that does not have a large national minority. However far decentralisation is carried out, different nationalities will always be found living together in different places (chiefly in urban communities); and it is democratism that surrenders a national minority to the national majority. But, as we know, VI [Lenin] is opposed to the federal state structure and the boundless decentralisation that exist in the Swiss Federation. The question is: what was his point in citing the example of Switzerland?

My object in citing the example of Switzerland has already been explained above. I have also explained that the problem of protecting the rights of a national minority can be solved *only* by a country-wide law promulgated in a consistently democratic state that does not depart from the principle of equality. But in the passage quoted above, Mr. Liebman repeats still another of the most common (and most fallacious) arguments (or sceptical remarks) which are usually made against the Marxist national programme, and which, therefore, deserve examination.

Marxists are, of course, opposed to federation and decentralisation, for the simple reason that capitalism requires for its development the largest and most centralised possible states. *Other conditions being equal*, the class-conscious proletariat will always stand for the larger state. It will always fight against medieval particularism, and will always welcome the closest possible economic amalgamation of large territories in which the proletariat's struggle against the bourgeoisie can develop on a broad basis.

Capitalism's broad and rapid development of the productive forces *calls for* large, politically compact and united territories, since only here can the bourgeois class – together with its inevitable antipode, the proletarian class – unite and sweep away all the old, medieval, caste, parochial, petty-national, religious and other barriers.

The right of nations to self-determination, i.e. the right to secede and form independent national states, will be dealt with elsewhere.[9] But while, and insofar as, different nations constitute a single state, Marxists will never, under any circumstances, advocate either the federal principle or decentralisation. The great centralised state is a tremendous historical step forward from medieval disunity to the future socialist unity of the whole world, and only *via* such a state (*inseparably* connected with capitalism), can there be any road to socialism.

It would, however, be inexcusable to forget that in advocating centralism we advocate exclusively *democratic* centralism. On this point all the philistines in general, and the nationalist philistines in particular (including the late Dragomanov), have so confused the issue that we are obliged again and again to spend time clarifying it.

Far from precluding local self-government, with *autonomy* for regions having special economic and social conditions, a distinct national composition of the population, and so forth, democratic centralism necessarily demands *both*. In Russia centralism is constantly confused with tyranny and bureaucracy. This confusion has naturally arisen from the history of Russia, but even so it is quite inexcusable for a Marxist to yield to it.

This can best be explained by a concrete example.

---

9   See Lenin, 'The Right of Nations to Self-Determination', in this volume, p. 33.

In her lengthy article 'The National Question and Autonomy', Rosa Luxemburg, among many other curious errors (which we shall deal with below), commits the exceptionally curious one of trying to *restrict* the demand for autonomy to Poland alone.

But first let us see *how* she defines autonomy.

Rosa Luxemburg admits – and being a Marxist she is of course bound to admit – that all the major and important economic and political questions of capitalist society must be dealt with exclusively by the central parliament of the whole country concerned, not by the autonomous Diets of the individual regions. These questions include tariff policy, laws governing commerce and industry, transport and means of communication (railways, post, telegraph, telephone, etc.), the army, the taxation system, civil[10] and criminal law, the general principles of education (for example, the law on purely secular schools, on universal education, on the minimum programme, on democratic school management, etc.), the labour protection laws, and political liberties (right of association), etc., etc.

The autonomous Diets – on the basis of the general laws of the country – should deal with questions of purely local, regional, or national significance. Amplifying this idea in great – not to say excessive – detail, Rosa Luxemburg mentions, for example, the construction of local railways (No. 12, p. 149) and local highways (No. 14-15, p. 376), etc.

Obviously, one cannot conceive of a modern, truly democratic state that did *not* grant such autonomy to every region having any appreciably distinct economic and social features, populations of a specific national composition, etc. The principle of centralism, which is essential for the development of capitalism, is not violated by this (local and regional) autonomy, but on the contrary is applied by it *democratically*, not bureaucratically. The broad, free and rapid development of capitalism would be impossible, or at least greatly impeded, by the *absence* of such autonomy, which *facilitates* the

---

10 In elaborating her ideas Rosa Luxemburg goes into details, mentioning, for example – and quite rightly – divorce laws (No. 12, p. 162 of the [journal *Przegląd Socjaldemokratyczny*, Kraków, 1908 and 1909]). – *Lenin*

concentration of capital, the development of the productive forces, the unity of the bourgeoisie and the unity of the proletariat on a *country-wide* scale; for bureaucratic interference in *purely* local (regional, national, and other) questions is one of the greatest obstacles to economic and political development in general, and an obstacle to *centralism* in serious, important and fundamental matters in particular.

One cannot help smiling, therefore, when reading how our magnificent Rosa Luxemburg tries to prove, with a very serious air and 'purely Marxist' phrases, that the demand for autonomy is applicable *only* to Poland and *only* by way of exception! Of course, there is not a grain of 'parochial' patriotism in this; we have here only 'practical' considerations... in the case of Lithuania, for example.

Rosa Luxemburg takes four gubernias – Vilna, Kovno, Grodno and Suvalki – assuring her readers (and herself) that these are inhabited 'mainly' by Lithuanians; and by adding the inhabitants of these gubernias together she finds that Lithuanians constitute 23 per cent of the total population, and if Zhmuds are added, they constitute 31 per cent – less than a third. The natural inference is that the idea of autonomy for Lithuania is "arbitrary and artificial" (No. 10, p. 807).

The reader who is familiar with the commonly known defects of our Russian official statistics will quickly see Rosa Luxemburg's mistake. Why take Grodno Gubernia where the Lithuanians constitute only 0.2 per cent, *one-fifth of 1 per cent*, of the population? Why take the whole Vilna Gubernia and not its Troki Uyezd alone, where the Lithuanians constitute the *majority* of the population? Why take the whole Suvalki Gubernia and put the number of Lithuanians at 52 per cent of the population, and not the Lithuanian uyezds of that gubernia, i.e. five out of the seven, in which Lithuanians constitute 72 per cent of the population?

It is ridiculous to talk about the conditions and demands of modern capitalism while at the same time taking not the 'modern', not the 'capitalist', but the medieval, feudal and official-bureaucratic administrative divisions of Russia, and in their crudest form at that (gubernias instead of uyezds). Plainly, there can be no question of any serious local reform in Russia until these divisions are abolished and superseded by a *really* 'modern' division that really meets the requirements, *not* of the Treasury, *not* of the bureaucracy, *not* of routine, *not* of the landlords, *not* of the priests, but of capitalism; and one of the modern requirements of capitalism is undoubtedly the greatest possible national uniformity of the population, for nationality and language identity are an important factor making for the complete conquest of the home market and for complete freedom of economic intercourse.

Oddly enough, this obvious mistake of Rosa Luxemburg's is repeated by the Bundist Medem, who sets out to prove, not that Poland's specific features are 'exceptional', but that the principle of national-territorial autonomy is unsuitable (the Bundists stand for national extra-territorial autonomy!). Our Bundists and liquidators collect from all over the world all the errors and all the opportunist vacillations of social-democrats of different countries and different nations and appropriate to themselves the *worst* they can find in world Social-Democracy. A scrapbook of Bundist and liquidator writings could, taken together, serve as a model social-democratic *museum of bad taste*.

Regional autonomy, Medem tells us didactically, is good for a region or a 'territory', but not for Lettish, Estonian, or other areas (okrugs), which have populations ranging from half a million to two million and areas equal to a gubernia. *"That would not be autonomy, but simply a zemstvo* [...] Over this zemstvo it would be necessary to establish real autonomy", and the author goes on to condemn the 'break-up' of the old gubernias and uyezds.

As a matter of fact, the preservation of the medieval, feudal, official administrative divisions means the 'break up' and mutilation of the conditions of modern capitalism. Only people imbued with the spirit of these divisions can, with the learned air of the expert, speculate on the contraposition of 'zemstvo' and 'autonomy', calling for the stereotyped application of 'autonomy' to large regions and of the zemstvo to small ones. Modern capitalism does not demand these bureaucratic stereotypes at all. Why national areas with populations, not only of half a million, but even of 50,000, should not be able to enjoy autonomy; why such areas should not be able to unite in the most diverse ways with neighbouring areas of different dimensions into a single autonomous 'territory' if that is convenient or necessary for economic intercourse – these things remain the secret of the Bundist Medem.

We would mention that the Brünn social-democratic national programme is based entirely on national-territorial autonomy; it proposes that Austria should be divided into "nationally distinct" areas "instead of the historical crown lands" (Clause 2 of the Brünn programme). We would not go as far as that. A uniform national population is undoubtedly one of the most reliable factors making for free, broad and really modern commercial intercourse. It is beyond doubt that not a single Marxist, and not even a single firm democrat, will stand up for the Austrian crown lands and the Russian gubernias and uyezds (the latter are not as bad as the Austrian crown lands, but they are very bad nevertheless), or challenge the necessity of replacing these obsolete divisions by others that will conform as far as possible with the national composition of the population, Lastly, it is beyond doubt that in order to eliminate all national oppression it is very important to create autonomous areas, however small, with entirely homogeneous populations, towards which members of the respective nationalities scattered all over the country, or even all over the world, could gravitate, and with which they could enter into relations and free associations of every kind. All this is indisputable, and can be argued against only from the hidebound, bureaucratic point of view.

The national composition of the population, however, is *one* of the very important economic factors, *but not the sole and not the most* important factor. Towns, for example, play an *extremely important* economic role under capitalism, and everywhere, in Poland, in Lithuania, in the Ukraine, in Great Russia, and elsewhere, the towns are marked by mixed populations. To cut the towns off from the villages and areas that economically gravitate towards them, for the sake of the 'national' factor, would be absurd and impossible. That is why Marxists must not take their stand entirely and exclusively on the 'national-territorial' principle.

The solution of the problem proposed by the last conference of Russian Marxists is far more correct than the Austrian. On this question, the conference advanced the following proposition:

> … must provide for wide regional autonomy (not for Poland alone, of course, but for all the regions of Russia) and fully democratic local self-government, and the boundaries of the self-governing and autonomous regions must he determined [not by the boundaries of the present gubernias, uyezds, etc., but] by the local inhabitants themselves on the basis of their economic and social conditions, national make-up of the population, etc.[11]

Here the national composition of the population is placed on the same level as the other conditions (economic first, then social, etc.) which must serve as a basis for determining the new boundaries that will meet the needs of modern capitalism, not of bureaucracy and Asiatic barbarism. The local population alone can 'assess' those conditions with full precision, and on that basis the central parliament of the country will determine the boundaries of the autonomous regions and the powers of autonomous Diets.

* * *

We have still to examine the question of the right of nations to self-determination. On this question a whole collection of opportunists of all nationalities – the liquidator Semkovsky, the Bundist Liebman and the Ukrainian nationalist-socialist Lev Yurkevich – have set to work to 'popularise' the errors of Rosa Luxemburg. This question, which has been so utterly confused by this whole 'collection', will be dealt with in our next article.

V Ilyin

---

11 See 'Resolution on the National Question', in this volume p. 221.

*Part 3:
During the Revolution and
in Power*

Reply to P Kievsky (G Pyatakov)

Written August–September 1916

Like every crisis in the life of individuals or in the history of nations, war oppresses and breaks some, steels and enlightens others.

The truth of that is making itself felt in social-democratic thinking on the war and in connection with the war. It is one thing to give serious thought to the causes and significance of an imperialist war that grows out of highly developed capitalism, social-democratic tactics in connection with such a war, the causes of the crisis within the social-democratic movement, and so on. But it is quite another to allow the war to *oppress* your thinking, to stop thinking and analysing *under the weight* of the terrible impressions and tormenting consequences or features of the war.

One such form of *oppression* or *repression* of human thinking caused by the war is the contemptuous attitude of imperialist Economism towards *democracy*. P Kievsky does not notice that running like a red thread through all his arguments is this war-inspired oppression, this fear, this refusal to analyse. What point is there in discussing defence of the fatherland when we are in the midst of such a terrible holocaust? What point is there in discussing nations' rights when outright strangulation is everywhere the rule? Self-determination and 'independence' of nations – but look what they have done to 'independent' Greece! What is the use of talking and thinking of 'rights', when rights are everywhere being trampled upon in the interests of the militarists! What sense is there in talking and thinking of a republic, when there is absolutely no difference whatsoever between the most democratic republics and the most reactionary monarchies, when the war has obliterated every trace of difference!

Kievsky is very angry when told that he has given way to fear, to the extent of rejecting democracy in general. He is angry and objects: I am not against democracy, only against *one* democratic demand, which I consider 'bad'. But though Kievsky is offended, and though he '*assures*' us (and himself as well, perhaps) that he is not at all "against" democracy, his *arguments* – or, more correctly, the endless *errors* in his arguments – prove the very opposite.

Defence of the fatherland is a lie in an imperialist war, but not in a democratic and revolutionary war. All talk of 'rights' seems absurd during a war, because *every* war replaces rights by direct and outright violence. But that should not lead us to forget that history has known in the past (and very likely will know, must know, in the future) wars (democratic and revolutionary wars) which, while replacing every kind of 'right', every kind of democracy, by violence during the war, nevertheless, in their social content and implications, *served* the cause of democracy, and *consequently* socialism. The example of Greece, it would seem, 'refutes' all national self-determination. But if you stop to think, analyse and weigh matters, and do not allow yourself to be deafened by the sound of words or frightened and oppressed by the nightmarish impressions of the war, then this example is no more serious or convincing than ridiculing the republican system because the 'democratic' republics, the most democratic – not only France, but also the United States, Portugal and Switzerland – have already introduced or are introducing, in the course of this war, exactly the same kind of militarist arbitrariness that exists in Russia.

That imperialist war obliterates the difference between republic and monarchy is a fact. But to therefore reject the republic, or even be contemptuous towards it, is to allow oneself to be frightened by the war, and one's thinking to be *oppressed* by its horrors. That is the mentality of many supporters of the 'disarmament' slogan (Roland-Holst, the younger element in Switzerland, the Scandinavian 'Lefts' and others).[1] What, they imply, is the use of discussing revolutionary utilisation of the army or a militia when there is no difference in this war between a republican militia and a monarchist standing army, and when militarism is *everywhere* doing its horrible work?

That is all *one* trend of thought, *one and the same* theoretical and practical political error Kievsky unwittingly makes at every step. He *thinks* he is arguing only against self-determination, he *wants* to argue only against self-determination, but the *result* – against his will and conscience, and that is the curious thing! – is that he has adduced *not a single* argument which could not be just as well applied to democracy in general!

The real source of all his curious logical errors and confusion – and this applies to not only self-determination, but also to defence of the fatherland, divorce, 'rights' in general – lies in the *oppression* of his thinking by the war, which makes him completely distort the Marxist position on democracy.

Imperialism is highly developed capitalism; imperialism is progressive; imperialism *is* the negation of democracy – 'hence', democracy is 'unattainable' under capitalism. Imperialist war is a flagrant violation of all democracy, whether in backward monarchies or progressive republics – 'hence', there is no point in talking of 'rights' (i.e. democracy!). The 'only' thing that can be 'opposed' to imperialist war is socialism; socialism alone is 'the way out'; 'hence', to advance democratic slogans in our minimum programme, i.e. under capitalism, is a deception or an illusion, befuddlement or postponement, etc., of the slogan of socialist revolution.

Though Kievsky does not realise it, that is the real source of all his mishaps. That is his *basic* logical error which, precisely because it is basic and is not realised by the author, *'explodes'* at every step

---

1 Henriette Roland-Holst was a left-wing Dutch social-democrat. Lenin is referring to the left wings of the Dutch, Swiss, Swedish and Norwegian social-democrats.

like a punctured bicycle tire. It 'bursts out' now on the question of defending the fatherland, now on the question of divorce, now in the phrase about 'rights', in this remarkable phrase (remarkable for its utter contempt for 'rights' and its utter failure to understand the issue): we shall discuss *not* rights, *but* the destruction of age-old slavery!

To say that is to show a lack of understanding of the relationship between capitalism and democracy, between socialism and democracy.

Capitalism in general, and imperialism in particular, turn democracy into an illusion – though at the same time capitalism engenders democratic aspirations in the masses, creates democratic institutions, aggravates the antagonism between imperialism's denial of democracy and the mass striving for democracy. Capitalism and imperialism can be overthrown only by economic revolution. They cannot be overthrown by democratic transformations, even the most 'ideal'. But a proletariat not schooled in the struggle for democracy is incapable of performing an economic revolution. Capitalism cannot be vanquished without *taking over the banks*, without repealing *private ownership* of the means of production. These revolutionary measures, however, cannot be implemented without organising the entire people for democratic administration of the means of production captured from the bourgeoisie, without enlisting the entire mass of the working people, the proletarians, semi-proletarians and small peasants, for the democratic organisation of their ranks, their forces, their participation in state affairs. Imperialist war may be said to be a triple negation of democracy:

a. Every war replaces 'rights' by violence;

b. Imperialism as such is the negation of democracy;

c. Imperialist war fully equates the republic with the monarchy.

But the awakening and growth of socialist revolt against imperialism are *indissolubly* linked with the growth of democratic resistance and unrest. Socialism leads to the withering away of *every* state, consequently also of every democracy, but socialism can be implemented only *through* the dictatorship of the proletariat, which combines violence against the bourgeoisie, i.e. the minority of the population, with full development of democracy, i.e. the genuinely equal and genuinely universal participation of the *entire* mass of the population in all *state* affairs and in all the complex problems of abolishing capitalism.

It is in these 'contradictions' that Kievsky, having forgotten the Marxist teaching on democracy, got himself confused. Figuratively speaking, the war has so oppressed his thinking that he uses the agitational slogan "break out of imperialism" to replace all thinking, just as the cry "get out of the colonies" is used to replace analysis of what, properly speaking, is the *meaning* – economically and politically – of the civilised nations "getting out of the colonies".

The Marxist solution of the problem of democracy is for the proletariat to *utilise all* democratic institutions and aspirations in its class struggle against the bourgeoisie in order to prepare for its overthrow and assure its own victory. Such utilisation is no easy task. To the Economists, Tolstoyans, etc., it often seems an unpardonable concession to 'bourgeois' and opportunist views, just as to Kievsky defence of national self-determination "in the epoch of finance capital" seems an unpardonable concession to bourgeois views. Marxism teaches us that to 'fight opportunism' by renouncing utilisation of the democratic institutions created and distorted by the bourgeoisie of the *given*, capitalist, society is to *completely surrender* to opportunism!

The slogan of *civil war* for socialism indicates the quickest way out of the imperialist war and *links* our struggle against the war with our struggle against opportunism. It is the only slogan that correctly takes into account both war-time peculiarities – the war is dragging out and threatening to grow into a whole 'epoch' of war – and the general character of our activities as distinct from opportunism with its pacifism, legalism and adaptation to one's 'own' bourgeoisie. In addition, civil war against the bourgeoisie is a *democratically* organised and *democratically* conducted war of the propertyless mass against the propertied minority. But civil war, like every other, must inevitably replace rights by violence. However, violence in the name of the interests and rights of the majority is of a different nature: it tramples on the 'rights' of the exploiters, the bourgeoisie, it is *unachievable* without democratic organisation of the army and the 'rear'. Civil war forcibly expropriates, immediately and first of all, the banks, factories, railways, the big estates, etc. But *in order* to expropriate all this, we shall have to introduce election of all officials and officers by the people, *completely merge* the army conducting the war against the bourgeoisie with the mass of the population, completely democratise administration of the food supply, the production and distribution of food, etc. The object of civil war is to seize the banks, factories, etc., destroy all possibility of resistance by the bourgeoisie, destroy *its* armed forces. But that aim cannot be achieved *either* in its purely military, *or* economic, *or* political aspects, unless we, during the war, simultaneously introduce and extend democracy among *our* armed forces and in *our* 'rear'. We tell the masses now (and they instinctively feel that we are right):

> 'They are deceiving you in making you fight for imperialist capitalism in a war disguised by the great slogans of democracy. You must, you shall wage a *genuinely* democratic war *against* the bourgeoisie for the achievement of genuine democracy and socialism.'

The present war unites and 'merges' nations into coalitions by means of violence and financial dependence. In our civil war against the bourgeoisie, *we* shall unite and merge the nations *not* by the force of the ruble, *not* by the force of the truncheon, not by violence, but by *voluntary* agreement and solidarity of the working people against the exploiters. For the bourgeoisie the proclamation of equal rights for all nations has become a deception. For us it will be the truth that will facilitate and accelerate the winning over of all nations. Without effectively organised *democratic* relations between nations – and, consequently, without freedom of secession – civil war of the workers and working people generally of all nations against the bourgeoisie is *impossible*.

Through utilisation of bourgeois democracy to socialist and consistently democratic organisation of the proletariat against the bourgeoisie and against opportunism. There is no other path. There is *no* other way out. Marxism, just as life itself, knows no other way out. We must direct free secession and free merging of nations along that path, not fight shy of them, not fear that this will 'defile' the 'purity' of our economic aims.

The Tasks of the Proletariat
in Our Revolution (Extract)

Draft Platform for the Proletarian Party

Written 10 April 1917

Editor's note: This pamphlet was written by Lenin in April 1917 in preparation for the April conference of the Bolsheviks where he waged a struggle for the rearming of the party. A few typed copies were circulated to delegates, and it served an important role in Lenin's polemic, but it was not published for general circulation until September 1917 due to logistical chaos at the printing press in St. Petersburg. The pamphlet develops the arguments summarised in his 'April Theses'. We publish here just the section dealing with the national question. We recommend reading the full text, published in *Lenin Selected Writings Volume 2: The Revolutions of 1917*, Wellred Books, 2024, pp. 77-113.

* * *

The agrarian and national programmes

14. As regards the national question, the proletarian party first of all must advocate the proclamation and immediate realisation of complete freedom of secession from Russia for all the nations and peoples who were oppressed by tsarism, or who were

forcibly joined to, or forcibly kept within the boundaries of, the state, i.e. annexed.

All statements, declarations and manifestos concerning renunciation of annexations that are not accompanied by the realisation of the right of secession in practice, are nothing but bourgeois deception of the people, or else pious petty-bourgeois wishes.

The proletarian party strives to create as large a state as possible, for this is to the advantage of the working people; it strives to *draw* nations *closer together*, and bring about their *further fusion*; but it desires to achieve this aim not by violence, but exclusively through a free fraternal union of the workers and the working people of all nations.

The more democratic the Russian Republic, and the more successfully it organises itself into a Republic of Soviets of Workers' and Peasants' Deputies, the more powerful will be the force of *voluntary* attraction to such a republic on the part of the working people of *all* nations.

Complete freedom of secession, the broadest local (and national) autonomy, and elaborate guarantees of the rights of national minorities – this is the programme of the revolutionary proletariat.

The Seventh (April) All-Russia Conference of the RSDLP(B)

24-29 April 1917

Editor's note: This was the conference which discussed Lenin's 'April Theses' for the rearming of the party. During the debate on the national question, Pyatakov spoke against Lenin's slogan of the right of nations to self-determination including secession and the formation of an independent state. In support of his resolution on the national question, Lenin said that this right alone ensured complete solidarity of workers and all working people of different nationalities; while the expediency of secession was to be decided by the proletarian party "in each particular case, having regard to the interests of social development as a whole and the interests of the class struggle of the proletariat for socialism".

* * *

Speech on the National Question

29 April 1917

Beginning from 1903, when our party adopted its programme, we have been encountering violent opposition on the part of the Polish comrades. If you study the minutes of the Second Congress you will see that they were using the same arguments then that they are using now, and that the Polish social-democrats walked out from that congress because they held that recognition of the right of nations to self-determination was unacceptable to them. Ever since then we have been coming up against the same question. Though imperialism already existed in 1903, the Polish social-democrats made no mention of it in their arguments. They are making the same strange and monstrous error now as they were then. These people want to put our party's stand on a par with that of the chauvinists.

Owing to long oppression by Russia, Poland's policy is a wholly nationalist one, and the whole Polish nation is obsessed with one idea – revenge on the Muscovites. No one has oppressed the Poles more than the Russian people, who served in the hands of the tsars as the executioner of Polish freedom. In no nation does hatred of Russia sit so deep as with the Poles; no nation dislikes Russia so intensely as the Poles. As a result we have a strange thing. Because of the Polish bourgeoisie, Poland has become an obstacle to the socialist movement. The whole world could go to the devil so long as Poland was free. Of course, this way of putting the question is a mockery of internationalism. Of course, Poland is now a victim of violence, but for the Polish nationalists to count on Russia liberating Poland – that would be treason to the International. The Polish nationalists have so imbued the Polish people with their views that this is how the situation is regarded in Poland.

The Polish social-democratic comrades have rendered a great historic service by advancing the slogan of internationalism and declaring that the fraternal union of the proletariat of all countries is of supreme importance to them and that they will never go to war for the liberation of Poland. This is to their credit, and this is why we have always regarded only these Polish social-democrats as socialists. The others are patriots, Polish Plekhanovs. But this peculiar position, when, in order to safeguard socialism, people were forced to struggle against a rabid and morbid nationalism, has produced a strange state of affairs: comrades come to us saying that we must give up the idea of Poland's freedom, her right to secession.

Why should we Great Russians, who have been oppressing more nations than any other people, deny the right to secession for Poland, Ukraine, or Finland? We are asked to become chauvinists, because by doing so we would make the position of social-democrats in Poland less difficult. We do not pretend to seek to liberate Poland, because the Polish people live between two states that are capable of fighting. Instead of telling the Polish workers that only those social-democrats are real democrats who maintain that the Polish people ought to be free, since there is no place for chauvinists in a socialist party, the Polish social-democrats argue that, just because they find the union with Russian workers advantageous, they are opposed to Poland's secession. They have a perfect right to do so. But people don't want to understand that to strengthen internationalism you do not have to repeat the same words. What you have to do is to stress, in Russia, the freedom of secession for oppressed nations and, in Poland, their freedom to unite. Freedom to unite implies freedom to secede. We Russians must emphasise freedom to secede, while the Poles must emphasise freedom to unite.

We notice here a number of sophisms involving a complete renunciation of Marxism. Comrade Pyatakov's stand repeats that of Rosa Luxemburg [...]¹ (Holland is an example.) This is how Comrade Pyatakov reasons, and this is how he refutes himself, for in theory he denies freedom of secession, but to the people he says that anyone opposing freedom of secession is not a socialist. Comrade Pyatakov has been saying things here that are hopelessly muddled. In Western Europe most countries settled their national questions long ago. It is Western Europe that is referred to when it is said that the national question has been settled. Comrade Pyatakov, however, puts this where it does not belong – to Eastern Europe, and we find ourselves in a ridiculous position.

---

1 The manuscript is incomplete in places, indicated by the ellipses in square brackets.

Just think of the dreadful mess that results! Finland is right next door to us. Comrade Pyatakov has no definite answer for Finland and gets all mixed up. In yesterday's *Rabochaya Gazeta*[2] you read that the movement for separation is growing in Finland. Finns arriving here tell us that separatism is growing there because the Cadets refuse to grant the country complete autonomy. A crisis is approaching there, dissatisfaction with Governor-General Rodichev[3] is rife, but *Rabochaya Gazeta* writes that the Finns should wait for the Constituent Assembly, because an agreement will there be reached between Finland and Russia. What do they mean by agreement? The Finns must declare that they are entitled to decide their destiny in their own way, and any Great Russian who denies this right is a chauvinist. It would be another thing if we said to the Finnish worker: Decide what is best for yourself [...]

Comrade Pyatakov simply rejects our slogan, saying that it means giving no slogan for the socialist revolution, but he himself gives no appropriate slogan. The method of socialist revolution under the slogan "Down with frontiers" is all muddled up. We have not succeeded in publishing the article in which I called this view 'Imperialist Economism'.[4] What does the 'method' of socialist revolution under the slogan "Down with frontiers" mean? We maintain that the state is necessary, and a state presupposes frontiers. The state, of course, may hold a bourgeois government, but we need the Soviets. But even Soviets are confronted with the question of frontiers. What does "Down with frontiers" mean? It is the beginning of anarchy... The 'method' of socialist revolution under the slogan "Down with frontiers" is simply a mess. When the time is ripe for socialist revolution, when it finally occurs, it will spread to other countries. We shall help it along, but in what manner, we do not know.

---

2 *Rabochaya Gazeta* (*Worker's Newspaper*) was the central organ of the Mensheviks, published daily from March-November 1917.
3 Fyodor Rodichev was a co-founder and leader of the Cadets.
4 See Lenin, 'A Caricature of Marxism and Imperialist Economism', *LCW*, Vol. 23, p. 28.

'The method of socialist revolution' is just a meaningless phrase. We stand for the settlement of problems which the bourgeois revolution has left unsolved. Our attitude to the separatist movement is indifferent, neutral. If Finland, Poland or Ukraine secede from Russia, there is nothing bad in that. What is wrong with it? Anyone who says that is a chauvinist. One must be mad to continue Tsar Nicholas' policy. Didn't Norway secede from Sweden? Alexander I and Napoleon once bartered nations, the tsars once traded Poland. Are we to continue this policy of the tsars? This is repudiation of the tactics of internationalism, this is chauvinism at its worst. What is wrong with Finland seceding? After the secession of Norway from Sweden mutual trust increased between the two peoples, between the proletariat of these countries. The Swedish landowners wanted to start a war, but the Swedish workers refused to be drawn into such a war.

All the Finns want now is autonomy. We are for Finland receiving complete freedom, because then there will be greater trust in Russian democracy and the Finns will not separate. While Mr. Rodichev goes to Finland to haggle over autonomy, our Finnish comrades come here and say, "We want autonomy." But what they get is a broadside, and the answer: "Wait for the Constituent Assembly." But we say: "Any Russian socialist who denies Finland freedom is a chauvinist."

We say that frontiers are determined by the will of the [local] population. Russia, don't you dare fight over Courland! Germany, get your armies out of Courland! That is how we solve the secession problem. The proletariat cannot use force, because it must not prevent the peoples from obtaining their freedom. Only when the socialist revolution has become a reality, and not a method, will the slogan "Down with frontiers" be a correct slogan. Then we shall say: "Comrades, come to us…" […]

War is a different matter entirely. If need be, we shall not draw the line at a revolutionary war. We are not pacifists… When we have Milyukov[5] sitting here and sending Rodichev to Finland to

---

5   Pavel Milyukov was a founder and leader of the Cadets, ideologue of the imperialist bourgeoisie. Foreign Minister in the first Provisional Government.

shamefully haggle with the Finnish people, we say to the Russian people: Don't you dare coerce Finland; no nation can be free that oppresses other nations. In the resolution concerning Borgbjerg we say: 'Withdraw your troops and let the nation settle the question itself'. But, if the Soviet takes over power tomorrow, that will not be a 'method of socialist revolution', and we shall then say: Germany, get your troops out of Poland, and Russia, get your troops out of Armenia. If we did otherwise we should be deceiving people.

Comrade Dzerzhinsky[6] tells us that in his oppressed Poland everybody is a chauvinist. But not a single Pole has said a word about Finland or Ukraine. We have been arguing over this so much since 1903 that it is becoming difficult to talk about it. Do as you please… Anyone who does not accept this point of view is an annexationist and a chauvinist. We are for a fraternal union of all nations. If there is a Ukrainian republic and a Russian republic, there will be closer contact and greater trust between the two. If the Ukrainians see that we have a Soviet republic, they will not secede, but if we have a Milyukov republic, they will. When Comrade Pyatakov said in self-contradiction that he is against the forcible retention of nations within the frontiers, he actually recognised the right of nations to self-determination. We certainly do not want the peasant in Khiva to live under the Khan of Khiva. By developing our revolution we shall influence the oppressed people. Propaganda among the oppressed mass must follow only this line.

Any Russian socialist who does not recognise Finland's and Ukraine's right to freedom will degenerate into a chauvinist. And no sophisms or references to his 'method' will ever help him to justify himself.

* * *

---

6   Felix Dzerzhinsky was a Polish revolutionary and a founding member of the SDKPiL, the Polish Social-Democratic Party. He was active in the Polish and Russian revolutionary movements. After the Russian Revolution he headed the Cheka from its formation in December 1917, and the Supreme Council of National Economy from 1924. He later became a supporter of Stalin.

Resolution on the National Question
29 April 1917

The policy of national oppression, inherited from the autocracy and monarchy, is maintained by the landowners, capitalists, and petty bourgeoisie in order to protect their class privileges and to cause disunity among the workers of the various nationalities. Modern imperialism, which increases the tendency to subjugate weaker nations, is a new factor intensifying national oppression.

The elimination of national oppression, if at all achievable in capitalist society, is possible only under a consistently democratic republican system and state administration that guarantee complete equality for all nations and languages.

The right of all the nations forming part of Russia freely to secede and form independent states must be recognised. To deny them this right, or to fail to take measures guaranteeing its practical realisation, is equivalent to supporting a policy of seizure or annexation. Only the recognition by the proletariat of the right of nations to secede can ensure complete solidarity among the workers of the various nations and help to bring the nations closer together on truly democratic lines.

The conflict which has arisen at the present time between Finland and the Russian Provisional Government strikingly demonstrates that denial of the right to free secession leads to a direct continuation of the policy of tsarism.

The right of nations freely to secede must not be confused with the advisability of secession by a given nation at a given moment. The party of the proletariat must decide the latter question quite independently in each particular case, having regard to the interests of social development as a whole and the interests of the class struggle of the proletariat for socialism.

The party demands broad regional autonomy, the abolition of supervision from above, the abolition of a compulsory official language, and the fixing of the boundaries of the self-governing and autonomous regions in accordance with the economic and social conditions, the national composition of the population, and so forth, as assessed by the local population itself.

The party of the proletariat emphatically rejects what is known as 'national cultural autonomy', under which education etc. is removed from the control of the state and put in the control of some kind of national diets. National cultural autonomy artificially divides the workers living in one locality, and even working in the same industrial enterprise, according to their various 'national cultures'; in other words, it strengthens the ties between the workers and the bourgeois culture of their nations, whereas the aim of the social-democrats is to develop the international culture of the world proletariat.

The party demands that a fundamental law be embodied in the constitution annulling all privileges enjoyed by any one nation and all infringements of the rights of national minorities.

The interests of the working class demand that the workers of all nationalities in Russia should have common proletarian organisations: political, trade union, co-operative educational institutions, and so forth. Only the merging of the workers of the various nationalities into such common organisations will make it possible for the proletariat to wage a successful struggle against international capital and bourgeois nationalism.

Finland and Russia

Published 15 May 1917

Finland's attitude to Russia has become the topic of the day. The Provisional Government has *failed* to meet the demand of the Finnish people, which, *so far*, is not for secession, but only for broad autonomy.

The Provisional Government's undemocratic, annexationist policy was formulated and 'defended' the other day by *Rabochaya Gazeta*. It could not have made a more 'damning' defence than it did. This is indeed a fundamental issue, an issue of state significance, which deserves the closest attention.

> The Organising Committee[1] believes, [writes *Rabochaya Gazeta*, No. 42] that the general problem of Finnish-Russian relations can and should be settled only by an agreement between the Finnish Diet and the Constituent Assembly. Pending this the Finnish comrades [the Organising Committee has had talks with the Finnish social-democrats] should bear in mind that if separate tendencies in Finland were to increase, this would be likely to strengthen the centralist tendencies of the Russian bourgeoisie.

That is the point of view of the capitalists, the bourgeoisie, the Cadets, but not of the proletariat. The programme of the Social-Democratic Party, namely, Section 9, which recognises the right of self-determination for all nation members of the state, has been

---

1 The Organising Committee (OC) was the leading body of the Mensheviks.

thrown overboard by the Menshevik social-democrats. They have, in effect, renounced this programme and taken sides with the bourgeoisie, just as they did on the question of the replacement of the standing army by the universally armed people, and so on.

The capitalists, the bourgeoisie, including the Cadet Party, never did recognise the right of nations to political self-determination, i.e. *freedom to secede* from Russia.

The Social-Democratic Party *recognised* this right in Section 9 of its programme, adopted in 1903.

When the Organising Committee 'recommended' to the Finnish social-democrats an 'agreement' between the Finnish Diet and the Constituent Assembly, they were, on this question, taking sides with the bourgeoisie. One merely has to compare the positions of *all* the principal classes and parties to see the truth of this.

The tsar, the Rights, the monarchists are not for an agreement between the Diet and the Constituent Assembly – they are for subjecting Finland to the Russian nation. The republican bourgeoisie are for an *agreement* between the Finnish Diet and the Constituent Assembly. The class-conscious proletariat and the social-democrats, *true* to their programme, are for the *right* of Finland, as of all the other underprivileged nations, to *secede from* Russia. We have here a clear, precise, and indisputable picture. Under the guise of an 'agreement', which cannot settle anything – for what are you going to do if an agreement is *not* reached? – the bourgeoisie is pursuing the same old tsarist policy of subjection and annexation.

For Finland was annexed by the Russian tsars as the result of a deal with the suppressor of the French revolution, Napoleon, etc. If we are really against annexations, we should say: *Give Finland the right of secession!* Not until this has been said and accomplished can an 'agreement' with Finland be a really free and voluntary agreement, a real agreement, and not just a fake.

Agreement is possible only between equals. If the agreement is to be a real agreement, and not a verbal screen for subjection, *both* parties to it must enjoy real equality of status, that is to say, both Russia *and Finland* must have the right to *disagree*. That is as clear as daylight.

Only by 'freedom of secession' can that right be expressed. Only when she is free to secede will Finland really be in a position to enter into an 'agreement' with Russia as to whether she should secede or not. *Without* this condition, without recognising the right of secession, all phrase-mongering about an 'agreement' is self-deception and deception of the people.

The Organising Committee should have told the Finns plainly whether it recognises the right of secession or not. It befogged the issue, like the Cadets, and thereby repudiated the right of secession. It should have attacked the Russian bourgeoisie for denying the oppressed nations the right to secede, a denial which is *tantamount to annexation*. Instead, the Organising Committee attacks the Finns and warns them that "separate" (they should have said separatist) tendencies would strengthen centralist inclinations! In other words, the Organising Committee threatens the Finns with the strengthening of the annexationist Great-Russian bourgeoisie – just what the Cadets have always done, the very guise under which Rodichev and co. are pursuing *their* annexationist policy.

We have here a clear and practical commentary on the question of annexations, which 'everybody' is now talking about, though afraid to face the issue squarely. *To be against the right of secession is to be for annexations.*

The tsars pursued a crude policy of annexation, bartering one nation for another by agreement with other monarchs (the partition of Poland, the deal with Napoleon over Finland, and so on), just like the landowners, who used to exchange peasant serfs. The bourgeoisie, on turning republican, is carrying on the *same* policy of annexation, only more subtly, less openly, by *promising* an 'agreement' while *taking away* the only effective guarantee of real equality in the making of an agreement, namely, the right of secession. The Organising Committee is dragging at the tail-end of the bourgeoisie, and in practice taking its side. (*Birzhevka*[2]

---

2   *Birzhevyie Vedomosti* (*Stock-Exchange Recorder*), *Birzhevka* (abb.) was a bourgeois daily published in St. Petersburg from 1880. Its abbreviated name, '*Birzhevka*' became a generic term for the unscrupulous and venal bourgeois press.

was therefore quite right in reprinting all the salient points of the *Rabochaya Gazeta* article and approving the Organising Committee's reply to the Finns, which it called a "lesson by Russian democracy" to the Finns. *Rabochaya Gazeta* deserved this kiss from *Birzhevka*.)

At its conference, the party of the proletariat (the 'Bolsheviks') once more confirmed the right of secession in its resolution on the national question.

The alignment of classes and parties is clear.

The petty bourgeois are letting themselves be frightened by the spectre of a frightened bourgeoisie – that is the whole crux of the policy of the Menshevik social-democrats and the Socialist-Revolutionaries. They are 'afraid' of secession. The class-conscious proletarians are *not* afraid of it. Both Norway and Sweden gained from Norway's free secession from Sweden in 1905: it made for mutual trust between the two nations, it drew them closer together on a voluntary basis, it did away with the stupid and destructive friction, it strengthened the economic and political, the cultural and social *gravitation* of the two nations to each other, and strengthened the fraternal alliance between the workers of the two countries.

Comrades, workers and peasants, do not be influenced by the annexationist policy of the Russian capitalists, Guchkov, Milyukov, and the Provisional Government towards Finland, Courland, Ukraine, etc.! Do not fear to recognise the right of all these nations to secede! Nations must be won over to the idea of an alliance with the Great Russians not by force, but by a really voluntary and really free agreement, which is *impossible* without the right of secession.

The freer Russia is, and the more resolutely our republic recognises the right of non-Great-Russian nations to secede, the more strongly will other nations be *attracted* towards an alliance with us, the less friction will there be, the more rarely will actual secession occur, the shorter the period of secession will last, and the closer and more enduring – in the long run – will the fraternal alliance be between the Russian proletarian and peasant republic and the republics of all other nations.

The Ukraine

Published 15 June 1917

Editor's note: In the aftermath of the overthrow of the tsarist regime in the February Revolution, the Ukrainian Central Rada, a bourgeois-nationalist government, was founded in April 1917. The Rada proclaimed its 'First Universal', an act which declared the autonomy of Ukraine. Lenin criticises the position of the bourgeois liberals of the Russian Provisional Government, which opposed the declaration, and explains how Russian revolutionary democrats had to defend Ukraine's rights in order to achieve the unity of the working class.

* * *

The new, coalition Provisional Government's policy failure is becoming more and more obvious. The Universal Act on the organisation of the Ukraine, issued by the Ukrainian Central Rada and adopted on 11 June 1917, by the All-Ukraine Army Congress, plainly exposes that policy and furnishes documentary proof of its failure.

Without seceding from Russia, without breaking away from the Russian state, [reads the Act] let the Ukrainian people have the right to shape their own life on their own soil [...] All laws by which order is to be established here in the Ukraine shall be passed solely by this Ukrainian Assembly. And laws establishing order throughout the Russian State must be passed by the All-Russia Parliament.

These are perfectly clear words. They state very specifically that the Ukrainian people do not wish to secede from Russia at present. They demand autonomy without denying the need for the supreme authority of the 'All-Russia Parliament'. No democrat, let alone a socialist, will venture to deny the complete legitimacy of the Ukraine's demands. And no democrat can deny the Ukraine's *right* to freely secede from Russia. Only unqualified recognition of this right makes it possible to advocate a free union of the Ukrainians and the Great Russians, a *voluntary* association of the two peoples in one state. Only unqualified recognition of this right can actually break completely and irrevocably with the accursed tsarist past, when *everything* was done to bring about a *mutual estrangement* of the two peoples so close to each other in language, territory, character and history. Accursed tsarism made the Great Russians executioners of the Ukrainian people, and fomented in them a hatred for those who even forbade Ukrainian children to speak and study in their native tongue.

Russia's revolutionary democrats, if they want to be truly revolutionary and truly democratic, must break with that past, must regain for themselves, for the workers and peasants of Russia, the brotherly trust of the Ukrainian workers and peasants. This cannot be done without full recognition of the Ukraine's rights, including the *right* to free secession.

We do not favour the existence of small states. We stand for the closest union of the workers of the world against 'their own' capitalists and those of all other countries. But for this union to be voluntary, the Russian worker, who does not for a moment trust the Russian or the Ukrainian bourgeoisie in anything, now stands for the right of the Ukrainians to secede, *without imposing* his friendship upon them, but *striving to win* their friendship by treating them as an equal, as an ally and brother in the struggle for socialism.

* * *

Rech, the paper of the embittered bourgeois counter-revolutionaries, who are half demented with rage, savagely attacks the Ukrainians for their 'unauthorised' decision. "That act by the Ukrainians", it says, "is a downright crime under the law, and calls for the immediate application of severe legitimate punitive measures." There is nothing to add to this attack by the savage bourgeois counter-revolutionaries. Down with the counter-revolutionary bourgeoisie! Long live the free union of free peasants and workers of a free Ukraine with the workers and peasants of revolutionary Russia!

Speech at the First All-Russia Congress of the Navy (Extract From Minutes)

Delivered 22 November 1917

Turning to the nationalities question, Lenin said, we should take note of Russia's highly patchy national composition, with the Russians making up only about 40 per cent, and the majority consisting of other nationalities. National oppression under the tsars, unmatched in savagery and absurdity, turned the rightless nationalities into great reservoirs of fierce hatred for the monarchs. It was not surprising that all Russians had been included in their hatred for those who went to the extent of prohibiting the use of the mother tongue, and doomed masses of people to illiteracy. It was assumed that the privileged Russians would try to retain the advantages which had been so assiduously preserved for them by Nicholas II and Kerensky.

We are told that Russia will disintegrate and split up into separate republics, but we have no reason to fear this. We have nothing to fear, whatever the number of independent republics. The important thing for us is not where the state border runs, but whether or not the working people of all nations remain allied in their struggle against the bourgeoisie, irrespective of nationality. (*Stormy applause.*)

If the Finnish bourgeoisie are buying arms from the Germans in order to use them against their workers, we offer the latter an alliance with the Russian working people. Let the bourgeoisie start their filthy petty squabbles and their trading over frontiers, the workers of all countries and nationalities will not fall out over that sort of thing. (*Stormy applause.*)

We are now 'conquering' Finland – this is using a nasty word – but not the way the robber barons of international capitalism conquered it. We are winning Finland over by giving her complete freedom to live in alliance with us or with others, guaranteeing full support for the working people of all nationalities against the bourgeoisie of all countries. It is not an alliance based on treaties, but on the solidarity of the exploited against the exploiters.

We now see a national movement in the Ukraine and we say that we stand unconditionally for the Ukrainian people's complete and unlimited freedom. We have to wipe out that old bloodstained and dirty past when the Russia of the capitalist oppressors acted as the executioner of other peoples. We are determined to wipe out that past, and leave no trace of it. (*Stormy applause.*)

We are going to tell the Ukrainians that as Ukrainians they can go ahead and arrange their life as they see fit. But we are going to stretch out a fraternal hand to the Ukrainian workers and tell them that together with them we are going to fight against their bourgeoisie and ours. Only a socialist alliance of the working people of all countries can remove all ground for national persecution and strife. (*Stormy applause.*)

Manifesto to the Ukrainian People with an Ultimatum to the Ukrainian Rada

Written 3 December 1917

Editor's note: After the victory of the October Revolution, 1917, in Russia, the Ukrainian Rada, dominated by bourgeois and petty-bourgeois nationalists, moved towards declaring independence from the Soviet government. It did so more from a class point of view (opposition to the workers and peasants taking power) than from a national point of view (it had only declared autonomy when the bourgeois Provisional government was in power in Russia). Furthermore, the Rada collaborated with the counter-revolutionary forces waging war against Soviet power and worked to suppress workers' and peasant's soviets in Ukraine. The manifesto and ultimatum were designed to unmask the real motives of the Rada in front of the Ukrainian masses. The Rada rejected the ultimatum and ended up supporting German imperialism.

* * *

Proceeding from the interests of the unity and fraternal alliance of factory workers and the working and exploited masses in the struggle for socialism, and also from the recognition of these principles by numerous decisions of the organs of revolutionary democracy, the soviets, and especially the Second All-Russia Congress of Soviets, the Council of People's Commissars – the socialist government of Russia – reaffirms that the right to self-determination belongs to all nations oppressed by tsarism and the Great-Russian bourgeoisie, up to and including the right of these nations to secede from Russia.

Accordingly we, the Council of People's Commissars, recognise the People's Ukrainian Republic, and its right to secede from Russia or enter into a treaty with the Russian Republic on federal or similar relations between them.

We, the Council of People's Commissars, recognise at once, unconditionally and without reservations everything that pertains to the Ukrainian people's national rights and national independence.

We have not taken a single step, in the sense of restricting the Finnish people's national rights or national independence, against the bourgeois Finnish Republic, which still remains bourgeois, nor shall we take any steps restricting the national independence of any nation which had been – or desires to be – a part of the Russian Republic.

We accuse the Rada of conducting, behind a screen of national phrases, a double-dealing bourgeois policy, which has long been expressed in the Rada's non-recognition of the Soviets and of Soviet power in the Ukraine (incidentally, the Rada has refused to convoke a territorial congress of the Ukrainian Soviets immediately, as the Soviets of the Ukraine had demanded). This ambiguous policy, which has made it impossible for us to recognise the Rada as a plenipotentiary representative of the working and exploited masses of the Ukrainian Republic, has lately led the Rada to steps which preclude all possibility of agreement.

These, firstly, were steps to disorganise the front.

The Rada has issued *unilateral* orders moving Ukrainian units and withdrawing them from the front, thereby breaking up the common united front *before* any demarcation, which can be carried out only through a formal agreement between the governments of the two republics.

Secondly, the Rada has started to disarm the Soviet troops stationed in the Ukraine.

Thirdly, the Rada has been extending support to the Cadet-Kaledin[1] plot and revolt against Soviet power. On the patently false plea of "the Don and the Kuban" having autonomous rights, a plea that serves to cover up Kaledin's counter-revolutionary moves, which clash with the interests and demands of the vast majority of the working Cossacks, the Rada has allowed its territory to be crossed by troops on their way to Kaledin, but *has refused transit to any anti-Kaledin troops*.

Even if the Rada had received full formal recognition as the uncontested organ of supreme state power of an independent bourgeois Ukrainian republic, we would have been forced to declare war on it without any hesitation, because of its attitude of unexampled betrayal of the revolution and support of the Cadets and the Kaledinites – the bitterest enemies of the national independence of the peoples of Russia, the enemies of Soviet power and of the working and exploited masses.

At the present time, in view of the circumstances set forth above, the Council of People's Commissars, with the full cognisance of the peoples of the Ukrainian and Russian Republics, asks the Rada to answer the following questions:[2]

1. Will the Rada undertake to give up its attempts to disorganise the common front?

2. Will the Rada undertake to refuse transit to any army units on their way to the Don, the Urals or elsewhere, unless it has the sanction of the Commander-in-Chief?

3. Will the Rada undertake to assist the revolutionary troops in their struggle against the counter-revolutionary Cadet-Kaledin revolt?

---

1 Alexey Kaledin was a tsarist general and a leader of the White armies, hostile to the revolution.

2 The text from this point on was written by Trotsky.

4. Will the Rada undertake to stop attempts to disarm the Soviet regiments and the workers' Red Guard in the Ukraine and immediately return arms to those who had been deprived of them?

In the event no satisfactory answer is received to these questions within forty-eight hours, the Council of People's Commissars will deem the Rada to be in a state of open war with Soviet power in Russia and the Ukraine.

Draft Resolution of the CC, RCP(B) on Soviet Rule in the Ukraine

Adopted 29 November 1919

1. The CC, RCP(B), having discussed the question of relations with the working people of the Ukraine now being liberated from the temporary conquest of Denikin's bands, is pursuing persistently the principle of the self-determination of nations and deems it essential to again affirm that the RCP holds consistently to the view that the independence of the Ukrainian Soviet Socialist Republic be recognised.

2. The RCP will work to establish federal relations between the RSFSR, and the Ukrainian SSR, basing itself on the decisions of the All-Russia Central Executive Committee of 1 June 1919, and the Ukrainian Central Executive Committee of 18 May 1919 (resolution attached).

3. In view of the fact that Ukrainian culture (language, school, etc.) has been suppressed for centuries by Russian tsarism and the exploiting classes, the CC, RCP makes it incumbent upon all party members to use every means to help remove all barriers in the way of the free development of the Ukrainian language and culture. Since the many centuries of oppression have given rise

to nationalist tendencies among the backward sections of the population, RCP members must exercise the greatest caution in respect of those tendencies and must oppose them with words of comradely explanation concerning the identity of interests of the working people of the Ukraine and Russia. RCP members on Ukrainian territory must put into practice the right of the working people to study in the Ukrainian language and to speak their native language in all Soviet institutions; they must in every way counteract attempts at Russification that push the Ukrainian language into the background and must convert that language into an instrument for the communist education of the working people. Steps must be taken immediately to ensure that in all Soviet institutions there are sufficient Ukrainian-speaking employees and that in future all employees are able to speak Ukrainian.

4. It is essential to ensure the closest contact between Soviet institutions and the native peasant population of the country, for which purpose it must be made the rule, even at the earliest stages, that when revolutionary committees and Soviets are being established the labouring peasants must have a majority in them with the poor peasants exercising a decisive influence.

5. Since the population of the Ukraine is predominantly peasant to an even greater extent than that of Russia, it is the task of the Soviet government in the Ukraine to win the confidence, not only of the poor peasants, but also of the broad sections of the middle peasantry whose real interests link them very closely with Soviet power. In particular, while retaining the food policy in principle (the state procurement of grain at fixed prices) the methods of its application must be changed.

    The immediate purpose of the food policy in the Ukraine must be the requisitioning of grain surpluses to the strictly limited extent necessary to supply the Ukrainian rural poor, the workers and the Red Army. When requisitioning surpluses, special attention must be paid to the interests of the middle peasants, who must be carefully distinguished from kulak elements. It is essential to expose to the Ukrainian peasantry the counter-revolutionary demagogy that tries to impress on them that the purpose of Soviet Russia is to channel grain and other food products from the Ukraine into Russia.

It must be made incumbent on all agents of the central authorities, all party officials, party instructors, etc., to draw the poor and middle peasantry extensively into the work of government.

For the same purpose (the establishment of the real power of the working people) measures must be immediately taken to prevent Soviet institutions from being flooded with Ukrainian urban petty bourgeoisie, who have no conception of the living conditions of the peasant masses and who frequently masquerade as communists.

A condition for the admission of such elements into the ranks of the party and into Soviet institutions must be a preliminary practical verification of their competence and their loyalty to the interests of the working people, primarily at the front, in the ranks of the army. Everywhere and under all circumstances such elements must be placed under the strict class control of the proletariat.

We know from experience that due to the unorganised state of the poor the large number of weapons in the hands of the Ukrainian rural population is inevitably being concentrated in the hands of the kulaks and counter-revolutionaries which actually leads to the domination of kulak bandits instead of the dictatorship of the working people; in view of this a primary task in organising Soviet Ukraine is to withdraw all weapons and concentrate them in the hands of the workers' and peasants' Red Army.

6. In the same way, the land policy must be effected with special attention paid to the farming of the poor and middle peasantry.

The tasks of the land policy in the Ukraine are:

1. The complete abolition of the landed proprietorship re-established by Denikin and the transfer of the landed estates to peasants possessing little or no land.

2. State farms to be organised in strictly limited numbers and of limited size and in each case in conformity with the interests of the surrounding peasantry.

3. In organising peasants in communes, cartels, etc., the party policy must be strictly adhered to, which in this respect does not permit any coercion, leaving it to the peasants to decide freely for themselves and penalising all attempts to introduce the principle of coercion.

Regarding it as beyond dispute for every communist and for every politically-conscious worker that the closest alliance of all Soviet republics in their struggle against the menacing forces of world imperialism is essential, the RCP maintains that the form of that alliance must be finally determined by the Ukrainian workers and labouring peasants themselves.

Letter to the Workers and Peasants of the Ukraine: Apropos of the Victories over Denikin

Written 28 December 1919

Editor's note: Between July and December 1919, the counter-revolutionary White armies, led by Anton Denikin, who had been a general in the Imperial Army, carried out an offensive against Moscow with the aim of taking over the capital. The defeat of the offensive in November-December was the prelude to the final defeat of the Whites. The defeat of Denikin in Ukraine played an important role in the overall collapse of his offensive. Lenin took advantage of the situation to explain the real policy of the Bolsheviks regarding the national rights of Ukraine, combining the recognition of her national rights with the need for the unity of Ukrainian and Great-Russian workers and peasants in the common struggle against the forces of counter-revolution. Alexander Kolchak, another general leading the counter-revolutionary armies in the east, had already been defeated in July 1919.

* * *

Comrades, four months ago, towards the end of August 1919, I had occasion to address a letter to the workers and peasants in connection with the victory over Kolchak.

I am now having this letter reprinted in full for the workers and peasants of the Ukraine in connection with the victories over Denikin.

Red troops have taken Kiev, Poltava and Kharkov and are advancing victoriously on Rostov. The Ukraine is seething with revolt against Denikin. All forces must be rallied for the final rout of Denikin's army, which has been trying to restore the power of the landowners and capitalists. We must destroy Denikin to safeguard ourselves against even the slightest possibility of a new incursion.

The workers and peasants of the Ukraine should familiarise themselves with the lessons which all Russian workers and peasants have drawn from the conquest of Siberia by Kolchak and her liberation by Red troops after many months of landowner and capitalist tyranny.

Denikin's rule in the Ukraine has been as severe an ordeal as Kolchak's rule was in Siberia. There can be no doubt that the lessons of this severe ordeal will give the Ukrainian workers and peasants – as they did the workers and peasants of the Urals and Siberia – a clearer understanding of the tasks of Soviet power and induce them to defend it more staunchly.

In Great Russia the system of landed estates has been completely abolished. The same must be done in the Ukraine, and the Soviet power of the Ukrainian workers and peasants must effect the complete abolition of the landed estates and the complete liberation of the Ukrainian workers and peasants from all oppression by the landowners, and from the landowners themselves.

But apart from this task, and a number of others which confronted and still confront both the Great-Russian and the Ukrainian working masses, Soviet power in the Ukraine has its own special tasks. One of these special tasks deserves the greatest attention at the present moment. It is the national question, or, in other words, the question of whether the Ukraine is to be a separate and independent Ukrainian Soviet Socialist Republic bound in alliance (federation) with the Russian Socialist Federative Soviet Republic, or whether the Ukraine is to amalgamate with Russia to form a single Soviet republic. All Bolsheviks and all politically-conscious workers and peasants must give careful thought to this question.

The independence of the Ukraine has been recognised both by the All-Russia Central Executive Committee of the RSFSR (Russian Socialist Federative Soviet Republic) and by the Russian Communist Party (Bolsheviks). It is therefore self-evident and generally recognised that only the Ukrainian workers and peasants themselves can and will decide at their All-Ukraine Congress of Soviets whether the Ukraine shall amalgamate with Russia, or whether she shall remain a separate and independent republic, and, in the latter case, what federal ties shall be established between that republic and Russia.

How should this question be decided insofar as concerns the interests of the working people and the promotion of their fight for the complete emancipation of labour from the yoke of capital?

In the first place, the interests of labour demand the fullest confidence and the closest alliance among the working people of different countries and nations. The supporters of the landowners and capitalists, of the bourgeoisie, strive to disunite the workers, to intensify national discord and enmity, in order to weaken the workers and strengthen the power of capital.

Capital is an international force. To vanquish it, an international workers' alliance, an international workers' brotherhood, is needed.

We are opposed to national enmity and discord, to national exclusiveness. We are internationalists. We stand for the close union and the complete amalgamation of the workers and peasants of all nations in a single world Soviet republic.

Secondly, the working people must not forget that capitalism has divided nations into a small number of oppressor, Great-Power (imperialist), sovereign and privileged nations and an overwhelming majority of oppressed, dependent and semi-dependent, non-sovereign nations. The arch-criminal and arch-reactionary war of 1914-18 still further accentuated this division and as a result aggravated rancour and hatred. For centuries the indignation and distrust of the non-sovereign and dependent nations towards the dominant and oppressor nations have been accumulating, of nations such as the Ukrainian towards nations such as the Great-Russian.

We want a *voluntary* union of nations – a union which precludes any coercion of one nation by another – a union founded on complete confidence, on a clear recognition of brotherly unity, on absolutely voluntary consent. Such a union cannot be effected at one stroke; we have to work towards it with the greatest patience and circumspection, so as not to spoil matters and not to arouse distrust, and so that the distrust inherited from centuries of landowner and capitalist oppression, centuries of private property and the enmity caused by its divisions and redivisions may have a chance to wear off.

We must, therefore, strive persistently for the unity of nations and ruthlessly suppress everything that tends to divide them, and in doing so we must be very cautious and patient, and make concessions to the survivals of national distrust. We must be adamant and uncompromising towards everything that affects the fundamental interests of labour in its fight for emancipation from the yoke of capital. The question of the demarcation of frontiers now, for the time being – for we are striving towards the complete abolition of frontiers – is a minor one, it is not fundamental or important. In this matter we can afford to wait, and must wait, because the national distrust among the broad mass of peasants and small owners is often extremely tenacious, and haste might only intensify it, in other words, jeopardise the cause of complete and ultimate unity.

The experience of the workers' and peasants' revolution in Russia, the revolution of October-November 1917, and of the two years of victorious struggle against the onslaught of international and Russian capitalists, has made it crystal clear that the capitalists have succeeded for a time in playing upon the national distrust of the Great Russians felt by Polish, Latvian, Estonian and Finnish peasants and small owners, that they have succeeded for a time in sowing dissension between them and us on the basis of this distrust. Experience has shown that this distrust wears off and disappears only very slowly, and that the more caution and patience displayed by the Great Russians, who have for so long been an oppressor nation, the more certainly this distrust will pass. It is by recognising the independence of the Polish, Latvian, Lithuanian, Estonian and Finnish states that we are slowly but steadily winning the confidence of the labouring masses of the neighbouring small states, who were more backward and more deceived and downtrodden by the capitalists. It is the surest way of wresting them from the influence of 'their' national capitalists, and leading them to full confidence, to the future united international Soviet republic.

As long as the Ukraine is not completely liberated from Denikin, her government, until the All-Ukraine Congress of Soviets meets, is the All-Ukraine Revolutionary Committee. Besides the Ukrainian Bolshevik communists, there are Ukrainian *Borotba* communists[1] working on this Revolutionary Committee as members of the government. One of the things distinguishing the Borotbists from the Bolsheviks is that they insist upon the unconditional independence of the Ukraine. The Bolsheviks will not make *this* a subject of difference and disunity, they do not regard *this* as an obstacle to concerted proletarian effort. There must be unity in the struggle against the yoke of capital and for the dictatorship of the proletariat, and there should be no parting of the ways among communists on the question of national frontiers, or whether there should be a federal or some other tie between the states. Among the Bolsheviks there are advocates of complete independence for the Ukraine, advocates of a more or less close federal tie, and advocates of the complete amalgamation of the Ukraine with Russia.

There must be no differences over these questions. They will be decided by the All-Ukraine Congress of Soviets.

If a Great-Russian communist insists upon the amalgamation of the Ukraine with Russia, Ukrainians might easily suspect him of advocating this policy not from the motive of uniting the proletarians

---

1 The Ukrainian Communist Party of Borotbists arose in May 1918 after the split in the Ukrainian Socialist-Revolutionary Party on the basis of supporting Soviet power in Ukraine. It was named for its paper, *Borotba* (*Struggle*). The Borotbists applied to join the Communist International. At their conference in the middle of March 1920, a majority agreed to merge with the Communist Party (Bolshevik) of Ukraine

in the fight against capital, but because of the prejudices of the old Great-Russian nationalism, of imperialism. Such mistrust is natural, and to a certain degree inevitable and legitimate, because the Great Russians, under the yoke of the landowners and capitalists, had for centuries imbibed the shameful and disgusting prejudices of Great-Russian chauvinism.

If a Ukrainian communist insists upon the unconditional state independence of the Ukraine, he lays himself open to the suspicion that he is supporting this policy not because of the temporary interests of the Ukrainian workers and peasants in their struggle against the yoke of capital, but on account of the petty-bourgeois national prejudices of the small owner. Experience has provided hundreds of instances of the petty-bourgeois 'socialists' of various countries – all the various Polish, Latvian and Lithuanian pseudo-socialists, Georgian Mensheviks, Socialist-Revolutionaries and the like – assuming the guise of supporters of the proletariat for the sole purpose of deceitfully promoting a policy of compromise with 'their' national bourgeoisie against the revolutionary workers. We saw this in the case of Kerensky's rule in Russia in the February-October period of 1917, and we have seen it and are seeing it in all other countries.

Mutual distrust between Great-Russian and Ukrainian communists can, therefore, arise very easily. How is this distrust to be combated? How is it to be overcome and mutual confidence established?

The best way to achieve this is by working together to uphold the dictatorship of the proletariat and Soviet power in the fight against the landowners and capitalists of all countries and against their attempts to restore their domination. This common fight will clearly show in practice that whatever the decision in regard to state independence or frontiers may be, there must be a close military and economic alliance between the Great-Russian and Ukrainian workers, for otherwise the capitalists of the 'Entente', in other words, the alliance of the richest capitalist countries – Britain, France, America, Japan and Italy – will crush and strangle us separately. Our fight against Kolchak and Denikin, whom these capitalists supplied with money and arms, is a clear illustration of this danger.

He who undermines the unity and closest alliance between the Great-Russian and Ukrainian workers and peasants is helping the Kolchaks, the Denikins, the capitalist bandits of all countries.

Consequently, we Great-Russian communists must repress with the utmost severity the slightest manifestation in our midst of Great-Russian nationalism, for such manifestations, which are a betrayal of communism in general, cause the gravest harm by dividing us from our Ukrainian comrades and thus playing into the hands of Denikin and his regime.

Consequently, we Great-Russian communists must make concessions when there are differences with the Ukrainian Bolshevik communists and Borotbists and these differences concern the state independence of the Ukraine, the forms of her alliance with Russia, and the national question in general. But all of us, Great-Russian communists, Ukrainian communists, and communists of any other nation, must be unyielding and irreconcilable in the underlying and fundamental questions which are the same for all nations, in questions of the proletarian struggle, of the proletarian dictatorship; we must not tolerate compromise with the bourgeoisie or any division of the forces which are protecting us against Denikin.

Denikin must be vanquished and destroyed, and such incursions as his not allowed to recur. That is to the fundamental interest of both the Great-Russian and the Ukrainian workers and peasants. The fight will be a long and hard one, for the capitalists of the whole world are helping Denikin and will help all other Denikins.

In this long and hard fight we Great-Russian and Ukrainian workers must maintain the closest alliance, for separately we shall most definitely be unable to cope with the task. Whatever the boundaries of the Ukraine and Russia may be, whatever may be the forms of their mutual state relationships, that is not so important; that is a matter in which concessions can and should be made, in which one thing, or another, or a third may be tried — the cause of the workers and peasants, of the victory over capitalism, will not perish because of that.

But if we fail to maintain the closest alliance, an alliance against Denikin, an alliance against the capitalists and kulaks of our countries and of all countries, the cause of labour will most certainly perish for many years to come in the sense that the capitalists *will be able* to crush and strangle both the Soviet Ukraine and Soviet Russia.

And what the bourgeoisie of all countries, and all manner of petty-bourgeois parties, i.e. 'compromising' parties which permit alliance with the bourgeoisie against the workers – try most of all to accomplish is to disunite the workers of different nationalities, to evoke distrust, and to disrupt a close international alliance and international brotherhood of the workers. Whenever the bourgeoisie succeeds in this the cause of the workers is lost. The communists of Russia and the Ukraine must therefore by patient, persistent, stubborn and concerted effort foil the nationalist machinations of the bourgeoisie and vanquish nationalist prejudices of every kind, and set the working people of the world an example of a really solid alliance of the workers and peasants of different nations in the fight for Soviet power, for the overthrow of the yoke of the landowners and capitalists, and for a world federal Soviet republic.

N Lenin

Eighth Congress of the RCP(B)

18-23 March 1919

Report On The Party Programme (extract)

19 March 1919

Comrades, according to the division of subjects agreed on between Comrade Bukharin[1] and myself, it is my task to explain the point of view of the commission on a number of concrete and most disputed points, or points which interest the party most at the present time.

* * *

We say that we have arrived at the dictatorship. But we must know how we arrived at it. The past keeps fast hold of us, grasps us with a thousand tentacles, and does not allow us to take a single forward step, or compels us to take these steps badly in the way we are taking them. And we say that for the situation we are arriving at to

1 Nikolai Bukharin joined the Bolsheviks in 1906 and became a leading figure in the party, joining its Central Committee and becoming the Editor-in-Chief of *Pravda* after the revolution. He opposed Lenin on the right of nations to self-determination and after the taking of power was a 'left communist'. After Lenin's death in 1924 he would become Stalin's most trusted ally until he was executed at the time of the purges.

be understood, it must be stated how we proceeded and what led us to the socialist revolution. We were led to it by imperialism, by capitalism in its early commodity production forms. All this must be understood, because it is only by reckoning with reality that we can solve such problems as, let us say, our attitude towards the middle peasants. And how is it, indeed, that there is such a category as a middle peasant in the era of purely imperialist capitalism? It did not exist even in countries that were simply capitalist. If we are to solve the problem of our attitude towards this almost medieval phenomenon (the middle peasants) purely from the point of view of imperialism and the dictatorship of the proletariat, we shall be absolutely unable to make ends meet, and we shall land in many difficulties. But if we are to change our attitude towards the middle peasant – then also have the goodness to say in the theoretical part where he came from and what he is. He is a small commodity producer. And this is the ABC of capitalism, of which we must speak, because we have not yet grown out of it. To brush this aside and say, "Why should we study the ABC when we have studied finance capitalism?" would be highly frivolous.

I have to say the same thing about the national question. Here too the wish is father to the thought with Comrade Bukharin. He says that we must not recognise the right of nations to self-determination. A nation means the bourgeoisie together with the proletariat. And are we, the proletarians, to recognise the right to self-determination of the despised bourgeoisie? That is absolutely incompatible! Pardon me, it is compatible with what actually exists. If you eliminate this, the result will be sheer fantasy. You refer to the process of differentiation which is taking place within the nations, the process of separation of the proletariat from the bourgeoisie. But let us see how this differentiation will proceed.

Take, for instance, Germany, the model of an advanced capitalist country whose organisation of capitalism, finance capitalism, was superior to that of America. She was inferior in many other respects, in technical development and production and in the political sphere, but in respect of the organisation of finance capitalism, in respect of the transformation of monopoly capitalism into state monopoly capitalism, Germany was superior to America. She is a model, it would seem. But what is taking place there? Has the German proletariat become differentiated from the bourgeoisie? No! It was reported that the majority of the workers are opposed to Scheidemann[2] in only a few of the large towns. But how did this come about? It was owing to the alliance between the Spartacists[3] and the thrice-accursed German Menshevik-Independents,[4] who make a muddle of everything and want to wed the system of workers' councils to a Constituent Assembly! And this is what is taking place in that very Germany! And she, mark you, is an advanced country.

Comrade Bukharin says, "Why do we need the right of nations to self-determination?" I must repeat what I said opposing him in the summer of 1917, when he proposed to delete the minimum programme and to leave only the maximum programme. I then retorted, "Don't halloo until you're out of the wood." When we have conquered power, and even then only after waiting a while, we shall do this.[5] We have conquered power, we have waited a while, and now I am willing to do it. We have gone directly into socialist construction, we have beaten off the first assault that threatened us – now it will be in place. The same applies to the right of nations to self-determination. "I want to recognise only the right of the working classes to self-determination", says Comrade Bukharin. That is to say, you want to recognise something that has not been achieved in a single country except Russia. That is ridiculous.

---

2 Philipp Scheidemann led the extreme right-wing section of the German SPD.

3 The Spartacists (*Spartakusbund*, Spartacus League) were German internationalists, headed by Rosa Luxemburg, Karl Liebknecht, Franz Mehring and others. They formed after the betrayal of the SPD at the start of the First World War. They would go on to found the Communist Party of Germany (KPD).

4 Lenin is referring to the Independent Social-Democratic Party of Germany (USPD), which split from the SPD over the war in 1917 and took a vacillating position between reformism and revolution.

5 See Lenin, 'Revision of the Party Programme', *LCW*, Vol. 26, p. 169.

Look at Finland; she is a democratic country, more developed, more cultured than we are. In Finland a process of separation, of the differentiation of the proletariat is taking a specific course, far more painful than was the case with us. The Finns have experienced the dictatorship of Germany; they are now experiencing the dictatorship of the Allied powers. But thanks to the fact that we have recognised the right of nations to self-determination, the process of differentiation has been facilitated there. I very well recall the scene when, at Smolny,[6] I handed the act to Svinhufvud[7] which in Russian means 'pighead' – the representative of the Finnish bourgeoisie, who played the part of a hangman. He amiably shook my hand, we exchanged compliments. How unpleasant that was! But it had to be done, because at that time the bourgeoisie were deceiving the people, were deceiving the working people by alleging that the Muscovites, the chauvinists, the Great Russians, wanted to crush the Finns. It had to be done.

Yesterday, was it not necessary to do the same thing in relation to the Bashkirian Republic?[8] When Comrade Bukharin said, "We can recognise this right in some cases", I even wrote down that he had included in the list the Hottentots, the Bushmen and the Indians.[9] Hearing this enumeration, I thought, how is it that Comrade Bukharin has forgotten a small tribe, the Bashkirs? There are no Bushmen in Russia, nor have I heard that the Hottentots have laid claim to an autonomous republic, but we have Bashkirs,

---

6   From August 1917, the Smolny Institute was the headquarters of the Bolshevik groups of the All-Russia Central Executive Committee, and the Petrograd Soviet of Workers' and Soldiers' Deputies.

7   On 18 December 1917, Lenin handed the decision of the Council of People's Commissars to recognise the independence of Finland to the head of the Finnish bourgeois government, Pehr Evind Svinhufvud.

8   Lenin refers to the negotiations in Moscow in March 1919 with a Bashkirian delegation on the question of forming an autonomous Bashkirian Soviet Republic. The Bashkir Autonomous Soviet Socialist Republic (ASSR) was the first autonomous republic of the RSFSR, established 23 March 1919.

9   'Hottentot' is a term, now considered offensive, used to refer to the indigenous Khoekhoe people of South Africa and Namibia. 'Bushmen' refers to a collection of hunter-gather peoples indigenous to southern Africa, also known as the 'San'.

Kyrghyz and a number of other peoples, and to these we cannot deny recognition. We cannot deny it to a single one of the peoples living within the boundaries of the former Russian Empire. Let us even assume that the Bashkirs have overthrown the exploiters and we have helped them to do so. This is possible only when a revolution has fully matured, and it must be done cautiously, so as not to retard by one's interference that very process of the differentiation of the proletariat which we ought to expedite. What, then, can we do in relation to such peoples as the Kyrghyz, the Uzbeks, the Tajiks, the Turkmen, who to this day are under the influence of their mullahs? Here, in Russia, the population, having had a long experience of the priests, helped us to overthrow them. But you know how badly the decree on civil marriage is still being put into effect. Can we approach these peoples and tell them that we shall overthrow their exploiters? We cannot do this, because they are entirely subordinated to their mullahs. In such cases we have to wait until the given nation develops, until the differentiation of the proletariat from the bourgeois elements, which is inevitable, has taken place.

Comrade Bukharin does not want to wait. He is possessed by impatience: 'Why should we? When we have ourselves overthrown the bourgeoisie, proclaimed Soviet power and the dictatorship of the proletariat, why should we act thus?' This has the effect of a rousing appeal, it contains an indication of our path, but if we were to proclaim only this in our programme, it would not be a programme, but a proclamation. We may proclaim Soviet power, and the dictatorship of the proletariat, and express the contempt for the bourgeoisie they deserve a thousand times over, but in the programme we must write just what actually exists with the greatest precision. And then our programme will be incontrovertible.

We hold a strictly class standpoint. What we are writing in the programme is a recognition of what has actually taken place since the time we wrote of the self-determination of nations in general. At that time there were still no proletarian republics. It was when they appeared, and only as they appeared, that we were able to write what is written here: "A federation of states organised after the Soviet type." The Soviet type is not yet soviets as they exist in Russia, but the Soviet type is becoming international. And this is all we can say. To go farther, one step farther, one hair's breadth farther, would be wrong, and therefore unsuitable for a programme.

We say that account must be taken of the stage reached by the given nation on its way from medievalism to bourgeois democracy, and from bourgeois democracy to proletarian democracy. That is absolutely correct. All nations have the right to self-determination – there is no need to speak specially of the Hottentots and the Bushmen. The vast majority, most likely nine-tenths of the population of the earth, perhaps 95 per cent, come under this description, since all countries are on the way from medievalism to bourgeois democracy or from bourgeois democracy to proletarian democracy. This is an absolutely inevitable course. More cannot be said, because it would be wrong, because it would not be what actually exists. To reject the self-determination of nations and insert the self-determination of the working people would be absolutely wrong, because this manner of settling the question does not reckon with the difficulties, with the zigzag course taken by differentiation within nations.

In Germany it is not proceeding in the same way as in our country – in certain respects more rapidly, and in other respects in a slower and more sanguinary way. Not a single party in our country accepted so monstrous an idea as a combination of workers' councils and a Constituent Assembly. And yet we have to live side by side with these nations. Now Scheidemann's party is already saying that we want to conquer Germany. That is of course ridiculous, nonsensical. But the bourgeoisie have their own interests and their own press, which is shouting this to the whole world in hundreds of millions of copies; Wilson,[10] too, is supporting this in his own interests. The Bolsheviks, they declare, have a large army, and they want, by means of conquest, to implant their Bolshevism in Germany. The best people in Germany – the Spartacists – told us that the German workers are being incited against the communists; look, they are told, how bad things are with the Bolsheviks! And we cannot say that things

---

10 Thomas Woodrow Wilson was President of the United States from 1913 to 1921.

with us are very good. And so our enemies in Germany influence the people with the argument that the proletarian revolution in Germany would result in the same disorders as in Russia.

Our disorders are a protracted illness. We are contending with desperate difficulties in creating the proletarian dictatorship in our country. As long as the bourgeoisie, or the petty bourgeoisie, or even part of the German workers, are under the influence of this bugbear – 'the Bolsheviks want to establish their system by force' – so long will the formula 'the self-determination of the working people' not help matters. We must arrange things so that the German traitor-socialists will not be able to say that the Bolsheviks are trying to impose their universal system, which, as it were, can be brought into Berlin on Red Army bayonets. And this is what may happen if the principle of the self-determination of nations is denied.

Our programme must not speak of the self-determination of the working people, because that would be wrong. It must speak of what actually exists. Since nations are at different stages on the road from medievalism to bourgeois democracy and from bourgeois democracy to proletarian democracy, this thesis of our programme is absolutely correct. With us there have been very many zigzags on this road. Every nation must obtain the right to self-determination, and that will make the self-determination of the working people easier. In Finland the process of separation of the proletariat from the bourgeoisie is remarkably clear, forceful and deep. At any rate, things will not proceed there as they do in our country. If we were to declare that we do not recognise any Finnish nation, but only the working people, that would be sheer nonsense. We cannot refuse to recognise what actually exists; it will itself compel us to recognise it.

The demarcation between the proletariat and the bourgeoisie is proceeding in different countries in their own specific ways. Here we must act with utmost caution. We must be particularly cautious with regard to the various nations, for there is nothing worse than lack of confidence on the part of a nation. Self-determination of the proletariat is proceeding among the Poles. Here are the latest figures on the composition of the Warsaw Soviet of Workers' Deputies.

Polish traitor-socialists: 333; Communists: 297. This shows that, according to our revolutionary calendar, October in that country is not very far off. It is somewhere about August or September 1917. But, firstly, no decree has yet been issued stating that all countries must live according to the Bolshevik revolutionary calendar; and even if it were issued, it would not be observed. And, secondly, the situation at present is such that the majority of the Polish workers, who are more advanced than ours and more cultured, share the standpoint of social-defencism, social-patriotism. We must wait. We cannot speak here of the self-determination of the working people. We must carry on propaganda on behalf of this differentiation. This is what we are doing, but there is not the slightest shadow of doubt that we must recognise the self-determination of the Polish nation now. That is clear. The Polish proletarian movement is taking the same course as ours, towards the dictatorship of the proletariat, but not in the same way as in Russia. And there the workers are being intimidated by statements to the effect that the Muscovites, the Great Russians, who have always oppressed the Poles, want to carry their Great-Russian chauvinism into Poland in the guise of communism. Communism cannot be imposed by force. When I said to one of the best comrades among the Polish communists, "You will do it in a different way", he replied, "No, we shall do the same thing, but better than you." To such an argument I had absolutely no objections. They must be given the opportunity of fulfilling a modest wish – to create a better Soviet power than ours. We cannot help reckoning with the fact that things there are proceeding in rather a peculiar way, and we cannot say: "Down with the right of nations to self-determination! We grant the right of self-determination only to the working people". This self-determination proceeds in a very complex and difficult way. It exists nowhere but in Russia, and, while foreseeing every stage of development in other countries, we must decree nothing from Moscow. That is why this proposal is unacceptable in principle.

* * *

Speech Closing the Debate on the Party Programme (extract)

19 March 1919

I must now deal with the question of self-determination of nations. Our criticism has served to exaggerate the importance of this question. The defect in our criticism was that it attached special significance to this question, which, in substance, is of less than secondary importance in the programme's general structure, in the sum total of programme demands.

While Comrade Pyatakov was speaking I was amazed and asked myself what it was, a debate on the programme, or a dispute between two Organising Bureaus? When Comrade Pyatakov said that the Ukrainian communists act in conformity with the instructions of the Central Committee of the RCP(B), I was not sure about the tone in which he said it. Was it regret? I do not suspect Comrade Pyatakov of that, but what he said was tantamount to asking what was the good of all this self-determination when we have a splendid Central Committee in Moscow. This is a childish point of view. The Ukraine was separated from Russia by exceptional circumstances, and the national movement did not take deep root there. Whatever there was of such a movement the Germans killed. This is a fact, but an exceptional fact. Even as regards the language it is not clear whether the Ukrainian language today is the language of the common people or not. The mass of working people of the other nations greatly distrusted the Great Russians whom they regarded as a kulak and oppressor nation. That is a fact. A Finnish representative told me that among the Finnish bourgeoisie, who hated the Great Russians, voices are to be heard saying: "The Germans proved to be more savage brutes, the Entente proved to be more savage, we had better have the Bolsheviks." This is the tremendous victory we have gained over the Finnish bourgeoisie in the national question. This does not in the least prevent us from fighting it as our class enemy and from choosing the proper methods for the purpose. The

Soviet Republic, which has been established in the country where tsarism formerly oppressed Finland, must declare that it respects the right of nations to independence. We concluded a treaty with the short-lived Red Finnish Government and agreed to certain territorial concessions, to which I heard quite a number of utterly chauvinistic objections, such as: "There are excellent fisheries there, and you have surrendered them." These are the kind of objections which induce me to say, "scratch some communists and you will find Great-Russian chauvinists".

I think that the case of Finland, as well as of the Bashkirs, shows that in dealing with the national question one cannot argue that economic unity should be effected under all circumstances. Of course, it is necessary! But we must endeavour to secure it by propaganda, by agitation, by a voluntary alliance. The Bashkirs distrust the Great Russians because the Great Russians are more cultured and have utilised their culture to rob the Bashkirs. That is why the term Great Russian is synonymous with the terms 'oppressor' or 'rogue' to Bashkirs in those remote places. This must be taken into account, it must be combated, but it will be a lengthy process. It cannot be eliminated by a decree. We must be very cautious in this matter. Exceptional caution must be displayed by a nation like the Great Russians, who earned the bitter hatred of all the other nations; we have only just learned how to remedy the situation, and then, not entirely. For instance, at the Commissariat of Education, or connected with it, there are communists, who say that our schools are uniform schools, and therefore don't dare to teach in any language but Russian. In my opinion, such a communist is a Great-Russian chauvinist. Many of us harbour such sentiments and they must be combated.

That is why we must tell the other nations that we are out-and-out internationalists and are striving for the voluntary alliance of the workers and peasants of all nations. This does not preclude wars in the least. War is another question, and arises out of the very nature of imperialism. If we are fighting Wilson, and Wilson uses a small nation as his tool, we say that we shall oppose that tool.

We have never said anything different. We have never said that a socialist republic can exist without military forces. War may be necessary under certain circumstances. But at present, the essence of the question of the self-determination of nations is that different nations are advancing in the same historical direction, but by very different zigzags and by-paths, and that the more cultured nations are obviously proceeding in a way that differs from that of the less cultured nations. Finland advanced in a different way. Germany is advancing in a different way. Comrade Pyatakov is a thousand times right when he says that we need unity. But we must strive for it by means of propaganda, by party influence, by forming united trade unions. But here, too, we must not act in a stereotyped way. If we do away with this point, or formulate it differently, we shall be deleting the national question from the programme. This might be done if there were people with no specific national features. But there are no such people, and we cannot build a socialist society in any other way.

I think, comrades, that the programme proposed here should be accepted as a basis and then referred back to the commission, which should be enlarged by the inclusion of representatives of the opposition, or rather, of comrades who have made practical proposals, and that the commission should put forward (1) the amendments to the draft that have been enumerated, and (2) the theoretical objections on which no agreement can be reached. I think this will be the most practical way of dealing with the matter, and one that will most speedily lead to a correct decision. (*Applause.*)

Declaration of the Rights of the People of Russia

Published 2 November 1917

The October Revolution of the workmen and peasants began under the common banner of emancipation. The peasants are being emancipated from the power of the landowners, for there is no longer the landowner's property right in the land – it has been abolished. The soldiers and sailors are being emancipated from the power of autocratic generals, for generals will henceforth be elective and subject to recall. The workingmen are being emancipated from the whims and arbitrary will of the capitalists, for henceforth there will be established the control of the workers over mills and factories. Everything living and capable of life is being emancipated from the hateful shackles. There remain only the peoples of Russia, who have suffered and are suffering oppression and arbitrariness, and whose emancipation must immediately be begun, whose liberation must be effected resolutely and definitely.

During the period of tsarism the peoples of Russia were systematically incited against one another. The results of such a policy are known; massacres and pogroms on the one hand, slavery of peoples on the other.

There can be and there must be no return to this disgraceful policy of instigation. Henceforth the policy of a voluntary and honest union of the peoples of Russia must be substituted.

In the period of imperialism; after the February Revolution, when the power was transferred to the hands of the Cadet bourgeoisie, the naked policy of instigation gave way to one of cowardly distrust of the peoples of Russia, to a policy of fault-finding and provocation, of 'freedom' and 'equality' of peoples. The results of such a policy are known; the growth of national enmity, the impairment of mutual trust.

An end must be put to this unworthy policy of falsehood and distrust, of fault-finding and provocation. Henceforth it must be replaced by an open and honest policy which leads to complete mutual trust of the people of Russia. Only as the result of such a trust can there be formed an honest and lasting union of the peoples of Russia. Only as the result of such a union can the workmen and peasants of the peoples of Russia be cemented into one revolutionary force able to resist all attempts on the part of the imperialist-annexationist bourgeoisie.

Starting with these assumptions, the First Congress of Soviets, in June of this year, proclaimed the right of the peoples of Russia to free self-determination.

The Second Congress of Soviets, in October of this year, reaffirmed this inalienable right of the peoples of Russia more decisively and definitely.

The united will of these Congresses, The Councils of the People's Commissars, resolved to base of their activity upon the question of the nationalities of Russia, as expressed in the following principles:

1. The equality and sovereignty of the peoples of Russia.

2. The right of the peoples of Russia to free self-determination, even to the point of separation and the formation of an independent state.

3. The abolition of any and all national and national-religious privileges and disabilities.

4. The free development of national minorities and ethnographic groups inhabiting the territory of Russia.

The concrete decrees that follow from these principles will be immediately elaborated after the setting up of a Commission of Nationality Affairs.

In the name of the Russian Republic,

Chairman of the Council of People's Commissars,
V Ulyanov (Lenin)

People's Commissar on Nationality Affairs,
Josef Dzhugashvili (Stalin)

Appeal of the Council of People's Commissars to the Moslems of Russia and the East

Dated 3 December 1917

Comrades! Brothers!

Great events are taking place in Russia! An end is drawing near to the murderous war, started by the bargainings of foreign powers. The rule of the plunderers who exploit the peoples of the world is tottering. The ancient citadel of slavery and serfdom is crumbling under the blows of the Russian Revolution. The world of violence and oppression is approaching its last days. A new world is being born, a world of the toilers and the liberated. At the head of this revolution stands the workers' and peasants' Government of Russia, the Council of People's Commissars.

Revolutionary councils of workers', soldiers' and peasants' deputies are scattered over the whole of Russia. Power in the country is in the hands of the people. The labouring masses of Russia burn with the single desire to achieve an honourable peace and to help the oppressed peoples of the world to win their freedom.

Russia is not alone in this sacred cause. The mighty call to freedom sounded by the Russian Revolution has been taken up by all the toilers in the East and West. The peoples of Europe, exhausted by war, are already stretching out their hands to us, in our work for peace. The workers and soldiers of the West are already rallying under the banner of socialism, storming the strongholds of imperialism. Even far-off India, that land which has been oppressed by the 'enlightened' European robbers for so many centuries, has raised the standard of revolt, organising its councils of deputies, throwing the hated yoke of slavery from its shoulders, and summoning the peoples of the East to the struggle and to freedom.

The empire of capitalist plunder and violence is falling in ruins. The ground is slipping from under the feet of the imperialist robbers.

In the face of these great events, we turn to you, toiling and disinherited Moslems of Russia and the East.

Moslems of Russia, Tatars of the Volga and the Crimea, Kyrghyz and Sarts of Siberia and Turkestan, Turks and Tatars of Transcaucasia, Chechens and mountain Cossacks! All you, whose mosques and shrines have been destroyed, whose faith and customs have been violated by the Tsars and oppressors of Russia! Henceforward your beliefs and customs, your national and cultural institutions, are declared free and inviolable! Build your national life freely and without hindrance. It is your right. Know that your rights, like those of all the peoples of Russia, will be protected by the might of the Revolution, by the Councils of Workers', Soldiers' and Peasants' Deputies!

Support this Revolution and its authorised Government!

Moslems of the East! Persians, Turks, Arabs, and Hindus! All you in whose lives and property, in whose freedom and native land the rapacious European plunderers have for centuries traded! All you whose countries the robbers who began the war now desire to share among themselves! We declare that the secret treaties of the dethroned Tsar regarding the annexation of Constantinople, confirmed by the deposed Kerensky, are now null and void. The Russian Republic and its Government, the Council of People's Commissars, are opposed to the seizure of foreign territory; Constantinople must remain in the hands of the Moslems.

We declare that the treaty for the partition of Persia is null and void. Immediately after the cessation of military operations the troops will be withdrawn from Persia and the Persians will be guaranteed the right freely to determine their own destiny.

We declare that the treaty for the partition of Turkey, which was to despoil it of Armenia, is null and void. Immediately after the cessation of military operations, the Armenians will be guaranteed the right freely to determine their political destiny.

It is not from Russia and its revolutionary Government that you have to fear enslavement, but from the European imperialist robbers, from those who laid waste your native lands and converted them into their colonies.

Overthrow these robbers and enslavers of your country! Now, when war and desolation are demolishing the pillars of the old order, when the entire world is blazing with indignation against the imperialist brigands, when the least spark of discontent bursts out in a mighty flame of revolution, when even the Indian Moslems, oppressed and tormented by the foreign yoke, are rising in revolt against their slave-drivers now it is impossible to keep silent. Lose no time in throwing off the yoke of the ancient oppressors of your land! Let them no longer violate your hearths! You must yourselves be masters in your own land! You yourselves must arrange your life as you yourselves see fit! You have the right to do this, for your fate is in your own hands!

Comrades! Brothers!

Advance firmly and resolutely towards a just and democratic peace!

We inscribe the liberation of the oppressed peoples of the world on our banners!

Moslems of Russia!

Moslems of the East!

We look to you for sympathy and support in the work of regenerating the world.

Draft Theses on National and Colonial Questions for the Second Congress of The Communist International

Written 5 June 1920

In submitting for discussion by the Second Congress of the Communist International the following draft theses on the national and the colonial questions I would request all comrades, especially those who possess concrete information on any of these very complex problems, to let me have their opinions, amendments, addenda and concrete remarks *in the most concise form* (*no more than two or three pages*), particularly on the following points:

– Austrian experience;

– Polish-Jewish and Ukrainian experience;

– Alsace-Lorraine and Belgium;

– Ireland;

– Danish-German, Italo-French and Italo-Slav relations;

– Balkan experience;

- Eastern peoples;

- The struggle against Pan-Islamism;

- Relations in the Caucasus;

- The Bashkir and Tatar Republics;

- Kyrghyzia; Turkestan, its experience;

- Negroes in America;

- Colonies;

- China-Korea-Japan.

N Lenin
5 June 1920

* * *

1. An abstract or formal posing of the problem of equality in general and national equality in particular is in the very nature of bourgeois democracy. Under the guise of the equality of the individual in general, bourgeois democracy proclaims the formal or legal equality of the property-owner and the proletarian, the exploiter and the exploited, thereby grossly deceiving the oppressed classes. On the plea that all men are absolutely equal, the bourgeoisie is transforming the idea of equality, which is itself a reflection of relations in commodity production, into a weapon in its struggle against the abolition of classes. The real meaning of the demand for equality consists in its being a demand for the abolition of classes.

2. In conformity with its fundamental task of combating bourgeois democracy and exposing its falseness and hypocrisy, the Communist Party, as the avowed champion of the proletarian struggle to overthrow the bourgeois yoke, must base its policy, in the national question too, not on abstract and formal principles but, first, on a precise appraisal of the specific historical

situation and, primarily, of economic conditions; second, on a clear distinction between the interests of the oppressed classes, of working and exploited people, and the general concept of national interests as a whole, which implies the interests of the ruling class; third, on an equally clear distinction between the oppressed, dependent and subject nations and the oppressing, exploiting and sovereign nations, in order to counter the bourgeois-democratic lies that play down this colonial and financial enslavement of the vast majority of the world's population by an insignificant minority of the richest and advanced capitalist countries, a feature characteristic of the era of finance capital and imperialism.

3. The imperialist war of 1914-18 has very clearly revealed to all nations and to the oppressed classes of the whole world the falseness of bourgeois-democratic phrases, by practically demonstrating that the Treaty of Versailles[1] of the celebrated 'Western democracies' is an even more brutal and foul act of violence against weak nations than was the Treaty of Brest-Litovsk[2] of the German Junkers[3] and the Kaiser. The League of Nations[4] and the entire post-war policy of the Entente reveal this truth with even greater clarity and distinctness. They are everywhere intensifying the revolutionary struggle both of the proletariat in the advanced countries and of the toiling masses in the colonial and dependent countries. They are hastening the collapse of the petty-bourgeois nationalist illusions that nations can live together in peace and equality under capitalism.

---

1   The Treaty of Versailles formally ended the First World War on 28 June 1919. It imposed crippling sanctions on Germany.

2   The Treaty of Brest-Litovsk was a separate peace treaty signed on 3 March 1918 between Soviet Russia and the Central Powers. Faced with a renewed aggression from the Central Powers, the new Bolshevik government was forced to sign the treaty, giving large concessions to Germany.

3   The Junkers were the landed nobility in Prussia.

4   The League of Nations was set up in 1920, following the end of the First World War. In the name of promoting 'peace' and 'diplomacy', it was in reality an imperialist alliance led by the US.

4. From these fundamental premises it follows that the Communist International's entire policy on the national and the colonial questions should rest primarily on a closer union of the proletarians and the working masses of all nations and countries for a joint revolutionary struggle to overthrow the landowners and the bourgeoisie. This union alone will guarantee victory over capitalism, without which the abolition of national oppression and inequality is impossible.

5. The world political situation has now placed the dictatorship of the proletariat on the order of the day. World political developments are of necessity concentrated on a single focus – the struggle of the world bourgeoisie against the Soviet Russian Republic, around which are inevitably grouped, on the one hand, the Soviet movements of the advanced workers in all countries, and, on the other, all the national liberation movements in the colonies and among the oppressed nationalities, who are learning from bitter experience that their only salvation lies in the Soviet system's victory over world imperialism.

6. Consequently, one cannot at present confine oneself to a bare recognition or proclamation of the need for closer union between the working people of the various nations; a policy must be pursued that will achieve the closest alliance, with Soviet Russia, of all the national and colonial liberation movements. The form of this alliance should be determined by the degree of development of the communist movement in the proletariat of each country, or of the bourgeois-democratic liberation movement of the workers and peasants in backward countries or among backward nationalities.

7. Federation is a transitional form to the complete unity of the working people of different nations. The feasibility of federation has already been demonstrated in practice both by the relations between the RSFSR and other Soviet Republics (the Hungarian, Finnish and Latvian in the past, and the Azerbaijani and

Ukrainian at present), and by the relations within the RSFSR in respect of nationalities which formerly enjoyed neither statehood nor autonomy (e.g. the Bashkir and Tatar autonomous republics in the RSFSR, founded in 1919 and 1920 respectively).

8. In this respect, it is the task of the Communist International to further develop and also to study and test by experience these new federations, which are arising on the basis of the Soviet system and the Soviet movement. In recognising that federation is a transitional form to complete unity, it is necessary to strive for ever closer federal unity, bearing in mind, first, that the Soviet republics, surrounded as they are by the imperialist powers of the whole world – which from the military standpoint are immeasurably stronger – cannot possibly continue to exist without the closest alliance; second, that a close economic alliance between the Soviet republics is necessary, otherwise the productive forces which have been ruined by imperialism cannot be restored and the well-being of the working people cannot be ensured; third, that there is a tendency towards the creation of a single world economy, regulated by the proletariat of all nations as an integral whole and according to a common plan. This tendency has already revealed itself quite clearly under capitalism and is bound to be further developed and consummated under socialism.

9. The Communist International's national policy in the sphere of relations within the state cannot be restricted to the bare, formal, purely declaratory and actually non-committal recognition of the equality of nations to which the bourgeois democrats confine themselves – both those who frankly admit being such, and those who assume the name of socialists (such as the socialists of the Second International).

    In all their propaganda and agitation – both within parliament and outside it – the communist parties must consistently expose that constant violation of the equality of nations and of the guaranteed rights of national minorities which is to be seen in all capitalist countries, despite their 'democratic' constitutions. It is also necessary, first, constantly to explain that only the Soviet system is capable of ensuring genuine equality of nations, by uniting first the proletarians and then the whole mass of the working population in the struggle against the bourgeoisie; and, second, that all communist parties should render direct aid to the revolutionary movements among the dependent and underprivileged nations (for example, Ireland, the American Negroes etc.) and in the colonies.

Without the latter condition, which is particularly important, the struggle against the oppression of dependent nations and colonies, as well as recognition of their right to secede, are but a false signboard, as is evidenced by the parties of the Second International.

10. Recognition of internationalism in word, and its replacement in deed by petty-bourgeois nationalism and pacifism, in all propaganda, agitation and practical work, is very common, not only among the parties of the Second International, but also among those which have withdrawn from it, and often even among parties which now call themselves communist. The urgency of the struggle against this evil, against the most deep-rooted petty-bourgeois national prejudices, looms ever larger with the mounting exigency of the task of converting the dictatorship of the proletariat from a national dictatorship (i.e. existing in a single country and incapable of determining world politics) into an international one (i.e. a dictatorship of the proletariat involving at least several advanced countries, and capable of exercising a decisive influence upon world politics as a whole). Petty-bourgeois nationalism proclaims as internationalism the mere recognition of the equality of nations, and nothing more. Quite apart from the fact that this recognition is purely verbal, petty-bourgeois nationalism preserves national self-interest intact, whereas proletarian internationalism demands, first, that the interests of the

proletarian struggle in any one country should be subordinated to the interests of that struggle on a world-wide scale, and, second, that a nation which is achieving victory over the bourgeoisie should be able and willing to make the greatest national sacrifices for the overthrow of international capital.

Thus, in countries that are already fully capitalist and have workers' parties that really act as the vanguard of the proletariat, the struggle against opportunist and petty-bourgeois pacifist distortions of the concept and policy of internationalism is a primary and cardinal task.

11. With regard to the more backward states and nations, in which feudal or patriarchal and patriarchal-peasant relations predominate, it is particularly important to bear in mind:

First, that all communist parties must assist the bourgeois-democratic liberation movement in these countries, and that the duty of rendering the most active assistance rests primarily with the workers of the country the backward nation is colonially or financially dependent on;

Second, the need for a struggle against the clergy and other influential reactionary and medieval elements in backward countries;

Third,[5] the need to combat Pan-Islamism and similar trends, which strive to combine the liberation movement against European and American imperialism with an attempt to strengthen the positions of the khans, landowners, mullahs, etc.;

Fourth, the need, in backward countries, to give special support to the peasant movement against the landowners, against landed proprietorship, and against all manifestations or survivals of feudalism, and to strive to lend the peasant movement the most revolutionary character by establishing the closest possible alliance between the West European communist proletariat and the revolutionary peasant movement in the East, in the colonies,

---

5   In the proofs, Lenin inserted a bracket opposite points 2 and 3 and wrote "2 and 3 to be united".

and in the backward countries generally. It is particularly necessary to exert every effort to apply the basic principles of the Soviet system in countries where pre-capitalist relations predominate – by setting up 'working people's Soviets' etc.;

Fifth, the need for a determined struggle against attempts to give a communist colouring to bourgeois-democratic liberation trends in the backward countries; the Communist International should support bourgeois-democratic national movements in colonial and backward countries only on condition that, in these countries, the elements of future proletarian parties, which will be communist not only in name, are brought together and trained to understand their special tasks, i.e. those of the struggle against the bourgeois-democratic movements within their own nations. The Communist International must enter into a temporary alliance with bourgeois democracy in the colonial and backward countries, but should not merge with it, and should under all circumstances uphold the independence of the proletarian movement even if it is in its most embryonic form;

Sixth, the need constantly to explain and expose among the broadest working masses of all countries, and particularly of the backward countries, the deception systematically practised by the imperialist powers, which, under the guise of politically independent states, set up states that are wholly dependent upon them economically, financially and militarily. Under present-day international conditions there is no salvation for dependent and weak nations except in a union of Soviet republics.

12. The age-old oppression of colonial and weak nationalities by the imperialist powers has not only filled the working masses of the oppressed countries with animosity towards the oppressor nations, but has also aroused distrust in these nations in general, even in their proletariat. The despicable betrayal of socialism by the majority of the official leaders of this proletariat in 1914-19, when 'defence of country' was used as a social-chauvinist cloak to conceal the defence of the 'right' of their 'own' bourgeoisie to

oppress colonies and fleece financially dependent countries, was certain to enhance this perfectly legitimate distrust. On the other hand, the more backward the country, the stronger is the hold of small-scale agricultural production, patriarchalism and isolation, which inevitably lend particular strength and tenacity to the deepest of petty-bourgeois prejudices, i.e. to national egoism and national narrow-mindedness. These prejudices are bound to die out very slowly, for they can disappear only after imperialism and capitalism have disappeared in the advanced countries, and after the entire foundation of the backward countries' economic life has radically changed. It is therefore the duty of the class-conscious communist proletariat of all countries to regard with particular caution and attention the survivals of national sentiments in the countries and among nationalities which have been oppressed the longest; it is equally necessary to make certain concessions with a view to more rapidly overcoming this distrust and these prejudices. Complete victory over capitalism cannot be won unless the proletariat and, following it, the mass of working people in all countries and nations throughout the world voluntarily strive for alliance and unity.

To the Comrades Communists
of Azerbaijan, Georgia,
Armenia, Dagestan, and
the Mountaineer Republic

Written 14 April 1921

Editor's note: The Mountaineer Republic (Mountain Autonomous Soviet Socialist Republic) was a short-lived Autonomous Republic within the RSFSR that existed from 20 January 1921 to 7 July 1924. It then split, with different national groups (Chechens, Ingush, North Ossetians, etc.) getting their own Autonomous Oblasts.

This letter was written in April 1921 after the Red Army had defeated the counter-revolutionary White forces in the Southern Front of the civil war in the Caucasus. This was at a time when the Bolshevik government was moving away from war communism and started to introduce the New Economic Policy, of concessions to the market and the peasantry. This policy was even more necessary in the Caucasus, due to the national question being entangled with the agrarian question.

* * *

I send my warmest greetings to the Soviet republics of the Caucasus, and should like to express the hope that their close alliance will serve as a model of national peace, unprecedented under the bourgeoisie and impossible under the capitalist system.

But important as national peace among the workers and peasants of the Caucasian nationalities is, the maintenance and development of the Soviet power, as the transition to socialism, are even more important. The task is difficult, but fully feasible. The most important thing for its successful fulfilment is that the communists of the Transcaucasus should be fully alive to the *singularity* of their position, and of the position of their republics, as distinct from the position and conditions of the RSFSR; that they should appreciate the need to refrain from copying our tactics, but thoughtfully vary them in adaptation to the differing concrete conditions.

The Soviet republic of Russia had no outside political or military assistance. On the contrary, for years and years, it fought the Entente military invasions and blockade.

The Soviet republics of the Caucasus have had political and some military assistance from the RSFSR. This alone has made a vast difference.

Second, there is now no cause to fear any Entente invasion or military assistance to the Georgian, Azerbaijani, Armenian, Dagestani and mountaineer White Guards. The Entente 'burnt their fingers' in Russia and that will probably compel them to be more cautious for some time.

Third, the Caucasian Republics have an even more pronounced peasant character than Russia.

Fourth, Russia has been, and to a considerable extent still is, economically isolated from the advanced capitalist countries. The Caucasus is in a position to start trading and 'living together' with the capitalist West sooner and with greater ease.

These are not all the differences, but they are sufficient to demonstrate the need for different tactics.

You will need to practice more moderation and caution, and show more readiness to make concessions to the petty bourgeoisie, the intelligentsia, and particularly the peasantry. You must make the swiftest, most intense and all possible economic use of the capitalist West through a policy of concessions and trade. Oil, manganese, coal (Tkvarcheli mines) and copper are some of your immense mineral resources. You have every possibility to develop an extensive policy of concessions and trade with foreign countries.

This must be done on a wide scale, with firmness, skill and circumspection, and it must be utilised to the utmost for improving the condition of the workers and peasants, and for enlisting the intelligentsia in the work of economic construction. Through trade with Italy, America and other countries, you must exert every effort to develop the productive forces of your rich land, your water resources and irrigation which is especially important as a means of advancing agriculture and livestock farming.

What the Republics of the Caucasus can and must do, as distinct from the RSFSR, is to effect a slower, more cautious and more systematic transition to socialism. That is what you must understand, and what you must be able to carry out, as distinct from our own tactics.

We fought to make the first breach in the wall of world capitalism. The breach has been made. We have maintained our positions in a fierce and superhuman war against the Whites, the Socialist-Revolutionaries and the Mensheviks, who were supported by the Entente countries, their blockade and military assistance.

You, Comrades communists of the Caucasus, have no need to force a breach. You must take advantage of the favourable international situation in 1921, and learn to build the new with greater caution and more method. In 1921, Europe and the world are not what they were in 1917 and 1918.

Do not copy our tactics, but analyse the reasons for their peculiar features, the conditions that gave rise to them, and their results; go beyond the letter, and apply the spirit, the essence and the lessons of the 1917-21 experience. You must make trade with the capitalist countries your economic foundation right away. The cost should be no object even if it means letting them have tens of millions' worth of valuable minerals.

You must make immediate efforts to improve the condition of the peasants and start on extensive electrification and irrigation projects. What you need most is irrigation, for more than anything else it will revive the area and regenerate it, bury the past and make the transition to socialism more certain.

I hope you will pardon my slipshod style: I have had to write the letter at very short notice, so as to send it along with Comrade Myasnikov.[1] Once again I send my best greetings and wishes to the workers and peasants of the Soviet Republics of the Caucasus.

N Lenin,
Moscow,
14 April 1921

---

1   Gavril Myasnikov was briefly an SR before joining the Bolsheviks from 1906.

On the Formation of a Federation of Transcaucasian Republics

Written 28 November 1921

Editor's note: In this article Lenin is pushing back against SG Ordzhonikidze and JV Stalin and their proposal for a Transcaucasian Federation (of Georgia, Armenia and Azerbaijan). The Georgian CC raised a series of objections to the formation of the Federation, but in March 1922, the Federal Union of Soviet Socialist Republics of Transcaucasia was established.

* * *

Comrade Stalin, in the main I agree with you, but I feel that the wording should be somewhat amended.

1. While a federation of Transcaucasian republics is absolutely correct in principle, and should be implemented without fail, its immediate practical realisation must be regarded as premature, i.e. a certain period of time will be required for its discussion, propagation and adoption by lower Soviet bodies;

2. The Central Committees of Georgia, Armenia and Azerbaijan shall be instructed (through the Caucasian Bureau) to submit the federation question for broad discussion in the party and by the *worker and peasant masses*, conduct vigorous propaganda *in*

favour of a federation and secure decisions to that effect by the congresses of Soviets in each of these republics. Should serious opposition arise, the Political Bureau[1] of the CC, RCP must be informed accurately and in good time.

Lenin

---

1 The Political Bureau was a body elected for the first time in October 1917 by the CC of the Russian Communist Party in order to give it day to day political leadership.

To the Communists of Turkestan

Published 7 November 1919

Editor's note: A Turkestan Soviet Federative Republic was established in April 1918, covering the territory of present day Turkmenistan, Kyrgyzstan, Uzbekistan and Tajikistan, taking into account the powerful pan-Turkic national sentiment. Lenin considered that this, as part of the general struggle against Great-Russian chauvinism, would have an impact in the struggle against imperialism in the East.

This letter was written by Lenin in connection with the dispatch to Turkestan of a commission of the All-Russian Central Executive Committee and the Council of People's Commissars.

* * *

Comrades, permit me to address you not as Chairman of the Council of People's Commissars and the Council of Defence, but as a member of the party.

It is no exaggeration to say that the establishment of proper relations with the peoples of Turkestan is now of immense, epochal importance for the Russian Socialist Federative Soviet Republic.

The attitude of the Soviet Workers' and Peasants' Republic to the weak and hitherto oppressed nations is of very practical significance for the whole of Asia and for all the colonies of the world, for thousands and millions of people.

I earnestly urge you to devote the closest attention to this question, to exert every effort to set an effective example of comradely relations with the peoples of Turkestan, to demonstrate to them by your actions that we are sincere in our desire to wipe out all traces of Great-Russian imperialism and wage an implacable struggle against world imperialism, headed by British imperialism. You should show the greatest confidence in our Turkestan Commission and adhere strictly to its directives, which have been framed precisely in this spirit by the All-Russia Central Executive Committee.

I would very much appreciate a reply to this letter indicating your attitude.

With communist greetings,
V Ulyanov (Lenin)

Letter to AA Joffe

Written 13 September 1921

Editor's note: At the beginning of August 1921, Adolph Joffe was sent to Turkestan by the Politburo to mediate the disagreement between Mikhail Tomsky and Georgii Safarov. The conflict, which was linked to the implementation of the New Economic Policy (of concessions to the market and the medium peasants), can be seen as a dress rehearsal for Lenin's 'last struggle' against Stalin on the national question.

Tomsky, the then Chairman of the Turkestan Commission of the All-Russia CEC, was demanding the introduction of tax in kind (in line with the NEP), but this became identified as a defence of the privileges of Russian settlers. Safarov, the head of the Comintern's 'Eastern Department', argued for the formation of committees of poor peasants, which should be given the land. He gathered support amongst the dispossessed Muslims because of his defence of the expropriation of the Russian colonists.

Lenin stressed that "the Muslim poor peasants should be treated with care and prudence, with a number of concessions", in order to "consolidate the line of wisdom and prudence"; for what was at stake, he reminded them, extended beyond Turkestan, and affected "our 'world policy' throughout the East."

* * *

Comrade Joffe,

You will find that today's Politbureau decision (which I enclose) largely meets your dispatch of 9 September.

Please be so kind as to send me a written report with more details.

In addition, as a personal request, to enable me to sort things out in this matter, I ask you to devote special attention (in your report or in a special annex to your report) to the question of protection of native interests against 'Russian' (Great-Russian or colonialist) exaggerations.

– What is the attitude of the natives to Safarov? Facts, facts and more facts.

– Who are the natives themselves (Safarov's supporters)? Names? Record? Prestige? (Facts, facts…)

– Will they be able to stand up for themselves? Is that sure? Even against such a subtle and firm and stubborn man as Tomsky?

– How many of them are there?

– 'The Union of the Poor' (set up by Safarov?) – its composition? importance? strength? role? Is it true that the natives were 'forcibly' stratified?

– Cotton? Its future? Is it true that Safarov is ruining the cotton? Facts, facts.

– The fronts in Ferghana? The Basmachi? Their attitude to the Tomsky and the Safarov 'line'?[1] Facts and exact decisions by Turkestan CEC concerning the Basmachi? The facts on what and when Tomsky and Safarov or their supporters differed in this question? (Extracts from relevant decisions, to show exactly when and on what precisely the formal differences occurred.)

There are some differences on this question inside the CC.

---

1   Ferghana is a city in Uzbekistan and was the centre of the Basmachi movement. The Basmachi movement was a movement of Islamic rebels who rose up against conscription into the tsarist army during the First World War. The movement later flared up again in 1918 against Soviet rule.

More exact information is highly important.

I personally very much suspect 'Tomsky's line' (perhaps it would be more correct to say Peter's line? or Pravdin's line? etc.)[2] of engaging in Great-Russian chauvinism, or, to put it more correctly, in deviating in that direction.

It is terribly important for all our *Weltpolitik* [world policy] to win the confidence of the natives; to win it over again and again; to prove that we are not imperialists, that we shall not tolerate any deviation in that direction.

This is a world-wide question, and that is no exaggeration.

There you must be especially strict.

It will have an effect on India and the East; it is no joke, it calls for exceptional caution.

With communist greetings,
Lenin

---

2   "Peter's line" is a reference to Tsar Peter I (Peter the Great). "Pravdin's line" is a reference to the Bolshevik leader AG Pravdin in Ufa who refused recognition to the Bashkirian Republic. Both are shorthand for Great-Russian chauvinism.

Letter To GK Ordzhonikidze

Written 2 March 1921

Editor's note: On 16 February 1921, the Red Army invaded Georgia. The invasion had been engineered by two high ranking Soviet and party officials of Georgian origin, Stalin (Peoples' Commissar for Nationalities and Politburo member) and Sergo Ordzhonikidze (Chief commissar of the Revolutionary War Council of the Caucasus and Chair of the Caucasian Bureau of the CC). Karl Radek opposed the decision and Trotsky, the head of the Red Army, had not been informed. Lenin was swayed by the pressure from the two Georgians, but he clearly had reservations. In this letter, written immediately after the invasion, he stresses the need to make concessions to Georgian petty-bourgeois nationalists, even to the point of reaching an agreement with Noe Zhordania, the head of the Georgian government before the invasion, and leader of the Georgian Mensheviks. He also insists on the need to create a Georgian Red Army by arming the workers and peasants (a decision which was sabotaged by Stalin), so that Soviet power would not be seen as a foreign invading force.

* * *

Please convey to the Georgian communists, and in particular to all members of the Georgian Revolutionary Committee, my warm greetings to Soviet Georgia. My special request to them is to inform me whether or not we are in complete agreement on the following three questions:

First, immediate arming of the workers and poor peasants and formation of a strong Georgian Red Army.

Second, there is need for a special policy of concessions with regard to the Georgian intelligentsia and small merchants. It should be realised that it is not only imprudent to nationalise them, but that there is even need for certain sacrifices in order to improve their position and enable them to continue their small trade.

Third, it is of tremendous importance to devise an acceptable compromise for a bloc with Zhordania[1] or similar Georgian Mensheviks, who before the uprising had not been absolutely opposed to the idea of Soviet power in Georgia on certain terms.

Please bear in mind that Georgia's domestic and international positions both require that her communists should avoid any mechanical copying of the Russian pattern. They must skilfully work out their own flexible tactics, based on bigger concessions to all the petty-bourgeois elements.

Please reply,
Lenin

---

1   Noe Zhordania was a Georgian Menshevik who joined the Social-Democratic movement in the 1890s. He would go on to become an opponent of the October Revolution.

*Letter to GK Ordzhonikidze
on the Strengthening of the
Georgian Red Army*

Written 13 February 1922

Comrade Sergo,

It is absolutely essential that the Congress of Soviets of Georgia should adopt a decision to strengthen the Georgian Red Army without fail, and that the decision is really carried out.

In the last resort, if the peasants are opposed to this, a decision, couched in the most general terms, should be adopted, such as it is deemed essential "without fail to strengthen the Georgian Red Army and to call upon all government bodies and all the working people to work to secure this", etc.

Actually, however, it is necessary, at all costs, and *immediately*, to develop and strengthen the Georgian Red Army. As a beginning let it consist only of one brigade or even less; two or three thousand Red cadets – of whom 1,500 should be communists – who (as cadres) could serve as the nucleus of an army *when the contingency arises*. This is absolutely essential.

Perhaps Stalin will enlarge on the military and technical methods of carrying this out.

I am confining myself to the political aspect of the matter: those who fail to carry this out will be expelled from the party *without compunction*. This is not a matter to be trifled with. It is absolutely essential politically; and you personally, and the entire Georgian Central Committee, will be held responsible to the whole party for this.

I await your reply.

Yours,
Lenin

PS: This is for Comrade Sergo and for all the members of the Central Committee of the Georgian Communist Party.

On the Establishment of the USSR

Letter to LB Kamenev for Members of the Politbureau

Written 26 September 1922

Editor's note: On 10 August 1922, the Politbureau set up a commission to go into the question of relations between the RSFSR and the independent national Soviet Republics in preparation for the next plenary meeting of the party's Central Committee Stalin had drafted a resolution entitled 'On the Relations Between the RSFSR and the Independent Republics', which discussed:

> ... treaties [to] be concluded between the Soviet Republics of the Ukraine, Byelorussia, Azerbaijan, Georgia, Armenia and the RSFSR for their formal entry into the RSFSR.

The CC of the Georgian Communist Party was against the draft resolution. At its meeting on 15 September 1922, it passed the following decision by a majority vote:

> The union in the form of autonomisation of the independent republics proposed on the basis of Stalin's theses is premature. A union of economic efforts and a common policy are necessary, but all attributes of independence should be preserved.

The CC of the Byelorussian Communist Party went on record for the preservation of treaty relations between the independent republics. The commission met 23-24 September 1922, and approved Stalin's draft (with one abstention – the representative from Georgia). In a special point the commission rejected the resolution of the CC of the Georgian Communist Party. Stalin's draft was gone over point by point and approved by a majority with certain minor amendments and addenda. The final wording of the commission's resolution, which Lenin deals with in his letter to the members of the Politbureau, was as follows:

1. It is considered advisable that treaties be concluded between the Soviet Republics of the Ukraine, Byelorussia, Azerbaijan, Georgia, Armenia and the RSFSR for their formal entry into the RSFSR, the question of Bokhara, Kharezm and the Far-Eastern Republic being left open and confined to agreements with them on customs arrangements, foreign trade, foreign and military affairs, and so on.

Note: Corresponding changes in the constitutions of the Republics mentioned in Point 1 and of the RSFSR to be made after enactment by Soviet procedure.

2. In accordance with this the decisions of the All-Russia Central Executive Committee of the RSFSR shall be considered binding upon the central bodies of the republics mentioned in Point 1, while the decisions of the Council of People's Commissars and the Council of Labour and Defence of the RSFSR shall be binding upon the unified commissariats of these republics.

Note: These republics are to be represented on the Presidium of the All-Russia CEC of the RSFSR

3. External affairs (foreign affairs and foreign trade), military affairs, ways of communication (with the exception of local transport) and Potel (the People's Commissariat for Post and Telegraph – Ed.) of the republics mentioned in Point 1 shall be merged with those of the RSFSR, the corresponding commissariats of the RSFSR having their agents and a small staff in the republics.

The agents are appointed by the People's Commissars of the RSFSR by arrangement with the Central Executive Committees of the republics.

It is considered advisable that the republics concerned be represented on the corresponding foreign agencies of the

People's Commissariat for Foreign Affairs and the People's Commissariat for Foreign Trade.

4. The Commissariats for Finance, Food, Labour and National Economy of the republics shall be formally subject to the directives of the corresponding RSFSR commissariats.

5. The remaining commissariats of the republics mentioned in Point 1, namely, the Commissariats for Justice, Education, Internal Affairs, Agriculture, Workers' and Peasants' Inspection, Public Health and Social Security, shall be considered independent.

Note 1: The agencies fighting counter-revolution in the aforementioned republics shall be subject to the directives of the GPU of the RSFSR.

Note 2: The Central Executive Committees of the republics shall be granted the right of amnesty only in civil cases.

6. This decision, if approved by the CC of the RCP, shall not be published, but shall be passed on to the national Central Committees as a circular directive to be enacted through the Central Executive Committee or the Congress of Soviets of the aforementioned republics pending the convocation of an All Russia Congress of Soviets, at which it is to be declared as the desire of these republics. (Central Party Archives of the Institute of Marxism-Leninism of the CC, CPSU).

Lenin found out about this proposal from Rakovsky, who was against it. Lenin also came out in opposition and insisted that there should be a formal union of equals, leading to the formation of a 'Union of Soviet Republics of Europe and the East' (note that the word Russian is not even part of the name). This was not a mere amendment, but two completely different and opposite approaches. Stalin was dismissive of and hurt by Lenin's corrections and in a memo to the Politburo he made the following comment:

> There is hardly a doubt that this 'hurriedness' [Lenin's], will 'supply fuel to the advocates of independence,' to the detriment of the national liberalism of comrade Lenin.

However, Stalin formally accepted the changes.

* * *

Comrade Kamenev,[1]

Stalin has probably already sent you the resolution of his commission on the entry of the independent republics into the RSFSR.

If he has not, please take it from the secretary at once, and read it. I spoke about it with Sokolnikov[2] yesterday, and with Stalin today. Tomorrow I shall see Mdivani (the Georgian communist suspected of 'independent' sentiments).[3]

In my opinion the matter is of utmost importance. Stalin tends to be somewhat hasty. Give the matter good thought (you once intended to deal with it, and even had a bit to do with it); Zinoviev too. Stalin has already consented to make one concession: in Clause 1, instead of 'entry' into the RSFSR, to put:

> Formal unification with the RSFSR in a Union of Soviet Republics of Europe and Asia.

I hope the purport of this concession is clear: we consider ourselves, the Ukrainian SSR and others, equal, and enter with them, on an equal basis, into a new union, a new federation, the Union of the Soviet Republics of Europe and Asia.

Clause 2 needs to be amended as well. What is needed besides the sessions of the All-Russia Central Executive Committee of the RSFSR is a: "Federal All-Union Central Executive Committee of the Union of the Soviet Republics of Europe and Asia".

If the former should hold sessions once a week, and the latter once a week (or once a fortnight even), this may be easily arranged.

The important thing is not to provide material for the 'pro-independence' people, not to destroy their *independence*, but to create another *new storey*, a federation of *equal* republics.

The second part of Clause 2 could stand: the dissatisfied will appeal (against decisions of the *Council of Labour and Defence, and*

---

1 Lev Kamenev was a leading 'old Bolshevik' and CC member.
2 Grigorii Sokolnikov was a Bolshevik who joined in 1905. He was a leading figure in Moscow in 1917 and a member of the CC as well as Commissar for Finance.
3 Polikarp Mdivani was a Georgian Bolshevik, leading the opposition against Stalin and Ordzhonikidze during the 'Georgian Affair'.

the Council of People's Commissars)[4] to the Federal All-Union Central Executive Committee, *without thereby suspending* implementation (just as in the RSFSR).

Clause 3 could stand, but its wording should be:

> … amalgamate in *federal* People's Commissariats whose seat shall be in Moscow, with the proviso that the respective People's Commissariats of the RSFSR have their authorised representatives with a small staff in all the Republics *that have joined the Union of Republics of Europe and Asia.*

Part 2 of Clause 3 remains; perhaps it could be said to emphasise equality:

> … by agreement of the *Central Executive Committees* of the member republics of the Union of the Soviet Republics of Europe and Asia.

Let's think about Part 3: perhaps we had better substitute *"mandatory"* for 'desirable'? Or perhaps insert *conditionally* mandatory at least in the form of a *request for instructions* and the authority to decide without such instructions solely in cases of 'specially urgent importance'?

Clause 4 could perhaps also be "amalgamate by agreement of the Central Executive Committees"?

Perhaps add to Clause 5:

> … with the establishment of joint (or general) conferences and congresses of a *purely consultative* nature (or perhaps of a *solely* consultative nature)?

Appropriate alterations in the first and second comments.

Stalin has agreed to delay submission of the resolution to the Political Bureau of the Central Committee until my return. I shall arrive on Monday, 2 October. I should like to see you and Rykov[5]

---

4 The Council of People's Commissars was the legislative body of the Soviet government, elected immediately on the day of the October Revolution, with Lenin as Chairman. The Council of Labour and Defence was set up under it's oversight near the end of the civil war, serving as the leading body on economic matters in the Soviet Union.

5 Alexei Rykov joined the RSDLP at the age of eighteen in 1899 and the Bolsheviks in 1903. He was Commissar of the Interior and later Chairman of the Council of People's Commissars after Lenin's death.

for about two hours in the morning, say 12 noon to 2 pm, and, if necessary, in the evening, say 5-7 or 6-8.

That is my tentative draft. I shall add or amend on the strength of talks with Mdivani and other comrades. I beg you to do the same, and to reply to me.

Yours,
Lenin

PS: Send copies to *all* members of the Political Bureau.

Memo Combatting Dominant Nation Chauvinism

Written 6 October 1922

Editor's note: By this time, Lenin was becoming increasingly alarmed by the Great-Russian chauvinist tendencies revealed by many leading communists, particularly Stalin and Ordzhonikidze. In this memo to the Politburo, he made a general statement and also a concrete proposal related to the Central Executive Committee of the USSR.

* * *

I declare war to the death on Great-Russian chauvinism. I shall eat it with all my healthy teeth as soon as I get rid of this accursed bad tooth.

It must be *absolutely* insisted that the Union Central Executive Committee should be *presided over* in turn by a:

– Russian,

– Ukrainian,

– Georgian, etc.

Absolutely!

Yours,
Lenin

The Question of Nationalities or 'Autonomisation'

Written 30-31 December 1922

Editor's note: Arising from the debate on the formation of the USSR and the Georgian incident, Lenin decided to dictate a series of general remarks about the national question and against what he described as Great-Russian chauvinism on the part of leading communists. 'Autonomisation' was the name given to Stalin's proposal of incorporating the different independent Soviet republics into the RSFSR. These notes, dictated by Lenin, form part of Lenin's Testament and were not published until 1956.

* * *

I suppose I have been very remiss with respect to the workers of Russia for not having intervened energetically and decisively enough in the notorious question of autonomisation, which, it appears, is officially called the question of the Union of Soviet Socialist Republics.

When this question arose last summer, I was ill; and then in autumn I relied too much on my recovery and on the October and December plenary meetings giving me an opportunity of intervening in this question. However, I did not manage to attend the October plenary meeting (when this question came up) or the one in December, and so the question passed me by almost completely.

I have only had time for a talk with Comrade Dzerzhinsky, who came from the Caucasus and told me how this matter stood in Georgia. I have also managed to exchange a few words with Comrade Zinoviev and express my apprehensions on this matter. From what I was told by Comrade Dzerzhinsky, who was at the head of the commission sent by the CC to 'investigate' the Georgian incident, I could only draw the greatest apprehensions. If matters had come to such a pass that Ordzhonikidze could go to the extreme of applying physical violence, as Comrade Dzerzhinsky informed me, we can imagine what a mess we have got ourselves into. Obviously the whole business of 'autonomisation' was radically wrong and badly timed.

It is said that a united apparatus was needed. Where did that assurance come from? Did it not come from that same Russian apparatus which, as I pointed out in one of the preceding sections of my diary, we took over from tsarism and slightly anointed with Soviet oil?

There is no doubt that that measure should have been delayed somewhat until we could say that we vouched for our apparatus as our own. But now, we must, in all conscience, admit the contrary; the apparatus we call ours is, in fact, still quite alien to us; it is a bourgeois and tsarist hotch-potch and there has been no possibility of getting rid of it in the course of the past five years without the help of other countries and because we have been 'busy' most of the time with military engagements and the fight against famine.

It is quite natural that in such circumstances the 'freedom to secede from the union' by which we justify ourselves will be a mere scrap of paper, unable to defend the non-Russians from the onslaught of that really Russian man, the Great-Russian chauvinist, in substance a rascal and a tyrant, such as the typical Russian bureaucrat is. There is no doubt that the infinitesimal percentage of Soviet and sovietised workers will drown in that tide of chauvinistic Great-Russian riff-raff like a fly in milk.

It is said in defence of this measure that the People's Commissariats directly concerned with national psychology and national education were set up as separate bodies. But there the question arises: can these People's Commissariats be made quite independent? and secondly:

were we careful enough to take measures to provide the non-Russians with a real safeguard against the truly Russian bully? I do not think we took such measures although we could and should have done so.

I think that Stalin's haste and his infatuation with pure administration, together with his spite against the notorious 'nationalist-socialism', played a fatal role here.[1] In politics spite generally plays the basest of roles.

I also fear that Comrade Dzerzhinsky, who went to the Caucasus to investigate the 'crime' of those 'nationalist-socialists', distinguished himself there by his truly Russian frame of mind (it is common knowledge that people of other nationalities who have become Russified over-do this Russian frame of mind) and that the impartiality of his whole commission was typified well enough by Ordzhonikidze's 'manhandling'. I think that no provocation or even insult can justify such Russian manhandling and that Comrade Dzerzhinsky was inexcusably guilty in adopting a light-hearted attitude towards it.

For all the citizens in the Caucasus Ordzhonikidze was the authority. Ordzhonikidze had no right to display that irritability to which he and Dzerzhinsky referred. On the contrary, Ordzhonikidze should have behaved with a restraint which cannot be demanded of any ordinary citizen, still less of a man accused of a 'political' crime. And, to tell the truth, those nationalist-socialists were citizens who were accused of a political crime, and the terms of the accusation were such that it could not be described otherwise.

Here we have an important question of principle: how is internationalism to be understood?

Lenin,
30 December 1922

Taken down by MV[2]

* * *

---

1 Stalin criticised the minority nations for not being 'internationalist' because they did not want to unite with Russia.
2 Maria Volodicheva was a secretary to the Council of People's Commissars.

Continuation of the notes

In my writings on the national question I have already said that an abstract presentation of the question of nationalism in general is of no use at all. A distinction must necessarily be made between the nationalism of an oppressor nation and that of an oppressed nation, the nationalism of a big nation and that of a small nation.

In respect of the second kind of nationalism we, nationals of a big nation, have nearly always been guilty, in historic practice, of an infinite number of cases of violence; furthermore, we commit violence and insult an infinite number of times without noticing it. It is sufficient to recall my Volga reminiscences of how non-Russians are treated; how the Poles are not called by any other name than Polyachiska, how the Tatar is nicknamed Prince, how the Ukrainians are always Khokhols and the Georgians and other Caucasian nationals always Kapkasians.

That is why internationalism on the part of oppressors or 'great' nations, as they are called (though they are great only in their violence, only great as bullies), must consist not only in the observance of the formal equality of nations but even in an inequality of the oppressor nation, the great nation, that must make up for the inequality which obtains in actual practice. Anybody who does not understand this has not grasped the real proletarian attitude to the national question, he is still essentially petty bourgeois in his point of view and is, therefore, sure to descend to the bourgeois point of view.

What is important for the proletarian? For the proletarian it is not only important, it is absolutely essential that he should be assured that the non-Russians place the greatest possible trust in the proletarian class struggle. What is needed to ensure this? Not merely formal equality. In one way or another, by one's attitude or by concessions, it is necessary to compensate the non-Russian for the lack of trust, for the suspicion and the insults to which the government of the 'dominant' nation subjected them in the past.

I think it is unnecessary to explain this to Bolsheviks, to communists, in greater detail. And I think that in the present instance, as far as the Georgian nation is concerned, we have a typical case in which a genuinely proletarian attitude makes profound caution, thoughtfulness and a readiness to compromise a matter of necessity for us. The Georgian[3] who is neglectful of this aspect of the question, or who carelessly flings about accusations of 'nationalist-socialism' (whereas he himself is a real and true 'nationalist-socialist', and even a vulgar Great-Russian bully), violates, in substance, the interests of proletarian class solidarity, for nothing holds up the development and strengthening of proletarian class solidarity so much as national injustice; 'offended' nationals are not sensitive to anything so much as to the feeling of equality and the violation of this equality, if only through negligence or jest, to the violation of that equality by their proletarian comrades. That is why in this case it is better to over-do rather than under-do the concessions and leniency towards the national minorities. That is why, in this case, the fundamental interest of proletarian class struggle, requires that we never adopt a formal attitude to the national question, but always take into account the specific attitude of the proletarian of the oppressed (or small) nation towards the oppressor (or great) nation.

* * *

What practical measures must be taken in the present situation?

Firstly, we must maintain and strengthen the union of socialist republics. Of this there can be no doubt. This measure is necessary for us and it is necessary for the world communist proletariat in its struggle against the world bourgeoisie and its defence against bourgeois intrigues.

Secondly, the union of socialist republics must be retained for its diplomatic apparatus. By the way, this apparatus is an exceptional component of our state apparatus. We have not allowed a single influential person from the old tsarist apparatus into it. All sections with any authority are composed of communists. That is why it has already won for itself (this may be said boldly) the name of a reliable communist apparatus purged to an incomparably greater extent of

---

3   Lenin is referring to JV Stalin.

the old tsarist, bourgeois and petty-bourgeois elements than that which we have had to make do with in other People's Commissariats.

Thirdly, exemplary punishment must be inflicted on Comrade Ordzhonikidze (I say this all the more regretfully as I am one of his personal friends and have worked with him abroad) and the investigation of all the material which Dzerzhinsky's commission has collected must be completed or started over again to correct the enormous mass of wrongs and biased judgments which it doubtlessly contains. The political responsibility for all this truly Great-Russian nationalist campaign must, of course, be laid on Stalin and Dzerzhinsky.

Fourthly, the strictest rules must be introduced on the use of the national language in the non-Russian republics of our union, and these rules must be checked with special care. There is no doubt that our apparatus being what it is, there is bound to be, on the pretext of unity in the railway service, unity in the fiscal service and so on, a mass of truly Russian abuses. Special ingenuity is necessary for the struggle against these abuses, not to mention special sincerity on the part of those who undertake this struggle. A detailed code will be required, and only the nationals living in the republic in question can draw it up at all successfully. And then we cannot be sure in advance that as a result of this work we shall not take a step backward at our next Congress of Soviets, i.e. retain the union of Soviet socialist republics only for military and diplomatic affairs, and in all other respects restore full independence to the individual People's Commissariats.

It must be borne in mind that the decentralisation of the People's Commissariats and the lack of co-ordination in their work as far as Moscow and other centres are concerned can be compensated sufficiently by party authority, if it is exercised with sufficient prudence and impartiality; the harm that can result to our state from a lack of unification between the national apparatuses and the Russian apparatus is infinitely less than that which will be done not only to us, but to the whole International, and to the hundreds of millions of the peoples of Asia, which is destined to follow us on to the stage of history in the near future. It would be unpardonable opportunism if, on the eve of debut of the East, just as it is awakening, we undermined our prestige with its peoples, even if only by the slightest crudity or injustice towards our own non-Russian nationalities. The need to rally against the imperialists of the West, who are defending the capitalist world, is one thing. There can be no doubt about that and it would be superfluous for me to speak about my unconditional approval of it. It is another thing when we ourselves lapse, even if only in trifles, into imperialist attitudes towards oppressed nationalities, thus undermining all our principled sincerity, all our principled defence of the struggle against imperialism. But the morrow of world history will be a day when the awakening peoples oppressed by imperialism are finally aroused and the decisive long and hard struggle for their liberation begins.

Lenin,
31 December 1922

Taken down by MV

Lenin's Last Letters

Written from 30 January – 16 March 1923

Editor's note: By the end of December 1922 and January 1923, as a result of the discussions on the formation of the USSR, the opposition and complaints of leading Georgian communists, etc., Lenin had become extremely worried about the bureaucratic and Great-Russian chauvinist tendencies he could see had developed in the party.

He saw the Georgian incident in which Ordzhonikidze had physically assaulted a leading Georgian communist, Akakii Kobakhidze, in opposition to him as a very serious and worrying manifestation of this. He insistently demanded to see the full contents of the report on the incident drawn up by Felix Dzerzhinsky, whom he did not trust on this question. He wanted to know the role Stalin had played in the affair.

He made it clear to the Georgians communists, whom Stalin had accused of 'nationalist deviations' that he was on their side and that he intended to defend their case at the forthcoming party congress. By March 1923, he realised that he may not be able to attend, and asked Trotsky to speak on his behalf. He was anxious that his point of view should be presented to the meeting, not only on the specific incident (where he stood against Stalin and Dzerzhinsky) but more generally on how to deal with the national question.

In effect, Lenin intended to launch a factional struggle against Stalin and his developing bureaucratic clique. That was not to be. On 9 March, Lenin suffered his third stroke which left him paralysed and more or less helpless until his death on 21 January 1924.

* * *

From the Journal of Lenin's Secretaries (extract)

Written 30-31 January 1923

Editor's note: These entries were taken by Lydia Fotieva, Lenin's personal secretary and a member of the Bolsheviks from 1904.

* * *

30 January 1923

On 24 January, Vladimir Ilyich sent for Fotieva and gave instructions to ask Dzerzhinsky or Stalin for the materials of the commission on the Georgian question and to make a detailed study of them. This assignment was given to Fotieva, Glyasser and Gorbunov. Object: report to Vladimir Ilyich, who wanted this for the party congress. Apparently, he did not know the question was up at the Politbureau. He said:

> Just before I got ill, Dzerzhinsky told me about the work of the commission and about the 'incident', and this had a very painful effect upon me.

On Thursday 25 January, he asked whether the materials had been received. I answered that Dzerzhinsky would not be arriving until Saturday. Therefore I had not yet been able to ask him.

On Saturday I asked Dzerzhinsky, he said Stalin had the materials. I sent Stalin a letter, but he was out of town. Yesterday, 29 January, Stalin phoned saying he could not give the materials without the Politbureau. Asked whether I had not been telling Vladimir Ilyich things he was not to be told – how was it he was posted about current affairs? For instance, his article about the WPI[1] showed that certain circumstances were known to him. I answered that I had not been telling anything and had no reason to believe he was posted about affairs. Today Vladimir Ilyich sent for me to learn the answer and said that he would fight to get the materials.

* * *

Evening of 14 February 1923

Called me in again. Impediment in speech, obviously tired. Spoke again on the three points of his instructions. In special detail on the subject that agitated him most of all, namely, the Georgian question. Asked to hurry things up. Gave certain instructions:

> Vladimir Ilyich's instructions that a hint be given to Soltz[2] that he (Lenin) was on the side of the injured party. Some one or other of the injured party was to be given to understand he was on their side.

> Three moments: (1) One should not fight. (2) Concessions should be made. (3) One cannot compare a large state with a small one.

> Did Stalin know? Why didn't he react?

> The name 'deviationist' for a deviation towards chauvinism and Menshevism proves the same deviation with the dominant-national chauvinists.

> Collect printed matter for Vladimir Ilyich.

* * *

---

1   The People's Commissariat of the Workers' and Peasants' Inspection, also known as the *Rabkrin* or WPI was a body set up in 1920 to scrutinise and maintain the effectiveness of the Soviet state and administration.

2   Aaron Soltz joined the Bolsheviks in 1898 and was a member of the presidium of the Communist Party Central Control Commission.

Letter to L Trotsky

Dictated 5 March 1923

Dear Comrade Trotsky:

It is my earnest request that you should undertake the defence of the Georgian case in the party CC. This case is now under 'persecution' by Stalin and Dzerzhinsky, and I cannot rely on their impartiality. Quite to the contrary. I would feel at ease if you agreed to undertake its defence. If you should refuse to do so for any reason, return the whole case to me. I shall consider it a sign that you do not accept.

With best comradely greetings,
Lenin

* * *

Letter to PG Mdivani,
FY Makharadze and Others

Dated 6 March 1923

Comrades Mdivani, Makharadze[3] and others
Copy to Comrades Trotsky and Kamenev

Dear Comrades:

I am following your case with all my heart. I am indignant over Ordzhonikidze's rudeness and the connivance of Stalin and Dzerzhinsky. I am preparing for you notes and a speech.

Respectfully yours,
Lenin

* * *

---

3   Filipp Makharadze was a Georgian Bolshevik.

To Comrade Kamenev
(Copy to Comrade Trotsky)

Dated 16 March 1923

Leon Borisovich,

Supplementing our telephone conversation, I communicated to you as acting chairman of the Political Bureau the following:

As I already told you, 31 December 1922, Vladimir Ilyich dictated an article on the national question.

This question has worried him extremely and he was preparing to speak on it at the party congress. Not long before his last illness he told me that he would publish this article, but later. After that he took sick without giving final directions.

Vladimir Ilyich considered this article to be a guiding one and extremely important. At his direction it was communicated to Comrade Trotsky whom Vladimir llyich authorised to defend his point of view upon the given question...

L Fotieva,
Personal secretary of Comrade Lenin

Appendices

Resolutions Adopted at the International Socialist Workers and Trade Union Congress, London, 1896

Adopted 30 July 1896

Lansbury [...] asks for the adoption of the following resolutions:

1. This Congress understands by 'political action' all forms of organised struggle for the conquest of political power and the use by the working class of the legislative and administrative institutions of the state and districts for the purposes of its emancipation.

2. The Congress declares that the most important means for the emancipation of the workers, as people and as citizens, and for the establishment of the international socialist republic, is the conquest of political power. It calls upon the workers of all countries to unite, and demand the following, independently of all bourgeois parties:

    – universal suffrage for all adults;

    – equal voting rights for every adult;

    – runoff voting

    – initiatives and referendums across the state and in the districts.

3. This Congress declares that it stands for the full right of all nations to self-determination and expresses its sympathy for the workers of every country now suffering under the yoke of military, national or other absolutism. This Congress calls upon the workers of all these countries to join the ranks of the class-conscious workers of the whole world in order jointly to fight for the defeat of international capitalism and for the achievement of the aims of international Social-Democracy.

4. The Congress declares that the emancipation of women is inseparable from the liberation of the working class and therefore calls on women in all countries to fight side by side with the workers, and to organise themselves politically together with them.

5. The Congress declares: Whatever the religious or civilising pretexts of colonial policy may be, its sole purpose is always the expansion of the area of capitalist exploitation in the exclusive interests of the capitalist class.

The resolutions of the commission receive near unanimous support.

The Nationalities Programme of the Social Democratic Workers' Party of Austria (Extract)

Adopted 29 September 1899

Since the national turmoil in Austria paralyses all political progress and all cultural development of the peoples, since this turmoil is primarily due to the political backwardness of our public institutions and since, in particular, the continuation of national division is one of the means by which the ruling classes secure their rule and prevent the real interests of the people from gaining any serious expression, the party congress declares:

The final settlement of the national question and the language question in Austria, in the spirit of equality, equal rights and reason, is above all a cultural demand. Therefore, in the vital interest of the proletariat; it is only possible in a truly democratic polity, founded on universal, equal and direct suffrage, in which all feudal privileges in the state and in the provinces are abolished. Only in such a polity can the working classes, who are, in truth, the elements sustaining the state and society, have their say. The cultivation and development of the national character of all peoples in Austria is only possible on the basis of equal rights and by avoiding all oppression; therefore, above all else, all bureaucratic-state centralism, as well as the feudal privileges of the provinces, must be combated.

Under these conditions, and only under these conditions, will it be possible to establish national order in Austria in place of national strife. This can only be done by recognising the following guiding principles:

1. Austria is to be reorganised into a democratic federation of nationalities.

2. In place of the historical crown lands, nationally delimited self-governing bodies shall be formed, whose legislation and administration shall be organised by national chambers elected on the basis of universal, equal and direct suffrage.

3. All self-governing territories of one and the same nation together form a nationally unified association that manages its national affairs completely autonomously.

4. The right of national minorities shall be safeguarded by a separate law to be passed by the Imperial Parliament.

5. We do not recognise any national privilege and therefore reject the demand for a national language; the extent to which a mediating language is necessary will be determined by the Imperial Parliament.

The party congress as the organ of international Social-Democracy in Austria, expresses the conviction that an understanding between peoples is possible on the basis of these guiding principles formally declares that it recognises the right of every nationality to national existence and national development; but that the peoples can only achieve any progress in their culture in close solidarity with each other, rather than in petty quarrels against each other. In particular, in the interests of each individual nation, as well as in the interests of the whole, the working class of all languages must adhere to the international community of struggle and fraternity, and conduct its struggle in politics and in the trade unions in complete unity.

Otto Bauer

Maps and Tables

The Union of Soviet Socialist Republics, 1936

Constituent Republics (1936):

Armenian, Azerbaijan, Byelorussian ("White Russian"), Georgian, Kazakh, Kyrghyz, Russian, Tajik, Turkmen, Ukrainian, Uzbek

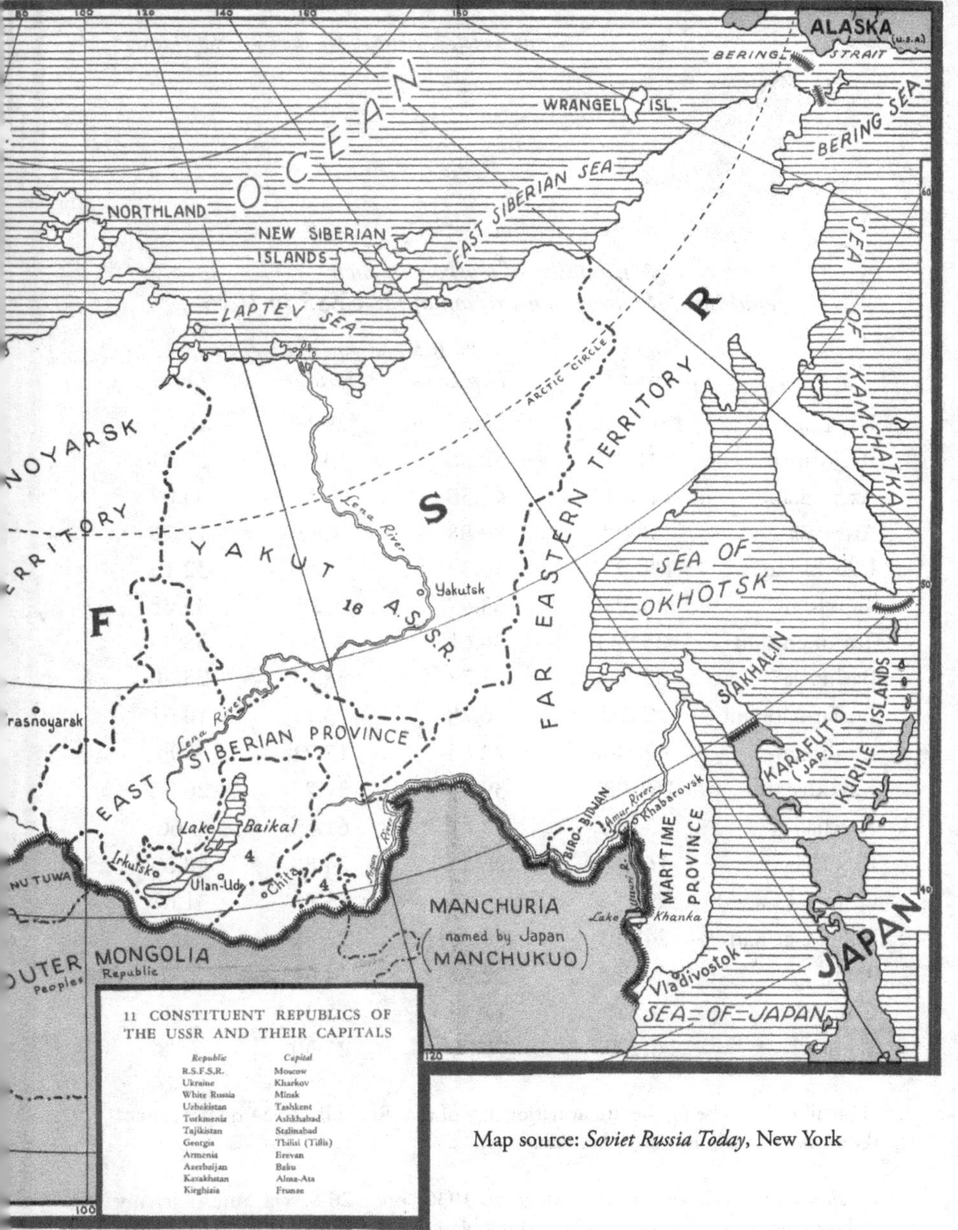

Map source: *Soviet Russia Today*, New York

Autonomous Republics included within the Constituent Republics:

1. Tatar 2. Bashkir 3. Dagestan 4. Buryat-Mongolian 5. Chechen-Ingush
6. Chuvash 7. Kabardino-Balkarian 8. Kalmyk 9. Karelian 10. Komi
11. Mariisk 12. Mordva 13. N. Osetian 14. Udmurt 15. Volga-German
16. Yakut 17. Moldavian 18. Nakhichevan 19. Abkhazian 20. Ajarian
21. Jara-Kalpak 22. Crimean

Nationality of workers in each republic and autonomous region of the USSR in 1926

	Total no. of workers	% Belonging to nationalities:		
		Titular	*Russian*	*Other*
Ukraine	1,071,856	54.64	29.17	16.19
Byelorussia	121,913	58.86	13.33	27.81
Azerbaijan	149,211	42.58	22.50	34.02
Armenia	28,295	80.88	1.42	17.70
Uzbekistan	136,921	50.37	17.50	32.13
Tajikistan	20,350	63.47	1.28	35.28
Turkmenistan	25,933	26.61	35.06	38.33
Bashkiria	69,196	17.77	58.83	23.40
Buriat-Mongol	10,857	16.28	73.11	10.61
Daghestan	42,180	72.84	17.21	9.93
Kazakhstan	151,987	39.43	34.25	26.32
Karelia	23,222	34.81	61.53	3.66
Kirghizia	16,453	26.49	24.88	48.63
Crimea (Tatars)	49,154	13.26	55.93	31.01
Volga Germans	24,091	58.24	27.89	13.87
Tatar	34,909	22.65	74.64	2.71
Chuvash	4,748	17.84	75.36	6.80
Yakuts	6,409	70.92	21.30	7.78

'Titular' refers to being the titular nationality of that Republic, so 54.64 per cent of the workers in Ukraine are Ukranian.

Natsional'naia politika VKP(b), Moscow, 1930, pp. 126-8, via Smith, Jeremy Robert Charnock, 'The Bolsheviks and the National Question, 1917-1923', 1996.

Linguistic composition of the Russian Empire in 1897

Language	Native speakers	%
Russian	55,667,469	44.31
Ukrainian	22,380,551	17.81
Polish	7,931,307	6.31
Belarusian	5,885,547	4.68
Jewish languages	5,063,156	4.03
Kyrgyz-Kaisak	4,084,139	3.25
Tatar	3,737,627	2.97
German	1,790,489	1.43
Latvian	1,435,937	1.14
Bashkir	1,321,363	1.05
Lithuanian	1,210,510	0.96
Armenian	1,173,096	0.93
Romanian	1,121,669	0.89
Mordovian	1,023,841	0.81
Estonian	1,002,738	0.80
Sartic	968,655	0.77
Chuvash	843,755	0.67
Georgian	823,968	0.66
Uzbek	726,534	0.58
Samogitian	448,022	0.36
Votyak	420,970	0.34
Mari	375,439	0.30
Tajik	350,397	0.28
Buryat	288,663	0.23
Turkmen	281,357	0.22
Mingrelian	239,625	0.19
Yakut	227,384	0.18
Chechen	226,496	0.18

A further seventy-six recorded languages are not presented here.

A General Summary for the Empire of the Results of the Development of Data From the First General Census of Population, Vol. 2, NA Troinitsky (ed.), St. Petersburg, 1905, via *Demoscope Weekly*, 2010.

Religious composition of the Russian Empire in 1897

Faith	Number	%
Eastern Orthodox	87,123,604	69.34
Muslim	13,906,972	11.07
Roman Catholic	11,467,994	9.13
Jewish	5,215,805	4.15
Lutherans	3,572,653	2.84
Old Believers	2,204,596	1.75
Armenian Apostolic	1,179,241	0.94
Buddhists	433,863	0.34
Reformed	85,400	0.07
Mennonite	66,564	0.05
Armenian Catholic	38,840	0.03
Baptist	38,139	0.03
Karaite	12,894	0.01
Anglican	4,183	0.00
Other Christian denominations	3,952	0.00
Other non-Christian denominations	285,321	0.23

A General Summary for the Empire of the Results of the Development of Data From the First General Census of Population, Vol. 2, NA Troinitsky (ed.), St. Petersburg, 1905, via *Demoscope Weekly*, 2010.

Timeline of the Georgian Affair

1922

12 March — Transcaucasian Soviet Federation is established, bringing together Georgia, Azerbaijan and Armenia.

22 October — Nine out of eleven Georgian Central Committee members resign in protest against the policies of Stalin and Ordzhonikidze on the national question.

Late November — Ordzhonikidze strikes Kobakhidze (dissident Georgian former Central Committee member). Dzerzhinsky is sent to produce a report on the situation in Georgia.

1923

24 January — Lenin requests, but is denied access to, Dzerzhinsky's report.

25 January — The Political Bureau endorses Dzerzhinsky's report and its findings, which defend Stalin and Ordzhonikidze.

1 February — Lenin is given access to Dzerzhinsky's report by the Political Bureau.

5 March — Lenin asks Trotsky to defend the dissident Georgian Central Committee members on his behalf.

6 March — Lenin writes to Georgian communist leaders offering his support against Stalin and Ordzhonikidze.

10 March — Lenin suffers his third stroke, preventing further political work.

Glossary

People

Axelrod, Pavel (1850-1928) – One of the founders of the Russian Emancipation of Labour group. After the Second Congress of the RSDLP he became a leading Menshevik.

Bauer, Otto (1881-1938) – The most prominent leader of the Austrian Social-Democratic Party. Prior to the First World War, Bauer was the secretary of the parliamentary faction of the SDAPÖ. He was the author of a number of books on the national and colonial questions. During the war, Bauer held a centrist position. In 1919 he became Minister of Foreign Affairs in the coalition government set up after the overthrow of the Habsburgs. Together with Friedrich Adler and others, Bauer participated both in creating the Two-and-a-half International and in fusing it with the Second International in 1923. He was a major theoretician of 'Austro-Marxism.'

Chkheidze, Nikolai (1864-1926) – Georgian Menshevik. President of the EC of the Soviet of Petrograd until September 1917.

Chkhenkeli, Akaki (1874-1959) – Georgian Menshevik.

Cunow, Heinrich (1862-1936) – Member of the SPD and a social-chauvinist who argued that backward nations should be denied the right to self-determination in the face of more advanced, 'progressive' imperialist nations.

David, Eduard (1863-1930) – Reichstag member for the German SPD after 1903, leading the social-chauvinist majority.

Dontsov, Dmytro (1883-1973) – Ukrainian nationalist. Started his political activity as a member of the Ukrainian Social-Democratic Worker's Party (USDRP). Became a fascist in the inter-war period.

Dragomanov, Mykhailo (1841-1895) – Ukrainian historian, ethnographer and publicist.

Fotieva, Lydia (1881-1945) – One of Lenin's personal secretaries.

Gvozdev, Kuzma (1859-1932) – Menshevik, on the Petrograd Soviet EC from February. Minister of Labour in the third Provisional Government.

Haecker, Emil (1875-1934) – Polish historian, member of the Social-Democratic Party of Galicia and Silesia, and Editor-in-Chief of Naprzód.

Hanecki, Yakov (born Jakub Fürstenberg) (1879-1937) – Polish Marxist, member of the SDKPiL and close collaborator with Lenin.

Hankiewicz, Mikolaj (1869-1931) – Ukrainian Social-Democrat and founder of the Ukrainian Social-Democratic Party.

Hindenburg, Paul von (1847-1934) – Prominent General who spent nearly fifty years in the Imperial German Army. He served in the Franco-Prussian war, was present at the crushing of the Paris Commune, and came out of retirement to lead the army during the First World War, becoming the Chief of the General Staff in 1916. He would later go on to be the last President of Germany, until his death and Hitler's rise to power in 1933.

Kamenev, Lev (1883-1936) – Joined the Bolshevik faction in 1903, elected to the CC in 1907. After the February Revolution, Kamenev sided with Zinoviev and Stalin and pursued a policy of conciliation with the Provisional Government. In October, Kamenev and Zinoviev went to the public press and disclosed the plans for an insurrection, for which Lenin called for their immediate expulsion. Executed in 1936 during the Great Purges.

Kautsky, Karl (1854-1938) – One of the leading theoreticians of the Social Democratic Party of Germany and the Second International. By the outbreak of the First World War, he had abandoned revolutionary Marxism and took up an indecisive position between revolutionary opposition to the war and patriotic support for the German bourgeoisie. As such, he became the theoretician of this 'centrism' in the socialist movement, and a bitter opponent of the Russian Revolution.

Kerensky, Alexander (1881-1970) – Lawyer and nominal member of the SRs. After the February Revolution, he became the outstanding representative of petty-bourgeois conciliationism, first as Minister of Justice, then as War Minister. Kerensky then headed the Provisional Government from July-October 1917, at which point he fled the country.

Kokoshkin, Fyodor (1841-1895) – A founding member of the Cadets.

Kolyubakin, Aleksandr (1868-1915) – A Cadet and Member of the Third Duma.

Kosovsky, Vladimir (born Levinson, Nokhem Mendel) (1867-1941) – A leading Bundist.

Lafargue, Paul (1842–1911) – French Marxist and Marx's son-in-law.

Lensch, Paul (1873-1926) – SPD Reichstag member elected in 1912. He took social-chauvinist positions which he dubbed "war socialism".

Liber, Mikhail (born Goldman) (1880-1937) – A leader of the Bund and a leading Menshevik.

Longuet, Jean (1876-1938) – French lawyer and socialist who in the First World War held a pacifist position but invariably voted for war credits.

Lopatin, German (1845-1918) – An early Russian Marxist and friend of Marx and Engels. Member of the General Council of the First International.

Luxemburg, Rosa (1871-1919) – Joined the SPD in Germany in 1898 and was on the bureau of the Second International from 1903. Luxemburg was the leader of the Left wing against the revisionist Right and, after 1910, against the Kautskyist group. She was a leading revolutionary opponent of the war and a founder of the Spartacus group. In prison for most of the war, she was murdered during the Spartacist Uprising in January 1919.

Martov, Yuri (Julius) (1873-1913) – A leading Menshevik, on its Left wing. He advocated against Mensheviks joining the Provisional Government. He strongly criticised Mensheviks such as Irakli Tsereteli and Fyodor Dan who, as members of the Russian government, supported the war effort.

Martynov, Alexandr (1865-1935) – Right-wing Menshevik before 1917. Strong advocate of the two stage theory. Joined the Communist Party in 1923, and became an opponent of the Left Opposition. Chief architect of the Stalinist theories used to justify subordinating the workers to the 'progressive' bourgeoisie, including the concept of the "bloc of four classes".

Mazzini, Giuseppe (1805-1872) – Italian nationalist and republican who played a leading role in the bourgeois revolutionary movement.

Mdivani, Polikarp (1877-1937) – Leading Georgian Bolshevik, leading the opposition to Stalin's centralising policies during the 'Georgian Affair' in 1922. Executed during the Great Purges.

Mehring, Franz (1846-1919) – Franz Mehring was a German communist, historian and art critic who was a veteran of the SPD and later the KPD. He was in correspondence with Engels and edited various papers including *Die Neue Zeit*. He played a leading role alongside Rosa Luxemburg and Karl Liebknecht in founding the Spartacus League.

Mogilyansky, Mikhail (1873-1942) – A leading Cadet, on its CC from 1907-1917. He was a lawyer and journalist who wrote for Rech.

Nekrasov, Nikolai (1879-1940) – A founder and leader of the Cadets. Transportation Minister in the first and Vice-president and Minister of Finance in the second Provisional Government. Supported Kornilov's revolt.

Ordzhonikidze, Sergo (born Orjonikidze, Grigol Konstantines dze) (1886-1937) – Georgian Bolshevik who joined the RSDLP and Bolsheviks in 1903. Close collaborator with Stalin. Appointed Commissar for the Ukraine, helped establish Soviet power in Ukraine. Played an active role as the leading Bolshevik in the Caucasus. Was appointed President of the Central Control Commission, responsible for expelling the Left Opposition from the party. Allegedly committed suicide during the purges.

Parvus, Alexander (born Gelfand, Israel) (Helphand) (1867-1924) – A Russian-German Social-Democrat, member of the SPD. During the Russian Revolution of 1905, he was active on the left wing of the Russian movement. He then fled to Germany where he settled. His credentials as a revolutionary were tainted by numerous scandals and business ventures that made him a wealthy war profiteer and his allegiances questionable.

Plekhanov, Georgi (1856-1918) – The founder of Russian Marxism and a leading member of the RSDLP. After joining the Menshevik faction in 1903, he became extremely hostile to Lenin and the Bolsheviks. He took a defencist, social-chauvinist position in the war. He initially opposed the February Revolution on the grounds that it disorganised the war effort, before supporting the Provisional Government.

Proudhon, Pierre-Joseph (1809-1865) – French petty-bourgeois anarchist.

Purishkevich, Vladimir (1870-1920) – Extreme reactionary and Russian monarchist Duma member who organised the Black Hundreds in the 1905 Revolution. He took part in the assassination of Rasputin in 1916.

Pyatakov, Georgy (pseudonym Kievsky) (1890-1937) – Ukrainian revolutionary and member of the Bolsheviks. chairman of the provisional Ukrainian workers and peasants' government formed at Kursk in November 1918, but was replaced by Christian Rakovsky, a Bolshevik, in the Kharkov-based Ukrainian Soviet government. Executed in 1937 during the Great Purges.

Renaudel, Pierre (1871-1935) – Leading French right-wing social-democrat; leader of the Socialist Party of France and editor of *l'Humanité*.

Renner, Karl (1870-1950) – Austrian social-democrat. Right-wing leader of Austrian SDP; Austrian chancellor 1918-20.

Rubanovich, Ilya (1859-1920) – Russian Narodnik, then Socialist-Revolutionary and social-chauvinist.

Ruge, Arnold (1802-1880) – German philosopher and associated with the Young Hegelians alongside Marx, Engels, Ludwig Feuerbach and others.

Rykov, Alexei (1881-1938) – Joined the RSDLP at the age of eighteen in 1899 and the Bolsheviks in 1903. He was Commissar of the Interior and later Chairman of the CPC after Lenin's death. He was executed in 1938 in the purges.

Scheidemann, Philipp (1865-1939) – Leader of the extreme right-wing section of the German SPD.

Sokolnikov, Grigorii (1888-1939) – Bolshevik who joined in 1905. He was a leading figure in Moscow in 1917 and a member of the CC. Commissar for Finance. Executed in 1939 in the purges.

Stirner, Max (1806-1856) – German anarchist philosopher, close to the Young Hegelians.

Struve, Peter (1870-1944) – Russian political economist, philosopher, historian and editor. He started his career as a Marxist, and exponent of 'legal Marxism'. He later became a liberal and leader of the Cadets. After the October Revolution he joined the White movement.

Prince Trubetskoy, Yevgeny (1863-1920) – Russian nobleman, lawyer and Cadet.

Tsar Nicholas II, Nikolai Romanov (1868-1918) – Last Emperor of Russia, King of Poland and Grand Duke of Finland, ruling from 1 November 1894 until his abdication on 15 March 1917.

Vandervelde, Émile (1866-1938) – Leader of the Belgian Workers' Party and chairman of the Brussels office of the Second International from 1900-14. Member of Belgian Council of Ministers 1916-21.

Kaiser Wilhelm II (1859-1941) – The last German Emperor and King of Prussia, from 1888 until his abdication in 1918 after the November Revolution.

Yurkevich, Lev (1883-1919) – A founding member of the Ukrainian Social-Democratic Workers Party (USDRP), a reformist, nationalist party in the Second International.

Zhordania, Noe (1868-1953) – Georgian Menshevik who took a social-chauvinist position in the war. He was an opponent of the October Revolution. He was elected chairman of the Tiflis Soviet in 1917, President of the Georgian Menshevik government in 1918-21, before being exiled in France from 1921.

Zinoviev, Grigory (1883-1936) – Joined the Bolshevik faction in 1903, elected to the CC in 1907. Lenin's closest collaborator in exile before and during the First World War. After the February Revolution, Zinoviev sided with Kamenev and Stalin and pursued a policy of conciliation with the Provisional Government. Zinoviev and Kamenev went to the public press and disclosed the plans for an insurrection in October, for which Lenin called for their immediate expulsion. Executed in 1936 during the Great Purges.

Groups, periodicals and other terms

Arbeiterstimme (*Worker's Voice*) – Central organ of the Bund from 1897 to 1905.

Basmachi – A movement of Islamic rebels who rose up against conscription into the tsarist army during the First World War. The movement later flared up again in 1918 against Soviet rule.

Beilis case – In 1913 the tsar's government staged a trial of Menahem Beilis, a Jewish man falsely accused of the ritual murder of a Christian boy. The murder was actually committed by the Black Hundreds. The government's aim was to stir up antisemitism and take advantage of anti-Jewish pogroms to divert the people's attention from the revolutionary movement growing throughout the country. The trial aroused public indignation. In a number of towns, workers held protest demonstrations. Beilis was eventually acquitted.

Bernsteinism – Eduard Bernstein was a German social-democrat who tried to revise Marx's revolutionary theory on the lines of bourgeois liberalism. Bernsteinism, the opportunist trend in German and International Social-Democracy, hostile to Marxism, derived its name from his ideas.

Birzhevka (abb.), *Birzhevyie Vedomosti* (*Stock-Exchange Recorder*) – A bourgeois daily published in St. Petersburg from 1880. Its abbreviated name, '*Birzhevka*' became a generic term for the unscrupulous and venal bourgeois press.

Black-Hundred, Black Hundreds (Union of the Russian People) – Ultra-reactionary terrorist bands, loyal to the tsar, responsible for state-sanctioned pogroms against Jews and social-democrats.

Bulletin of the International Socialist Committee – The Bulletin of the International Socialist Committee in Berne was published by the executive of the Zimmerwald organisation, an organisation of socialists who took a revolutionary, anti-imperialist and anti-war stance after the majority of the Second International lent its support to their own nation's bourgeoisie in the First World War. It was, Lenin said, the first step in the development of the internationalist movement against the war.

Bund – See General Jewish Workers' Union of Lithuania, Poland and Russia.

Cadets – Abbreviated name for the Constitutional-Democratic Party, a bourgeois liberal party in tsarist Russia, founded 1905. They advocated for constitutional monarchy, opposed the October Revolution and supported the Whites in the Civil War

Chartism – A mass revolutionary movement in Britain in the 1840s.

Der Čechoslavische Sozialdemokrat (*The Czechoslovak Social-Democrat*) – The German-language paper of the Czech social-democrats.

Die Glocke (*The Bell*) – A magazine published by Parvus. Lensch was an editor. The magazine put forward a social-chauvinist position, arguing that socialists should support the German war effort.

Dyen (*Day*) – A daily newspaper of a liberal-bourgeois trend, published in St. Petersburg from 1912. Among its contributors were Menshevik liquidators, who took over complete control of the paper after February 1917.

Dzvin (*The Bell*) – A Ukrainian language nationalist journal with a Menshevik trend, published in Kiev from January 1913 to the middle of 1914.

Economism – An opportunist trend in Russian Social-Democracy at the turn of the century. The Economists limited the tasks of the working-class movement to the economic struggle for higher wages, better working conditions etc., maintaining that the political struggle should be left to the liberal bourgeoisie.

Fabian Society – A British reformist organisation founded in 1884.

Fenianism – Referring to the revolutionary movement for Irish independence.

Gazeta Robotnicza (*Worker's Gazette*) – The illegal paper of the Warsaw Committee of the Social-Democratic Party of Poland and Lithuania.

General Jewish Workers' Union of Lithuania, Poland and Russia (The Bund) – A secular Jewish socialist party initially formed in the Russian Empire and active between 1897 and 1920. Opposed Zionism. Sided with the Menshevik faction of the Russian Social Democratic Labour Party. The majority faction of the Russian Bund was dissolved in 1921 and incorporated into the Communist Party.

Hohenzollern – The House of Hohenzollern was the royal dynasty which ruled Germany. It was overthrown in the November Revolution of 1918 where Kaiser Wilhelm II was forced to abdicate.

Iskra (*The Spark*) – The first all-Russian illegal Marxist newspaper, founded by Lenin in 1900. It played a decisive part in the establishment of the revolutionary Marxist party of the working class.

JSLP (Jewish Socialist Labour Party) – A petty-bourgeois nationalist organisation, founded in 1906.

Junkers – Members of the landed nobility in Prussia and subsequently Germany.

Kievskaya Mysl (*Kiev Thought*) – A Russian paper aligned with the intelligentsia.

La Petite République (*The Little Republic*) – Organ of the French reformist socialists.

Libre Belgique (*Free Belgium*) – An illegal journal of the Belgian Labour Party, Brussels (1915-18).

Liquidators, liquidationists – A set of tendencies within the RSDLP after the 1905 Revolution, where the question of the combining of legal and illegal work came under contention. The Liquidators were split between the 'lefts', who fetishised illegal work, and the 'right', chiefly the Mensheviks, who insisted on solely using legal methods of struggle. Lenin for some considerable time waged a ruthless struggle against both of these tendencies.

Mazeppists – Moniker for Ukrainian nationalists, named after Ivan Stepanovych Mazepa, who attempted to separate Ukraine from Russia through a treaty with Sweden, but was defeated by Tsar Peter I at the Battle of Poltava.

Mensheviks – Originated as the opposition faction in the RSDLP. They pursued a policy of class collaboration with the bourgeoisie. Their leading body was the Organising Committee (OC).

Naprzód (*Forward*) – central organ of the Social-Democratic Party of Galicia and Silesia, published in Kraków beginning with 1892. The newspaper, which was a vehicle of petty-bourgeois nationalist ideas, was described by Lenin as "a very bad, and not at all Marxist organ".

Narodnik – Members of the Narodnaya Volya, a revolutionary movement active in the 1860s and 70s, led by students and the intelligentsia, who believed the peasantry was the revolutionary class that would overthrow the monarchy. They regarded the village commune as the embryo of socialism.

Narodowa Demokracja (National Democracy) – A reactionary, chauvinist party of the Polish bourgeoisie, founded in 1897.

Nash Golos (*Our Voice*) – A Menshevik social-chauvinist newspaper.

Nasha Zarya (*Our Dawn*) – A legal monthly paper of the Menshevik liquidators.

Nashe Dyelo (*Our Cause*) – A journal of the Mensheviks, which succeeded *Nasha Zarya*.

Nashe Slovo (*Our Cause*) – An Internationalist daily paper published in Paris from January 1915 to September 1916. Trotsky was the main editor and attended the Zimmerwald Conference as a representative of *Nashe Slovo*. The paper was banned by the French authorities on 15 September 1916 and Trotsky was ordered to leave France.

Nauchnaya Mysl (*Scientific Thought*) – Journal of a Menshevik trend.

Die Neue Rheinische Zeitung (*The New Rhenish Gazette*) – Paper of Marx and Engels, appeared in Cologne from 1 June 1848 until 19 May 1849. Marx and Engels were managers of this newspaper, Marx being editor-in-chief. As Lenin put it, the newspaper was "the best, the unsurpassed organ of the revolutionary proletariat". It educated the masses, roused them to fight the counter-revolution, and made its influence felt throughout Germany. Because of its resolute and irreconcilable position and its militant internationalism, the *Neue Rheinische Zeitung* was from the first months of its existence persecuted by the feudal-monarchist and liberal-bourgeois press, and also by the government. Marx's deportation by the Prussian Government and the repressive measures against its other editors led to the paper ceasing publication, with its famous last 'red issue' on 19 May 1849.

Die Neue Zeit (*The New Times*) – The theoretical organ of the German Social-Democratic Party (SPD), published in Stuttgart from 1883 to 1923.

Novaya Rabochaya Gazeta (*New Workers' Paper*) – A legal daily paper of the Menshevik liquidators.

Novoye Vremya (*New Times*) – A daily newspaper, published in St. Petersburg from 1868. In 1905 it became an organ of the Black Hundreds. Lenin called it a model of a corrupted newspaper.

Octobrists (The League of October Seventeenth) – Party of the big merchants, industrialists and big landowners who ran their estates on capitalist lines. Their name derives from their support for the tsar's 'October Manifesto' in 1905.

Peredonov, Peredonovism – A character from Fyodor Sologub's novel, The Petty Demon. A sadistic, hateful and nihilistic schoolteacher, his name became symbolic of this mentality. Lenin describes Peredonov as "a type of teacher-spy and dull lout".

Political Bureau (abbreviated Politbureau or Politburo) – A body elected for the first time in October 1917 by the Central Committee of the party in order to give it day to day political leadership.

Posledniye Izvestia (*Latest News*) – A periodical bulletin issued by the Foreign Committee of the Bund from 1901 to 1906.

Pravda (*Truth*)– Main organ of the Bolsheviks.

Prosveshcheniye (*Enlightenment*) – A legal Bolshevik monthly journal.

Przedświt (*Daybreak*) – The magazine of the Polish Socialist Party.

Przegląd Socjaldemokratyczny (*Social-Democratic Review*) – The monthly journal of the Social-Democratic Party of the Kingdom of Poland and Lithuania (SDKPiL).

Polish Socialist Party (PSP) – A petty-bourgeois nationalist party, founded in 1892.

Rabochaya Mysl (*Workers' Thought*) – A newspaper published by a group of Economists in Russia from October 1897 to December 1902.

Rech (*Speech*) – A daily newspaper and the central organ of the Cadet Party. It was published in St. Petersburg from February 1906.

Revolutsionnaya Rossiya (*Revolutionary Russia*) – A paper of the SRs.

Russian Soviet Federative Socialist Republic (RSFSR) – The state created after the October Revolution in Russia, which in 1922 became the largest republic in the USSR.

Russian Social-Democratic Labour Party (RSDLP) – The Russian Marxist party formed in 1898 in Minsk. It united the various isolated revolutionary groups in Russia into a single, unified party based on the principles of Marxism. At its Second Congress, the party was divided into the Bolshevik and Menshevik factions, before forming separate parties in 1912. Until 1918, the Bolsheviks went under the name Russian Social-Democratic Labour Party (Bolsheviks), abbreviated as RSDLP(B).

Russkaya Molva (*Russian Tidings*) – A bourgeois daily paper that was the organ of the Progressists, founded in 1912.

Russkaya Mysl (*Russian Thought*) – A monthly magazine published by Struve, which while not formally affiliated, argued along the lines of the Cadets.

Russkoye Bogatstvo (*Russian Wealth*) – A monthly magazine of the liberal Narodniks.

Russkoye Slovo (*Russian Word*) – A daily newspaper, published in Moscow from 1895 to 1918. The paper defended the interests of the Russian bourgeoisie from a liberal platform.

Shlyakhi (*Paths*) – The organ of the Ukrainian Students' Union, a nationalistic organisation, published in Lvov from April 1913 to March 1914.

Social-Democratic Party of Galicia and Silesia – A Social-Democratic Party that formed originally as a section of the Austrian Social-Democratic Party, later splitting away in 1907. Its work covered the region spanning the border between modern Poland and Ukraine.

Social Democratic Party of Germany (SPD) – Considered the leading party in the Second International, with over 1 million members in 1914. The near-unanimous vote for war credits amongst its members in the Reichstag at the opening of the First World War signified the death of the International.

Sotsial-Demokrat (The Social-Democrat) – An illegal paper published from 1908 to January 1917. The paper was run by Lenin and was the central organ of the RSDLP as a whole.

Spartacus League (Spartacists, Internationale Group) – The Internationale group, who produced the organ *Die Internationale*, was formed by the German Left social-democrats Karl Liebknecht, Rosa Luxemburg, Franz Mehring, Clara Zetkin and others at the beginning of the First World War. Soon after, the group denounced the SPD, and formed the Spartacus League. They carried out propaganda among the masses against the imperialist war, exposing the aggressive policy of German imperialism and the treachery of the leaders of Social-Democracy. In 1917 they became affiliated to the centrist Independent Social-Democratic Party of Germany, preserving their organisational independence.

State Duma – During the reign of Nicholas II the State Duma was the name given to the national parliament, which only had an advisory role. There were also local dumas, the equivalent of local councils.

Stirnerism – Referring to the individualist anarchism of Max Stirner, which emphasises self-interest and individual freedom, rejecting all forms of external authority and abstract ideals.

The New York Daily Tribune – An American newspaper published from 1841 to 1924. Until the 1850s it was the organ of the Left wing of the American Whigs, and thereafter the organ of the Republican Party. Karl Marx contributed to the paper from August 1851 to March 1862, and at his request Friedrich Engels wrote numerous articles for it.

The People's Commissariat of the Workers' and Peasants' Inspection (*Rabkrin*, WPI) – A body set up in 1920 to scrutinise and maintain the effectiveness of the Soviet state and administration.

Der Vorbote (*The Herald*) – A German-language paper published in the Netherlands by Anton Pannekoek, a Dutch socialist, astronomer and member of the German SPD.

Vorwärts (*Forwards*) – The central organ of the German Social-Democratic Party, published daily in Berlin from 1891 to 1933.

Zarya (*Dawn*) – A Marxist scientific and political journal published in Stuttgart in 1901-02 by the editors of *Iskra*.

Titles by Wellred Books

Wellred Books is a publishing house specialising in works of Marxist theory. Among the titles we publish are:

Anti-Dühring, Friedrich Engels

Bolshevism: The Road to Revolution, Alan Woods

Chartist Revolution, Rob Sewell

China: From Permanent Revolution to Counter-Revolution, John Peter Roberts

The Civil War in France, Karl Marx

Class Struggle in the Roman Republic, Alan Woods

The Class Struggles in France, 1848-1850, Karl Marx

The Classics of Marxism: Volumes One & Two, Various authors

Dialectics of Nature, Friedrich Engels

The Eighteenth Brumaire of Louis Bonaparte, Karl Marx

The First Five Years of the Communist International, Leon Trotsky

The First World War: A Marxist Analysis of the Great Slaughter, Alan Woods

Germany: From Revolution to Counter-Revolution, Rob Sewell

Germany 1918-1933: Socialism or Barbarism, Rob Sewell

History of British Trotskyism, Ted Grant

The History of Philosophy: A Marxist Perspective, Alan Woods

The History of the Russian Revolution: All Volumes, Leon Trotsky

The History of the Russian Revolution to Brest-Litovsk, Leon Trotsky

The Ideas of Karl Marx, Alan Woods

Imperialism: The Highest Stage of Capitalism, VI Lenin

In Defence of Lenin, Rob Sewell & Alan Woods

In Defence of Marxism, Leon Trotsky

In the Cause of Labour, Rob Sewell

Ireland: Republicanism and Revolution, Alan Woods

'Left-Wing' Communism: An Infantile Disorder, VI Lenin

Lenin and Trotsky: What They Really Stood For,
   Alan Woods & Ted Grant

Lenin Selected Writings, VI Lenin
    On Imperialist War
    On the National Question
    The Revolutions of 1917

Lenin, Trotsky & the Theory of the Permanent Revolution, John Roberts

Marxism and Anarchism, Various authors

Marxism and the USA, Alan Woods

Materialism and Empirio-criticism, VI Lenin

My Life, Leon Trotsky

Not Guilty, Dewey Commission Report

The Origin of the Family, Private Property & the State, Friedrich Engels

The Permanent Revolution and Results & Prospects, Leon Trotsky

Permanent Revolution in Latin America, John Roberts & Jorge Martin

Reason in Revolt, Alan Woods & Ted Grant

Reformism or Revolution, Alan Woods

Revolution and Counter-Revolution in Spain, Felix Morrow

The Revolution Betrayed, Leon Trotsky

The Revolutionary Legacy of Rosa Luxemburg, Marie Frederiksen

The Revolutionary Philosophy of Marxism, John Peterson (Ed.)

Russia: From Revolution to Counter-Revolution, Ted Grant

Spain's Revolution Against Franco, Alan Woods

Stalin, Leon Trotsky

The State and Revolution, VI Lenin

Ted Grant: The Permanent Revolutionary, Alan Woods

Ted Grant Writings: Volumes One and Two, Ted Grant

Thawra hatta'l nasr! - Revolution until Victory!, Alan Woods & others

What Is Marxism?, Rob Sewell & Alan Woods

What Is to Be Done?, VI Lenin

Women, Family and the Russian Revolution,
     John Roberts & Fred Weston

Writings on Britain, Leon Trotsky

To make an order or for more information, visit wellred-books.com or email books@wellred-books.com.